D1126076

Sources Of
American Spirituality

American Jesuit Spirituality

THE MARYLAND TRADITION, 1634-1900

Edited by Robert Emmett Curran, S.J.

PAULIST PRESS
New York ◆ Mahwah

Cover art:
Map of the Maryland Jesuit Stations reproduced from Thomas Hughes, S.J., *The History of the Society of Jesus in North America: Colonial and Federal*, Text, Vol. 2, London, 1917. Adapted from Louis Carrez, S.J., *Atlas Geographicus Societatis Jesu*, plate 37, Paris, 1900.

Library of Congress Cataloging-in-Publication Data

    American Jesuit spirituality.

    (Sources of American spirituality)
    Bibliography: p.
    Includes index.
    1. Jesuits—United States—Spiritual life.
2. Spiritual life—Catholic authors. I. Curran,
Robert Emmett. II. Series.
BX3708.A48   1988   271'.53'0752   87-25905
ISBN 0-8091-0381-8

Published by Paulist Press
997 Macarthur Boulevard
Mahwah, N.J. 07430

Printed and bound in the United States of America

CONTENTS

v

Contents

GENERAL INTRODUCTION

Readers of this volume of the *Sources of American Spirituality* are in for a treat. The documents of the Maryland Jesuits, who during the seventeenth, eighteenth, and nineteenth centuries were such an important part of the American Catholic scene, have for the most part remained untranslated and unappreciated by both scholar and lay person alike. Few would recognize the names of men like Andrew White, Stephen Dubuisson, Joseph Mosley, Peter Atwood, John McElroy, and Benedict J. Sestini. Yet many certainly would be familiar with the substance of their thought and would recognize how it fit into the larger picture of American Catholic life. For those reasons this volume is an important contribution.

But I said that this work was, in fact, a treat. The writings of the members of the Maryland Province of the Society, which we recall extended the entire length of the Eastern seaboard during the time surveyed in this work, reveal, along with a myriad of facts about the life and times of their authors, a substratum of personal religious belief upon which was built the entire work of those men. That substratum, grounded on the *Spiritual Exercises* of St. Ignatius Loyola, focused the individual's whole being on the life and mission of Jesus. This attempt to set apart all of one's being, and indeed all of creation, for the greater glory of God manifested itself in very different ways during the nearly three centuries covered by this work. In some cases, like that of John Carroll's Enlightenment-inspired Republican piety or Edward Holker Welch's Yankee Catholic synthetic spirituality, the influence of the American experiment is clear. Yet in other cases like the sentimental, delicate piety of Stephen Dubuisson, or the European-style devotion to the Sacred Heart championed by Benedict Sestini we see an attempt to transplant European religious styles and sensitivities practically unchanged. By respecting the integrity of the original documents and by choosing large enough portions of text that enable the reader to get a sense of the documents

1

as literature, not merely as artifacts, the editor has enabled us to experience the richness of these materials.

As pleasurable as is the reading of these texts, the treat does not end there. The broad time frame herein encompassed and the complexity and even nebulousness of the proposed focus on "spirituality" are potential problems for any student of these materials. Yet the notes and introductions steer clear of those obstacles and provide a lucid commentary on the material that places it in the larger context of American Catholic religious history. In addition to providing new information on the history of the Maryland Jesuits, this work brings to light aspects of the devotional life of U.S. Catholics, the importance of which we have become increasingly aware, thanks to the recent works of Joseph P. Chinnici, Jay Dolan, Ann Taves and others. This work combines the freshness of a pioneering effort with the polish of a well-rehearsed rendering of the past, and as such is a fitting addition to our series.

John Farina

PREFACE

When one thinks of the Jesuits in North America prior to this century, images of Eusebio Kino or Isaac Jogues probably spring to mind, or perhaps composites of their French or Spanish confreres. Except for Joseph deSmet among the Indians of the Northwest, the Jesuits of British America seem a rather prosaic group. No canonized saints; no heroic chronicles; no dreams of Christian empires. Yet the Maryland Mission of the Society of Jesus was by far the most important in laying the foundations for the Church in America. During the colonial period it constituted, almost exclusively, the institutional church in British America, its limits stretching from New York to Virginia. Out of that mission came John Carroll, the first bishop of the United States, and the Select Body of the Clergy, the prototype of the national church that Carroll organized in the wake of the American revolution.

In the nineteenth century the Maryland mission/province embraced most of the east coast, from Maine to South Carolina. The Missouri Province, which sent Jesuits (including deSmet) to the far reaches of the West, was an offspring. Among the network of colleges that Jesuits established, Boston College, Brooklyn, Fordham, Georgetown, Gonzaga (Washington), Holy Cross, Loyola (Baltimore), Xavier (New York), St. Joseph's (Philadelphia), and St. Peter's (Jersey City) were all part of the Maryland Province. Associated with nearly all of these colleges (Fordham and Holy Cross being the exceptions) were prominent parish churches. One of the most popular magazines of Catholic piety in the late nineteenth century, *The Messenger of the Sacred Heart,* was edited by Maryland Jesuits. In brief, from the colonial period to the end of the nineteenth century, the Maryland Jesuits played an important part in shaping American Catholic culture.

This volume in the *Sources of American Spirituality* attempts to examine Jesuit spirituality as it was refracted under the pressures of American experience and European influence. That spirituality was already a century

3

old when it spurred Andrew White and his companions to join the Maryland adventurers in 1633. Horace's dictum about changing skies but unchanged minds surely applies to the Jesuit missioners, so far as Ignatian spirituality is concerned. But their social situation from the beginning was different and those differences in time had implications for the faith life as well. As conservative as the Maryland Jesuits were, attitudes developed about the experience of God, devotionalism, and the ideal environment for spreading the kingdom that brought the Maryland Jesuits under heavy suspicion in Rome by the early nineteenth century. Although that distrust of Maryland Jesuits in both Jesuit and non-Jesuit Roman circles continued, several factors had combined to produce a flowering of ultramontane piety among Maryland Jesuits by the end of the century.

Given the very broad dimensions of spirituality that range from the inner life to popular devotions, I have tried to select those documents that reveal significant aspects of Ignatian spirituality, from the private experience of individual Jesuits to mass media devotions, as it evolved over the course of two and a half centuries in America. Thus I have used diaries, sermons, correspondence, community exhortations, a devotional manual, and issues of *The Messenger*. More than half of the material is here published for the first time. Most of it was transcribed from manuscripts. Except for completing some consistent abbreviations, substituting th for the thorn (y) in colonial manuscripts, and inserting within brackets some necessary punctuation and clarifying words, I have respected the integrity of the documents. Some materials (parts 1 and 3 of the chapter concerning the founding of the Maryland Mission, as well as the report on the evangelical apostolate in 1851) were in Latin. Unless noted otherwise, the translations are mine.

I am grateful to Constance Fitzgerald, O.C.D. and Felicitas Powers, R.S.M. for the use of the archives of the Carmelite Monastery in Baltimore and Archdiocese of Baltimore respectively; to the staff of the Woodstock Library of Georgetown University; and to the Special Collections division of the Lauinger Library of Georgetown, with special thanks to George M. Barringer and Jon Reynolds, for all their assistance and advice in locating and editing so many of the documents in this book. John Farina first suggested this topic to me five years ago. He has been a remarkably supportive and patient editor in shaping the volume and bringing it finally to press.

This book is dedicated to Sydney Ahlstrom, mentor for a generation of American religious historians, including the present writer, whom two decades ago he encouraged to explore the distinctive patterns of the Jesuit tradition in the United States. May this work be a modest start in that direction.

INTRODUCTION

"To follow Jesus Christ in the most intimate union possible":
The Roots of Ignatian Spirituality

The heart of Jesuit spirituality is the *Spiritual Exercises* of Ignatius
Loyola, the manual of reformation that Saint Ignatius put together from
his personal experience for the members of the society that he founded.
These *Exercises*, made for a month at least twice during each Jesuit's
formation and for eight days annually, are the basic instrument for the
shaping of a Jesuit's relationship with God and his creation through the
radical reworking of his imagination. For Ignatius the imagination is the
key to the affections or emotions which are the source of behavior. By
educating the imagination to perceive the roots of reality in the Christian
dispensation, Ignatian spirituality aims at ordering the affections for a
proper response. Thus the four phases of the *Spiritual Exercises* are designed to give the individual making them an opportunity to encounter
a God who has given of himself superabundantly in his creation, whom
humans, individually and collectively, have nonetheless rejected in their
self-centeredness, but who persists in his love of the world through the
sending of his son. In pondering Jesus and his "standard" of poverty,
contempt for the world, and humility, against Satan's "standard" of
riches, honor, and pride, the individual is led to seek his identity with
Jesus by imitating him as completely as he can, by God's grace. The
stakes are no less than the soul of the world itself; the call of Christ
the king for active campaigners to make it over in his image is an urgent
one. The only response to such a loving call is expected to be the gift
of all one has freely received—mind, heart, will—for the service of the
kingdom.

Indeed the focus of Jesuit spirituality is service, of "active and generous conformity to the will of God.''[1] The most noted commentator on the spirituality of the Society observes:

> . . . this seems to be the message which God entrusted to Ignatius through the mystical favors with which He almost overwhelmed him: service through love, apostolic service for the greatest possible glory to God, a service given in generous conformity to the will of God, in the abnegation or sacrifice of all self-love and personal interest in order to follow Christ, the Leader who is ardently loved.[2]

Ignatius's *Exercises* are the means he discovered for discerning the will of God. The key meditations allow the person making the retreat the opportunity to examine his own dispositions and open himself to the Spirit's movements; in so doing he discovers the possibility of breaking free of self-love to respond to the divine love that inspires service. Discernment is crucial to the process. It is rooted in Ignatius's sense of an extraordinarily dynamic Providence, of a God working ''simply and quietly'' in the world to complete the revolution that He has begun in the Incarnation of His Son out of love for His creation.[3] In confronting our changing moods and situations we confront a God who calls us to respond. Ignatian discernment involves a testing of one's thoughts and feelings through prayer to verify that they are of the Spirit. A profound interior peace that flows from decisions often painful, if not repugnant, is the immediate confirmation. Protracted experience, ultimately history, is the ultimate one.[4]

Individual direction is the norm in order to adapt the *Exercises* to the movements the person is experiencing and to help ensure that the retreatant is remaining open to the Spirit. The high point of the *Exercises* is the individual's ''electing'' to dispose of his life in a particular way in the light of the discernment he has made. In this process Ignatius leads the person to rely upon reason as well as intuition. There is a relentless logic about the *Exercises* which builds from beginning to end. But joined closely to this logic is a confidence in the direct perception of divine truth which will make the person react with an enthusiasm and abandon that runs far beyond the dictates of reason. It envisions a retreatant being able to say to the Lord Jesus: ''I am moved by your grace to offer myself to you and to your work. I deeply desire to be with you in accepting all wrongs and all abuse and all poverty, both actual and spiritual—and I deliberately choose this, if it is for your greater service and praise.''[5] And later: ''I so much want the truth of Christ's life to be fully the truth of my own that I find myself, moved by grace, with a love and a desire for poverty in order to be with the poor Christ; a love and a desire for insults in order to be closer to Christ in his own rejection by people; a love and a desire to be considered worthless and a fool for Christ, rather than to be esteemed as wise and prudent according to the standards of the world. By grace, I find myself so moved to follow Jesus Christ in the most intimate union possible, that his experiences are reflected in my own. In that, I find my delight."[6]

Such enthusiasm stems from an intimate knowledge of Jesus gained through a series of contemplations in which the imagination is intensively used to recreate the living Jesus in his full humanity and to bring the retreatant—as much as imagination can—to encounter Christ "at a deeply personal level in such a way that one is changed . . . in an ordering of one's whole self. . . . "[7] Experiencing Christ as one's provider, protector, model, and companion, the person is moved to make a whole-hearted and single-minded commitment to serve him. An intimate yet hierarchical relationship results from this mutual giving and fidelity.[8]

The *magis* or the greater glory of God is the ultimate criterion for the follower of Christ according to Ignatius. And glory is promoted by service. How God is to be better served becomes the constant question for the Jesuits, as individuals and as a community, who would be faithful to the call they have experienced in the *Exercises*. Although Ignatius was convinced that "the interior law of charity and love which the Holy Spirit writes and engraves upon hearts" would be the best means toward the preservation of the Society's fidelity, still he spent the last decade of his life refining the *Constitutions of the Society of Jesus* in order to provide a structure and rules for the implementation of the goals he and his companions had been inspired to strive for and to help dispose the members of the Society for the continuing influence of the Spirit within their ranks.

Discernment thus was intended to be a part of every Jesuit's ordinary life. The examination of conscience that Ignatius prescribed to be made twice daily by members of the Society—a reflection on one's behavior and dispositions or consciousness—is a continuation of the process of the retreat of reordering the imagination to remain faithful to God's will in the midst of changing circumstances. The various kinds of prayer—vocal, mental, contemplative—are all further means to the same end. The account of conscience, which every Jesuit is to render yearly to his superior, is to enable the latter to direct him and make decisions about his service according to the superior's understanding of the pattern of spiritual motions his subject has been experiencing.

The service that the Jesuit is driven to give to his Lord is not the personal service that can fulfil itself in monastic confinement or isolated pilgrimages. The Jesuit, like Ignatius, is not merely the pilgrim, but "a kind of apostolic vagabond."[9] His service is apostolic. Its boundaries are worldwide, seeking Christ "in ten thousand places" through the men and women whose first born brother he is.[10] As Ignatius stated it in the *Constitutions,* "our vocation is to travel through the world and to live in any part of it whatsoever where there is hope of greater service to God and of help of souls. . . . The aim and end of this Society is, by traveling through the various regions of the world at the order of the supreme vicar of Christ our Lord or of the superior of the Society itself, to preach, hear confessions, and use all the other means it can with the grace of God to help souls."[11] The vows of poverty, chastity, and obedience are taken to ensure the individual the corporate freedom necessary for such mobility and selfless service. In addition those chosen for profession or solemn vows take a fourth vow of "special obedience to the sovereign pontiff in regard to the missions" precisely because Ignatius considered that the pope as universal pastor alone had the breadth of vision that his men required to direct their apostolic energies across the globe.[12]

"To spend and more than spend myself":
Maryland and the Ignatian Vision

England in the 16th century seemed to its Jesuit members a microcosm of the struggle between the camps of Jesus and Satan. There was certainly opportunity in spades for finding humiliation, contempt, persecution, and even death in attempting to restore the ancient faith in Elizabethan England. From their sanctuaries in the Lowlands, at St. Omers, Liège, Watten, and elsewhere, English Jesuits prepared themselves for this *ad majorem dei gloriam* mission.

With conditions for Catholics and even Jesuits beginning to improve in the early 17th century under the Stuarts, it was natural that the perspective of English Jesuits on the kingdom should alter somewhat. When a Catholic convert, George Calvert, undertook to plant a colony in America in the 1630s, English Jesuits saw the providential possibilities for carrying Christ's standard into new parts. As the author (likely a Jesuit) of a 1633 advertisement for the colony observed: "I call the work of aiding and saving souls glorious: for it was the work of Christ, the king of glory."[13]

The *Exercises* reinforced for the Jesuit Andrew White St. Paul's conviction that "all things work together for good to them that love God." As we have noted, Ignatian spirituality involved at its roots a providential sensibility. Not that its sense of the providential nature of the world was unique, either in Catholic or Protestant circles in the seventeenth century. White's prayer of petition during the storm at sea, his finding the finger of God in their late sailing from England, his rationale about the miraculous availability of land in the Chesapeake region—all are reminiscent of parallel passages in John Winthrop's Journal or William Bradford's *Of Plymouth*

Plantation. In the worldviews of both Jesuit and Puritan providence is vindictive, although the cause in the latter's cautionary tales is typically blasphemy while for the former it is some insult to Mary or the saints. But, on the whole, in the Ignatian vision God's providence was exercised not so much in leading his chosen people on an errand into a wilderness, but in reclaiming the good earth from the power of Satan. Ignatian spirituality is predicated on a fundamental goodness in nature, including man, that is the indelible work of God in his creation and ongoing redemption. Jesuit anthropology is essentially positive.

Like their Spanish and French counterparts English Jesuits came to the new world to convert the Amerindians. The inauguration of the mission to Maryland produced among some English Jesuits an irrepressible urge to bring Christianity to the natives. A colony in America, under Catholic auspices, was clearly a sign of God's will that the good news be at last made known to them. As one applicant for America wrote after receiving the announcement of the need for volunteers, "it hath bin like an ocean able to drowne all other sorrows & crosses. . . . " "To tell you the truth," he admitted, "my joy was so great, that no thought nor word for a long time could come from me which resounded not 'Maryland'."[14] But instant generosity, no matter how zealous, was not enough. Superiors were of Roger Rigby's mind, who pleaded in his late application, that the best policy was "not always first come, first sped."[15] In the early selection of missioners for Maryland, Ignatian discernment, the testing of the movements of spirit over time and shifting circumstances, seems to have been a crucial criterion. Those were chosen who weighed the call to Maryland over the course of months and still found it driving them. Among them was John Cooper who testified in 1640 that he had for "many years no smale inclination towards such a mission." Now with the actual possibility before him "I find the fier of charity so to increase that I can no longer hold from asking the favour, that I may be sent forthwith into those parts, there to spend *et superimpendere meipsum* in reducing those soules so deare to Christ our Lord, and for His sake more deare to me than my very life."[16]

Another aspect of discernment that marks the applications of these 17th century Jesuits is the recognition of gifts that qualify them to meet specific apostolic needs. Christopher Morris, for instance, counted his linguistic and musical skills particular assets for a mission trying to bridge cultures. Morris, however, with his wide-ranging talents, including a command of both theology and philosophy, could not be spared for Maryland. As one superior remarked of him: "We have few missioners in our Province like him, ready for everything."[17] Indeed throughout the colonial period those distinguished for academic or intellectual attainments tended to be kept in the seminaries and colleges on the continent.

Those who were chosen seemed sober enough in their assessment of Maryland. As one of the successful applicants wrote: "Tis true I conceive the mission not only happie and glorious, but withall hard and humble, in regard of the raw state things as yet are in; yet the love of Jesus neyther feares labour nor low imployment."[18] In truth they found life in Maryland in the first decade all they had anticipated. Eight of the 12 first Jesuits in Maryland died by violence or disease; among the survivors only Andrew White and Thomas Copley, the first two superiors, were there for more than two years. Three of them died in 1645–46, apparent victims of the Ingle rebellion. Another, Ferdinand Poulton, was shot by accident. The average missionary in Maryland in the seventeenth century lived less than 10 years from the time of his arrival in the colony. Small pox, yellow fever, a poor diet, and overwork made for a fearsome seasoning. So wasting was the climate and demands of the mission on Jesuits that by the late 17th century superiors in Europe were accelerating the training of native American Jesuits in order to fill the manpower needs in America.

During the first five years of the colony's history, Governor Calvert refused to allow the Jesuits to live in the Indian villages. When they finally took up residence among the Piscataway and others, the baptism of key tribal leaders gave substance to their dreams of evangelizing the Amerindians. "For the greatest hope," they reported in 1639, "is that, when the family of the king [of the Piscataway] is baptized, the conversion of the whole empire will speedily take place." Given the few Jesuits in Maryland (by 1641 lack of manpower had forced them to substitute a kind of circuit boating for their residential missions in order to serve the Indians), and their frustrations in attempting to acquire a working knowledge of native languages and culture, such dreams were probably unrealistic under the best circumstances, much more so under the ones in which White and his companions struggled.[19] In 1640 illness struck down both White and John Altham, the latter fatally. Then the overthrow of the Calverts in 1645 drove the Jesuits from the colony itself. When the first Jesuit returned to Maryland three years later, he reported that "the Indians summon me to their aid. . . . I scarcely know what to do, but cannot attend to all. God grant that I may do His will to the greater glory of His name. Truly flowers appear in our land—may they attain to fruit."[20] But the Patuxent, the Piscataway, and other tribes that the Jesuits had been ministering to were being pressed by the English on one side and the Susquehanna on the other. The result was the end of a promising apostolate for the Maryland Jesuits in which their accomplishments, if modest in comparison to the record of their French brethren in Canada, were nonetheless impressive.[21]

By 1650 the Jesuit mission in Maryland was limited to the Catholic minority of the English population. As early as 1638 they were giving the

Spiritual Exercises to laymen in Maryland. Although the Calverts discouraged any proselytizing of the Protestant majority, conversions in the first generation were high, partly due to the lack of any Church of England or Protestant ministers. Conversions continued throughout the colonial period, giving agents of the Anglican Society for the Propagation of the Faith cause to complain that Jesuits were threatening the religious establishment (the Church of England became the established religion in 1702) by taking advantage of the indifferent ministry and scandalous private lives of too many clergymen of the Church of England to win converts to Rome. A number of prominent Protestant families such as the Hansons and the Stones had Catholic branches by the middle of the eighteenth century but the Catholic portion of the population never exceeded a twelfth.

Within the first five years of settlement the Jesuits had begun to develop the plantations which became the center of their ministry. Without the support of the proprietor (Calvert had decided that there would be no established religion in Maryland) the Jesuits were forced to provide for their ministry by their own means. By grants from the proprietor under the conditions of plantation, acquisitions and grants, the Jesuits came to possess six plantations in southern Maryland and the Eastern Shore, as well as two farms in southeastern Pennsylvania. There were several advantages in the Jesuit position. For one thing, the Jesuits in Maryland never became dependent upon the Catholic laity as their counterparts in England did. The Maryland Jesuits' status as large landowners gave them an equality that the English clergy never had. In 1759 the English Provincial of the Society of Jesus acknowledged that the desire of the Maryland Jesuits to be independent of seculars was honorable but, he went on, in their impoverished circumstances "highly unreasonable," when their own plantations were not supporting them and they were forcing their equally poor English brethren to make up the difference. The Maryland Jesuits, if truth be told, were poor planters for much of the colonial period, although the social and psychological standing that their property gave them may have outweighed their lack of economic success.

In effect they became a combination of priest-planters and circuit riders. With indentured servants (in Maryland slaves from the late 17th century on) they raised tobacco and wheat as money crops to sustain their ministry. Their plantations served as liturgical centers for the Catholics in the areas; Catholics in outlying districts were visited by horseback or boat once a month or more frequently. In 1773 John Mattingly, a Maryland native who had remained in Europe to teach theology at the English College in Rome, reported on the observance of the Lord's day in Maryland. Except for a few details (a church at Newtown as the site for services instead of a manor house), the description would have as easily fit the rhythm of Catholic life on Sundays in the 1720s or the 1820s. Mattingly wrote that the priests

> travel to various chapels [from their central residences], which are called congregations, 10, 15, or even more than twenty miles away, to carry out their duties on Sundays and feast days; so that Mass is celebrated in each chapel at least once a month, the sacraments administered, and the word of God preached; in the principal places, however, twice or more frequently, according to the number and the needs of the faithful. Everything is done more or less in the following manner: from early morning until 11 o'clock they hear confessions: then they celebrate Mass, & distribute holy communion: once Mass is finished they preach to the congregation, and Christian doctrine is explained.[22]

"Liberty of Conscience . . . the chief and fundamental part . . . ":
Maryland Jesuits and the Penal Era

After the Glorious Revolution in 1689 Catholics in Maryland found themselves, at least theoretically, under the same penal laws they had left England to escape. Catholics could not vote, practice certain professions, bear arms, educate their children in their faith, or worship publicly. Priests were subject to life imprisonment for being in the colony. Although Maryland Catholics rarely if ever felt the full material impact of the legislation, there was still a psychological cost. As an historian has remarked about the Irish under similar penal legislation, the "codes had an almost mythical power and could be periodically invoked as a threat. . . . They were a constant reminder of the inferior status of Catholicism. . . . "[23] In Maryland, such a reminder had a particular appeal to a new establishment which feared that the Catholic gentry would somehow regain power. The threat to invoke penal laws was exercised in Maryland several times in the 18th century, such as in the 1750s when the Assembly doubled the property taxes of Catholics. Jesuits were arrested on a few occasions and charged with offenses that ranged from saying Mass to conspiring with France but no Jesuit was ever imprisoned.

For the Maryland Catholic gentry economic loss did not follow as a consequence of political disability. Indeed the period from 1720 to 1750 was one of great prosperity for Catholics like Charles Carroll and James Digges. With this prosperity came an apparent religious revival, at least as gauged by religious vocations. By the second quarter of the eighteenth century a steady stream of children of the Maryland gentry were entering religious orders in Europe. No Marylanders, for instance, had joined the

Society of Jesus from 1689 to 1724. From 1724 to 1773 there were 36 Jesuit novices from Maryland. The Carmelites, the Poor Claires, and the Benedictines had similar harvests from the daughters of Maryland families like the Semmes, Boones, Brookes, and Spaldings.

The number of Maryland Jesuits during this period of eighty years was always small, never more than five priests at any time in the 17th century, only 23 as late as 1772. After the wave of enthusiasm of the first decade, the English Province seemed to give distinctly less attention to its Maryland Mission.[24] A few superiors became politically active, such as Peter Attwood and George Hunter. Disenfranchisement and other disabilities provided an occasion for reflecting on the meaning of the experiment in religious toleration that the Calverts had launched in 1634. In 1720 Attwood wrote a long treatise entitled: "Liberty and Property or the Beauty of Maryland displayed in a brief and candid search into her Charter, Fundamental Laws & Constitution." To Attwood "the Law of Liberty of Conscience . . . [was] the chief and fundamental part of" the Maryland Constitution. He contended that this liberty had been religiously observed for the first sixty years of the settlement and that it had been esteemed by the inhabitants "as their birth-Right. . . . " A person's "religion," according to Attwood, "was neither a help nor a hindrance and nothing came under a consideration but his integrity, parts and Capacity, were he Churchman or Presbyterian, Quaker or R. Catholic and hence it is to be presumed that the country was never better served, nor could it be, than in those halcyon days. . . . " Attwood was arguing that religious freedom was the fundamental right upon which rested the enjoyment of all other rights and privileges, including the right to property. He was claiming the intrinsic connection between liberty and property that would underlay the next generation's rationale for revolution.[25] Thirty-five years later Hunter returned to England in an unsuccessful effort to persuade the proprietor of the colony to protect the fundamental rights of the Catholics in Maryland.

In general, however, Maryland Jesuits lived quietly on their plantations and ministered to their scattered Catholic congregations. The large majority were Englishmen who came to British America fully expecting to serve in that mission for the rest of their lives. Most, like Joseph Mosley, continued to be volunteers, responding, as Mosley wrote his sister in 1758, not to "the Law of Nature" but "the Law of Grace . . . to seek what tends more to the honour and glory of God." He found a grinding regimen of long and frequent horse rides, often in rain or freezing cold, that aggravated the kidney stone that eventually plagued him. He felt keenly his isolation from English civilization, an isolation that became even worse when he was sent to begin a new mission in a remote section of the Eastern Shore of Maryland. Still he could count himself "perhaps the happiest man that breathes.'' To a brother back in England who was worried about what this raw country was doing to his health, Mosley responded: ''You hope, I'll be a better steward of a life, not at my disposal: but it is at God's, and he is welcome to it, to spend it in the service of my fellow-creatures, or Brethren in Christ.'' ''Poor Mick,'' Mosley wrote to his sister about their brother, ''he can't enjoy that health at Bath, as I enjoy with all the dangers and fatigues of Maryland. . . . '' Even when the severe climate and wasting lifestyle took its toll on Mosley, he could still not ''as yet hear of quitting my stand. . . . '' For this English Jesuit only death or incapacitation could force a companion of Jesus to abandon the fields.

Jesuit preaching in colonial Maryland showed the strong influence of the French spirituality of the Lowlands, where the English Jesuits were largely trained (Joseph Greaton was a rare exception). Part of the humanistic tradition of French piety associated with Francis de Sales and Jacques Bénigne Bossuet, it was rooted in an anthropology that was moderately positive about human nature and promoted a spirituality that stressed virtuous living as a key to happiness. Against the countervailing spiritual doctrines of Jansenism and Quietism, this French spirituality enunciated by Etienne Binet (1569–1639) and Jean Pierre de Caussade (1675–1751) among others, sought a middle course between rigorism and indulgence. Rhetoric played an important role in this ''devout humanism.'' Through the skillful orchestration of images and biblical allusions in familiar and concrete tones, Jesuit writer-preachers such as Louis Bordaloue (1632–1704) and Claude de la Columbière (1641–1682) developed a theme in a relentlessly logical manner with the calculated intention of producing certain emotional effects in readers or listeners.[26]

The sermons of the Maryland Jesuits in the eighteenth century were highly derivative, freely utilizing the published works of Bordaloue, Columbière and others. Also in their libraries would have been compilations such as Vincent Houdrey's *La Bibliothèque des prédicateurs* (1712–1724) which listed appropriate passages in Scripture and the writings of the Fathers, as well as quotations from modern theologians for traditional catechetical and liturgical topics. This, no doubt, accounts in large part for the impression the sermons give of being out of time and place. It also explains their baroque style, somewhat toned down in scale of imagery in deference to their colonial audiences. The structure follows the traditional format of Jesuit meditations, consisting of three points. Unlike the classical sermons of the court preachers, however, there is no elaborate substructure of points within points. Many of the sermons are practical instructions, a tradition from the earliest days in the colony: the routine matters of how to hear Mass, how to confess. But more distinctively Ignatian themes are also present such as the Two Standards (see Attwood's sermon on the Incarnation, Greaton's on Good Friday), and the wellspring of Christian action: God's glory and the neighbor's good (Mosley on Ignatius).

In Peter Attwood's Ash Wednesday sermon we see an example of the blending of logic and emotion for maximal impact upon a congregation. Attwood underscores the irrationality of the behavior of those who knowing "that we are made of dust and ashes" yet live "as if . . . we were to pitch our tabernacles . . . eternally upon earth." "What folly, what stupidity, what madness is this," he observes, "to believe as we do, and live and act so contrary to what we believe."

Their sermons also effectively engage the listener, either by putting him in the place of the preacher, or by the speaker assuming a praeternatural persona (see Mosley's sermon on St. Ignatius) or by employing an extended image that dramatizes the theme (Attwood's use of the Ninevites in the Ash Wednesday sermon). And there is the call to action. They are not without hope or means of salvation. There is much they can do "to prevent this threatning blow." God's grace is still abundant for those who respond by mortifying themselves in order to become "a New Man" and "labor efficaciously for God's church." If God calls them to be faithful, he provides the grace which makes it possible for them to do their "Duty & reclaim 'em from their disorders." Indeed Mosley can ask: "Why are you not Saints as well as [Ignatius]?" since he believes God has provided sufficient means for every one's sanctification. For Mosley reason and revelation combine to teach the earthly pilgrim the wisdom of weaning himself from all disordered affection for the world. The Christian has the means and every reason to use his time and talents economically for the building up of God's kingdom. If life is hard and unfair, so was it for Christ. As Greaton points out to his congregation, "It does not become a servant to fare better than his M[aste]r" (see "Whipps & Thorns").

How the Catholic laity in Pennsylvania and Maryland received these highly formal sermons one can only speculate. In 1785 Robert Molyneux admitted that he found it harder to preach than formerly. "I wish I had the talent of doing it *ex tempore*. To preach with a paper does not suit this place [Philadelphia] so well; and now, from want of time and habit, I should find it difficult to speak without."[27] By that time the Great Awakening had transformed the art of preaching in America but its impact upon the Jesuit pulpit style seems to have been minimal.

For the Catholic gentry the Jesuits often served as agents for obtaining works on scripture, theology, apologetics, or the spiritual life. They also maintained lending libraries. Besides the Old and New Testaments, instructional books and manuals of instruction, such as John Gother's *Instructions for Particular States and Conditions of Life* and Richard Challoner's *Garden of the Soul,* were in particular demand.

"He has hurt his own cause, not us":
Maryland Jesuits, Enlightenment, and Revolution

When Pope Clement XIV suppressed the Society of Jesus in 1773, even the Maryland Jesuits, as removed as they were from European affairs, were not surprised. Joseph Mosley wrote his sister in October 1774 that they had been dreading it. The event still sent shockwaves through Maryland Jesuits from the Eastern Shore to the Low Countries. "I know no fault we are guilty off," Mosley confessed. "I am convinced that our labors are pure, upright and sincere, for God's honour and our neighbour's good. What our Supreme Judge on Earth may think of our labours is a mystery to me. He has hurt his own cause, not us."[28] John Carroll, writing to his brother from Bruges, admitted that he "perhaps never shall be, recovered from the shock of this dreadful intelligence." Quite clearly both Carroll and Mosley identified mission and Society. "In me," Mosley confided to his sister, "the Jesuit and the Missioner was always combined together; if one falls, the other must of consequence fall with it."

Despite such identifications, none of the Maryland Jesuits left America or the priesthood in the wake of the suppression or the revolution against England that followed less than two years later. Mosley felt himself "between hawk and buzzard," and subsequently was barred from preaching when he failed to take the oath of allegiance to the new Maryland government. The apolitical Mosley ("a Clergyman's call has little to do with civil broils and troubled waters") eventually subscribed and remained at his station in Maryland until his death in 1787.

John Carroll who had returned from Europe in the spring of 1774, soon found himself a participant in the revolution. Despite his conviction that "ministers of Religion" who became political activists generally made fools of themselves or their cause, he agreed to serve on an abortive mission to Canada in 1776 to persuade the inhabitants to join the revolt against England. Carroll remained a staunch celebrator of the revolution, including the civil and religious liberties that followed the Declaration of Independence. By 1784 Carroll had reorganized the dispirited ex-Jesuits under a constitutional government and the following year Rome named him superior of the church in the United States. Five years later his fellow priests elected him bishop. His diocese, he once remarked, was without boundaries. By 1803 it stretched from Vermont to Louisiana. For thirty years he administered it, traveling by coach and boat, working eighteen hour days, penning without a secretary responses to his mounting volume of mail.

His episcopal duties allowed him little time for reflection; still his correspondence and pastoral letters reveal a distinct vision, the product of enlightened French and English Catholic influences. Drawing heavily upon the ideas of English Catholics such as Joseph Berington and John Fletcher, Carroll's enlightened Catholicism stressed the reasonable person, the intelligibility of Christianity, the continuity between nature and grace, and a latitudinarian ecclesiology that included all believers.[29]

In the tradition of his Maryland ancestors Carroll championed religious liberty because he found it such a rich matrix not only for enlightened inquiry but also for the Spirit's stirrings. "In matters of faith," he preached, "everything must be free & voluntary" (see "Confess our Faith Exteriorly"). Like Berington he was convinced that toleration promoted the free and full discussion that exposed truth and cultivated "unity of Opinion on matters of Religious concern."[30] His Protestant neighbors he already regards as "Brethren in J. Christ." For Carroll they are already members of the Church, although not in communion.

Carroll's spirituality, like his ideology, is moderately rational. God's world is the temperate world. What he asks is "a just and reasonable homage" (see "Confess Our Faith Exteriorly"). For Carroll faith is largely intellectual. "The clearest principles of reasoning" have more credibility than "pious prophecies & visions."[31] The Revolution for Carroll was a part of sacred history because it had established a society in which people are free to govern themselves and worship according to their own consciences. In the open society of America, Catholics now know a liberty that stands in sharp contrast to the lack of freedom that has marked the Church's history. Through the Revolution America has claimed Catholics as its "own," taken them under "her protection," but a protection that does not stifle but liberates (see "Sermon on Independence of Church in America").

In his later years Carroll had some misgivings about the wisdom of a free trade in ideas. He stressed more the limits of reason in revealing God's dispensation for mankind. Reason is not autonomous; by itself it can ruin society. If the United States is founded on the bedrock of a moral people, that people's virtue can survive only as long as their religion flourishes, and that religion must have a divine origin, that is, be known to men and women by revelation. In a republic that counts the pursuit of happiness as a God-given right, that pursuit is ultimately frustrated without the guidance of revelation. For Carroll the problem lies not in the mind, but in the heart. Revelation alone can constitute a democracy of knowledge in which piety and justice can flourish. Rational religion is elitist, excluding the young, uneducated, weak-minded, those without leisure—in short, most of society. Ultimately such a rationalistic epistemology guarantees an heuristic paralysis, as the history of the intellectuals who have tried to construct such natural religions demonstrates (see "Necessity of Revelation").

Only the Holy Spirit who dwells in all members of the church can ensure institutional fidelity to revelation and enhance the natural dignity of the individual. Carroll distinguished between the indwelling of the Spirit within individuals and within the Church. "To private persons," he affirmed, "the Holy Ghost is given as the spirit of sanctification; but to the church as the spirit of truth, as well as sanctification, guiding him into all truth, and directly excluding all error from her."[32] If scripture and tradition are complementary, it is because both emanate from the apostles and their successors.[33]

Carroll's sermons presuppose a mature and open Christian at home in a society that respects his spiritual nature. The Mystical Body Carroll sees as a republic of the spirit in which Christian "projectors" build up the body of believers through their prayer and work. If American Catholics enjoy unprecedented religious liberty, all the greater is the "duty of honoring your Religion. A duty extending itself to all of us, . . . " especially to the laity whose words and deeds will have more influence in a republic than those of a clergyman fulfilling his office (see "Confess Our Religion Exteriorly"). He continued to take seriously the duty of ministers of religion to enlighten the understanding of mankind, but he had also come to appreciate that the greater need was to stir the heart, "to reanimate the grace" of those who already possessed the Spirit (see "Two Sermons on Confirmation").

"He will stand you in lieu of everything else":
The Jesuit Tradition Between Suppression and Restoration

Because Catherine the Great valued the Jesuit schools in White Russia, she had refused to allow the brief of suppression to be promulgated in areas under her rule. That remnant of the Society of Jesus in Russia spurred the hopes of reestablishment for Jesuits in many places, including America. Ten years after *Dominus ac Redemptor* the ex-Jesuits in Maryland and Pennsylvania, under Carroll's leadership, formally organized themselves, partly to preserve the Society's property toward the day when it might again be revived in what was now the United States. In 1788 thirteen former Jesuits determined to do everything possible to join the Society that had survived in Russia. "[W]e conceive this government of the Society," they declared, "to be the only one that can procure us the happiness our hearts are in search after. We have felt her controul, we have experienced her influence, which has stamped impressions on our souls not to be erased."[34] In 1804 permission came from Rome for the ex-Jesuits in the United States to affiliate with the Society in Russia.

The Pious Guide to Prayer and Devotion (1791), edited by some ex-Jesuits in Georgetown, reflects the persistence of the Jesuit tradition of spirituality two decades after suppression. The guide is largely a compilation of Jesuit devotions, including two of the most characteristic ones, devotion to the Sacred Heart and the Novena in honor of St. Francis Xavier.

The Sacred Heart Devotion, stressing God's love and Christ's humanity, had been one of the issues which opponents had raised against the Society before the suppression, with Jansenists especially attacking the benevolent cast of its anthropology and soteriology. That ex-Jesuits gave it such a prominent place in their manual said much about their defiant loyalty to their heritage. How deeply rooted it was in the British American Catholic community is uncertain. Devotional literature on the Sacred Heart was circulating in some volume in Maryland by the 1760s. Although some later Jesuits found it unsuitable for the United States, it fit well the social conditions of 18th century Maryland Catholics. As the *Guide* explained: "What more beneficial, than a devotion, which so far from being confined to some barren and outward practices chiefly consists in a constant study of the interior dispositions of this adorable Heart, and in an uninterrupted endeavour to model ourselves on it, and transcribe its virtues into our own lives[.]" The devotion lent itself to the private nature of Maryland Catholicism. With its centerpiece in the morning act of consecration, it was a lay person's way of practicing the Ignatian spirituality that found God in all things, even the most mundane. "He will stand you in lieu of everything else," the *Guide* assured its readers in the section on the Sacred Heart, "if you but know how to seek all things in him."

The Novena in honor of St. Francis Xavier became an annual high point of popular piety in Jesuit circles in the United States in the late nineteenth century. "The Novena of Grace" drew thousands to the urban Jesuit churches. Mission bands and newly ordained Jesuits preached the novena in many other parishes in towns, villages, and countryside. Reaching across classes to men and women alike, the novena functioned as an annual minimission for adults too busy to spend more than a half-hour in church during workdays. There was also the central premise of Xavier's power in obtaining material and spiritual favors. Even if the person experienced no such intervention, there was still the church's spiritual rewards for those who fulfilled the conditions set down for the proper making of the novena. In the late nineteenth century Leo XIII granted a plenary indulgence for anyone who made the novena in a Jesuit church; in the twentieth century Pius XI extended it to any church.

The novena dated to the early seventeenth century on the continent. Instructions in English for making the novena were published at St. Omers in 1690 (*The Manner of Performing the Novena Or The Nine Days of Devotion to St. Francis Xaverius: Of the Society of Jesus and Apostle of India*) but the *Guide* is the first mention of the devotion in Maryland. What is significant is that this manual seems to presuppose a private novena, either read

or listened to at home. The authors point out that it can be made at any time
during the year. It is in sharp contrast, not only with the practice of a century
later, but even with the St. Omers edition which pointed out that performing
the novena in the church, "with great Solemnity, great concourse of People, and daily Sermons upon the Vertues of St. Francis Xaverius . . . is the
better way, not only because God in the Church . . . is more inclined to
grant our requests; but also, because the Prayer of many together is more
acceptable to God; and when all be for all, every individual the more easily
obtains his desire, by reason that Charity adds Force to Prayer. . . . "[35] The
theology upon which this preference is based may be sounder, but the Maryland ex-Jesuits chose to follow the 1765 Bruges version of *The Manner,*
which omitted this section, presumably in deference to the tenuous status
of the Society at that time in the Lowlands. They also prescribed a corporal
or spiritual work of mercy, as well as the spreading of the devotion to others, guidelines that disappeared from the nineteenth century manuals.

In general there is a democratic thrust to the spirituality of the *Guide*
which perhaps accounts for its remarkable popularity. It presupposes a
Catholic laity controlling its own devotional life. As Joseph Chinnici has
pointed out, it is very much within the humanistic tradition of piety, Chris-
tocentric and optimistic in its encouragement of individuals to pursue piety
interiorly with relatively little reliance on intermediaries or official structures.[36] By 1852 it had gone through at least twelve editions.[37]

"This is the worst of all provinces":
Restoration and Pluralism

In June 1844, shortly after Isaac Hecker had decided to enter the Roman Catholic Church, he visited the college which the Maryland Province
had recently established in Worcester, Massachusetts. He found the Jesuits
there well educated within a rather narrow circle of scripture and church
history, but dogmatic in their approach to problems and "profoundly ignorant" of philosophy. "These men *seem to me,*" he wrote his friend Orestes Brownson,

> . . . [to be] wanting that vital consciousness of divine eternal life
> and high spiritual aspirations which have animated so many of the
> children of the true Church. I had to ask them repeatedly if that
> was the ground on which they based a true christian life[,] the
> lowest and the least that the Church demands of us.

Still he was willing to believe that if he really got to know them, their "private virtues" would surface.[38]

Many European Jesuits, had they been privy to Hecker's letter, would have responded that the convert had been too generous in judging his Jesuit hosts. From the generals of the Society to the Jesuit emigrés in this country, the conviction was that the Maryland Jesuits in the post-restoration period were utterly lacking religious discipline and zeal. It was no accident that from 1840 to 1877 only one native American was made provincial. In that time four immigrant members of the province were appointed to that office, and three foreign Jesuits brought in with the explicit mission of reforming the province and regenerating its spiritual life. There was also an official visitor sent from the general to promote the same ends. As late as 1897 an English Jesuit was appointed provincial and visitor with a reform mandate.

From the time that the Society was restored in America in 1805 until the late nineteenth century, foreign Jesuits constituted a substantial portion of the Maryland mission/province. In the first three decades when Maryland was an international mission, foreigners were in the majority. In the 1850s they were still a third of the province. Their reports to Rome contributed greatly to the negative image of the Maryland Jesuits there.

The immigrant Jesuits found their American brethren too much the children of their culture, too imbued with the national spirit of liberty and materialism. Many of these Europeans, such as the Germans and Italians who arrived in 1848, were refugees from revolutions. They tended to be very suspicious of American society and of the liberal principles upon which it was based. One Italian immigrant was appalled that the Maryland Jesuits at Georgetown enthusiastically took part in the "national feasts" of Washington's birthday and the Fourth of July by staging grand banquets. "By thus praising the founding fathers," he observed, "they think they will win popular respect which they love too much and are too much influenced by."[39] The Europeans were forever complaining about the lack of religious order in the province: the overindulgence in alcohol, the lack of silence during sacred hours, the going out at night or without a companion or both, the receiving of lay guests, both male and female, in the private rooms of the houses. As one European concluded in 1838: "This is the worst of all provinces."[40]

Other immigrant Jesuits thought this judgment an exaggeration but were convinced that the Maryland Province was far from the spirit of the Society. Too many of the native Jesuits, they found, were too preoccupied with temporal things and too little with those of the spirit.

In a religious order that had lost absolutely all of its property in Europe at the time of its suppression in 1773, the Maryland Jesuits with their huge estates in Maryland and Pennsylvania seemed an anomaly. For the superiors general the land was more a curse than a blessing. Both Aloysius Fortis and John Roothaan worried that the planter-pastor lifestyle in Maryland and

Pennsylvania did not really promote the Institute of the Society. By 1831 there were 400 slaves on the six estates in southern and eastern Maryland. There were fears about the corrupting effects of the Peculiar Institution upon their personal morality and apostolic zeal. Moreover the Maryland Jesuits in the 1810s and 1820s seemed to be bankrupting their future by their cavalier attitude about the formation of their scholastics and novices. An open admissions policy prevailed, and novices were either undersupervised or pulled away to teach school; in hard times, the Mission closed the novitiate and sent the novices home as an economy measure.

When the Maryland Jesuits resisted the Archbishop of Baltimore, the general, and the pope in the 1820s in response to the archbishop's claim that the lands were juridically his, it deepened Fortis' suspicions that the Maryland Jesuits loved their land more than the Society or the Church. Even after most of the slaves were sold in 1838 and the apostolic focus shifted to the cities and the founding of urban colleges, the manorial heritage still seemed to prevail: the Roman Catholic gentlemen of Maryland were now becoming expectant capitalists.

In 1839 the provincial, Thomas Mulledy, was forced to resign because of the scandal he had given in the mass sale of the province's slaves in the preceding year (some families had been unwittingly separated; the slaves were sold to buyers in the Deep South). When Mulledy's successor, William McSherry, died of cancer six months later, Francis Dzierozynski was appointed superior.

Dzierozynski, a missionary from the Russian Province, had been superior of the Maryland Mission during the controversy with Archbishop Marechal in the 1820s. Dzierozynski had been responsible for breaking the autonomy of the Corporation of Roman Catholic Clergymen of Maryland, the civil body that administered the Jesuit estates in Maryland. He brought with him much the same wariness about American republican values that most of the emigrés brought. But if his fellow emigrés expected Dzierozynski to put the province into the order they thought proper, they were quickly disappointed. Unlike many of the other Europeans, Dzierozynski had learned much about America since coming here in 1821. He had also come to appreciate the Ignatian principle of adaptation according to circumstances. What worked in Europe, what could ideally govern behavior there was not *a priori* to be set down as a code to be rigidly observed. It might be the ideal, he wrote Father General Roothaan in 1841, to have no visitors at a college, but "considering the circumstances of this society, namely a new world and a new population, and many of them Protestants," (including a good portion of the students at Georgetown) an absolute prohibition was out of the question. Dzierozynski also now vehemently denied that the Americans suffered from a spirit of nationalism. Such complaints, as well as those concerning the degenerate state of the province, were to him the products of overvivid imaginations with no foundation in reality.[41]

Unfortunately the general had ceased listening to Dzierozynski. Newer immigrants like Anthony Rey had his ear. Rey from France had been in the country less than two years. He nonetheless reported to Roothaan that there was an "urgent need" for a provincial who would combine talent, prudence, knowledge of the Institute, "and the desire to have it observed to the letter, as the circumstances and your instructions permit." The Maryland Jesuits especially needed "an interior man, who will give his special attention to the morale of our Province, and motivate us to that interior and truly religious spirit, which we now more or less are lacking."[42] Two years later the General brought in a Belgian from the Missouri Vice-Province, Peter Verhaegen, who ironically had been a novice in Maryland in 1823 when the superior had closed the novitiate. Verhaegen made Anthony Rey his assistant.

Verhaegen, however, also disappointed the general. By 1847 the provincial was pleading that the opposition of certain key Roman trained Maryland Jesuits (Thomas Mulledy and his brother Samuel, James Ryder, George Fenwick) was nullifying his attempts to reform the province. In his place Roothaan sent Ignatius Brocard from Switzerland. Brocard too could not escape *miramurs* from Rome. But Brocard was a wise choice. He knew the Society and he quickly came to know America. He realized early that which has confounded so many idealists—how differently "things work out in America from what is planned; even," he once told the general, "when your Paternity has intervened. . . . "[43] Brocard was compassionate but decisive. He dismissed several ne'er-do-wells, including Samuel Mulledy, from the province ranks. He seized upon the availability of many distinguished German, Swiss, and Italian Jesuit emigrés to provide for the first time an adequate faculty for the formation of Jesuit scholastics and to expand the educational apostolate of the province. He lessened the ethnic tensions.[44] Then in March 1852 he died suddenly from typhoid fever, probably the worst loss the province had suffered in its brief history.

Roothaan's successor, Peter Beckx, also had difficulty understanding American Jesuits and attempted to impose special regulations that would bring their mores into line with their European brothers. The first provincial that the new general appointed in Maryland, Burchard Villiger, was, like Brochard, a Swiss emigré. He was keenly aware of being an outsider but, also like Brochard, had rapidly acculturated himself to his new country. He suggested to Beckx in 1859: " . . . Americans can not be forced to sanctity, cannot be forced to perfection, but nonetheless they can more quickly and securely be brought [to this state] with gentleness and exhortation than with rigor. . . . In time the Americans will be equal to the Europeans but give them time. . . . "[45]

The Americans, Villiger found, simply did not know "the Spirituality of the Society." They were not malicious, simply badly formed. A minimalist attitude prevailed. "They seemed to rejoice," he noted, "that Holy father Ignatius said that His rules do not oblige under sin."[46] Villiger thought that Beckx's regulations would merely aggravate the nativist charges about the unamerican character of the Jesuits. More importantly, he argued, they failed to take circumstances into account. He warned that enforcing them would take more of his time than all the rest of his governance of the province. "But if your Paternity thinks it necessary to make the rules public," he concluded, "then it will be necessary to elect an American Provincial, because I can not succeed in this barring a miracle."[47]

A few months later the general informed Villiger that he was sending still another official visitor, the third in less than twenty years. The new delegate, Felix Sopranis, was no stranger to Maryland. He had originally come to the province as a refugee in 1848. As the general's visitor he quickly put into effect the regulations that Villiger had balked at. His decrees for the spiritual renewal of the province were detailed and comprehensive. Superiors, especially the presidents of colleges, were reminded that their major concern was the direction of their subjects toward perfection; to do that they themselves needed to know the Constitution and Rules of the Society, and to "apply them gently but efficaciously." A set daily order was an absolute necessity. Individuals could not be free to rise when they wished or to make their spiritual exercises as they would. Meals should be at least in silence, if common reading could not be provided. There should be an annual eight day retreat for everyone. Those renewing vows should make a triduum of recollection. In addition the reading of newspapers was to be restricted to superiors and those whom the superior judged had a legitimate reason to use them. All should be home before nightfall, except those engaged in the care of souls. There should be particular vigilance about going out alone, although the visitor admitted there were often circumstances that made this impossible in this country. The scholasticate would be transferred from Georgetown to Conewago, a province farm in southeastern Pennsylvania, where the seminarians could concentrate on their studies and be free from the corrupting influences of Washington. "Let everyone understand," he concluded, "that there does not exist in the Society nor can it exist in any province—a general dispensation from the minimal observance of the Rules."[48]

A wave of protest swept through the province houses at the release of these decrees. Villiger found it necessary to convene the local superiors, without the visitor's knowledge, in order to get them to put into practice voluntarily "what they would scarcely consent to do under orders."[49] He pointed out to the general that Sopranis' decrees were too rigidly detailed for the American religious.[50] "Fr. Sopranis is indeed a holy and most beloved man of the Society," he commented; "however[,] it will be good to remember that although in theory he is especially sound, in practice, because of his age . . . he does not appreciate how things can be affected by many circumstances of time and place with the most serious consequences. . . . "[51]

For twenty years Maryland provincials, whether natives or immigrants, had been saying the same thing. They differed on their appraisal of the spiritual health of the province but agreed that the rigid imposition of European customs would not promote spirituality in America. Such an Old World matrix would merely repel American Jesuits and confirm nativist prejudices. Still the reputation of the Maryland Jesuits as spiritual vagrants persisted. As late as 1879, one of the reasons for merging the New York mission to the Maryland Province and moving the provincial's headquarters to New York City was the hope that religious discipline would be strengthened and the Maryland "tradition" of easy living be broken by new blood and a new location for provincial authority. In 1895 still another general regarded the Maryland Province as being in virtual "secession" from the Society.

"Digitus Dei est hic":
Stephen Dubuisson and Continental Piety

"I'm very glad that Dubuisson does not return with you," James Ryder wrote from Rome in 1828 to a fellow American Jesuit on his way home. "I'd rather he was left in Rome . . . he would thus be serviceable to America and escape the odium of the Americans."[52] Dubuisson, a French emigré (from both Santo Domingo and the continent), had been in the United States for a decade before being called to Rome in 1826. To many of the American Jesuits he represented the worst of the rigid monastic piety of the Europeans, pursuing a bubble-tent spirituality that absolutized rules and isolated the individual from the world. His early diary reveals a fragile, somewhat narcissistic idealist cultivating a rather hot-house variety of spirituality. It is clear from the diary and other sources that in his gentle way he felt quite alien to American society. He tended to consider monarchy as the ideal in both the temporal and spiritual orders. Nothing upset him more than the prospect of a position of authority for himself.

But if America repelled him, he was increasingly attracted to Rome. He confessed to Father General Fortis in 1823 that he had long had a desire to go to Rome and see the Society of Jesus.[53] This ultramontanist perception of the Society won him few friends among the American Jesuits but endeared him to Rome. When he finally got his opportunity to live there for three years, he greatly impressed superiors by his zeal and simplicity. John Roothaan was especially taken with him. In 1839 Dubuisson's letters to the general decrying the scandal of the mass sale of the slaves to the Deep South probably had more to do with the removal of Mulledy than anything else.

Dubuisson's private apostolate in the United States became the promotion of miracles. In his diary in 1818 he wrote: "It is dangerous to pray for extraordinary favours from above; yet it is very laudable to act so as to deserve them. Chiefly men of prayer and contemplation obtain them. Frequently at least such favours are not granted us for us only; but also for the sake of promoting God's glory among our fellow-creatures, and then we must publish them." Whatever the danger, six years later Dubuisson was the leading advocate in the United States of the European priest-healer, the Prince Alexander Hohenlohe. Together with Anthony Kohlmann, another European Jesuit immigrant and Dubuisson's former theology instructor, he promoted the miraculous cures of more than a dozen individuals, virtually all women, and mostly members of religious orders, in a span of fourteen years between 1824 and 1838. The major ones all occurred at the very moment the individual received the Eucharist. Pamphlets were published; reports were written to Rome to show that God could work such wonders even in the United States.

Faith healing, of course, was by no means a phenomenon unique to American Catholics in the nineteenth century. One need only consider the interest in mesmerism and Christian Science, for example, to appreciate the widespread appeal of cults and esoteric wisdom that promised cures of mind and body. And the prominence of women in these circles was common enough. Still the Catholic cures had their own significance.

Miraculous cures had roots in the American Catholic community as far back as Andrew White. But the phenomenon had seemed to die with the first generation. By the 1820s faith healing was something foreign to the community whose approach to religion stressed common sense and practicality. To Dubuisson the miracles were palpable proof that "digitus dei est hic"; they revealed in this sensational way the wonder working effects of the Real Presence in the Catholic sacrament and confirmed the superior claim of Catholicism to the mantle of Christianity in a society in which denominations had to compete for popular support. Dubuisson's isolation from the larger culture and preoccupation with the miraculous as the sign of God's presence in society prefigured the authoritarian and ultramontanist patterns that proved dominant in the American church by the close of the century. In the phenomenon of the cures of the 1820s and 1830s one gets a glimpse of the passage of the American Catholic community from "enlightened" to "devotional" Catholicism.[54] They reflect a religious sensibility that was replacing the older humanistic piety characteristic of a John Carroll or *The Pius Guide,* a sensibility that "separated the Church from the world, facilitated the mystification of authority, and placed order, external conformity, at the center of the spiritual life."[55]

"The most profitable part of our Ministry":
John McElroy and Catholic Revivalism

In 1842 there were 107 persons in the province: 35 priests, 31 scholastics, and 41 coadjutors. Over one half of them were engaged in the two colleges at Georgetown and Frederick, including all of the 14 scholastics in theology and philosophy at Georgetown. There were 24 missions or parishes, only three of which were urban (in Alexandria, Georgetown, and Philadelphia). There were nearly 30 more Jesuits than there had been ten years before, but the number of priests was virtually the same. In that same period the Catholic population in the United States had doubled (from an estimated 600,000 to approximately 1,300,000).

One of the reasons Father General Roothaan wanted the Maryland Jesuits to give up the rural missions and farms was to free some of them for "bands of missionaries" who would be ready to give retreats to clergy or laity throughout the eastern part of the United States. A few American Jesuits were already engaged in this work. As we have noted, Jesuits were giving the *Spiritual Exercises* in Maryland as early as the 1630s. After the first decade, however, all mention of retreat giving drops out of the annual reports. The practice of giving missions went back to the late eighteenth century in Maryland but it was not part of the English Catholic tradition. Early proponents of missions in Maryland had been continental immigrants, like John Baptist M. David from France and Anthony Kohlmann from White Russia.[56] During the antebellum period the two most active Jesuits on the East Coast in this apostolate were John McElroy and James Ryder, both from Ireland, where missions had strong roots, especially in the Scotch-Irish north where Presbyterian evangelicalism had been flourishing since the seventeenth century.

As early as 1827 McElroy was engaged in this work at St. John's, Frederick. Deeply concerned about the poor, his vision transcended the boundaries of the Catholic community. Conversions became a pressing matter for him and missions or retreats became the key to his apostolate to preserve and spread the faith. Whatever the origins of McElroy's commitment to missions, it gave him an advantage in America where revivalism was sweeping and resweeping the land, leaving "burned over districts" and a transformed culture. Missions in effect were the Catholic counterpart of revivals in regenerating the faith of natives and immigrants alike through the week-long exercises that included Mass, instructions, meditations, litanies, the rosary, benediction, and the sacrament of reconciliation.

By 1840 McElroy was pleading to the general that missions should be the top priority for Jesuit apostolates in America.

> From my little experience in . . . retreats . . . I am convinced it is the *most profitable part* of our ministry, and to *form a band exclusively for such,* say 3 or 4, would deserve almost any sacrifice, this *be the means under God, of laying solidly, the foundations of our holy religion in this new world* of renovating the Clergy, and through them the Laity. . . . I w[oul]d willingly offer myself as the last & the least, to labor with them in this glorious enterprise—by such a band it is not only a single city or village, that would profit by our labors; but *the whole United States!*[57]

The immigrant provincials in the 1840s and 1850s supported McElroy's efforts. Father General Roothaan authorized the creation of a mission band, but it proved premature; there was no one to spare from the colleges and parishes for such work. Nonetheless, by 1851 the priests completing their formation were giving missions in Maryland and Pennsylvania to blacks and whites, slaves and masters, with thousands of communicants and scores of converts. Three years later the young priests were not only working the towns and villages of Maryland and Pennsylvania but as far south as Georgia.

The 1850s witnessed the rise of the parish mission as a major instrument of revitalization and evangelization within the American church. In this development the mission movement within circles of Catholic Europe, the success of Protestant revivalism, and concern about unchurched immigrants were all influential. The Jesuits were but one of several religious orders that began to specialize in this apostolate. The Passionists, the Redemptorists, and the Paulists, founded by former Redemptorists principally for the work of parish missions, were all heavily engaged in Catholic revivalism. The differences were in the structure and themes of the missions that the religious ordered conducted. While the Jesuits promoted the devotion to the Sacred Heart, the Redemptorists gave a special place to Mary and the Passionists predictably enough focused on the Passion. All were in the business of fostering *metanoia* through their sermons and devotional exercises.[58]

McElroy himself, despite his many other involvements, remained incredibly active on this circuit for over thirty years. As late as 1863, in the middle of the Civil War, when he was 81, he travelled over 2000 miles by steamer, rail, and carriage in less than four months to give retreats in Baltimore, New York, St. John's (New Brunswick) and Halifax.

John McElroy was largely self-educated. That included the spiritual life. For years he tried to set aside an hour a day to study moral theology to better meet the needs of his people. He wanted to keep a traditional schedule that included a set time for Mass, meditation, spiritual reading, the divine office, and the examination of conscience. In 1823, shortly after moving to Frederick, he vowed to improve his "interior recollection" by increased periods of silence, isolation, and prayer. But McElroy's own apostolic activity kept conflicting with his asceticism and devotional routine. In his yearly retreats he continued to censure himself for neglecting his mental prayer and spiritual reading and set a new schedule for himself. In later years he seemed to realize that what was most important was the promotion of God's glory (the phrase becomes much more frequent with him; indeed the Ignatian concept of "the greater glory"), not the keeping of his schedule or even of all the exercises he set for himself. He was realizing the consolation of finding God in all things, even though the tensions between contemplation and action never disappeared entirely.

John McElroy was showing in his unspeculative way how the Ignatian spirit of contemplation in action could find rich soil in America. As John Wright has pointed out, the Ignatian charism "does not map out a field, giving [Jesuits] . . . a definite area within which [their] efforts are to be enclosed. . . . rather it is a basic drive in [their] . . . lives . . . [;] not a platonic ideal, some remote and changeless idea existing in a world apart."[59] John McElroy incarnated this Ignatian legacy in a way that eluded many of his more formally trained Jesuit brothers. It allowed him to serve with such unselfishness and flexibility, knowing that the work was essentially God's and not his.

"Americans, you are marked for their prey":
The Maryland Jesuits and Nativism

Benedict Fenwick wrote about his arrival in Boston in 1825 in language reminiscent of Bradford's *Plymouth Plantation:*

He saw himself in a situation far from being enviable—in a section of the country to which he was a perfect stranger, without a single confidential friend of ancient acquaintance, and in the midst of a congregation wholly unknown to him and particularly devoted and attached to their late Pastor. He found at his disposal only one Clergyman at Boston, and two at the distance of one hundred miles from it, who had each his own congregation to attend to. He had no other Priests for the various calls which might be made upon him from other parts of the Diocess—nor had he any means of increasing his Clergy, or even a prospect of being able to add to their number. . . . The Bishop, however, did not yield to despondence—he had put his whole confidence in God, who was the strength of the weak, and who could *out of the very stones raise up children* to Levi as well as *to Abraham. He did not take the honor to himself, but was called of God,* through his Vicar Leo, *as Aaron was,*—and he knew that he who had called him, could impart to him sufficient strength and grace to accomplish his end, and could also furnish him, in due time, with all the means requisite for its full accomplishment.[60]

Over the next two decades Fenwick's faith in the Lord was matched by the remarkable development of Catholicism in New England. The bishop founded churches, schools, a journal, even a rural colony in Maine for poor Catholics, as his diocese grew from a tiny community whose most prominent members were French emigrés to a sprawling body dominated by Irish immigrants. Such growth had its costs, among which was the ecumenism which Fenwick assiduously cultivated in his early days in Boston. The turning point was the burning of the Ursuline convent at Charlestown in 1834 and its frustrating aftermath in the courts, as the alleged arsonists were acquitted and the Sisters denied compensation. Fenwick seems to have concluded that the irenic approach of his beloved predecessor, Jean-Louis Chevrus, had no place in Boston by the mid-thirties.[61]

By the second quarter of the century Roman Catholicism had replaced deism or infidelity as the greatest threat to America's becoming a Protestant empire. The sharp influx of Catholic immigrants, the conversion of prominent Protestants to Catholicism, the attempts of Catholic prelates to secure public funds for their schools—all combined to alarm many evangelical Protestants. Anti-Catholic tracts became something of a cottage industry in the three decades before the Civil War. The Society of Jesus received a disproportionate share of attention. Samuel F. B. Morse, in a tract published in 1835 shrilly warned:

[The Jesuits] have already sent their chains and oh! to our shame be it spoken, you are fastening them upon a *sleeping victim.* Americans you are marked for their prey, not by foreign bayonets, but by weapons surer of effecting the conquest of liberty, than all the munitions of physical combat in the military or naval storehouses of Europe. Will you not awake to the apprehension

of the reality and extent of your danger? . . . Up! Up! I beseech
you, Awake! To your posts! Let the tocsin sound from Maine to
Louisiana. Fly to protect the vulnerable places of your Constitution and laws. . . . "[62]

Most attacks, like Morse's, were rhetorical but there was occasional
violence, as at Charlestown. Nativism flared both in the forties and fifties.
In the latter decade attempts to secure public funds for parochial schools,
and restiveness over the growing sectional crisis nurtured a xenophobia
which found convenient targets in Catholics, especially Jesuits. In 1854 in
Ellsworth, Maine a crowd tarred and feathered John Bapst, a Swiss Jesuit
refugee who was working with Indians and Irish immigrants.

Nowhere was the American Party, the political organ of the nativists,
stronger than in Maryland. In 1854 it elected its candidate mayor of Baltimore. The following year it captured the state legislature. In 1856 Maryland became the only state to cast its presidential vote for the American or
Know-Nothing Party candidate, Millard Fillmore. By 1850 twenty percent
of the city's population was foreign born. During the decade, German and
Irish immigrants, many of them Catholics, streamed into the city from the
docks in increasing numbers. In 1852 a Catholic delegate in the legislature
introduced a bill to secure funds for sectarian schools. That same year the
First Plenary Council of the church hierarchy convened in Baltimore. And
the Maryland Province finally opened Loyola College. To many Marylanders the growing power of the church seemed all too evident. In a community disrupted by demographic and socio-economic changes that
included the decline of slavery, immigrants and Catholics "served, like
lightning rods, to attract the apprehensive attentions of citizens whose old
ways of life were disappearing. . . . "[63]

In the district of Columbia, Charles Stonestreet felt the shockwaves
from Maryland. " . . . [We] are in a crisis," he wrote Father General
Beckx in 1856. Stonestreet worried that nativism might poison the presidential election that year. "In such a situation prudence seems very much
in order for us, so that we . . . project an image of calm regarding the outside world."[64] Calmness, though, did not mean absolute silence. In February 1855 the provincial wrote a letter to *The Metropolitan*, a Baltimore
magazine, to respond to the hoary charge that Jesuits took an oath to overthrow non-Catholic rulers. "I am humiliated as a Marylander," he wrote,

> to . . . repel the charge of more than latent treason! The Western
> shore of Maryland, the home of my childhood, has ever been a
> classic place, cherished in my heart with patriotic pride. There
> are the remains of my grandfather, a revolutionary soldier, and

there, in an adjoining country, is the landing place of "The Pilgrims of St. Mary's," whose brightest scenes and best memories are imperishably connected with the Jesuits' name.

. . . I can not help seeing in this, an effort to render me and my brethren in religion, aliens at home and strangers by our own fireplace.[65]

Of course many of the Jesuits in Maryland *were* aliens. The persistence of Germans and Italians in clinging to their native languages and openly decrying American ways was providing welcome ammunition for the nativist attacks. As one Marylander warned the general, ethnic differences that had previously "unsettled only our houses and colleges" now had much larger repercussions.[66] No one was more sensitive to the delicate position of foreign Jesuits than Villiger. "Would that we had an American Provincial in this region!" he wrote the general in 1859.[67] Villiger thought that Father General Beckx was making his position even worse by attempting to impose certain regulations regarding nocturnal visits and the like.

When Civil War broke out in 1861 the new provincial Angelo Paresce urged that his subjects abstain "from every spirit of party."[68] Such non-involvement in politics was part of the Maryland Jesuit tradition. John Carroll himself, realizing that priests and politics rarely mix well, had warily consented to being part of the mission to pursue the Canadians to join the Revolution in 1776. But Carroll had not only gone but became a staunch supporter of the patriot cause. Maryland Jesuits had prided themselves on their patriotism, as we have noted. As recently as the Mexican War the province had taken advantage of the opportunity to demonstrate its allegiance by appointing John McElroy and other Jesuit chaplains. 1861 was not 1846, of course. This was civil war.

But if the English ex-Jesuits in America had found themselves confused in the face of divided loyalties in the American Revolution, there was something new in the policy of caution and silence that superiors imposed at the outbreak of the Civil War. To understand it one must appreciate not only the damage that nativism had done to the Jesuit psyche over the past generation, but more importantly the defensive attitude that refugee Jesuits brought with them. Being uprooted in a revolution could make one very sensitive to giving the least pretext for offense. Thus Stephen Dubuisson, himself a refugee as a young child from revolution in Santo Domingo, agonized over what liturgical acknowledgement he should make of President Harrison's death in 1841 when Dubuisson was pastor of St. Mary's Church in Alexandria. For Dubuisson even a sermon and prayer for a dead president smacked of politics. That the Society in Italy was itself in the midst of a revolution that was threatening Rome by 1860 conditioned the fears that some American Jesuits harbored about the American situation. Father General Beckx kept instructing Paresce that he do everything possible to ensure that no cause be given for offending one side or the other.

Thomas Mulledy and Antebellum Jesuit Preaching

If John McElroy and James Ryder were utilizing extemporaneous sermons to give soul to their missions, the older form of preaching hung on tenaciously among Maryland Jesuits. Thomas Mulledy was the most renowned of the traditional preachers on the Catholic circuit that stretched from Boston to southern Maryland. John Hughes had him preach at his installation in 1838 as Coadjutor Bishop of New York. In the Maryland tradition Mulledy depended, at least in part, upon European models. Some sermons he explicitly attributed to others, such as the Italian Jesuits, Giovanni Grannelli (1703–1770) and Francesco Finetti (1762–1842). Others seem to have been derivative sermons extensively reworked. Still others seem largely original.

If all we knew of Thomas Mulledy were his sermons, we would think him some grim-visaged Catholic Calvinist. The topics of sin and death preoccupy him. "The Dying Sinner," "Forgetfulness of Death," and "The Thought of Death" are typical titles. Other titles seemingly unrelated to death are nonetheless woven into that context, as in his sermon on the "Examination of our Charity" which is framed in the constant expectation we should have of our last day. Even his sermon on the feast of the Immaculate Conception, given four times between 1852 and 1859, stresses the connection between sanctifying grace and death. Death had long been a favorite theme with Jesuit preachers given to concentrate on the eschatological themes of the first week of the *Exercises*. But with Mulledy the tragic has become the pathetic. One can readily imagine how Isaac Hecker would have reacted to such an approach; why he felt it an appeal to "the lowest and least that the Church demands of us."

Mulledy was usually preaching to Catholic gentry or commercial classes of Georgetown or Philadelphia or Baltimore. Leisure and the dangers of the good life are another recurring theme. Foppery and the obsession with pleasure—what he calls "the spirit of effeminacy"—are particular targets for his wrath. To those for whom "plays, visits, amours, parties, are the entire, or at least, the principal employments of their days," Mulledy offers the model of John the Baptist, no clotheshorse or *bon vivant*. If they can not live as John did, at least let them develop the desire to be "not addicted to a delicate pleasing life, . . . not a lover of effeminacy: . . . not . . . a man of fine times."[69]

At times Mulledy seems to be decrying not the loss of Christian as-

ceticism but the strenuous life. It should be said, however, that he is not
condemning the goods and pleasures that his hearers' society makes available to them, but rather the excessive pursuit of them. The *tantum quantum*
of the *Spiritual Exercises* has to be their guide. Use the creatures to the
extent that they aid the soul; "if any one of these transitory goods can
impede my salvation, I willingly sacrifice it to thee [O Lord]." Let his listeners "do their duty to God and neighbor; then they may enjoy the good
things of the world, but always in moderation."[70]

For Mulledy the ideal attitude for the Christian is a balance of fear and
hope. In a sermon delivered in Nice in 1840, he said:

> When in the gospel we observe that God like a good & loving
> shepherd . . . always watches over our defense[?], who is there
> that does not cherish the greatest hope? But if we reflect that the
> devil like a ravenous wolf, exerts all his arts & finally succeeds
> in decoying off the less cautious of the flock—& tears them to
> pieces & devours them . . . who can refrain from feeling the great
> fear? . . . The only road which can securely lead us to the happy
> end of our journey—a happy death—lies between these two ex-
> tremes.[71]

Striking a balance between presumption and paralysis, this sermon surely
offers sound enough Christian advice, but it is hardly the hallmark of Jesuit
spirituality. Even in his most explicitly Jesuit sermon, "Duty of Promoting
the Glory of God," the dynamic is one of obligation rather than of love
responding to love. In truth with Mulledy the Ignatian principles have become very domesticated. One promotes the glory of God for worldly success. "The art of inducing God to think upon you," he told his congregation
in 1857, "is for you to think upon him alone" (see "Duty of Promoting the
Glory of God"). Ignatian spirituality has become thoroughly bourgeois.

But in Mulledy's sermons, rhetoric dominates content. They are exceedingly dramatic, indeed voyeuristic at times. In his preaching Mulledy
has become an ecclesiastical showman, competing for the attention of an
audience with the leisure and money for other entertainments. Death, God's
glory, sin and freedom: all have become themes for his homiletic theatre.
Spiritually the whole seems less than the sum of the parts.

The Flowering of Ultramontane Piety

"The afflictions of the Holy Father have made ultramontanes of all of
us here who have any good within," Keller reported to Beckx in December

1870.[72] Earlier the provincial reported the attention that the topic of personal infallibility was getting in the journals:

> We think that that article can be proclaimed by acclamation. Let it happen! For whoever knows well the idea of the Church as the body of Jesus Christ can not doubt for a moment the infallibility of its head. It is the head that directs, it is the head who speaks for all the members, and if the Church is infallible, she is so by her head . . . in a word in the Pope, as the visible head of the body.
>
> Pardon that speech—I presume on your goodness and your sympathies: above all I ardently desire that a *coup de grace* will be dealt to those nonCatholicly catholic systems which exist in the Church as spies in the camp, as enemies disguised as friends.[73]

Keller's "speech" would have puzzled, if not embarrassed, John Carroll and his confreres of the colonial and early national periods. For them infallibility was a character of the Church, not a personal charism of the pope. As late as 1849 charges were raised in the *Freeman's Journal* and elsewhere that Jesuits were not sufficiently obedient toward the pope, that the philosophy they taught gave too much autonomy to reason and led to infidelity. The European refugees, of whom Keller was one, undoubtedly set the intellectual life of the province in a much more conservative direction. Woodstock, the theologate of the province, by the 1890s was the intellectual center of the ultramontanist forces in the American Church.

Through the pages of *The Messenger of the Sacred Heart,* the magazine founded at Georgetown in 1866 by an Italian immigrant, Benedict Sestini, and moved to Woodstock when it opened in 1869, one can trace the shift in perspective and piety. In its initial issue, Sestini set down the manifesto. In the Christian realm that encompassed contemplation and action, the apostolate of action was basically reserved by Jesus to "his Apostles and their legitimate successors, the Bishops, united to the visible head of the church. . . . " Priests were to assist; "the rest of the faithful . . . cannot, without arrogance and danger, intermeddle with their office." The good news for the laity was that contemplation, which had the higher status, had no such restrictions. Any lay person could pray; indeed one had the obligation to do so to make reparation to the Sacred Heart for the offenses committed in response to Jesus' love of the world. Women were considered in a superior position for this apostolic ministry of prayer since, as Sestini suggested in the introductory essay, their prayer, more often than that of men, "ascends from a heart that is humble and has been purified in the fire of tribulation." Women's lowly status, their long suffering nature, made them more Christ-like and models of Christian asceticism. Their humility and acceptance of place stood in stark contrast to the male liberals who were defying God and Church in leading the world into modernity.

Although some American Jesuits, including Anthony Kohlmann, thought the Sacred Heart devotion would not do well in the United States, *The Messenger* quickly proved them wrong. Within a few months its circulation exceeded 2,000. Far larger than the circulation list of *The Messenger* itself was the membership of the Apostleship of Prayer in the United States, the voluntary association for practicing and spreading devotion to the Sacred Heart. The association became a prominent element in the spiritual culture of late 19th century American Catholicism. Although its primary base was in religious communities, colleges, and seminaries, it included a broad cross section of the middle class Catholic community, especially females and certain ethnic groups, particularly Germans. It abetted the development of certain features of American Catholic spirituality, including a sentimentalization of devotion and the promotion of frequent communion.

The Messenger followed closely the declining temporal power of Pope Pius IX. Ann Taves has pointed out the nineteenth century tendency in Catholic circles to identify the Blessed Sacrament with the Roman pontiff.[74] As Jesus revealed his love most fully through suffering, including that which he continued to endure through his Real Presence in the tabernacle, nowhere could the suffering Jesus be more visibly found than in the Holy See and its bishop. Increasingly the devotion to the Sacred Heart was put in the service of papal primacy and infallibility. Peter and his successors, as "the brain of the Mystical Body," had the lion's share of Jesus' love, which guaranteed ultimate victory, no matter how much worldly forces seemed to prevail.

"To this great work of malice and of pride," *The Messenger* commented in July 1869 about the attacks on the Papal States,

> hailed by multitudes, encouraged or urged on by rulers, the Man-God has opposed the mildness of His oppressed Vicar on earth, abandoned to the rage of his enemies, and despoiled by sacrilegious robbers, of the patrimony of the Church. The world, looking on at the struggles, sees the heart of Christ's Vicar reflecting a ray of that divine mildness and charity which fills the Saviour's Heart; and in the hearts of the faithful, a corresponding fire is enkindled. . . .[75]

In the world of redemptive suffering, Rome also had primacy.

In the late eighteen-sixties *The Messenger* gave much coverage to those who engaged in the highest form of Catholic action available to the laity, defense of the Holy See itself in the pope's army. Those who could not join the Papal Zouaves could at least make reparation through their prayers for all the onslaughts, military or moral, against God's kingdom. And when Rome finally fell, a captive pope seemed more than ever the vicar of Christ on earth.

The Church of *The Messenger* was obviously not above the *sturm und drang* of the modern world; yet it still had the answers that alone could bring peace for the world and for the individual. In December 1869, the editor admitted that the Church was sadly sharing the "fearful restlessness" that pervaded society. But added, "she alone endeavors to remedy; she proposes to reestablish the tottering social edifice on a divine, indestructible basis. . . . " What the Church held out to the world, *The Messenger* explained in an 1873 article, were the very lessons of humility and unity which the devotion to the Sacred Heart taught as the antidote to the independence of mind which was unraveling the modern world. Submissiveness, whether to pope or monarch or industrial aristocracy, was not only the guarantor of peace and order but also the only means of saving modern man from self-destruction. Paternalism was the key to social justice and private tranquility.

Edward Holker Welch and Synthesis

From the mid-nineteenth century on, converts began to join the Maryland Jesuits in increasing numbers. They gradually came to hold key posts within the province. In 1888 Joseph Havens Richards, the son of a Congregational minister, was named president of Georgetown University. By the turn of the century both the provincial and the rector of Georgetown were converts. One of the earliest was Edward Holker Welch of Boston, who from the fringes of the Oxford movement was brought to Rome and eventually to the Society of Jesus in 1851. Reading a commentary on the Two Standards proved decisive in persuading him that he could better spend his life for God as a Jesuit than a lawyer.

When Welch died a half century later, one editor of a Catholic magazine wrote that although "his name rarely appeared in print . . . [,] perhaps no priest or prelate in this country has done more to promote the glory of God and the salvation of souls."[76] The editor, the Holy Cross Father Daniel Hudson, was no doubt prejudiced from the impact that Welch had had upon him as a young boy in Boston. In the late nineteenth century Boston was no longer the intellectual hub of the country. Welch's sermons may have drawn overflow crowds to the Immaculate Conception Church but they were not published for larger audiences. He was reputed to have converted many Protestants, but even granting that, it is a very limited gauge of apostolic achievement.

Still within the Maryland Province Hudson's appraisal may well be true, in the sense that Welch as an outsider, no cradle Catholic of either Europe or America, was able more freely to appropriate the Ignatian tradition within a perspective that valued both Rome and America. A John Carroll had chosen not to rejoin the Society, partly because of lingering distrust of the papacy, partly because of serious misgivings about the Society's ability to adapt to the modern world that the intellectual and political revolutions were making. The Jesuits who worked in America in the nineteenth century seem to have been caught between the two worlds of Rome and America, of heritage and environment that remained segmented in their vision and praxis, if not at odds. The native Americans, even the Roman trained ones like Thomas Mulledy, tended to read the Ignatian tradition through heavily American lenses that distorted as well as refracted. Many of the immigrants, like Stephen Dubuisson, never felt at home in America. It was for them a place alien to the ideals and values of the Society. John McElroy found his own resolution but not in a way that reconciled practice with theory. Even those who were sympathetic to American culture never lost the sense of being strangers in the land. Welch was no stranger. He made deliberate decisions to embrace both the Church and the Society. In the process he seems to have laid the ground for a synthesis between the Ignatian and American cultures that eluded most of his companions, either native or immigrant.

Welch was clearly no modernist, but no obscurantist either. If there was a conflict between the claims of science and the teachings of the Church, there was no question where he stood. For Welch truth comes from the revelation that transcends the "narrow limits of our reason." But there is little or no attempt to emphasize the personal infallibility of the pope.

He had no illusions that the religious life he had chosen was nature's own. "We must all acknowledge," he once told his fellow Jesuits at Georgetown, "that the life of a true Religious is a *supernatural* life. It is not in accordance with the cravings of nature. . . . "[77] It is the Spirit that makes it possible to sustain the apostolic life, that is its very wellspring in living under Christ's standard. The discernment of spirits with Welch is very consciously the discernment of the Spirit, the source of affections, the source of the knowledge that transcends the wisdom of the world, the source of love.

Welch's spirituality was socially sensitive. If his New England heritage led him to stress charity rather than justice, it was the charity of a Winthrop that saw the seamless garment of society and felt obliged to respond to the cry of the poor. And he did not hesitate to point out to his Jesuit brethren that they too often were "inclined to labor rather among the refined and educated than the ignorant and uncultivated," that they too naturally discriminated between the rich and the poor, even though the latter were in need of their help.

From Andrew White to Holker Welch the Maryland Jesuits had struggled to bring the Ignatian tradition to an American society that was more than an ocean away from the Old World in which the order had taken shape. Often under suspicion from Rome, often at odds with themselves, still they managed, not only to keep the tradition alive, but to give it new life in a new land. By 1900 there were 634 Jesuits in the Maryland-New York Province involved in apostolates that ranged from universities to mission bands to prisons. More importantly, one could discern that there was well in the making an authentic American Jesuit tradition, faithful to the spirit and *Constitutions* of the Society, but reflecting the unique environment of the United States.

NOTES

1. Joseph de Guibert, S.J., *The Jesuits. Their Spiritual Doctrine and Practice: A Historical Study* (Chicago, 1964), 128.

2. de Guibert, 180–181.

3. "The First Day and the First Contemplation: The Incarnation," in David L. Fleming, S.J., *Modern Spiritual Exercises: A Contemporary Reading of The Spiritual Exercises of St. Ignatius* (New York, 1983), 50.

4. John Carroll Futrell, S.J., "Ignatian Discernment," *Studies in the Spirituality of Jesuits* II (April 1970), 49, 65. Futrell observes: "Ignatian contentment is the profound peace experienced in recognizing that one has heard and responded to the word of God—a word which is often disconcerting and unexpected and a call to share in the Cross of Christ. This deep contentment can co-exist with very great repugnance on the level of spontaneous emotions" (66).

5. Fleming, "Christ the King and His Call," in *Modern Spiritual Exercises,* 48–49.

6. Fleming, 66–67.

7. Robert L. Schmitt, S.J., "The Christ-Experience and Relationship Fostered in the Spiritual Exercises of St. Ignatius of Loyola," *Studies in the Spirituality of Jesuits* VI (October 1974), 219.

8. Schmitt, 233, 242. Schmitt traces the feudal ideal of the lord-vassal relationship which provided the image for Ignatius's model of the relationship between Jesus and his follower.

9. Brian E. Daley, S.J., " 'In Ten Thousand Places': Christian Universality and the Jesuit Mission," *Studies in the Spirituality of Jesuits* XVII (March 1985), 3.

10. The phrase is Gerard Manley Hopkins' from his sonnet "As Kingfishers Catch Fire":

For Christ plays in ten thousand places,
Lovely in limbs, and lovely in eyes not his
To the Father through the features of men's faces.

Quoted in Daley, 28.

11. *The Constitutions of the Society of Jesus,* translated by George E. Ganss, S.J. (St. Louis, 1970), 170, 172.

12. John W. O'Malley, S.J., "The Fourth Vow in Its Ignatian Context. A Historical Study," *Studies in the Spirituality of Jesuits* XV (January 1983), 26. From virtually its beginning, the Society of Jesus divided its members into certain classes or "grades": those having solemn vows (the professed), those having simple but final vows (spiritual and temporal coadjutors [priests and brothers respectively]), and those having simple vows only (all those without final vows, including scholastics or those in formation).

13. *Declaratio Coloniae Domini Baronis de Baltimoro,* Fund Publication No. 7, Maryland Historical Society (Baltimore, 1874), 48.

14. Thomas Hughes, *The History of the Society of Jesus in North America, Colonial & Federal. Text,* I (London, 1908), 461.

15. Hughes, I, 472.

16. Hughes, I, 473.

17. Verdier to Vincenzo Carafa, S.J., June 24, 1649, in Henry Foley, S.J., *Records of the English Province of the Society of Jesus,* VII, Part I (London, 1882), 526.

18. Hughes, I, 472.

19. See James Axtell, "White Legend: The Jesuit Missions in Maryland," *Maryland Historical Magazine* (Spring 1986), 5.

20. Philip Fisher to Caraffa, March 1, 1648, quoted in Foley, *Records,* I, 256.

21. From 1632 to 1643, the French Jesuits had baptized over 2700 natives; the Maryland Jesuits fewer than 150 from 1634 to 1643. During that same period, however, the French Province had 53 of its members in Canada as opposed to 14 from the English Province in Maryland. Léon Pouliot, *Etude sur les Relations des Jésuites de la Nouvelle-France (1632–1672)* (Montreal, 1940), 308n.1), cited in Axtell, 5, 7; A.M.D.G. (Arthur Melançon), *Liste des Missionnaires-Jésuites, Nouvelle-France et Louisiane, 1611–1800* (Montreal, 1929), 75–76 and *passim;* cited in Axtell, 5,7.

22. Archives of the Sacred Congregation for Propagation of the Faith, Congressi, America Centrale, I, fols. 557r-v and 558r.

23. Patrick Carey, *An Immigrant Bishop: John England's Adaptation of Irish Catholicism to American Republicanism* (Yonkers, 1982), 6.

24. Even during the founding of the colony, only a minority of English Jesuits seem to have considered volunteering for Maryland. "I make bold to tell you," one Jesuit wrote his provincial in 1640 about the latter's call for missioners, "that as

much as I can percyve, & yett I have spoake with many, there be very few who imagine your Rev[eren]c[e]s letter touched themselves'' (Maryland Province Archives [hereafter MPA] 2 Z, Francis Parker to Edward Knott, [Antwerp], 26 July 1640).

25. Georgetown University Special Collections (hereafter GUSC). A printed version of the treatise was edited by John Gilmary Shea in the *United States Catholic Historical Magazine* 3 (1889–1890), 237–263.

26. See de Guibert, 349–373, 402–412, 431–436; also "Jésuites. IV. Le 17ᵉ Siècle Français," in *Dictionnaire de Spiritualité. Ascétique et Mystique. Doctrine et Histoire* VIII (Paris, 1974), 994–1015.

27. GUSC, Shea Transcripts, Molyneux to John Carroll, March 28, 1785.

28. GUSC, Mosley Papers, Joseph Mosley to Mrs. Dunn, Oct. 3, 1774.

29. See Joseph Chinnici, OSF, "Politics and Theology: From Enlightenment Catholicism to the Condemnation of Americanism," *Working Papers Series, Center for the Study of American Catholicism* (Spring 1981).

30. "An Address to the Roman Catholics of the United States of America By a Catholic Clergyman," in Thomas O'Brien Hanley, S.J., ed., *The John Carroll Papers* I (Notre Dame, 1976), 140; Carroll to Joseph Berington, July 10, 1784, ibid., 148.

31. Carroll to Charles Plowden, April 10, 1784, in Hanley, *Papers*, I, 145.

32. "An Address," Hanley, *Papers*, I, 102.

33. Ibid., 137.

34. Circular of Maryland ex-Jesuits, April 25, 1788, in Hughes, *History, Documents*, I, Part II, 684.

35. *Manner*, 5.

36. "Organization of the Spiritual Life: American Catholic Devotional Works, 1791–1866," *Theological Studies* 40 (June 1979), 236–237.

37. Chinnici, "Politics and Theology," 19.

38. "I feel so in their presence," he confessed, "that if it was to them that I was to be united I should shrink but it is not to them but the Church" (Hecker to Brownson [24 June 1844], in Joseph F. Gower and Richard M. Leliaert, eds., *The Brownson-Hecker Correspondence* [Notre Dame, 1979], 104–106).

39. *Archivum Romanum Societatis Jesu* (hereafter ARSI), *Provincia Marylandia* (hereafter MD) 7 III 1, Philip Sacci to Jan Roothaan, Georgetown, July 22, 1838.

40. ARSI, MD 7 I 6. Stephen Dubuisson to Roothaan, Alexandria, August 10, 1838. The Jesuit cited was Stephen Gabaria, who was evidently so estranged from American culture that seven years after arriving had still not learned English.

41. ARSI, MD 7 I 35, Dzierozynski to Roothaan, Frederick, June 29, 1841. A college like Georgetown, serving as a scholasticate and boarding school, was something unknown on the continent. One European marveled that it was neither urban nor rural, neither a religious house nor a secular boarding school, but some strange combination of them all (ARSI, MD 7 III 4, Philip Sacci to Roothaan, Georgetown, January 23, 1839).

42. ARSI, MD 7 I 51, Rey to Roothaan, Georgetown, July 22, 1842.

43. ARSI, MD 8 II 27, Brocard to Roothaan, Georgetown, August 12, 1850.

44. An ironic twist in these ethnic-related issues occurred over the use of alcohol. By the end of the forties it was the foreigners, especially the Italians, who were decrying the elimination of wine at table. Native or naturalized Americans, like Ryder, were among the advocates of this measure in order to refute the reputation the Society had acquired in this country. Brocard thought it was a small price the Europeans could pay to avoid any possible occasion for scandal.

45. ARSI, MD 8 IV 9, Villiger to Beckx, Georgetown, June 23, 1859.

46. ARSI, MD 8 IV 4, Villiger to Beckx, Georgetown, December 1, 1858.

47. Ibid.

48. ARSI, MD 8 VI, Ordinations of Felix Sopranis, 1860.

49. Literally: "what they would scarcely consent to in another fashion" (ARSI, MD IV 18, Villiger to Beckx, Georgetown, July 13, 1860).

50. " . . . fewer words and fewer rules," he suggested, "might have had a better effect" (ARSI, MD 8 IV 21, Villiger to Beckx, Baltimore, September, 1860).

51. ARSI, MD 8 IV 26, Villiger to Beckx, Baltimore, February 17, 1861.

52. Ryder to William McSherry, Sept. 16, 1828, quoted in *Woodstock Letters* 44 (1915), 324–325.

53. Quoted in Hughes, "History, Text III" (Redaction of 1926), 659, ms. copy in GUSC.

54. The phrase "devotional Catholicism" has been coined by Jay Dolan to describe the peculiar ethos of American Catholicism from the mid-nineteenth century to the mid-twentieth, with its distinguishing attitudes toward sin, authority, ritual, and the miraculous (*The American Catholic Experience* [New York, 1985], chapter VIII).

55. Chinnici, "Organization of Spiritual Life," 255.

56. Jay P. Dolan, *Catholic Revivalism: The American Experience, 1830–1900* (Notre Dame, 1978), 16–20.

57. ARSI, MD 7 V 6, McElroy to Roothaan, Frederick, June 4, 1840.

58. Dolan, *Catholic Revivalism*, 36–43, 64.

59. John H. Wright, "The Grace of our Founder and the Grace of Our Vocation," *Studies in the Spirituality of Jesuits* Vol. III, No. 1 (February, 1971), 18–19.

60. Benedict Joseph Fenwick, S.J., *Memoirs to Serve for the Future* (Joseph M. McCarthy, ed., Yonkers, N.Y., 1978), 182–183.

61. Fenwick had been considering founding a college. After the events of Charlestown, he vowed to his brother, George: "I shall erect a College into which no Protestant shall ever set foot" (Maryland Province Archives, Fenwick to George Fenwick, November 29, 1838). He was as good as his word. When the College of the Holy Cross opened in Worcester in the fall of 1843, it was for Catholics only.

62. *Imminent Dangers to the Free Institutions of the United States Through Foreign Immigrations.*

63. Jean H. Baker, *Ambivalent Americans: The Know-Nothing Party in Maryland* (Baltimore and London, 1977), 23.

64. ARSI, MD 8 III 17, Stonestreet to Beckx, Boston, March 11, 1856. Two

years earlier Stonestreet had already begun to consider opening houses in the deep South where he thought there was less opposition to Catholics and danger of persecution (ARSI, MD 8 III 8, Stonestreet to Beckx, Georgetown, November 4, 1854).

65. *Woodstock Letters* 31 (1902), 221–222.

66. ARSI, MD 8 III 9, James Ward to Beckx, Baltimore, November 17, 1854.

67. ARSI, MD 8 IV 8, Villiger to Beckx, Worcester, May 21, 1859.

68. ARSI, MD 8 V 1, Paresce to Peter Beckx, Frederick, April 22, 1861.

69. GUSC, Mulledy Papers, "Deceptions Unmasked," 3; "Amusements," 14.

70. GUSC, Mulledy Papers, Box 2, Folder 2, "Deceptions Unmasked," 15; "Amusements," 14.

71. GUSC, Mulledy Papers, Box 2, Folder 6, "Fear and Hope."

72. ARSI, MD 10 II 14, Keller to Beckx, Baltimore, December 23, 1870.

73. ARSI, MD 10 II 7, Keller to Beckx, Baltimore, January 6, 1870. It is revealing to compare Keller's attitude to that of Brocard and his fellows in 1850 when the papal declaration of the doctrine of the Immaculate Conception was being considered. The American Jesuits urged that no such declaration be made for several reasons (ARSI, MD 8 II 21, Brocard to Roothaan, Georgetown, January 6, 1850).

74. "Context and Meaning: Roman Catholic Devotion to the Blessed Sacrament in Mid-Nineteenth-Century America," *Church History,* 54 (December 1985), 490–491.

75. *Messenger,* 278.

76. Daniel Hudson, C.S.C., *Ave Maria* 59 (December 24, 1904), 822.

77. GUSC, Welch Papers, Exhortation to the Community, Georgetown, Sept. 18, 1898.

Part I

THE ANGLO-AMERICAN TRADITION, 1634–1805

I

ANDREW WHITE AND THE BEGINNINGS IN MARYLAND

NARRATIVE OF A VOYAGE TO MARYLAND[1] (1634)

Written towards the end of April, 1634, to the Very Reverend Father, General Mutius Vitelleschi.

[*Andrew White (1579–1656) had joined the Society of Jesus in 1606, shortly after he had been expelled from England in the reaction to the Gunpowder Plot of 1605. White, who was already a priest when he entered the Jesuit novitiate in Louvain, soon returned to England. He subsequently taught at the Jesuit colleges at Valladolid, Louvain and Liège. His rigid view that Thomistic theology was the only orthodox interpretation of revelation cost White his position at Liège in 1629. By that time he had already volunteered for America, partly in response to George Calvert's urgings. As Lord Baltimore made his plans for his second colony (he had briefly attempted a settlement in Newfoundland), White was in London assisting him. It is highly likely that his hand was in the "Declaratio" that Baltimore had drawn up in 1633 about the prospects for the colony. Certainly the language of part of the report resonates with the tone and spirit of the Spiritual Exercises of Ignatius.*]

The first and most important design of the Most Illustrious Baron, which also ought to be the aim of the rest, who go in the same ship, is, not to think so much of planting fruits and trees in a land so fruitful, as of sowing the seeds of Religion and piety. Surely a design worthy of Christians, worthy of *angels,* worthy of *Englishmen.* The English nation, renowned for so many ancient victories, never undertook anything more noble or glorious

47

than this. Behold the lands are white for the harvest, prepared for receiving the seed of the Gospel into their fruitful bosom. They themselves are everywhere sending out messengers, to seek after fit men to instruct the inhabitants in saving doctrine, and to regenerate them with the *sacred* water. There are also men here in the city, at this very time, who declare that they have seen Ambassadors, who were sent by their Kings, for this same purpose; to Jamestown in Virginia; and infants brought to New England to be washed in the saving waters. Who then can doubt, that by one such glorious work as this, many thousands of souls will be brought to Christ? I call the work of aiding and saving souls glorious: for it was the work of Christ, the king of glory. For the rest, since all men have not such enthusiastic souls and noble minds, as to think of nothing but divine things, and to consider nothing but heavenly things; because men are more in love, as it were, with pleasures, honors, and riches, (than with the Glory of Christ;) it was ordained by some hidden influence, or rather by the manifest (and) wonderful wisdom of God, that this one enterprise should offer to men every kind of inducement and reward.[2]

[*Father General Mutius Vitelleschi finally gave permission for White to accompany Lord Baltimore's party to Maryland, despite the general's apparent reservations about White's prudence in such a delicate mission. White was appointed superior of the Jesuit trio of missioners, which also included the priest, John Altham (alias Gravenor), and a coadjutor brother, Thomas Gervase.*

The Baltimore ships, the Ark and the Dove, sailed from Gravesend, England in the fall of 1633 after all aboard took the oath of allegiance to King Charles. The three Jesuits and most, if not all of the Catholic adventurers boarded the ship in late November at Cowes in order to avoid the antipapist oath. The following is the account of the crossing that White sent to Rome. It is obvious that he had a keen eye for natural detail as well as a deep faith in God's abiding blessing on their venture.]

On the Twenty Second of the month of November, in the year 1633, being St. Cecilia's day, we set sail from Cowes, in the Isle of Wight, with a gentle east wind blowing. And, after committing the principal parts of the ship to the protection of God especially, and of His most Holy Mother, and St. Ignatius, and all the guardian angels of Maryland, we sailed on a little way between the two shores, and the wind failing us, we stopped opposite Yarmouth Castle, which is near the southern end of the same island, (Isle of Wight). Here we were received with a cheerful salute of artillery. Yet we were not without apprehension; for the sailors were murmuring among themselves, saying that they were expecting a messenger with letters from London, and from this it seemed as if they were even contriving to delay us. But God brought their plans to confusion. For that very night, a favorable but strong wind, arose; and a French cutter, which had put into the same harbor with us, being forced to set sail, came near running into our pinnace. The latter, therefore, to avoid being run down, having cut away and lost an anchor, set sail without delay; and since it was dangerous to drift about in that place, made haste to get farther out to sea. And so that we might not lose sight of our pinnace, we determined to follow. Thus the designs of the sailors, who were plotting against us, were frustrated. This happened on the 23rd of November, St. Clement's day, who, because he had been tied to an anchor and thrown into the sea, obtained the crown of martyrdom, and afforded to his people a way to land, as the miracles of God declare.

Now on that day, we were again greeted with a cheerful salute, about ten o'clock in the morning, from Hurst Castle, and then sailed past a number of rocks near the end of the Isle of Wight, which, from their shape, are called the Needles. These also are a terror to sailors, on account of the double tide of the sea, which whirls away the ships, dashing them against the rocks on the one side, or the neighboring shore on the other; to say nothing, meanwhile, of the other risk we ran near Yarmouth Castle. For while we were waiting there, before we had weighed anchor, the wind and tide pressing hard upon us, the ship came near being driven on shore. And this would have certainly happened, had we not been suddenly turned away with great force; and driving out to sea, escaped the danger by the mercy of God, who deigned to give us this additional pledge of his protection, through the merits of St. Clement.

On that day, which fell on the Sabbath, and the following night, we had such favorable winds, that early on the next day, about nine o'clock, we left behind us the western promontory of England and the Scilly Isles, and sailing easily on, we directed our course more towards the west, passing over the British channel. Yet we did not go as fast as we could, fearing, if we left the pinnace too far behind us, that it would become the prey of the Turks and Pirates, who generally infest that sea.

Hence it came to pass, that a fine merchant ship of six hundred tons, named the Dragon, on her way from London to Angola, overtook us, about three o'clock in the afternoon. And as we now had time to enjoy a little pleasure, after getting out of danger, it was delightful to see these two ships, with fair weather and a favorable wind, trying for a whole hour to outstrip each other, with a great noise of trumpets. And our ship would have beaten the other, though we did not use our topsail, if we had not been obliged to stop on account of the pinnace, which was slower; and so we yielded the palm to the merchant ship, and she sailed by us before evening, and passed out of sight.

Now on Sunday the 24th, and Monday the 25th of November, we had fair sailing all the time until evening. But presently, the wind getting round to the north, such a terrible storm arose, that the merchant ship I spoke of from London, being driven back on her course, returned to England, and reached a harbor much resorted to, among the Paumonians. Those on board our pinnace also, since she was a vessel of only 40 tons, began to lose confidence in her strength, and sailing near, they warned us, that if they apprehended shipwreck, they would notify us by hanging out lights from the mast-head. We meanwhile sailed on in our strong ship of four hundred tons—a better could not be built of wood and iron. We had a very skilful captain, and so he was given his choice, whether he would return to England, or keep on struggling with the winds: if he yielded to these, the Irish shore close by awaited us, which is noted for its hidden rocks and frequent shipwrecks. Nevertheless his bold spirit, and his desire to test the strength of the new ship, which he then managed for the first time, prevailed with the captain. He resolved to try the sea, although he confessed that it was the more dangerous, on account of being so narrow.

And the danger was near at hand; for the winds increasing, and the sea growing more boisterous, we could see the pinnace in the distance, showing two lights at her masthead. Then indeed we thought it was all over with her, and that she had been swallowed up in the deep whirlpools; for in a moment she had passed out of sight, and we saw nothing of her for the next six or seven weeks. Accordingly we were all of us certain the pinnace had been lost; yet God had better things in store for us, for the fact was, that finding herself no match for the violence of the waves, she had avoided the Virginia sea, with which we were already contending, by returning to England, to the Scilly Isles. And making a fresh start from thence, in company with the Dragon, she overtook us, as we shall relate, at a large harbor in the Antilles. Thus God, who oversees the smallest things, guided, protected, and took care of the little vessel.

We, however, being ignorant of the event, were distressed with grief and anxiety, which the gloomy night, filled with manifold terrors, increased. When the day dawned, although the wind was against us, being from the south-west, yet, as it did not blow very hard, we sailed on gradually by making frequent tacks. So Tuesday, Wednesday, and Thursday passed with variable winds, and we made small progress. On Friday, a south-east wind prevailing, and driving before it thick and dark clouds, so fierce a tempest broke forth towards evening, that it seemed every minute as if we must be swallowed up by the waves. Nor was the weather more promising on the next day, which was the festival of Andrew the Apostle. The clouds, accumulating in a frightful manner, were fearful to behold, before they separated, and excited the belief that all the malicious spirits of the storm, and all the evil spirits of Maryland had come forth to battle against us. Towards evening, the captain saw a Sunfish swimming, with great efforts, against the course of the sun, which is a very sure sign of a terrible storm; nor did the omen prove a false one. For about ten o'clock at night a dark cloud poured forth a violent shower. And such a furious hurricane followed close upon it, that it was necessary to run with all speed to take in sail; and this could not be done quickly enough to prevent the mainsail, the only one we were carrying, from being torn in the middle from top to bottom. A part of it was blown over into the sea, and was recovered with difficulty.

At this juncture, the minds of the bravest among us, both passengers and sailors, were struck with terror; for they acknowledged that they had seen other ships wrecked in a less severe storm; but now, this hurricane called forth the prayers and vows of the Catholics in honor of the Blessed Virgin Mary and her Immaculate Conception, of Saint Ignatius, the Patron Saint of Maryland, Saint Michael, and all the guardian angels of the same country. And each one hastened to purge his soul by the Sacrament of penance. For all control over the rudder being lost, the ship now drifted about like a dish in the water, at the mercy of the winds and the waves, until God showed us a way of safety. At first, I confess, I had been engrossed with the apprehension of the ship's being lost, and of losing my own life; but after I had spent some time, in praying more fervently than was my usual custom, and had set forth to Christ the Lord, to the Blessed Virgin, St. Ignatius, and the angels of Maryland, that the purpose of this journey was to glorify the Blood of Our Redeemer in the salvation of barbarians, and also to raise up a kingdom for the Saviour (if he would choose to favor our poor efforts,) to consecrate another gift to the Immaculate Virgin, His Mother, and many things to the same effect; great comfort shone in upon my soul, and at the same time so firm a conviction that we should be delivered, not only from this storm, but from every other during that voyage, that no shade of doubt remained with me. I had given myself to prayer, when the sea was raging its worst, and (may this be to the glory of God) I had scarcely finished, when they observed that the storm was abating. That indeed brought me to a new frame of mind, and filled me at the same time with great joy and admiration, since I understood much more clearly the greatness of God's love towards the people of Maryland, to whom your Reverence has sent us. Eternal praises to the most sweet graciousness of the Redeemer!!

When the sea had thus immediately abated, we had delightful weather for three months, so that the captain and his men declared they had never had a calmer or more pleasant voyage; for we suffered no inconvenience, not even for a single hour. However, when I speak of three months, I do not mean to say we were that long at sea, but I include the whole voyage, and also the time we stopped at the Antilles. For the actual voyage occupied only seven weeks, and two days; and that is considered a quick passage. . . .

And here also I cannot pass on, without praising the Divine Goodness, which brings it to pass, that all things work together for good to them that love God. For if, meeting with no delay, we had been allowed to sail at the time we had appointed, namely on the twentieth of the month of August, the sun being on this side of the equator, and striking down vertically, the intense heat would not only have ruined our provisions, but would have brought disease and death upon almost all of us. We were saved by the delay, for by embarking in the winter time, we escaped misfortunes of this kind; and if you except the usual sea-sickness, no one was attacked by any disease, until the Festival of the Nativity of our Lord. In order that that day might be better kept, wine was given out; and those who drank of it too freely, were seized the next day with a fever; and of these, not long afterwards, about twelve died, among whom were two Catholics. The loss of Nicholas Fairfax and James Barefote was deeply felt among us.

[*They decide to stop at Barbados to secure merchandise that the ship can carry back to England in order to defray some of Lord Baltimore's expenses.*]

This is the remotest of the Caribee or Antilles Islands, 13 degrees distant from the equator, and serves as a granary for all the rest, which extend in a long line in the shape of a bow, clear to the Gulf of Mexico. When we reached this island, on the third of January, we had hope of securing many articles of trade from the English inhabitants, and from the governor, who was our fellow countryman; but forming a combination, they determined not to sell us any wheat, (which was selling in the island at half a Belgic florin a bushel,) for less than five times that price, that is two florins and a half. . . .

Reflecting on Divine Providence consoled us amid this cruel treatment. For we understood that a Spanish fleet was stationed off the island of Buenavista, to keep all foreigners from engaging in the salt trade. If, keeping to our appointed route, we had gone on thither, we should have fallen into the net, and become the prey of our enemies. In the meantime, we were delivered from a greater danger at Barbados: the servants throughout the whole island had conspired to kill their masters; then, indeed, after having gained their liberty, it was their intention to possess themselves of the first ship which should touch there, and venture to sea. The conspiracy was disclosed by one who was deterred by the atrocious cruelty of the enterprise; and the punishment of one of the leaders was sufficient for the security of the island and our own safety. For our ship, as being the first to touch there, had been marked for their prey; and on the very day we landed, we found eight hundred men in arms to oppose this wicked design, which had just transpired.

[*After short stops at Matalina and Maevius in the Caribee Islands, they spent ten days on St. Christopher's, before beginning the final leg of the journey to the Chesapeake.*]

At length, sailing from this place, we reached the *cape,* which they call *Point Comfort,* in Virginia, on the 27th of February, full of apprehension, lest the English inhabitants, who were much displeased at our settling, should be plotting something against us. Nevertheless the letters we carried from the King, and from the high treasurer of England, served to allay their anger, and to procure those things which would afterwards be useful to us. For the Governor of Virginia hoped, that by this kindness toward us, he would more easily recover from the Royal treasury a large sum of money which was due him. They only told us that a rumor prevailed, that six ships were coming to reduce everything under the power of the Spaniards, and that for this reason, all the natives were in arms; this we afterwards found to be true. Yet I fear the rumor had its origin with the English.

After being kindly treated for eight or nine days, we set sail on the third of March, and entering the Chesapeake Bay, we turned our course to the north to reach the *Potomac* River. The Chesapeake Bay, ten leagues (30 Italian miles) wide, flows gently between its shores: it is four, five and six fathoms deep, and abounds in fish when the season is favorable; you will scarcely find a more beautiful body of water. Yet it yields the palm to the Potomac River, which we named after St. Gregory.

. . . Never have I beheld a larger or more beautiful river. The Thames seems a mere rivulet in comparison with it. . . . Just at the mouth of the river, we observed the natives in arms. That night, fires blazed through the whole country, and since they had never seen such a large ship, messengers were sent in all directions, who reported that a *Canoe,* like an island had come with as many men as there were trees in the woods. We went on, however, to Herons' Islands, so called from the immense numbers of these birds. The first island we came to, [we called] St. Clement's Island, and as it has a sloping shore, there is no way of getting to it except by wading. Here the women, who had left the ship to do the washing, upset the boat and came near being drowned, losing also a large part of my linen clothes, no small loss in these parts.

This island abounds in cedar and sassafras trees, and flowers and herbs, for making all kinds of salads, and it also produces a wild nut tree, which bears a very hard walnut with a thick shell and a small but very delicious kernel. Since, however, the island contains only four hundred acres, we saw that it would not afford room enough for the new settlement. Yet we looked for a suitable place to build only a Fort (perhaps on the island itself) to keep off strangers, and to protect the trade of the river and our boundaries; for this was the narrowest crossing-place on the river.

On the day of the *Annunciation of the Most Holy Virgin* Mary in the year 1634, we celebrated the mass for the first time, on this island. This had never been done before in this part of the world. After we had completed the sacrifice, we took upon our shoulders a great cross, which we had hewn out of a tree, and advancing in order to the appointed place, with the assistance of the Governor and his associates and the other Catholics, we erected a trophy to Christ the Saviour, humbly reciting, on our bended knees, the Litanies of the Sacred Cross, with great emotion.

Now when the Governor had understood that many Princes were subject to the Emperor of Pascataway, he determined to visit him, in order that, after explaining the reason of our voyage, and gaining his good will, he might secure an easier access to the others. Accordingly, putting with our pinnace (the Dove) another, which he had procured in Virginia, and leaving the ship (the Ark) at anchor, he sailed round and landed on the southern side of the river. And when he had learned that the Savages had fled inland, he went on to a city which takes its name from the river, being also called Potomeack. Here the young King's uncle named Archihu was his guardian, and ruled in his stead; a sober and discreet man. He willingly listened to Father (John) Altham, who had been selected to accompany the Governor, (for the latter kept me still with the ship's cargo.) And when the Father explained, as far as he could through the interpreter . . . the errors of the heathen, he would, every little while, acknowledge his own: and when he was informed that we had come thither, not to make war, but out of good will towards them, in order to impart civilized instruction to his ignorant race, and show them the way to heaven, and at the same time with the intention of communicating to them the advantages of distant countries, he gave us to understand that he was pleased at our coming. The interpreter was one of the Protestants of Virginia. And so, as the Father could not stop for further discourse at the time, he promised that he would return before very long. "That is just what I wish," said Archihu, "we will eat at the same table; my followers too shall go to hunt for you, and we will have all things in common.'' . . .

. . . We landed on the right-hand side [of St. Mary's River], and going in about a mile from the shore, we laid out the plan of a city, naming it after St. Mary. And, in order to avoid every appearance of injustice, and afford no opportunity for hostility, we bought from the King thirty miles of that land, delivering in exchange, axes, hatchets, rakes, and several yards of cloth. . . . The *Susquehanoes,* a tribe inured to war, the bitterest enemies of King *Yaocomico,* making repeated inroads, ravage his whole territory, and have driven the inhabitants, from their apprehension of danger, to seek homes elsewhere. This is the reason why we so easily secured a part of his kingdom: God by this means opening a way for His own Everlasting Law and Light. They move away every day, first one party and then another, and leave us their houses, lands and cultivated fields. Surely this is like a miracle, that barbarous men, a few days before arrayed in arms against us, should so willingly surrender themselves to us like lambs, and deliver up to us themselves and their property. The hand of God is in this, and He purposes some great benefit to this nation. Some few, however, are allowed to dwell among us until next year. But then the land is to be left entirely to us.

LETTERS OF ENGLISH JESUITS
VOLUNTEERING FOR MARYLAND[3]

Although Jesuits by their vow of obedience could be assigned any work, including foreign missions, it was common for missionaries to be chosen from those who had volunteered for a specific mission. White, along with most of the early Jesuit missioners, volunteered for America in order to work among the Indians, as the letters below make clear. Of the four applicants two, Francis Parker and Christopher Morris, were rejected, presumably because their academic talents made them more valuable to the Society in Europe than in America. The two who were sent in response to their requests, Roger Rigby and John Cooper, both apparently met in Maryland the violent deaths they anticipated, but at the hands of Englishmen rather than Amerindians.

Francis Parker[4] to Edward Knott, Provincial[5]

[Antwerp] 26 July 1640
At the very readinge of your Reverence his letter concerninge Mari-

land, I confesse I found myself very strongly moved to the undertakinge of soe greate a worke; and, although I was then in a very quyett moode, as havinge the self same day ended the spirituall exercise, yett, that I might more assuredly knowe the devyne Will in a matter of such consequence, I resolved to take some days of mature consideration before I would wryte unto you. Havinge therefore all this whyle seriously debated the question with myself in the sight of Allmighty God, directinge all my devotions to knowe Jesus his Will in this poynt, after all I fynd in my self a most earnest desyre to live and dye in an employment soe gratefull to his devyne Majesty, soe directly expressinge the holy apostles lyfe, and soe advantageous for the assistinge of soe many poore needy soules as famish there dayly for want of the breade of lyfe.

The chiefest objections which occurred unto me were these: That, if I went now, perchance I should fynd some difficulty in matter of controversy with heretiques there, having yett read but little in that kynde, and had no practise at all. 2ly, That I should want all those spirituall helpes of the third yeare [novitiate] under Father Stafford,[6] to whose idea in matter of vertue I have ever had a greate ambition wholy to frame myself; and now the tyme iust seemed to be come, in which I might most fitly compasse my desyre.[7] Lastly, that my eldest brother, 2 sisters with their husbands and children are all heretiques; my Mother very ould and soe weake a Catholique, that I have iust reason to thinke her allmost in extreame want of present help; which many others of my friends, since Father Scroope[8] came out of those parts [Lancashire], doe allsoe very much stand in neede of, and I seemed now to be come to the poynt when Allmighty God might dispose of me soe, that perchance I might afford them some small succour. Yett for all this, betwixt sweete Jesus and my self, I have soe clearly solved not only these, but alsoe all other objections, of a hard journey, want of all humane comfort, paynes to be necessarily undergone in the gayninge of soules, continuall hazard of lyfe, etc. that I verily think I could securely defend this question without a President. I will not rehearse my motives because I have almost infinite, amongst others this is none of the smallest, that herein I shall soe neerely resemble glorious St. Xaverius, to whom above all other Saynts I have ever since my conversion bine most especially devoted. Wherefore I doe most humbly prostrate my self at your Reverences feete, and beg of you for the appretiative & tender love you bear to all the glorious Saints of our Society,[9] and to the pretious blood sweete Jesus shed for all the soules of Mariland, that you will graunt me this iubily of hart for the only favour I begge of you this iubily yeare,[10] as to employ me freely, if you judge me worthy of so greate a benefite. . . . I make bould to tell you that as much as I can perceyve, & yett I have spoake with many, there be very few who imagine your Rev[eren]ces letter touched themselves. . . .

Christopher Morris[11] *to Edward Knott*

Liège, 27 July 1640

The ardent zeal and earnest desire of concurring to the conversion of those poore Indians of Maryland, which your Reverence in your exhorting letter doth sufficiently declare, stirred up in me a confidence that no employment whatsoever, is like to prove an obstacle to such as find in themselves a true desire of going to assist those needy soules, so dearly bought, and so long neglected. Wherefore after having heard your letter upon Saturday, and suppressing the flame then begun to be enkindled in my hart, omitted to write upon Sunday, to the end I might take some daies to deliberate in so weighty a matter. I find it rather to encrease, then any way to diminish, and now do beg as a favour that which hitherto I never was able even to think on but with repugnance and horrour. The considerations that move me thereunto are these following: First & chiefly, the great want of succour which those poore soules, as deare unto Christ our Lord & redeemed with as great a price as the best in Europe, do stand in need of, and yet that they for so many years since Christ his suffering seeme to have beene so neglected, and as it were forgotten, by the permission of God's secret and inscrutable providence—as if Christ had not suffered for them, but for the Europeans alone, so far they have hitherto been from reaping the fruite of that *copiosa redemptio,* for lacke of external helpes which the Europeans have more then abundance.

Secondly, the facility which God of his goodness hath bestowed upon me in learning of what language soever, the want of which seemeth to have been the chiefe impediment to the charitable endeavours of such as are already setled there. To which may be added the knowledge of Musicke, which may perchaunce be of speciall use in the beginning of that young primitive Church. Things which heere by reason of aboundance are of no great use unto me, and may be there of special consequence.

Thirdly, (but this is a motive of another straine, and a grace which I do acknowledge my selfe most unworthy of), the desire of Martyrdome. for can the Catholicke Church be firmly established in any country without persecutions, and martyrdomes? Will not the devill be as busy in raising oppositions against the Christian faith as well in Maryland as in China, Japony, & other places? At least, if we misse of martyrdome, there cannot want sufferances of labour and afflictions which, joyned with a true desire of martyrdome on my part, I hope will be accepted of Almighty God as part of satisfaction for my manifould former sinnes.

Now what is there besides my sinnes and imperfections, that can hinder your designes, and my desires? The courses of Philosophy which I have in hand? Certaintly this cannot hinder anything: there being those that can supply in this who perhaps have no calling for that. . . . Againe on my part there can be no difficulty, which might arise out of humane considerations, to whom it cannot but be glorious for Almighty God's sake, and the help of souls, to have forsaken an employment of credit, at such a time as the chief labour was overcome and passed, and what remained was rather a glorious crowne of my former[12] pains, then otherwise. And if any shall so interprete my desires as to account me rash, in neglecting what commodious and honourable employment I might expect in our Province heere, and inconsiderately covetous of novelty, rather then moved with a true desire of helping soules, I do contemne his judgement and more highly esteeme of the teaching of Christ's crosse in all sences in Maryland then of the most honourable Chaire either in Liège or all Europe besides.

And as for other dangers and difficulties, either of the journey, or function which there may befall me, I am most ready to undergo all for the love of Christ, and hope by the assistance of his holy grace, never to sinke under the burthen. These dangers and difficulties I have perused as much as I was able in particular . . . [;] whether I die by sea in my journey or by land in Maryland, sure I am I shall have as good, yea more glorious a sepulcher than in Liège. The Cause will ennoble the death. the inconveniences of diet, apparell and lodging will be made easy and supportable by the frequent memory of my Saviours vinegar and gall, nakednesse & hard bed of his crosse. And I hope to feele this stomache that in honourable employment used sometimes to be squeamish, by the influence of the soules hunger and thirst after souls and a good toilsome daies work and labour of body to that effect, to become so hungry as to leape at a browne loaf. He little cared for the want of corporall goods who saied, *Meus cibus est facere voluntatem Patris.*[13] If I can gett no meate, I pray God I may starve in so good an employment, & I shall be happy. Temporal commodities I neither wish for, nor expect among those, I had almost called them Barbarians, whom I hope shortly to see worthy Members of Christ his mystical Body. I beseech Alm. God to give me grace ever to remaine in the same readiness and fervour on my part, and to inspire your Reverence [to do] that which shall be most to his honour and glory. . . .

Roger Rigbie[14] *to Edward Knott*

31 July 1640

I had thought to have petitioned for a favour at your Reverence's last being here; but your sudden, and indeed to me unknowne, departure prevented me. Howsoever, I hope it was not without God Allmighties particular providence, that I might maturely deliberate of soe waightie a matter before I proposed it. My request is only to intreate the happiness to bee made partaker of that happie Mission of Maryland. Tis true I conceive the mission not only happie and glorious, but withall hard and humble, in regard of the raw state things as yet are in; yet the love of Jesus neyther feares labour nor low imployment. Your Reverence's letter inkindled in my mind a great desire of this voyage, renewed former good purposes to that effect, and made me in fine resolve upon it. This resolution hath bin verie much strengthened this tyme of holy exercises both in prayer, holy Mass, & other occasions, which I have taken to deliberate of this point. I confesse the deliberation hath bin long; and the resolution, I feare, will come late both for others speedier petitions, and the tyme of the year. Nevertheless, not always first come, first sped; sometimes *novissimi* become *primi;* and, being neare at hand, I confide I may bee ready in due tyme for that voyage the next opportunitie. Besyd's, thoughe others farr better deserving, & more able to found that new spirituall plantation, will have allreadie presented themselves, yet I should be glad to joyne my meanest endeavours with their best; and the little experience I have had gives mee good hopes that my health and strength will bee able to break through occurrent difficulties, and accompanie others in their greatest labours.

I fear I have hindred your more serious thoughts too long. Wherefore, in a word, I leave the matter wholly to your prudent charitie, desiring you would freely dispose of me as you judge best. If you be allreadie furnished with workmen, it may bee you will want the next spring to provide for a new harvest, then you know where to find one. . . .

John Cooper[15] to Edward Knott

17 July 1640

Your R[everen]ces exhortatory letter towards Marylands mission caused such comfort and joy in my hart, that I was inforced to use no smale indeavour to keep it from breaking forth to others; for I conceived immediately uppon the reading there of, that there was now hope of compassing my desires in helping to reduce such barbarous people to the knowledg of one God and the true faith of Christ. I have had these many years no smale inclination towards such a mission; but, not finding how to compass it, this litle sparke of zeale for soules was in a manner cover'd with the ashes of dispaire, which now begins againe to shew it self; and, by reason of new fewel of hopes added, I find the fier of charity so to increase that I can no longer hold from asking the favour, that I may be sent fortwith into those parts, there to spend *et superimpendere meipsum*[16] in reducing those soules so deare to Christ our Lord, and for His sake more deare to me than my very life. For alas! how is it possible but that I should burne with this fier, behoulding[17] with my interiours eyes my dearest Saviour hinging uppon the crosse, and with as many mouths as he had woundes in his virginall body inviting me to this most Christian and truly apostolicall worke? and indeed, the confidence I have in His divine providence mak's all apprehension of difficulties to vanish quite out of thought; and, although I might perchaunce have some fals apparent reasons to disswade me from this most holy enterprise, yettt of such force I find this present motion that I can admit of none. Wherefore I most earnestly beseech your Reverence, out of that affection you bare my souls good, that you will value my health & life no more than I my selfe do value them, who shall be most happy to spend a thousand lives (if I had them) in so good a cause. I would have your R[everen]ce to know that I care not to live nor feare to dye: death will free me from infinite miseries this world affords; and life is already so distastfull, by reason of my smale increase of love towards Almighty god, that I esteeme it more than a perpetuall death to live any longer. O, how happy should I be eyther to dye in this iourney, or in the midst of so glorious a harvest! Verily, Father, I cannot but speake this with much feeling, and so much the more, speaking it to one who I doubt not but understands me. But why do I mention death, who perswade myself that life & health will rather be increased then lesned by reason of this journey? For why may I not hope that, as for leaving a father and brother in the world to follow Christ I have found a hundred as welwishers in religion, so for hazarding (if I may so terme it) my life & health for his love I shall also find both health increased and life prolonged, according unto those his most true words, *Qui perdiderit animam suam propter me inveniet eam.*[18] Moreover, my meane parts and small sufficiency will not, as I immagin, prove so beneficiall to Europeians as to these barbarians, thos of Europe requiring more learning then I for my part professe to have. Besids, this country of Maryland, taking its name from so great a patronesse as is the ever immaculate Virgin, gives me no smale assurance of doing some-thing to her honour and glory, in whose help and assistance I trust next to God. . . .

John Cooper to Edward Knott

May 9, 1642

I write to you an other way, that so at least one [letter] might not faile you. My business wer only to lett you understand that never was my desire greater for the place ye know, then at this present. The more I propose the occurring difficultyes, the more I find my affections inflamed that way, & I hope the very ocean will not squinch this fier. Deer Sir, let me know what hopes there is of obtaining this great happynesse. If you send none this yeare, I must intreat the favour in the interim, you would lett me be where I may imploy the strength & health God hath lately given me, in helping the poore and travelling a foot in that great work. I am confident I shall be able to perform it, for in experience I find no difficulty in it. Where I live, I am abriged of liberty in doing the good I could wish; which makes me more earnest to be els where imployed; but I[19] leave myselfe to your prudence to dispose, as you shall thinke fitting. Only this I must tell you, that, considering my health is so much increased, I thought it my obligation to propose these motions to you, and so to rest in your advice and counsell.

ANNUAL LETTERS CONCERNING THE JESUIT MISSION IN MARYLAND: EXCERPTS[20]

The Calverts, unfortunately, did not share the Jesuit zeal for carrying the gospel to the natives and tended to hamper the efforts of White and the others to proselytize them. The acceptance of land from the Patuxents also did not endear the Jesuits to the governor, Leonard Calvert. Despite deteriorating relations with the Calverts and serious losses from disease or violence (only White and one other Jesuit survived for more than two years in the first decade), the missionaries were remarkably successful in converting the tribes in the region, most notably the Piscataway and the Anacostians. White, committed to bringing Christianity to the natives in their own language, composed a catechism in Piscataway, as well as a grammar and dictionary. The Indian mission continued until 1645 when the Calverts were overthrown by invaders from Virginia. Three Jesuits disappeared into Virginia; White and another Jesuit were carried off in chains to England. Although it was a capital offense for a priest to come into that country, the Puritans chose instead to exile them to the continent, from where White, nearly seventy, tried to get back to America, but his superiors refused his request. He did once more return to England and died there peacefully.

The following are annual reports sent to Rome by the superiors of the mission.

1638

Four Fathers gave their attention to the mission, and along with them one lay-brother,[21] who, after enduring severe toils for the space of five years with the greatest patience, humility and ardent love, was seized by the disease prevalent at the time, and happily exchanged this wretched life for that which is eternal.

He was shortly followed by one of the Fathers, who, though young, possessed remarkable qualities of mind, which gave great promise for the future.[22] He had scarcely spent two months in this mission, when, to the great grief of all of us, he was carried off by the sickness so general in the colony, from which none of the three remaining priests have entirely escaped, yet we have not ceased to labor to the best of our ability among the neighboring people.

Though the authorities of this colony have not yet allowed us to dwell among the savages, on account both of the prevailing sickness and of the hostile disposition shown by the savages towards the English, to the extent of murdering a man from this colony, who had gone amongst them for the sake of trade, and also of entering into a conspiracy against our whole nation; still we hope that one of us will shortly secure a station among the savages. Meanwhile, we devote ourselves more zealously to the English settlers; and since there are Protestants as well as Catholics in the colony, we have labored for both, and God has blessed our labors.

For among the Protestants, nearly all who came out from England this year (1638) and many others, have been converted to the faith, together with four servants whom we purchased in Virginia (another of our colonies) for necessary services, and five mechanics whom we hired for a month, and have in the meantime won to God. . . .

A certain person, a zealous Protestant, entirely unknown to us, was staying with a friend who was still more fervent in his religion, and having been bitten by one of the snakes that abound in these parts, he was in great danger of death. One of our Fathers, on learning this, took a surgeon with him and hurried to the sick man, with the hope of being of some benefit to his soul, though it was reported that he was already delirious. His friend, however, sensing this intention, tried to thwart its success. The priest, unable to think of any other plan, determined to stay all night with the sick man. But his friend prevented this also, and, lest the Father should gain entry during the night, he stationed a guard on a bed laid across the door of the room occupied by the sick man. The priest, nevertheless, returning at midnight, when he supposed the guard would probably be asleep, managed, without disturbing him, to enter the sick man's room; and, at his own request, received him into the Church. Although, under the circumstances, it was impossible that the man could be taught much, or be very firmly established in his belief, yet when, contrary to all expectation, he was cured by our surgeon, the grace of God gave him courage to choose to be put out of his friend's house rather than retract what he had done; nay, he even came to us of his own accord, and happily completed the work which he had begun.

As for the Catholics, the attendance on the sacraments here is so large, that it is not greater among the faithful in Europe, in proportion to their respective numbers. The unlettered have been taught catechism and the others have heard catechetical lectures every Sunday; on feast days a sermon has rarely been omitted. The sick, and the dying, who were numerous this year, and dwelt far apart, we have assisted in every way, so that not even a single one has died without the sacraments. We have buried a great many, as well as baptized a number of persons. And although there are not wanting frequent occasions of dissension, yet none of any importance has arisen here in the last nine months, which we have not immediately allayed. By the blessing of God, we have this consolation, that no vices spring up among the new Catholics, although settlements of this kind are not usually supplied from the best class of men.

We bought the contracts of two Catholic indentured servants in Virginia. Nor was the money ill-spent, for both showed themselves good Christians; one, indeed, is extraordinary. Some others have performed the same charitable act in buying from that place Catholic servants, of whom there are a great number. For every year a great many sell themselves into bondage for Virginia, and, as they live among persons of the worst example and are utterly deprived of any spiritual means, they generally make shipwrecks of their souls.

Several of the leading men of the colony we have led through the Spiritual Exercises to a devout state by the incalculable grace of God. In one case, of a man bedeviled with so many worldly cares and lately living in Virginia as a virtual pagan, we are dumbstruck at the remarkable providence and mercy of God in bringing him to make the Exercises shortly before his death; he made such progress through them that he had resolved to lead his life henceforward from the highest motives. This intention was only frustrated by a fatal disease, which he accepted with the greatest resignation, his mind fixed wholly on God, and having received all the sacraments, in a most peaceful manner that was in stark contrast to the troubles and worries of his former life, gave his soul back to his Creator. . . .

1639

There are in this mission four priests and one coadjutor. All are in places far distant—this, no doubt, with the hope of being able to learn more quickly the local language, and propagate more widely the sacred faith of the gospel. . . . Father Andrew White is distant . . . one hundred and twenty miles, to wit: at Kittamaquidi, the metropolis of Pascatoway, having lived in the palace with the king himself, whom they call Tayac, from the month of June, 1639. . . .

. . . The cause of this remarkable affection for the father, is to be found in two dreams (unless you think them worthy of another name). Uwanno, the king's blood brother and former king, whom he had removed in the middle of his reign, had the first dream. In his sleep he seemed to see Fathers White and Gravenor and heard a voice admonishing him, "These are the men, who from their hearts loved him with all his tribe, and brought with them those blessings, which would make him happy, if he wished." Thereafter so vivid an impression of these strangers remained with him, that even at first sight, he recognized them coming toward him and embraced them warmly. He was also accustomed to call Father White his parent; to whose instruction he wants to entrust for seven years his dear son (indeed the whole tribe is very fond of children, and almost never let them out of their sight). The other dream happened to the Tayac, which he frequently repeats; as he slept, his dead father appeared to be present before his eyes, accompanied by a god of a black color, whom he worshipped, beseeching him that he would not desert him. Standing there with this hideous god was a certain Snow, an obstinate heretic from England; and lastly, standing apart were the governor of the colony and Father White, also accompanied by a god, but one of great beauty, who excelled the unstained snow in whiteness and was gently calling the king to him. From that time on the king treated both the governor and the father with the greatest affection.

Shortly after Father White's arrival, the Tayac was in danger of death from a severe disease; and when forty conjurers had in vain tried every remedy, the Father, by permission of the sick man, administered medicine, that is, a certain powder of known efficacy mixed with holy water, and the next day, with the assistance of the boy whom he had with him, opened one of his veins for blood letting. After this, the sick man began daily to grow better, and soon was completely cured. Having recuperated, he resolved to be initiated in the Christian rites as soon as possible; not only himself, but his wife also and his two daughters; for as yet he had no male offspring. Father White is now diligently engaged in their instruction; nor do they idly receive the heavenly doctrine, for by the grace poured upon them, they have long since discovered the errors of their former life. The king has exchanged the skins, with which he was heretofore clothed, for a garment made in our fashion; he makes also a little effort to learn our language. Having put away his concubines, he lives content with one wife, that he may the more freely (as he says) have leisure to pray to God. He abstains from meat on the days, in which it is forbidden by the christian laws; and thinks that those who do otherwise should be considered heretics or bad christians. He greatly delights in spiritual conversation, and indeed seems to esteem earthly wealth as nothing, in comparison with its heavenly counterpart, as he told the Governor, who was explaining to him what great advantages he could gain from trading with the English. "Truly," he said, "I consider these trifles when compared with this one advantage, that through these preachers, I have come to the knowledge of the one God; than which there is nothing greater to me or ought to be.''

Not long ago, when he held a council of the tribe, in a crowded assembly of the chiefs and people, with Father White and some of the English present, he publicly attested that it was his advice, together with that of his wife and children, that they should forsake their native superstition and give themselves to Christ; for there was no other true god but that of the Christians, nor could men in any other way save their immortal souls; indeed the stones and herbs, which, through blindness of mind, he had formerly joined his people in the worship of, are the humblest things created by Almighty God for the use and assistance of mankind. Saying this, he cast from him a stone which he happened to have in his hand, and ground it under his foot. A murmur of applause from the people indicated well enough how these things had fallen on their ears. For the greatest hope is that, when the family of the king is baptized, the conversion of the whole empire will speedily take place. In the meantime, we heartily thank God for such an encouraging start, and particularly take hope when we daily witness the contempt with which the natives now regard their idols, who lately were counted among the deities. . . .

If we could look over the entire world, nowhere, perhaps, would we find men more abject in appearance than these Indians, who, nevertheless, have souls, if you consider the ransom paid by Christ, no less precious than the most cultivated Europeans. They are inclined indeed to vices, though not very many, in such darkness of ignorance, such barbarism, and in so unrestrained and nomadic a life; nevertheless, in their disposition they are docile, nor will you find, except rarely, their passions carrying them away. They are most patient in bearing hardships, and easily endure contempt and injuries, if these do not involve any danger to life. They have few or no idols, to whose worship they are greatly addicted. Nor are there among them priests or mystics who have charge of the administration of sacrifice; though there are certainly those who interpret superstitions, and sell them to the people; but even these are commonly not at all numerous. They acknowledge one God of heaven; notwithstanding, they are not sure how he should be worshiped, how he should be honored; thus they readily listen to those who convey this knowledge. They rarely give thought to the immortality of the soul, or of the things after death. If, at any time, they meet a teacher clearly explaining these things, they show themselves very attentive as well as docile; and by and by are seriously brought to think of their souls, so as to be ready to obtain those things, which, they perceive, conduce to the salvation of the same. They are readily swayed by reason, nor do they withhold their assent obstinately from the truth set forth in a credible manner. This natural disposition of the tribe, aided by the seasonable assistance of divine grace, gives us hope of the most desirable harvest hereafter, and animates us to continue our labors in this vineyard with the greatest exertion. And the same ought to be an incitement to all those who in future, by the will of God, may come here to help us. . . .

1640

In the mission this year were four priests and one coadjutor. We stated in our last letter what hope we had of converting the Tayac, or the King of the Pascataway. In the meantime, such is the goodness of God, the result has not disappointed our expectations. He has indeed converted and brought over to our faith some others with him. . . .

. . . Another king, that of the Anacostans, whose territory is not far distant, is anxious for one of Ours to settle among them. From this it is evident that a rich harvest awaits us, on which we may work to great advantage; though we fear that we will lack the workers to realize the full fruits of this harvest. There are other villages lying near, which, I doubt not, would run promptly and joyfully to the light of evangelical truth, if there was any one to bring them the word of eternal life. We should not, however, be too concerned about winning over others, lest we give the impression that we are prematurely abandoning our present flock. Nor must those who are sent here to assist us fear that they will lack the necessities of life, since he, who clothes the lilies and feeds the birds of the air, will not leave destitute those who are laboring to build up his kingdom.

To Father Philip Fisher,[23] now residing at St. Mary's, the capital of the colony, nothing would have been more agreeable than to labor in the Indian harvest, but Superiors could not afford to dispense with his services there. Still his good will does not go unrewarded; for while many Indians are being baptized, just as many, thanks to his industry, are being at the same time brought back into the bosom of the church from heretical depravity. The Catholic settlers are not inferior in piety to those in other countries; in urbanity of manners, according to the judgment of those who have visited other colonies, they are considered far superior to them. Everywhere the hope of an abundant harvest has dawned; and while each one of us is anxious to help even unto death as many as we can, various events are happening that deserve record. Two of the most prominent are narrated here, one manifesting the divine mercy, and the other the divine justice.

On the day on which a certain man was about to abjure heresy and expiate the sins of his past life by confession, his house caught fire, and the flames rapidly burst through the roof. He was at a little distance when this occurred, and lost no time in calling his neighbors, of whom two only would come to his help; and although all this time the fire was burning in a house that was built only of dry logs, yet it was put out before any great damage had been done. Some feared lest this unexpected calamity might deter him from converting. The result was just the opposite; for the marvelous preservation of his house led him to the conclusion that God was showing his approval of his intention to become a Catholic.

Another man felt some internal stirrings of the grace of God, and for a long time took steps which seemed to be leading him to conversion, but then, casting aside all such thoughts, decided to revert to all his old ways. This man, while he had been considering his spiritual health, had acquired a rosary for himself; but after his change of heart, he had the rosary ground into powder, which he mixed with tobacco for his pipe, and often joked that in a way he had swallowed his Avemaria (for so he called his rosary). But divine vengeance did not let this wicked deed go long unpunished. Scarcely a year had passed, indeed it was nearly the anniversary of the day on which he had abandoned his purpose of embracing the catholic faith, when his companions noticed he was becoming especially ribald and sacrilegious. During his daily afternoon bath in the river, he had scarcely touched the water when a huge fish suddenly seized the wretched man, and before he could reach the bank it tore away at one bite a large portion of flesh from his thigh, inflicting a mortal but merited wound which in a short time took him from the living; the divine justice thus ordained that he, who a little while before had boasted of eating his Avemarias, should see his own flesh devoured while he was still alive.

1641[24]

A year ago I wrote to you that Almighty God seemed to be opening the way for the conversion of many thousands of souls, namely by calling to his orthodox faith the emperor or grand king of the Pascatoway. . . . Nor is there any doubt but that very many following in the footsteps of their chief would have been washed as quickly as possible at the same font of baptism, had not Fathers White and Altam, who were engaged in that mission, been seized with sickness, and to regain their health had to retire to the town of St. Mary's in the English colony, where Father Altam died on the 5th of November following, and Father White, having had a relapse, was for many days after his sickness unable to return to his Mission on account of his weakness. But in February last, having partially recovered his strength, he returned and joined me at Pascatoway, in order to restore, and as far as possible, solidly establish that mission, and to propagate the Christian faith, the seeds of which it had pleased God so happily to sow. However, shortly after our arrival Father White again fell sick, and has not as yet recovered his strength; and, indeed, I fear that from his age and increasing infirmities, nature will shortly put an end to his great labors. I will use my utmost endeavors to preserve his life, that this great work of God, the conversion of so many infidels, may prosperously and happily progress, because, with his grasp of their language, (which is better than the rest of us can claim) he has the greatest influence over them. . . . I hope that by God's favor, if we do not lack assistance, there will be great progress for the Christian faith within a very short time amid these nations of barbarians. And this, although, on account of the dearness of corn, and the increased expenses and deficiency of means of living, we are pressed by great difficulties; nor are there here in this colony any who are either able or willing to furnish us with alms, and divine providence shows that neither by our own exertions, nor of those for whose salvation we labour, be they christians or pagans, can we hope for support. I can, however, fear nothing. He who feeds the birds of the air that neither sow nor reap, and who supplied the apostles, whom he sent forth without staff or scrip to preach the gospel, will provide us with everything we need. . . . Having set out on this mission, certainly the very thought of recalling us, or of not sending others to help us in this glorious work of the salvation of souls, would in a manner betray our faith in God's providence and his care for his servants, as if he were wanting now where he had not been wanting before. So, let no such thoughts sap the courage of any one, but rather increase and strengthen it; since God has now taken us under his protection to provide for us himself; especially as it has pleased the divine goodness to draw some fruit from our labours. Howsoever it shall seem good to the divine Majesty to dispose of us, let his will be done; for my own part, I should prefer to work here among the Indians for their conversion, and, destitute of all human aid and reduced by hunger, to die lying on the bare ground under the open sky, than even once to think of abandoning this holy work of God through any fear of privation. God grant me but the grace to do him some service, and the rest I leave to his providence. . . .

1642

In the mission of Maryland for the year 1642, just elapsed, we have had only three companions and those all priests, one of whom was confined by sickness of three months' duration. This was Father Roger Rigby. The other two were Father Philip Fisher, superior of the mission, and Father Andrew White, who separated themselves in different places for the purpose of gathering greater harvests. The superior, Father Philip, remained for the most part at St. Mary's, the chief town of the colony, in order that he might take care of the English, who live there in greater numbers, and also of the Indians not living far distant, as well as those who pass through there. Father Andrew returned to his former station at Piscataway; but Father Roger went to a new settlement, which the natives call Patuxent, in order to learn more easily the Indian language; also, that he might better instruct some neophytes, and scatter along the bank of that great river the seed of faith.

. . . An attack having been recently made on one of our places, [the Susquehanna Indians] slew the men whom we had there, and carried away our goods, with great loss. And unless they be restrained by force of arms, which we little expect from the English who are at odds with themselves, we will not be safe there. So we have to be content with excursions, many of which we have made this year in ascending the river, which they call Patuxent. This much we can show for it: the conversion of the young queen of the town of that place, of the same name with the river there, and her mother; also of the young queen of Portobacco; of the wife and two sons of Tayac the great, as they call him—that is the king, who died last year; and of one hundred and thirty others besides. The following is our manner of making an excursion. We are carried in a pinnace or galley, that is the Father, the interpreter, and a servant. . . . In our excursions we endeavor, as much as we can, to reach by evening some English house, or Indian village, but if not, we land and to the Father falls the care of mooring the boat fast to the shore, then of collecting wood and making a fire, while in the meantime the two others go to hunt, so that whatever they take may be prepared. But if not, having refreshed ourselves with our provisions, we lie down by the fire and take our rest. If rain threatens, we erect our hut and cover it with a larger mat spread over; nor, praise be to God, do we enjoy this humble fare and hard couch with a less joyful mind, than more luxurious provisions in Europe; having this comfort, that God now imparts to us a foretaste of what he is about to give to those who labor faithfully in this life, and mitigates all hardships with a degree of pleasantness; so that his divine majesty appears to be present with us, in an extraordinary manner.

The difficulty of this language is so great, that none of us can yet converse with the Indians without an interpreter. Father Rigby has made a little progress, so that he hopes he will be able by a short time to converse with them, upon things of ordinary importance, as far as may be necessary to instruct them to be admitted to baptism; for he had composed a short catechism by the aid of an interpreter. These things, I say, being considered, it appears miraculous that we have been able to effect anything with them; especially when we have no interpreter, except a young man, who is not himself so well acquainted with their language, but that he sometimes excites their laughter; so that when, for a time, we seemed almost to despair, nevertheless, by patience we are succeeding, and in a gradual way are bringing them over to what we desire.

It has also pleased the divine goodness, by the virtue of his cross, to effect something beyond mere human power. The circumstances are these: a certain Indian, called an Anacostan, now a Christian, while he was making his way with others through a forest, fell behind his companions a little, when some savages of the tribe of Susquehanna . . . attacked him suddenly from an ambush, and with a strong and light spear of locust wood . . . pierced him through from the right side to the left, at a hand's breadth below the armpit near the heart itself with a wound two fingers broad at each side. When the man had fallen, his enemies quickly retreated; but his friends who had gone on before, hearing the sudden noise and shouting, returned and carried the man from the land to the boat, which was not far distant, and from there to his home at Piscataway, where they left him speechless and out of his senses. The thing being reported to Father White, who by chance was but a short distance off, he hastened to him the following morning, and found the man in front of the entrance, lying on a mat before the fire and enclosed by a circle of his tribe, not indeed completely speechless, or out of his senses, as the day before, but expecting certain death almost every moment; and with a mournful voice joining in the song with his friends that stood around, as is the custom in the case of the more distinguished of these men, when they are thought to be certainly about to die. But some of his friends were Christians, and their song, which they raised in a plaintive tone, was: "may he live, oh God! if it so please thee;" and they repeated it again and again, until the Father attempted to address the dying man, who immediately recognized the Father, and showed him his wounds. The Father pitied him exceedingly; but when he saw the danger was imminent, he briefly ran over the principal articles of faith; and repentance of his sins being elicited, he heard his confession; then filling the man's soul with hope and confidence in God, he recited the gospel which is appointed to be read for the sick, and the litany of the Blessed Virgin, and told him to commend himself to her most holy intercession and to call unceasingly upon the most sacred name of Jesus. Then the Father, applied to the wound on each side the sacred relic of the Most Holy Cross, which he carried in a case around his neck, but had now taken off. He himself had to leave to baptize an aged Indian who was expected to die that very day. But he directed the bystanders, when the man should breathe his last, to carry him to the chapel for the purpose of burial.

It was noon when the Father departed; and the following day, at the same hour, when by chance he was borne along in his canoe, he saw two Indians propelling a canoe with oars towards him; and when they had come along side, one of them put his foot into the boat, in which the Father was sitting. While he stared at the man, being in doubt, (for he easily recognized him by his features, but could not forget the state in which he had left him the day before) the man, on a sudden, threw open his cloak, and showed him the scars of his wounds, or rather a red spot on each side, the only trace of the wounds. All doubt immediately vanished. The man exclaimed with great exultation that he was completely well, and that from the hour at which the Father had left the day before he had not ceased to invoke the most holy name of Jesus, to whom he attributed his recovered health. All who were in the boat with the Father, after they confirmed his claim, broke forth in praise of God and thanksgiving. They rejoiced greatly and found their faith strengthened by this miracle.

The Father, having counseled the man that he should forever be thankful for so great and manifest a blessing, and continue to treat that holy name and most holy Cross with love and reverence, sent him on his way. The latter returned to his boat with a companion, and boldly propelled it with the oar, which he could not have done, unless he had been healthy and in full use of his powers. . . .

NOTES

1. Translated from *Relatio Itineris in Marylandiam. Declaratio Coloniae Domini Baronis de Baltimoro. Excerpta Ex Diversis Litteris Missionariorum ab Anno 1635, Ad Annum 1638,* Fund Publication No. 7, Maryland Historical Society (Baltimore, 1874), 10–17, 20–21, 23–24, 30–34, 36–37.

2. *Declaratio Coloniae Domini Baronis de Baltimoro,* Fund Publication No. 7, 47–48.

3. Maryland Province Archives (hereafter MPA), 2 Z. These archives are located in the Special Collections division of the Lauinger Library of Georgetown University.

4. Francis Parker (1606–1679), a native of Lancashire. After completing his studies in 1641, he was on the faculty at St. Omer's and rector of the novitiate at Watten, then returned to England in 1644. In 1678 he was implicated in the Titus Oates Plot and forced to flee to the continent.

5. Edward Knott, alias Matthew Wilson (1582–1656). He was provincial twice (1640–1645; 1653–1656), his residence being in London.

6. Henry Stafford (1606–1657), at this time a professor at St. Omer's College.

7. After a Jesuit completes his studies, he spends an additional year in ascetical studies and practices, including the making of the full (month-long) Spiritual Exercises. Together with his first two years in the Society, this constitutes a third year of novitiate, formally known as tertianship. Since the Maryland Mission had no novitiate, superiors would not have considered sending Parker until he had made

tertianship on the continent. Later in the century generals complained when the English Province, in its attempt to provide for the mission, cut short the tertianship of some Americans. In Parker's case, there were family considerations that may also have been a factor in the failure to assign him to Maryland. But his academic abilities seem to have persuaded superiors to keep him in Europe.

8. Laurence Anderton, alias Scroop (1576–1643), a Lancashire convert and former Anglican minister. His Jesuit ministry was mostly spent in Lancashire; he was reassigned there two years after Parker's letter.

9. Crossed out: "this Je."

10. The year 1640 marked the centenary of the foundation of the Society.

11. A native of Wales, Christopher Morris (1603–1667) had been appointed Professor of Philosophy at Liège the preceding year. Several years after applying for Maryland, Morris was kidnapped at sea and taken to Ireland. He finally got back to Liège in 1651.

12. Crossed out: "and."

13. "My food is to do the will of the Father."

14. Robert Knowles, alias Roger Rigby, also from Lancashire. He worked in Maryland until he was captured during the Ingle-Claibourne invasion in 1645 and died in Virginia a year later.

15. John Cooper (1610–1646[?]).

16. "overspend myself."

17. Crossed out: "Christ."

18. "Whosoever shall lose his life for me shall find it."

19. Crossed out: "and I."

20. I have followed the translation in the *Woodstock Letters* (Vol. 10 [1881], 220–224; Vol. 11 [1882], 3–17, 117–123), with certain revisions made according to the Latin text in Thomas Hughes, S.J., *The History of the Society of Jesus in North America: Colonial and Federal,* Documents, Vol. I, Part I (London, 1908), 109–125.

21. Thomas Gervase (1590–1637) died of yellow fever in August.

22. John Knowles (1607–1637) died on September 24.

23. The alias for Thomas Copley (1596–1652). Copley managed to flee the colony during the invasion of 1645 and returned three years later to resume his ministry.

24. This letter, as well as the previous two, was written by Ferdinand Pulton (1601–1641), who was killed, apparently by accident, a few weeks afterward.

II

MARYLAND JESUITS AND THE PENAL ERA

PETER ATTWOOD

Peter Attwood (1682–1734) was a native of Worcestershire and educated in the recusant schools in the Lowlands. He joined the Society of Jesus in 1703 or 1704. In 1711 he was sent to the Maryland Mission and eventually became its superior in 1720. Two years earlier the Maryland Assembly had disenfranchised Catholics and affirmed that the penal laws in England were binding in Maryland as well. In response Attwood wrote a long treatise on "Liberty and Property or the Beauty of Maryland displayed in a brief and candid Search into her Charter, Fundamental Laws & Constitution." Attwood argued that "the Law of Liberty of Conscience" was "the chief and fundamental part" of the constitution of the colony upon which depended all other rights and privileges, including the right to property, itself a guaranty of liberty. In imposing disabilities upon Catholics or any other members of its community, Maryland was turning its back upon its own honorable tradition.[1] What role, if any, Attwood's treatise played in the subsequent relaxation of the pressures against Catholics is unclear. What is significant is his willingness to participate in political dissent, despite the fragile status of priests in Maryland in the wake of the Glorious Revolution. But he was primarily a pastor, severely concerned with the inner life of his congregations. The following sermons seem closely modelled on the court sermons of the age. Their neat copybook form suggests a date of composition prior to Attwood's coming to Maryland. At the very least they reveal the austere spirituality in which the Jesuits of the eighteenth century were formed and which they carried to the new world.

73

ASH WEDNESDAY: DANGEROUS TO LIVE IN SIN[1a]

Memento homo[2] *quia pulvis es et in pulverem reverteris.* Gen. 3:19.

I appear this morning D[ear] C[ongregation] in this sacred place to imitate the prophet Michael who caryed the happy tydings to king Ahab; I come to speak on a sad and malancholy subject to proclame a mournfull case and bring the most unwelcome news you can hear. I find the task hard and difficult in execution least I shoud turn this chappell into a vaile of tears and I shoud hear that execration of Ahab echoing from evry breast. My soul hates that man because he announces to me evill things; and therefore like the prophet Jonah pitched uppon by heaven to warn Nineve of its approaching ruin out of a human prudence I coud decline the office imposed upon me. But yet I presume I shall not be rude for delivring the mesage (tho unpleasant) which[3] the holy church, and the Sa[cred]: Scrip[ture]: has put into my mouth, wherefore I will not dessemble but faithfully discharge my commission.

There is a sentence which suffers no appeal thundered out against us by divine Justice that we are made of dust and ashes, and that we must return again into dust and ashes. *Memento homo, quia pulvis es et in pulverem reverteris.* Remember Man that dust thou art, and into dust thou shalt return, that we must all dye and quit this world, tho we are never so well placed here, and seated in it, we must leave it together with all these amusements, that take up our time, and employ our thoughts and steal our hearts from God; nothing can pass into eternity with us but our virtues and our vices, these to be chastized, and those to be rewarded. This sentence pronounced against all the poor children of Adam is without limitation, it reaches the whole species and takes in all the mass of mankind, and altho' the Alm: sometimes dispenses with his other laws this will remain inviolable never to be reversed. *Pulvis es et in pulverem reduceris.*

We scarce know of any errour, that has not found some abetter, some patron to defend it; the atheist denys the being of a god[,] the Manacheans set up two and the pagans a 1000, but we never yet read of any so extravagantly madd up to deny mortality; we must all dye[;] neither the power of an alexander; nor the valour, and glory of a Caesar, nor the riches of a Solomon, nor the beauty of an Absolom, neither the meekness of a Moses nor the piety of a David can keep off the fatal stroke of death. It will assault the king even sitting on his royal throne, and environed with huge lifeguards; it will attack the conqueror at the head of his army, and tho he has subdued countrys[,] fetterd the liberty of nations[,] coulored his purple in the blood of dying monarchs, tho' Europe, Africa, and Asia have drawn his triumphant chariot, and America brought up his glorious train, yet he himself shall become the slave, and captive, and augment the triumphs of death. It

shall surprise [. . .] the rich man in the midst of his treasures, the voluptuous man in the midst of his pleasures,[4] and the great ones[5] of the world
in the midst of their honours: crowns and scepters, croisers and miters all
must become the spoils of death; Robes, and purple must drop to its standard; rich and poor, young and old, beautiful, and deformed, kings and pe-
sants, merchants[,] tradsmen all must buckle and bend to the yoke of death.
It will snatch from the arms of the father and the bosome of the mother that
darling child, so well acomplishd and sett out by nature, who was all the
hopes of the family, who so charmingly flattered the designs of his father,
and was all the delight of his mother, and upon whose green and florishing
years they believed they coud securely reckon, and form great projects for
their future happiness, and prosperity. It will carry off the young woman in
the bloom and flower of her age, in the pride of nature, and in the luster of
a most perfect beauty, by which she thought to have made her fortune and
to have gained a fair, and large possession in this world. In fine the pittilys
syth of death will cutt all down; without mercy or compassion. But me
thinks I see your thoughts, and hear you say wherein your own escap be;
here is nothing recounted but what you knew before: we stand in need of
no one to put us in mind of our mortality in the midst of the soothings of
fortune as the Romans were wont to doe to their triumphing conquerors; nor
in the stings and inticements of concupiscence to tell us that we are dust and
ashes as was practiced amongst the [h]ermits of thebais[?]; nor in the Assaults of the world, that its treasures are vain and perishable, as the Apostle
warns us. If we cast but an eye into the grave and look on that dismall spectacle which lyes within[,] [. . .] that sight [. . .] will make as[6] moving
and powerfull a sermon as that of the prophet Daniel, who at the sight of
the murdering dragon which for many years was adored upon the altar, but
now lay extended upon the ground, and wallowing in mire, and stench induced his people to penance only while saying to them *ecce quem colebatis.*
behold him whom you adored[,] see what this body is, so much idolized in
this life, about which as on an Idoll so much incense is burnt, so much precious time is lost, so much treasure is consumed, so much labour is blown
away, so much pain is spent, *ecce quem colebatis,* see that which you
adored so much.

Me thinks I hear you still run on very eloquently on this subject and
say that we are all convinced we must dye; that fate is rung in our ears[,] it
is the common topick of evry man's discourse; this truth we read engraven
on every created object[:] the church yards proclaim it, the marble monuments of so many kings and princes divulge it, and our dead parents in a
mute but pathetick langage tell us that we must follow [th]em into an other
world. *Memento hoc quia pulvis es etc.*

Never did Alm. God make a decree, which he observed more rigor-ously than this of death. It is a[bout] 5000 years since the penal law of mortality was put in execution, and in all this space he has never, so much as once dispenced with it. He give the sun general orders when he created it, to run round and enlighten the earth, but he stopt it for a Josue, and totally eclypsed it at the death of our agonizing Redeemer. He appointed bounds for the sea [. . .] but how often has he permitted it to swell over its banks, and drown whole nations in its mercyless floods? Yet in this decree of death, no exemption, no dispensation was ever yet granted, no it is a decree so sacred as never to be violated[;] so general, as to suffer no exception; stand sinner, learned and unlearned, prince and pesant, rich and poor all must dye, there is no sanctuary so sacred, no [. . .] hermitage so private, no fortress so strong no princes bed chamber so watchfully guarded which death does not find entrance into. Nor does it pity innocents nor spare youth, or regard wisdom, or hear eloquence or fear armes, or dread majesty. No Abells and Absoloms, Solomons, and Ciceros, Caesars, and Alexanders[,] Pauls and Neroes all must dye, this we all know, this we are all convinced of. This is an article of Xtian religion, and all Xtians believe it. Doe we then all know that we are made of dust, and ashes, and that we must dye and bid adiue to all things on this side of heaven? how is this possible? are not we the men who live as if we were never to dye? are not we the men who stunned w[i]th the noise of a busy clamorous world, distracted with the variety of present objects, and as if living we were to pitch our tabernacles, and fixe our seats eternally upon earth; as for heaven it is slighted, as for eternity it is forgotten, as for judgment it is not feared, as for hell it is not thought on. Are not we the men who injurious to our selves and ungreatfull to God spend our desires, consume our love, and cast away our thoughts on vain transitory things, on trifles, and toys? What folly? What stupidity? What madness is this? to believe as we do, and live and act so contrary to what we believe. I thought from the consideration of our mortality to have drawn an irrefragable motive to stop us in this carreer of sin, and lead us to a hearty sorrow and repentance for our past offences, by minding us of our ashes, and our last end. I thought to have found a strong argument against the vanities, amusements and flattery of the world. But I see my hopes are dwindled to nothing whilst I behold Xtians notwithstanding such pressing motives live without rules and sin without restraint. What then must I doe? Must I yield and retire, and leave Xtians lulled asleep in the bloom of sin, and wallowing in the mire and filth of corruption? Must I permit them become a prey to the infernal dragon? Must I suffer them to slip out of this world in a sinful lethargy unreconciled to their great master, and plunge into that deep abyss where the fire never goes out nor torments end. So far be it from me, so unXtian an action, so ungodly and uncharitable a design. behold then I'll draw another consequnce from this antecedent. We all grant that we are compounded of dust and ashes, which every wind may blow before it, we are all convinced we must dye, and quit this world w[it]h all the vain amusements therein. How great a folly, and presumption then is it, supposing we must dye to live one moment in mortal sin? what a boldness and temerity is it?

Man is naturally more prone to fear, and tremble in great dangers, than he is disposed to remain secure, and unshaken. In the vessel which carryed the prophet Jonah, whilst angry heaven thundered over their heads whilst the winds were unfeatterd and death appreared riding on every wave, he alone lay quietly buried in sleep, all the rest of the ship crew either in loud cries bemoaned their case, or laboured and toyld to rescue themselves from the threatening danger; this principle is true when we speak of temporal dangers, but not of eternal, which are more dreadfull, and irreversible. These perills men doe not only not fear, but run in quest after them, not only not fly from them, but goe out to meet and embrace [th]em.

Sinner, what is your state but the menace and threat of an eternal ruin and destruction? You know that in the very moment in which you consummated that sin, either in thought[,] word, or deed, the sentence of eternal damnation was thundered out against you, the breath of d[ivine] Justice has already enkindled that fire which is to be your bed for eternity. *Ignis successus est in furore meo.*[7] Says Al[mighty] G[od:] your never ending torments are prepared and the cruel executioners stand ready expecting the fatal moment, nothing is wanting but the cutting asunder the small thread of life by which you hang over this dreadful abyss [. . . .] What atonment[,] what a trouble, what a consternation, must it be to the poor sailor, when the vessel tossed, and broken w[it]h a dreadful storm he sees himself within two fingers of death? and here near to eternal death is the man in the state of sin? Nothing supports him but that small thread of life which the least wind may break[,] nothing but one spark of health, which the least breath may extinguish; can any danger be greater or more threatening than yours?

The Ninivites no sooner heard from the prophet Jonas that their city was within 40 days to be buried in a pile of ashes, if they did not repent but immediately they changed their garments[,] put on a penitential weed[,] fasting and sackcloth became the mode, the people and town are presently in it, and follow it with so much eagerness and vigour, that they expected not the edict of their prince, who tho' later than his people yet no sooner receivd so unpleasant a message, but he casts the purple from his sholdiers, which he had not only stained but even drenched with his repeated crimes; sackcloth, and haire cloth imperiously invade and banish the royal robes, and dust and ashes tarnish the crowns lustre. But why such hast, and precipitation? did they not know the threatening danger stood off at the distance of 40 days? Why was not their language and behavour still the same. ''Let us still crown ourselves with robes, baith our temples in rich wines, shed sweet ointments on our heads, and leave marks of our luxury, and riot when ever we can[;] God is merciful and good; many hours are not requisite to appease his anger, and dissarme his justice. One timely sigh, one season-able tear, one act of contrition is sufficient to operate that great work[.] the 40th day we will seriously begin to sett hand to work. But if they had argued thus would you not have condemned them of folly and madness, and deemed them unworthy of all pardon? yet your case is worse, you cannot permit yourselves 40 days. The ruin and destruction of your bodys may not only not be far off but may be at your gates; death may seize you in this very week which is now running, nea this hour, this moment; it will come upon you like a theif as Xt. tell us, who does not make his attack at noon day whilst we are upon watch, and guard, but steels upon us at midnight whilst we are buried in sleep & the Son of man, says the Scripture will surprise you when you are least upon your guard, when you are asleep in the night of sin, when you are dissolved in pleasure, intoxicated with vine, when you are in sad forgetfullness of god in a deplorable neglect of your salvation; and if you are left for ever without possibility of a mediation or atonement. And will you make no endevour to prevent this threatning blow?

[THE INCARNATION][7a]

The following sermon has the marks of a translation, perhaps with some revisions, of a French text. It may well date to the period of Attwood's the-ological studies at Liège, prior to 1711. Whatever its source, this reflection on the central mystery of Christianity reveals some proto-characteristics of an enlightened spirituality: the symmetry of the divine economy, the ability of man to appreciate that economy, the positive state of human nature, and its dynamic development in Christ. The underlying theme is the mystery's embodiment of the standard of Christ. Also revealing is the high Mariology that Attwood enunciates.

Ne timeas Maria ingenisti gratiam apud Deum; ecce concipies in utero filum, et vocabitur altissimi filius. Luke 1.

Shall I follow here, D[ear] C[hristians], the example of this angel, who brings today from god so happy tydings to Mary? Shall I announce of what he announces and shall I undertake to explicate to terrestial man and with a terrestial tongue the grandeur of the misteries which are revealed this day. The angel which advertises Mary to fear nothing had nothing to fear for himself, announcing, and explicating to her this great mystery. He knew this divin creature woud receive them with faith, that she woud consent to them with obedience, and submission[,] that she woud answer with the most profound humility confessing herself the handservant of him to whom she was promised to be mother.

But DC, are not all these things here to be feared for you, and me? how can I understand to speak and explicate with a mortal tongue the greatest and highest of all the misteries of the divinity? and how will you receive these words, which have troubled the most holy, & most pure and the most elevated of all creatures? Yet it must be done; it is an indispensible obligation today for me to speak of so great a mistery, it is an indispensible obligation for you to hear because it is the foundation of our Religion.

Holy virgin it is in your bosom that this great mystery commenced, it is in you that the economy of the incarnation of the word is accomplished[,] made us your partakers of those graces, and those divine lights which you received at that moment when the Angel say'd Ave.

All that which the Xtian Religion has of the most great, but what do I say? all that God himself could doe of the most great is found shutt up in those 3 great works, a god who becomes man, a virgin who becomes the mother of god, men who become the children of a god, in effect. What can be greater than this work which is called by excellency in a God *domine opus tuum*. I woud say the incarnation of the word in which a god is abased, a god is humbled, or rather anihilated. I woud speak of the admirable mixture of the divinity with the humanity, of an all with the nothing, of darkness with light, I woud speak of that incomparable temper which makes that he who is by himself in eternity begins to be by another in time; that he who is uncreated and who has created all things, is himself created, and that he who has given being to all[8] creatures, receives it himself, and that he whom all the universe cant contain, is contained in the womb of a virgin.[9]

It is today DC it is in this great day, that these 3 great works come from the hand of god. conceive if you can what a veneration you ought to have for it, it is today that god becomes man, tis today that a virgin becomes a mother of god, it's today that we become the children of god. A god becomes man, a god makes himself man, a god takes the figure of man, and why? to correct the manners of men; what an example for men? a virgin becomes the Mother of God, and why? to the end she may be placed in a state of being the mediatrix, and protextrix of men; what a succor for men? men become the children of god, and why? to the end that partaking of his nature by adoption, they may be sharers of the inheritance of his glory, what an honour for men? But also if they follow not this example, if they slight this succour, if they dishonour this quality by a life opposite to that of children of a god alas what punishment, what misfortune, what shame for men? [. . .]

The first thing on which we must set our thoughts this day, and which
even demands our adorations is a man god, is a god made man, but a god
made man to correct men, its a god who begins to see the light of this world,
that men may begin to enjoy the light of eternity. Its a god who begins to
live the life of man, that men may begin to live the life of a god. Its a god
who enters into the world to the end he may condemn all the crimes, and
maxims of the world[,] that he may set up virtue in place of vice, humility
in place of pride, obedience in place of rebellion[,] a spirit of suffring and
of the cross, of poverty[,] of mortification, in the place of pleasures. Riches,
delights, and saisfactions; in fine tis a god who comes to expose his life to
all manner of danger, and disgraces to the end he may propose it as an example to all men; behold all the end of the incarnation[,] behold all the fruit
the incarnate word hopes for as St. Aug[ustine]. says; if this be not done;
if this does not happen to what purpose should he make himself man? [. . .]
I dont pretend to wander from my subject, nor from my aime to prove the
verity of this mystery.[10] In effect let us consider a little nearer this mystery,
and we shall find that he is annihilated there, that he adores there his father,
and that he there offers sacrifice. Behold then from the beginning[11] of the
life of our Sav: anihilations, adorations and sacrifices. By these anihilations
he begins to give men an example of humility and debaisment to draw them
from pride, and arrogances, an inheritance they received from Adam: by
those adorations he begins to give men a great example of reverence for
God: to draw them from a forgetfulness of them, in which they pass almost
all their lives, in fine by those sacrifices, by which he acknowledges the
grandeur, and soveranity of his father; he begins to give men a great example of mortification, suffrings, and the cross to draw them from criminal
pleasures, and delights in which they spend all their life. What examples
[. . .]? what wonderful Lessons? but above all what confusion, and condemnation for us if we dont hearken to them, and follow them? for let us
examine the first lesson he made us by his anihilation or abasement.

He who was equal to the eternal father makes himself equal to man;
he who enjoyd all the treasures of the wisdom, knowledge and power of
god becomes ignorant[,] poor, and weak like men, he who was incomprehensible shut himelf up in the bosome of a creature; he who had the forme
of God takes upon him that of a slave, what mystery! what lessons for us!
Tertullian speaking against the heritick Manion who sayd the body of the
son of god was formed of heavenly matter and even of the substance of the
stares, because it semed as if it woud have been unworthy to have done
otherwise addresses to him these few words. *Quid distruit dedecus necessarium q[uo]d deo indignum mihi expedit?* don't destroy with your ignorance & shame so necessary, that which is unworthy a god can be worthy
men, and it is sufficient for the goodness of god. Faith without sin woud

have been a glorious faith, that is to say, it woud not have had for object but a god elevated in glory, but a god in his majesty, and grandeur; but man having sinned, faith must become shameful and propose to us nothing but shameful objects in appearance *dedecus necessarium,* to punish our sin and rebellion; man who lost himself by pride, must be reestablished by humility, this shameful anihilation must be the subject of our faith, this is necessary for the allaying those humours, which pride raisd in our souls; as man by his pride and presumption makes himself equal, and like unto God, [. . .] so also to pull down this pride a god must become like unto man, [. . .] Behold DC, the great design of god in the incarn[ation]: tis to teach humility to men: see how JC begins his life by anihilation to the end that men begin theirs the same way. See how to facilitate to us a thing, which was so contrary to the innate pride of men; he woud himself be given us as an example; for JC, is not JC but by anihilations, and you're not Xtians but by the same; Xtian Religion is not grounded but on this; if you dont anihilate yourselves, you are not truly Xtians, that is to say you resemble no more JC, you belong no more to him, Jes Xt quits the form of god to take up that of a slave and you think on nothing, but raising yourself to something great, an indifferent condition seems to you insupportable, you know not how to look but with horrour on those who are in humility, you seek nothing but glory, you aspire to nothing but honor, and for this you make your selves the slaves of the world, and divill. What will you have him say of your strange opposition of your life, with that of JC, and to what purpose is JC anihilated so low, if you yet walk in pride and arrogance, as before, *ut q[uo]d deus factus e[st] homo.*

But DC, if we dont profit by the example which JC gives us by his humiliations, and anihilations, we profit less by that which he gives us by his adorations with which he gives his new life, and which he dayly continues from that moment to the end thereof; He's no sooner conceived, no sooner united to our nature, but he begins his adorations, but he turns himself to his father to pay the homage and respect which is due to him, he says already before hand, what he has since sayd in the D[ivine] sermon he makes to men, *sicut misit me univers pater; et ego propter Patrem.*[12] Ah! What sense is there in these words! Strive DC to penetrate all the misteries. The son of God does not only live by his father, but he lives also for his father; but is also sent for his father. *Propter Patrem.* because his father is not only the beginning of his mission, but also the end thereof, because in eternity in truth he's made not for his father altho' he be produced by his father being equal to him in all things. But from the moment in which he is conceived in the bowels of Mary, from the moment in which he is united to our nature, Ah he does not only acknowledge by his respect, and adoration the eternal father of his beginning, but also as his end, *sicut misit me*

&c. Ah my father[,] says your D[ivine] Sav[ior] to him whilst I dwelt, and
remaind in your bosom I had nothing to consecrate to your divine majesty,
I coud not acknowledge your grandeur, by any homage by reason of our
equality, but now since I've received a mortal and passible life, now since
I'm subject to you, now since I'm made for you, I shall not spare this life
to acknowledge your grandeur, I have consecrated it entirely to it, I will not
make use of it but to make it be adored by all nations of the world. Behold
that which is here most considerable for God in this mistery; never woud
God have received so much honour; in fine what makes this mistery so considerable is not only because his mercy and justice, his goodness and wisdome did never appear with more lustre; But it is because he begins to have
an adorer worthy of himself; tis because he begins to be adored as much,
and according as he deserves. To make an adorer worthy of God, was necessary to joyn sanctity and anihilation together; God had much sanctity, but
not anihilation, man had much anihilation but he had not sanctity, what has
the eternal word done? he has united himself to the nature of man, and
joyn'd his sanctity with mans anihilation, so that this godman being a com-
pound of sanctity and annihilation was an adorer worthy of god. Behold
then that Jesus Xt acknowledges the Eternal father for his sovereign from
the womb of his mother as he tells us by his prophet. *De ventro matris meae
deus meus es tu.*[13] What examples DC, but also what condemnations, that
1st moment of our Sav[iour] is consecrated to the respect which he ows, in
quality of man, to his Eternal father, he begins his life by adorations, but
by adorations which he continued to his last breath, and how can it be sayd
of us that we consecrate our lives to the adorations which we owe to God?
[. . .] how many are there amongst us who plunged in the affairs, pleasure,
and vanities of the world give not so much as a moment to this adoration
of god, which is so lawfully due to him? and not content to remain there[14]
they carry their boldness yet farther, they neglect the adoration of god, to
adore things, which are totally opposite to him, they pass their life in the
adoration of fortunes, of greatness, of creatures, in which they see some
appearance of beauty, in a word they pass their lives in the adoration of so
many goods, as they are creatures not troubling themselves about the adorations which is due to the creator, and thereby rendring themselves abominable to god as well, as what they adore, et *facti sunt abominabiles sicut
ea quae dilexerant.*[15]

   Let us end this first part, and see how JC begins his life, not only by
annihilations, not by adorations, but also by sacrifices. The womb of Mary
is the first altar where this D priest coming to the world, has made the first
sacrifice. Dont imagine him an ordinary infant, for the prophets have represented him to us in the state of a perfect man, *faemina circumdabit virum.*
he was not such in regard to the quality of his body, but by the lights and

wisdome of his soul, because the treasures of divine wisdome are inclosed in him[,] . . .] he knew as well that he came not to the world but to sacrifice to his father, all that he was and its for this reason says the apostle, that he already sacrifices himself in entring into the world without expecting untill he's entred. *Ingrediens mundum dixit ecce venio* Ah, my father, says our D Sav: hereto you have refused the sacrifice of men, [. . .] but you have framed me a body which I offer to you in place of theirs, and from the very moment I consecrate it to the pains to the labours, to the thorns, and crosses, and to death itself *Ingrediens mundum.* Behold after what manner JC comes into the world, and behold in what manner[16] we ought to goe to him; his life beginning must be the rule of ours, no less than his painful, and dying death, by the acception of his cross, which he begins to embrace, tis thus a god begins today to live in the world, But [. . .] DC, how far distant is your lives from his? you to whom the least thought of a cross strikes a horrour, you who can suffer nothing, who will have your ease in all things, who mortify yourselves in nothing, who run to shews, pleas[ures], and divertisments even in time of lent consecrated by the church to the cross and Xtian penance you who far from accepting the cross which divine providence sends you from time to time[17] for your good murmur against his S Orders. Ah beginning of the life of my infant Sav: how little are you imitated by Xtians, and how will you be one day the subject of a severe condemnation for them, for DC, these are trials which the Church obliges me to announce to you; JC is not made man but to oblige you to quite like forgetfulness, which makes you unmindful of god, and your salvation, for to make you quite your life of pleasure, of sensuality, and of delights, that you may begin one of humility adoration and sacrifice for if this be not so why should a god have taken such pains. . . . Behold the first wonder of the mistery of this day, but let us pass to the 2d, because not only a god becomes men, to correct men but also because a virgin becomes mother of god to succour him: which is the subject of my 2d point.

After the great works, of a god man, after the ineffable union of human and divine nature, its certain there is nothing greater, or higher than the quality of mother of god, and in effect what is greater to a creature than to enter into alliance with the eternal father, and to engender in time the same son which he begot from all Eternity, than to partake with him of the title of principle or beginning, than to give a human birth to him on earth who received a divine one from him in heaven, for my part I think this is the highest, and most sublime quality to which a creature can ever aspire, and this also I find today in this glorious mistery. No only because the Eternal Word is the son of the one, and the other, but also because she engenders them both; and produces them the same way, for its by the way of contemplation that the father engenders him, from all Eternity, but it is also by

contemplation that Mary brings him forth in time, to show that his generation is noble, S Luke has not forgot to observe that this great mistery was
begun by Mary both in words, and thoughts, turbata e[st] in *sermone isto,
et cogitabat qualis esset haec salutatio.* [. . .] Let us leave the words there,
and fix ourselves on the thoughts. H[oly] Virgin I am not surprised to see
you to day in so profound, and secret thoughts; to engender the Eternal
thought is necessary for to think; but I woud willingly penetrate a little into
the mistery, I woud enter into the sanctuary, where so noble, and so sublime
thoughts are produced. The father teaches us that the Eternal Word was related to our human nature in those happy moments in which the H. virgin
thought of the greatness of this mistery which according to the prophecies
and promises of the scrip[tures]. was soon to be accomplished, it was in
these thoughts that the Angel surprised her, when he announced to her this
great news, and its this which caused her astonishment, when absorpt as she
was in the infinite grandeur of this mystery she learnt that it was to be accomplished in her. But how did this happen? it was by pronouncing that *fiat*
so much desired by all the patriarchs and prophets. it was in giving her consent that she began to produce the word. Ah I dont doubt says she to the
angel[,] returned as she was from her first trouble into which his arrival has
cast her. Ah I doubt not of the promises of God, altho' their greatness, and
my lowness frighten me, I am but the handmaid of him of whom you pronounce me mother, but in this quality I owe both my faith, and my obedience, therefore, *fiat mihi secundum verbum tuum.*[18] Behold DC how by the
means of faith, of contemplation, and pious reflections Mary has begun to
produce the word. She produces it in time, as the Eternal father produced
it in Eternity; it is in contemplating that the Eternal father produced the word
it is in contemplating herself Mary produces it to men, all the difference is
that the Eternal father produces it by contemplating his grandeurs, and that
Mary there mixes her contemplation of her baseness, and humiliations; she
produces a word but it is a word made flesh, to correct the pride, forgetfulness and sensuality of men, by his abasements and its by this means that
she is most gloriously associated to the production of the word. But why
think you has she been so raised? was it necessary for the word of God to
assume a body of a virgin? could he not have made himself man, without
being the son of man? yes by the means of creation he coud have produced
himself a body as well as he produced that of Adam, and there one shoud
have had a man its true, but we should not have had a mother of God. But
was it necessary that we shoud have a mother of God? Ah, hearken here to
the great designs of the D providence over men, and prepare yourselves, to
love and acknowledgement for not only all the fund of this mistery is for
us, because tis only for us that a god became man, but also the circumstances of the mistery are for us, because to have a mother of god was but

a circumstance and yet this mother was not chosen, and elevated unto this high rank but for us; god man is all entire for sinners and the mother is wholy for the same; for if man had never transgressed the law of god, never had this grand design of the incarnation been decreed in Eternity, or executed in time. No my D. Sav: without us you never woud have been man, without us you never woud have been incarnate, without us you never woud have quitted your glory, or the bosome of your Eternal father. It is sin therefore that is the occasion of your incarnation and it[19] be true that JC is all entire for man because the design of the law of the world in taking a virgin for mother is to the end that this mother be all entire for sinners, and that we might find in her person a mediatrix, and advocate to god. JC presents his wounds to the Eternal father, which are so many mouths that plead in our behalf, the mother presents her breasts to her son in our favour. the eternal father can refuse nothing to this son, this son can refuse nothing to his mother. Ah never let us limite her power with god, let us not judge it ill that she showers down so many graces on sinners and impenitants. It's true, she does not cause them to be poured down upon them but to the end that they may be no longer sinners, the graces which she offers for us are the graces of the mother of god, that is to say of a mother that would yet form her son in the hearts of men, as she had already formed him in her womb according to that of the Apostle, *Domine, formetur in nobis Xtus.*[20]

But what means this to form JC in ones heart? it is to forme there his love, it is to chase away all other love, it is to fly the world, and all its vanities, its to love suffrings[,] its to love rather mortification than pleasure, its to renounce freely and generously all the satisfactions of sense, Ah sinner will you forme JC in your heart? *donec formetur.*[21] Strip yourselves of the perishable goods of this world, and renounce them entirely, imitate JC on the cross where he's naked, deprived of all things. *donec formetur.* Behold the graces which Mary asks for us[.] She would form JC in us and its in these hopes that she causes all the celestial showers to fall upon us, its to destroy all that is opposite to[22] him, that she continually petitions graces of god, it is therefore to affront her to demand any of her graces, to remain in sin under a pretext that we have a devotion for her, and that we make profession to honour her; is this the way to obtain that great help, which we hope from her, if we don't imitate her? is this to imitate her virtues? She is in the midst of graces, an Angel salutes her, and says that she is filled therewith; yet she anihilates herself, she is employed only in her nothingness, she confesses god beholds nothing in this mistery but the lowliness of his servant, q[ui]a *respescit humilitatem.* Yet she is so much taken up with her baseness that in the time when she was to be raised, she seems to make some resistance, in saying she was nothing but the handmaid of him whose mother she was to be. *Ecce Ancilla domi[ni].* Where shall we find nowadays, such humble sentiments? have we humility whilst we run after greatness? Whilst in all things we seek nothing but glory? whilst the best advantage of witt, of beauty, of eloquence, so much pass and swell our hearts, as if they were the greatest goods, and whilst we joyn to that haughty ingratitude a contempt of Eternal goods, the BV is so pure, and chast that altho' an angel comes to announce the conception of a god in her bowels, she woud not consent[23] to the honour without the Angel assured her it woud be without the loss of her virginity. Whilst Xtians remain in the filth of an impure life, staining their souls, with all the blemishes of the flesh and yet believe they imitate the purity of the BV. Ah Sinners Mary is the Mother of the beautifull fear, yet I dare say with all your pretended devotion towards her, if you fear not to offend her son she wont obtain you any help. She is the mother of beautiful fear, yet I dare venture to say that if you continue to nourish filthy love in your heart, she'll disown you for her children. She is the mother of beautiful hope yet I dare say that if by your presumption you neglect the amendment of your life, and the correction of your manner she'll neglect you, and abandon you, at the hour of your death. Let us then DC, this day take a firm Resolution; Let us endevour to correspond with all the graces, she dayly obtains for us lest with all those graces ill employed we miserably come to fall into the eternal Abyss, we for whom god is become man, we for whom a virgin was made his mother, we in fine who receive the power to become the children of god which is the subject of my 3rd point.

The 2 greatest pledges of love which god has ever given to men are without doubt the presents which he has made them of his son by nature, and of the power to become his child by adoption. by the first he descended even to us, by the 2d he made us mount up to himself, by the first he became partaker of our mortality, by the 2d he made us partakers of his immortality, by the first god became man, by the 2d man has been made god; when the Sav: of the world speaks of the first he makes use of terms the most tender and affectionate that can be found *sic Deus dilexit mundum.*[24] When the apostle speaks of the 2d he uses expressions which mark the excess of love and tenderness that God had for men. *Videte qualem charitatem dedit nobis pater, ut filii dei nominemur et simus.*[25] Learn by this how venerable this feast ought to be to you; tis today that god makes us these 2 presents, its today that god made man, its today he gives us power to be his children, and how is this? it is that as by one only sin, and that of one only man, the whole mass of men was corrupted, so the same spirite which produces the word produces also the children of god, the same spirit, which forms JC forms also Christians, and by this the word unites itself to all mankind. Behold what has made Origine speak a word very bold and which I woud not say had I not so good a warrant. *Per unum solum multi Xtiani transformati ad imaginem ejus qui imago patris.* Yes says this learned man by the incarnation of one JC, there are made as many JC, as there are men who have been transformed to the resemblance of him, who is the image of his father; is not this the same as the Apostle would say when he says that god has loved us in JC, with all sorts of spiritual benedictions and celestial gifts [. . .] for hearken to the nobly thought of S. Aug[ustine] hereupon, who remarks that god did not give his benediction in the beginning of the world but to things which were to multiply; so says this holy father, after that god had created the heavens, it is not marked that he gave them his blessing because they were *not* to multiply; benediction therefore concludes Augustine implys multiplication. *benedictio igitur ad multiplicamem valet.* Ah Christians says the Apostle: God has blessed us in Jesus Christ, he woud that Jesus Christ shoud be the Eldest amongst so many Brothers *ut sit primogenitus in multis fratribus.* He woud that he who's the image of the Eternal father, shoud give to men by his incarnation, as by the impression of a seal the perfect resemblance of this d[ivine] original, for that is very remarkable. The Scrip: says well that god had made man according to his own image, but it says not that he made him according to his own resemblance, why so? because an image is the representation of a thing, but its not a perfect one of the thing represented according to the original; man therefore in the moment of his creation was not made but according to the image of god and not according to the Resemblance, because the image was to pass thro the hands of a god creator to those of a god redeemer: this god redeemer was to retouch it, and set the finishing stroke to it, it belonged only to Jesus Christ to give the last perfection to it. Also when god had made a perfect creature [. . .] the Scripture says that as soon as he spoke it was made et *facta e[st] lux, et facti sunt coeli* but it was not so in regard of man, the scripture notes that god sayd faciamus hominem *ad imaginem nostram* but it does not speak as of all other creatures, *et factus e[st] hoc.* God began to form man in his creation, but there was yet a *fiat,* so much desired by which we receive power to be the sons of god. Dedit *illis potestatem filios dei fieri.*[26]

What honour for us DC can I find thoughts, and words to make you conceive to what a high degree and eminent pitch these illustrations carry us. Ah if you woud but stop here a little, and consider what is the dignity, and graciousness of this glorious title, how woud all the grandeurs of the world, all its pomp, and vanity soon vanish, and appear to yourselves, like a shadow, and smoke? Yet we scarce make any account of this eminent quality, speak to a Xtian of his birth, nobility, the grandeur of his ancestors and dignity of his family presently his heart is swelled with pride; tell him that he is a child of god, a quality so glorious for a creature, that there's none after that of mother of god which is more elevated[,] he's not touched with it, he's as cold as before, whence come this? its because he does not only not forme an Idea high and noble enough of it but even vilifys it by his manner of life, and conduct. Become Dear Congregation, true imitators of your heavenly father[;] be perfect as he is perfect, and if you say [you] can't imitate him, imitate at least his Son, love what he loved, and despise what he despised, Lay aside those vain grandeurs, of the world, run no more after fleet, and passing shadows; behold what the glorious quality of son of god ought to inspire into you, to the end you may not only be fitted with graces in this world, but that by this means you may gaine a right to eternal glory which God grant *us all. Amen.*

JOSEPH GREATON

A convert and a priest before he entered the Jesuits in 1708, Greaton was one of the few Maryland Jesuits not trained in the Netherlands and deeply influenced by French Jesuit spirituality. His own theological studies were made at the English seminary at Valladolid. Greaton spent thirty-one years in the Maryland Mission. After a decade in Maryland he was sent into Pennsylvania to open missions for the German and other Catholic settlers (some from Maryland) attracted to the land and toleration of this middle colony. In Philadelphia he founded the first urban church for Catholics in British America. He died in 1753 at Bohemia, on the Eastern Shore of Maryland.

METHOD OF CONFESSING[26a]

Greaton gave this sermon at least six times, from 1723 to 1748. It is a good example of the practical instruction that Jesuits in colonial Maryland and Pennsylvania regularly gave, either during the Mass or afterwards. The sacrament of Penance or Reconciliation was part of the regular sabbath liturgy. Catholics were obliged to receive communion at least once a year, and were accustomed to confess before receiving. The limited evidence from diaries, sermons, and reports suggests that the reception of both sacraments was infrequent.

Fili mi, da gloriam D[o]m[in]o Deo Israel et confitere atque indica mihi quid feceris, ne abscondas Jos[ue] 7.19.

Al[mighty] G[od], having commanded Josue to burne the city of Jericho & all things in it, it happened that Achan took some things & hid them in his tent. But the theft being discovered, Josue exhorted him to confess the bare truth: which[27] he did with g[reat] humility & c[on]viction, faithfully relating every circumstance & quality of the theft. W[ith] the same candour & sincerity ought all penitents confess their sins. These words they must imagine as directed to them by the H[oly] God. They must regard their confessor not as a rigorous judge but as a tender F[athe]r, not as an ordinary man, but as the minister of Xt. Fili mi, da gloriae Deo. they must glorify G[od] of truth by an entire & humble confession. indica q[uo]d feceris, they must discover wherein they have transgressed the law of G[od] ne abscondas. not concealing any mortal sin.[28] Today I shall speak of the conditions which ought to accompany confession. viz. humility, clarity, sincerity, & integrity.

Humility is a very necessary disposition to a good confession. For he approaches in quality of a sinner loaden with the heavy burden of their sins, he comes to owne himself as such & to be eased of that troublesome load. he comes as an enemy of G[od],[29] as one sentenced to e[terna]l flames to recover the greace & favour of his L[ord] & obtain reversion of that sentence. he comes as a slave of hell found with the chains of sins and fetters of vicious habits to implore the benefits[30] of Xts. Redemption. With what humility then ought he to appear, with what confusion ought he; how was the prodigal son ashamd to stand before his F[ather] in his filthy cloaths in which he had served the swine, with what confusion fear & shame does a criminal convicted of heanous crimes stand before his judge[;] with the same sentiments ought a penitent to appear at the s[ai]d tribunal of confession. Such persons as relate their sins with the same indifferences as if it were an idle story. Such as argue the case with the confessor, such as to excuse themselves[,] lay the fault on others, such as repine at the pennance enjoynd or do not patiently harken to the confessors reprimands & advice evidently show that they want the requisite humility, & that tho they bend their knees yet their heart is still stiff & obstinate.

2. Confession ought to be clear, declaring the sin such as it realy is. mortal as mortal, venial as venial. They ought not to mince the matter but to desire that the confessor s[hou]d know perfectly the true state of their soul, & th[erefo]re they must clearly explaine themselves which if they did they w[oul]d deliver themselves & the priest from a g[reat] deal of trouble. Its very ungratefull to penitents & troublesom to confessors to ask questions & some may complaine of their confessors as being very inquisitive, but it is the penitents fault for not sufficiently explaining themselves, for they must discover & [a] confessor know the true nature of their sin. So e.g. its not enough to say I have had several idle thoughts; you must specify those thoughts whether they were against charity justice faith, chastity &c. whether you rejected [th]em & how speedily[,] whether you dallied with them, took satisfaction, assented to them. again, if you accuse yourself of violating a fasting day, if it was out of ignorance, forgetfulness, or some just cause that is to be mentioned because it changes the nature or destroyes the sin. If he accuse himself of swearing & cursing, he must mention what sort of curses & imprecations he usd, whether against his neighbour or other

creatures, whether he desird[31] from his heart during his passion that those evills might befall his neighbour which he wisht. for wh[en] one is in a passion they matter not what they say[,] what they wish . & all must know that tho' w[hen] their passion is over they are perfectly reconcild & desire[32] no such evills may befall their neighbour, that this is no sign that they did not sin by anger, but that they do not still continue in that evill & malicious mind. They may have sind tho for one moment & th[ere]f[or]e they must examen themselves which thoughts & desires may have passd in their minds during their passion. If with t[hi]s candour & clarity he discovers the state of his soul he'll rid himself & confessor of the ever greatfull trouble of asking necessary questions, & will render confession much more easy & sweet. 3. These [do] not discover the sin of another by saying I sind with such a person: & if the sin can not be confessd without naming the party; its advisable to confess to another priest who is not acquainted with that person. 4. brevity is to be observd, so as not to relate passages & circumstances nothing to the purpose. eg I went to such a place, where I met such a person & we fell into such a discourse. all this is superfluous, its enough to say I've committed this or that sin, so often. 5. Confession is a self accusation & th[ere]f[or]e he is not to charge others with sin by saying such a person provokd me & tempted me above my strength. had it not been for him I should never have sinnd. whe[re]fore this [is] but to aggravate their sin, by excusing their sins as the Ps[almist] says ad excusandas excusationes in pec[cat]is [Ps. 140, v.4]. which they came not to excuse & clear themselves from but to accuse themselves of. Few people see their owne faults. few are willing to owne themselves guilty of pride[,] luxery[,] covetousness prodigality, hatred, impiety. They can easily cloak their vices under specious pretences. pride must pass for a just regard to their honour. covetousness for a care of their children. prodigality for generosity. hatred for a just revenge. This art of excusing oneself is learnt from our f[irs]t parents. For when Al[mighty] G[od] charged Adam w[i]th eating the forbidden fruit, he laid the fault on Eve, saying the woman whom thou gavest me, gave me to eat. & she chargd the serpent saying it had deceived her. But what did these excuses justify them in the sight of G[od]? ought not Adam as being superiour[33] to have reprimanded her, whereas he encouraged her in her sin. ought not he rather to harken to the voice of G[od] from whom he had received imediate prohibition, than so a woman. Did he not aggravate his sin by seeming to lay the blame on G[od] himself. the woman whom thou gavest me, as much as to say if you had not given her for my companion I s[houl]d not have sind. was not also Eve highly to blame by suffering herself to be deluded by a vile & malicious serpent? Do not those do the like, who attribute their sins to the malice of the divel, violence of temptations, frailty of nature, bad companions & example. But will these excuses justify them any more than Adam's did? If the infernal serpent hisses, can not he stop his ears? if temptations are violent can not he overcome them by the greace of G[od]? if nature is frail can not he resist it? if passions are strong can not he curb[34] [th]em? if companions invite him can not he quit their conversation. the fault is our owne & none but our owne. we may overcome if we will cooperate with the grace of G[od]. if we do not whom can we blame, but ourselves.

6. The number of the sins, as near as one can is to be expressd. w[hi]ch if it can not be, the continuance of time wherein you have perseverd in sin, as likewise those circumstances which notably aggrevate the sin. All doubtfull sins also are to be confessd as doubtfull. If for ex[am]ple after mature consideration with good reasons you fear you may have committed such a sin or assented to such a thought, he is to accuse himself of it to the best of his knowledge, for fear of invalidating the S[acrame]nt. But the chief difficulty consists in duly accusing themselves of several internal sins w[hi]ch unless one uses very singular care & diligence easily escapes his knowledge for not only the external action but even internal thoughts are grievous offences of Al[mighty] G[od]. it is not only a sin to steal & commit adultery but even the very desires of both are forbidden by Al[mighty] G[od] The 2 last commandments. Many through gross ignorance imagin that those thoughts & desires which have pasd in their mind were not grievous sins because they did not proceed to action, or have soon retracted the same. The very desire to commit a sin provided they had an opportunity is almost as g[reat] a sin as the very deed itself. one single moment is sufficient to compleat the malice of a sin. Lucifer & his A[n]g[el]s. committed but one & that of thought & that only for one moment, & yet are justly damnd for it for all eternity. & alass how many souls are now frying in hell, for a momentary thought. & particularly this is to be observd in point of chastity that even the very thoughts against chastity are m[ortal] sins if one takes wilfull pleasure & delight in them tho they never intended or even disired to do any thing amiss. But those thoughts are not sinfull as long as one detests [th]em[,] resists [th]em[,] & endeavours to put [th]em away. G[reat] care & vigilance is right on these occasions & th[ere]f[o]re one must carefully examen how they behave themselves on those occasions. Moreover its very advisable & the common practice of such as are well instructed & a very p[ro]per means to supply all defects which commonly happen in confession, to accuse themselves of besides the sins which have happened since their last confession of some remarkable sin in their life past as eg to conclude their confession in this forme. I accuse myself of these sins & all rash oaths, sacrilegious confessions, impurities of my life, if I say you may have committed any such sin. its true theres no obligation to confess a sin over again. nevertheless its very beneficiall to do it. 1. its [a] greater act of

humility & so disposes us better for the reception of grace. 2. one receives
a more perfect & full pardon of their sin & punishment. but chiefly because
it often happens that one has not a sin, especially such as accuse themselves
only of trifling sins, & a sufficient sorrow for their sins &[35] yet its absolutely
necessary to be sorry for those sins they confess; now w[he]n they accuse
themselves of some notorius sin they can not fail of being sorrowfull for
that sin.

Last condition is ne abscondas[,] conceale nothing[,] all m[ortal] sins
are sincerely to be confessed; if one m[ortal] sin is wilfully omitted the
confession is sinfull & sacrilegious. that sin & all others committed & confessd since that sacrilegious confession are to be confest again or else they
can not be pardond & forgiven. let none be ashamd to confess their sins let
[th]em be never [sic] so enormous. the confessor will never have a worse
opinion of you. he'll not upbraide & reproach you. & know that those sins
you have not the courage now to confess will be reveald to all the world in
the day of judgment. is it not then better to discover your shame to one
person bound to invioable secrecy than be exposed to general confession.

Behold I have in short explaind those conditions which ought to accompany confession. 1. that it ought to be made with profound humility
shame & confession. 2. with clarity laying open the sincere & plain state
of your souls. 3. brevity by not relating unnecessary circumstances. 4. not
to accuse others especially to clear ourselves. 5. the number is to be deliverd
in as near as one can. 6. dubious sin & particularly sins of thoughts & desires are to be searchd into & as faithfull an account to be given as one is
able. 7. its commendable alwaies to add some notorious sin of our life past
that the contrition may be more assurd & compleat. lastly no m[ortal] sin
is to be conceald. What ease & content & comfort, confession affords to a
disturbed & uneasy mind, the following example evinces related by several
authors [. . .] Of toads coming out of a womans mouth [. . .]

WHIPPS & THORNS[35a]

*Not only did the Maryland Jesuits repeat their sermons, they shared them.
Greaton's following Good Friday Sermon was used as late as 1775, more
than two decades after his death. It is a good example of how the baroque
sermon continued to survive in the colonies. Its portrayal of the Jewish role
in the passion is a reminder of another long-lived tradition within the Catholic worldview.*

Ad Majorem Dei Deiparae St. Ang. Cust: Gloriam[36]
Apprehendit Pil[atus]: Jesum et flagellavit. J.19.1[37]

Solomon seeing in spirit the coronation of our S[avio]r invites all faithfull souls seriously to contemplate that mistery. Egredimini f[ili]ae Sion & videte R[eg]em Sal[omonem]: in diademate, quo coronavit illum m[ater] sua in die despons[ationis] illius.[38] i.e. go forth O pious souls & behold Xt. the true Solo[mon] in the crown of thorns w[hi]ch his m[othe]r the Sinagogue or rather stepm[othe]r has put on his head in the day of his espousals to the C[hurch]. He allud[ed] to the ancient custome of crowning Bridegroom & bride on the day of marriage, with flowers. The day of Xts death was the day of his marriage to the C. then he was crowned not with roses but with thorns. In my former discourses I treated of our L[ord's] grief in the garden[,] of the injuries in the house of Caiphas. now I shall probe the cruel scourging & whipping at the pillar & crowning with thorns. Go forth th[ere]f[o]re pious souls, contemplate your L[ord] cruelly torn with whips & crownd with thorns to espouse you to hims[el]f. Behold &c.

It was the custom of the jews at Easter to release to the people a malefactor out of prison whom they w[ishe]d. Pilate th[erefo]re desirous X s[hou]d be the man p[ro]p[o]sd him & Bar[abbus]: not doubting but that they w[oul]d choose X before Bar: who was a thief, murderer & seditious fellow. But the priests & elders went about to[39] persuade people to preferr Bar: saying undoubtedly that X was more deserving of death than Barrab: that he was more seditious having disturbd the whole nation, that he was an enemy to Caesar pretending to make hims[el]f king. That he was an imposteur, a frend of the divel Blasphemer so that movd with the authority of grave & learned persons & more through spleen they cryd out[:] release to us Bar: away with X & crucify him. O Loving S[aviou]r how soon are you forgot by men. O the ingratitude & perversness of mankind. a thief a murder[er] can gain the peoples favour, can find patrons & advocats, but you who did good to all wheresoever you went, curing all sorts of diseases have none to speak in your favour. where are the lame you heald let [th]em come appear in your behalf. where are the blind & deaf let [th]em employ the speech you gave [th]em in your favour. But alass X is forgotten Oblivioni datus sum ps.30.13. all those good deeds are buried in oblivion. all are silent none dares speak one word in X['s] behalf, w[ha]t an injury[,] w[ha]t an affront for the splendour of heaven to be compard with darkness[,] the author of life with a murderer, liberal benefactor with a thief, the H[oly] of h[olies] with an infamous sinner. But what a disgrace must it be to be set behind,[40] so vile a wretch. With good reason then did you say by the R[oyal] P[salmist] Vermis sum,[41] I am ac[cursed]. for all cast thee of, & trample upon thee as a worm. We here condemne the jews ingratitude to their greatest benefactor. we blame their mad & foolish choise but if we look at home we shall find ours[elve]s guilty of far greater ingratitude & folly. For w[he]n we consent to m[ortal] sin what do we else but prefer Bar: to X. i.e. some momentary delight & forbidden pleasure before et[ernal] good[,] a vile

creature before the creator. honours[,] riches & pleasures of this world before the joys of heaven. W[ha]t is it[42] to set our disordinate passions at liberty giving full scope unto them but to release Bar. & crucify X, for he that
sins mortally crucifys X. . . . When the divel tempts to sin he asks which
we'll set a liberty X or Bar: O let us answer with S Ber[nard]: Let X live
let Bar be crucified. Crucify this irregular passion, crucify that disordinate
affection, its like a Bar: a thief robbing us of grace. its a murtherer killing
our souls with e[terna]l death, its seditious rebelling against Al[mighty]
G[od] let it the[re]f[o]re dye, its guilty of death, & live long Je[sus;] live in
my soul.

Pilate[,] amazd that they s[houl]d prefer Bar: askt what he s[houl]d do
with X. They all cryd out crucify him. But what harm has he done replyd
Pilate. But they redouble their cryes crucifigatur. These clamours so
daunted his spirits in the defense of X that he durst not set him at liberty for
fear of the peoples displeasure, nor condemne him on whom he ownd he
c[oul]d fix no crime. He th[ere]f[o]re invented a cruel expedient w[hi]ch he
hopd w[oul]d assuage their fury & save his life w[hi]ch was severely to
chastice him & so dismiss him. His sentence was most unjust, as being
pro[n]ouncd against a person whom the judg declare to be innocent; it was
most unreasonable, because it was not to correct a delinquent, but to satiate
the malice of an enragd populace. it was most ignominious as being the
common punishment of the vilest slaves, yet X joyfully accepts it saying to
his E[terna]l F[ather] those words of the R P 37.18. Ego in flagella paratus
sum. *I am prepared for scorges* I am willing to pour out streams of blood,
for the redemption of the world. The sentence no sooner past but the soldiers
strip our L[ord] of his cloaths, they bind his hands fast & tye him to a pillar.
X c[oul]d more easily have broken these cords than Samson did if he
w[oul]d, but his hands were faster bound with fetters of love, love made
him joyfully submit to this cruel punishment. love made him refuse no torment, love made him not regard shame & infamy. But O Xtians, what
tongue is able to express the sharpness & cruelty of this scourging. 1. In
regard of the inst[ru]m[en]ts which are said to have been of 3 sorts. sinews
of beasts which raised the flesh & beat it black & blue. Sharp rods w[hi]ch
cut the skin. & chains armd with pointed rowels w[hi]ch tore the flesh off
the bones. 2. This scourging was most painful[43] to X by reason of his most
tender & delicate complexion and thusly was more sensible[44] of the least
pain, and especially being weakned [sic] by the bloody sweat & all nights
rude treatment from the soldiers. 3. they, chiefly from the cruelty of the
executioners who instigated by the divel to move X to impatience, & animated by the High priests Scribes & Pharasies to revenge thems[elve]s on
him, exerted all their fury upon his S[acre]d body. A whole band that is
godless fell upon our L[ord] by turns succeeding each other.[45] O how many

& cruel blows did they inflict, they regarded not the law of Moyses [sic] w[hi]ch allowed not above 40 stripes;[46] they offered no law but their owne malice & strength laying on as long as they were able to stand it. Such cruelty soon tore all his flesh; & no entire place being left they wounded even the wounds th[e]ms[elve]s, fulfilling that of the P[ro]p[het] Is[aiah] 1.6 A planta pedis usque ad verticem capitis non est in eo sanitas.[47] & & 3. "There is no beauty in him. we have seen him & there is no sightliness, he is despised & the most abject of men; a man of sorrows & knowing infirmities. He hath born our infirmities, & our sorrows he hath carryed. We toke[48] him for a Leper & stricken by Al[mighty] G[od]; but he was wounded for our iniq[ui]ties, he was broken for our sins. The L[ord] has put upon him all our iniq[ui]ties, he was offerd because hims[el]f w[ille]d; he was lead [sic] to slaughter like a sheep dumb & not opening his mouth." Thus far the P[ro]p[het].

S. Aug[ustine] relates that a certain person movd wth compassion cryd out. Numq[uo]d int[e]rficietis eum non judicatum. & with this cut the rope with which he was tyed. So that X weakned with the effusion of so much blood fell downe & lay wallowing in his owne gore. But the inhumain & barbarous jews fell upon him kicking him.[49] O what a mournfull[50] sight is this to behold our sweet Redeemer fainting unde[r] stripes, rowling in his blood, none helping nor even compassionating [sic] him. O, P A [?], let us not be more insensible than the senseless jews, let this dolefull sight moves us at least to compassion. Let it wring tears from our eies to wash his bleeding wounds. Lets kiss the ground sprinkled with his pretious blood, lets kiss the whips & scourges, lets embrace the pillar to which he was bound, applying our hearts unto it, wth bitter grief[,] lamenting our sins for which he was so cruelly scourged.

This dismal spectacle of a man flead from head to foot, methinks w[oul]d move any rational heart to compassion, but alass its not enough to satiate a jews cruelty. Their thirst is not assuagd at the effusion of so much blood but like elephants rather increasd. For elephants are said in Mac[cabees] 6.34 to be excited to battle at the sight of blood. they are not content wth that cruel scourging nor willing to let him live a miserable life even worse than death its[el]f. Their malice goes yet further, & invents a torment which none but a jew c[oul]d ever have thought of, or at least have had the heart to inflict, which was 1. To violently pull of his cloaths which had cloven fast to his ribs with the goreblood, & then planting a crown of thorns[,] fixt it upon his S[acre]d head. But what[,] was it not enough to have rent all the flesh of his sides, legs & thighs, or at least had not his head sufferd enough by buffets, by plucking of his hair & beard? no X said he was a K[ing] & th[ere]f[o]re the jews resolve to crowne him as such, & with such a crown as his pretended ambition deservd. Then they flung a tatterd

purple garment about his shoulders for royal robes, put a reed into his hand
for a mock scepter, to signify that his kingdom was like a reed, hollow,
vaine empty & tottering without strength & substance. Others in derision
bending their knee saluted him saying Ave X & then spit in his face. O
w[ha]t torments what indignities were these. The thorns piercd his head in
72 places as was reveald to[blank] & even to the very brains which w[oul]d
have bereavd him of life, had he not reservd it for a more cruel martyrdome.
Some struck the crowne with the reed[;] others beat it further in with sticks,
others toke hold of it with their hands saying lets see how it sits thy head.
What blasphemies did they spit out of their sacrilegious mouths together
with[51] phlegme & spitle. They cald him a phantastical K[ing] an empty &
crazy brain, that now they had given him the scepter robes & crowne
w[hi]ch he deservd. They ript up their old slanders of glutton[,] imposter,
blasphemer, possest of the divel &c. that now he had receivd the just reward
of his deserts. X endurd all these torments & affronts wth invincible constancy, as if his body had been made of steel; he resisted not his strikers,
he turnd not away his face from the spitters, he receivd their blasphemies
without the least resentment; tho their spite & malice afflicted his tender
heart.

In this condition Pilate brings our B[lessed] L[ord] into a balcony to
show him to the people not doubting but that dolefull sight being wounded
from head to foot & crownd with thorns w[oul]d movd [sic] them to compassion & make them desist from desiring his death because he was so disfigurd that one c[oul]d scarce tell what he was, Pilate said ecce ho[mo].
Moreover he plaided in favour of X. by this punishment; he declares his
innocence, signifying that if he so severely punisht him, whom he found
free from crime, much more severely w[oul]d he punish him even with
death if he was really guilty. & in case he had committed any fault worthy
of chasticement, that now he had receivd condigne punishment. & lastly if
he pretended[52] to be a K[ing], & rebell against the Roman Emp[eror] that
now they s[houl]d be convincd that he was a phantastical K[ing], & nothing
to be apprehended from so mean & contemptible a person. Lastly he
doubted not but that the invincible patience he showd w[oul]d be an irrefragable proof of his innocence. For if he was not a H[oly] man, nay more
than a pure man, it w[oul]d be impossible for flesh & blood to endure such
cruel torments without expressing signs of impatience. But alass the malice
of the jews crost all his designs, their hearts were overruld with malice, they
thirsted after the blood of X & they were resolvd to have him sentencd to
death, innocent or guilty. Exivit J[esus] portans coronam spineam & pur-
puream vestimentur.[53] O dolefull sight O malancholy scene!

Go forth then the daughters of Sion, the pious souls, to contemplate your K[ing] Sol: your L[ord] your Messias crownd by his cruel M[o]t[he]r the synagogue with a crown of thorns. Ecce ho[mo]. Thus said Pil to the people to move them to compassion, but the E[terna]l F[ather] directs the same words to us in a more divine sence. Behold the man, who tho he appears as a poor & contemptible man, is nevertheless the son of G[od] equal to his F[ather] in wisdom power & majesty & as man is head of the A[n]g[el]s[,] L[ord] of heaven & earth; he is the Messias, the Redeemr of the world whose love for man was such that he sufferd hims[el]f to be thus disfigurd for him Ecce ho. behold the man whom I sent into the world to be a pattern of all sorts of vertue, for you to imitate. Behold his humilty admidst such contempts. his poverty in such want, his meekness in such injuries, his patience in such torments his silence amidst calumnies. his obedience to such painfull commands, his charity to those that persecute him. Behold this patterne & follow the example. Behold the man crownd as a K[ing] to cure your pride & ambition in aspiring to dignities & preferments. Behold his head crownd with thorns to punish your sinfull thoughts which piercd his head more sensibly than the thorns did. behold his body rent & torn from head to foot to chastice your lurery & sensuality. O P A what must be our sentiments at this dolefull spectacle. Can we yield to the desires of the flesh w[he]n we see X['s] flesh so cruelly mangled for the sins of ours. can we be proud & ambitious w[he]n we see X so humble. Can we think much to suffer some slight affliction for love of him who has endurd so much for us. O no our bodyes have sind, Xts is innocent they ought then rather suffer than his. Our S[avio]r is covered with wounds, its not fitt we s[houl]d live without wounds. X is our head[,] hes crowd with thorns, we his membres, its not fitting th[ere]f[o]re to indulge sensuality. for as S. Ber[nard]: says non decet sub capite spinass ex membra ac mollia & delicate. a tender & delicate body does not become a thorny head. W[he]n any temptations arises lets set this man before our eies ecce ho. saying how can I be so ungratefull as to sin w[he]n I see what X has done to destroy sin. W[he]n any afflictions disturbe us, let us comfort our s[elve]s with the consideration of X sufferings, saying to our heart, Mat: 10.24 non e[st] discipulus sup[e]r M[agistrum]. nec servus sup[er] Dom[inu]m. It does not become a servant to fare better than his M[aste]r. If then X our L[ord] & M[aster] has sufferd, sufferings are due to us.

Lastly let us address these words to the E[terna]l F[ather] ecce ho. Behold the man thy D[ivi]ne Sone. Respice in faciem Xi tui. Let his blood wash away our sins. Let his torments satisfy for our crimes. Let his humilty, let his patience move us to follow his example, that so we may behold the same man not disfigurd with thorns but beautifull & resplendent crownd with glory & immortality which &c.

NOTES

1. Georgetown University Archives. A version, edited by John Gilmary Shea, appeared in the *United States Catholic Historical Magazine*, III (1889–1890), 237–263.

1a. Georgetown University Special Collections (hereafter GUSC), American Catholic Sermon Collection.

2. Crossed out: "man."

3. Attwood consistently abbreviates "which" to "wch" and "with" to "wh."

4. "the voluptuous in the midst of his pleasures" is repeated in the text.

5. Crossed out "great ones."

6. Crossed out: "sinner."

7. "The impending fire crazes me."

7a. GUSC, American Catholic Sermon Collection.

8. Crossed out: "things."

9. Crossed out: "And that who by this humble conception becomes the mother in time of him who has no beginning, who shutes him up who is immense, who give a new being to Eternity, and new life to immortality. this work is so admirable, that the angel of the schools dares assert it is inimatable, and that God cant communicate to a creature, a dignity more noble, more eminent, more elevated, than this to be mother of god. after this what is there yet more great? that men who are all terrestiall, and plunged in the corruption of their nature shoud become the children of god even really, and truly, for all other works are referred to this, all being expect with patience the manifestation of the children of god. . . ."

10. There follows: "I find in the beginning of the life of the Eternal word wherewith to continue you."

11. Crossed out: "from the beginning."

12. "As the universal Father has sent me, so do I send you because of the Father."

13. "From my mother's womb my father is you."

14. Crossed out: "amongst."

15. "And they become as abominable as the things they delight in."

16. Crossed out: "JC comes into the world."

17. Crossed out: "consecrated by the."

18. "Be it done unto me according to your word."

19. "It" is repeated in the text.

20. "Lord, let Christ be formed in us."

21. "until he be formed."

22. Crossed out: "affront."

23. Crossed out: "Confess."

24. "God so loved the world."

25. "See what love the father has for us, that we are named and become sons of God."

26. "He gave to them the power to become sons of God."

26a. GUSC, American Catholic Sermon Collection.

27. Greaton, like Attwood, consistently abbreviates ''which'' to ''wch''. He also eliminates the ''i'' from ''with'' and the ''ha'' from ''what''.

28. Crossed out is ''thing of moment.''

29. Crossed out, ''as one deserving et[ernal] torments.''

30. Crossed out: ''be set at liberty.''

31. Crossed out: ''sincerely wished.''

32. Crossed out: ''wish.''

33. Crossed out: ''and having received imediate prohibition.''

34. Crossed out: ''resist.''

35. Crossed out: ''yet they must be sorry for the sins they confess.''

35a. GUSC, American Catholic Sermon Collection.

36. First given in 1728. The heading expands upon the Jesuit phrase *Ad majorem dei gloriam* to include Mary and the Guardian Angels as well.

37. ''Pilate took Jesus and had him scourged.'' (John 19:1)

38. ''Daughters of Zion, come and see King Solomon, wearing the diadem with which his mother crowned him on his wedding day.'' (Song of Songs 3:11)

39. Crossed out: ''raise friends.''

40. Crossed out: ''him.''

41. Psalm 22:6.

42. Crossed out: ''I say.''

43. Crossed out: ''sensible.''

44. Crossed out: ''most painful.''

45. Crossed out: ''When one was weary.''

46. In margin: ''no less than 5000 stripes did they discharge upon our B[lessed] L[ord] as was reveald to S. Brigit.''

47. ''From head to toe there is not a sound spot.''

48. Crossed out: ''thought.''

49. Crossed out ''about like a football with their feet.''

50. Crossed out ''pittyful.''

51. Crossed out ''gobs of.''

52. Crossed out ''they pretended.''

53. ''Jesus went out, wearing his crown of thorns and cloathed in purple.''

III

JOSEPH MOSLEY AND THE
EIGHTEENTH CENTURY MISSION

*Like most of his fellow Jesuits in British America, Joseph Mosley (1731–
1787) was English, of an old Catholic family of modest means. A native of
Lincolnshire, Mosley left home at eleven to be educated at St. Omers, the
recusant school that had been established in Flanders in 1593. As was the
custom with those sent abroad for a Catholic education, Mosley used an
alias (Joseph Frambeck). He entered the Society in 1748. Ten years later
he volunteered for the Maryland Mission. His first seven years as a missionary were spent in southern Maryland. In 1764 he began to work on the
Eastern Shore, first at Bohemia and then farther south in Queen Ann's and
Talbot counties. A year later he established the mission of St. Joseph's at
Tuckahoe near the Wye river in Talbot county. Like the other rural missions, St. Joseph's had a farm or plantation to support the apostolic work.
This, along with its slaves, was also Mosley's care. It was hardly a manorial
existence. John Carroll described Mosley's living quarters as "a cell such
as the woman of Sumanite prepared for the prephet Elisus (4th Book of
kings, c. 4), containing just space enough for a bed, a table and a stool."[1]
It was certainly a very lonely life, with rare opportunities to visit with his
Jesuit brothers. One can appreciate his confusion in the 1770s when in par-
alyzing succession the Society of Jesus was suppressed and the colonies
revolted against Great Britain. In his isolated position he delayed taking the
oath of loyalty to the new government until he could ascertain what common
course of action the other former Jesuits were taking. For this indecision he
was barred from preaching, but once apprised that the Jesuits on the western
shore had pledged their loyalty, he followed suit in 1778. As his correspondence with his sister indicates, he was a troubled priest during the Revolution, "between hawk and buzzard" but was willing to stay where he was
needed. Whatever his natural feelings, he never returned home. His letters*

to his family seem in part to have served as a spiritual journal for him, to contemplate what sent him to Maryland and what kept him there.

LETTERS TO HIS FAMILY[2] (1757–1786)

23 October, 1757
Dear Sister,[3]
      . . . I left Liege, the 1st of last March; lived some while at St. Omer; and am now at Graveline, Director to the English Nuns there[4] . . . and God knows how long I shall stay here. I only supply till a Secular comes: I've been here since May last, and probably shall be here some time. . . . I expect to be in England next Spring on my road to Maryland: so, if I can't get time to see you, which happiness I can't hardly expect, I hope you will give me leave to trouble you with a parting line from London. And so, if we see one another no more in this world, I hope we shall meet in the next.

London, 25th of Feb. 1758
Dear Sister,
      I've arrived safe to London at last. Again I am come to see my own country, from whence I've been, as I may say, banished now above 16 years. I really have not time to descend as far as the North to see you. So I write you this parting Letter according to my promise. I set off for America the 10th of next month; not to be banished from my own country for only 16 years, but for Love of God and the conversion of souls, to abandon it and you for always: nothing but what I've mentioned should ever have brought me to it, for if I consider things according to the Law of Nature, what can indulge it more than to live at home amongst our own friends and relations: but if we examine for what we were born, it was not to give way to the whole Law of Nature, but according to even one's call let the Law of Nature be ruled and governed by the Law of Grace. This I write that you may not condemn my undertaking, which was entirely my own choice. For, if I consider the call of my state of life with which God has blessed me, I am not in all things to follow what is even innocently delightful, but to seek what tends more to the honour and glory of God. . . . Whenever an occasion serves of any ship to New-Castle, from America, you may be assured you shall not fail hearing from me, and then I will give you proper directions to me; which correspondence will be at least some satisfaction to me, when seeing you can't be granted: but for my part, I think that seeing one another is of little satisfaction, unless our lives are such that we may see one another in a happy Eternity: when there we meet, we meet for ever. In this life nothing is certain, but that we must sooner or later separate: So, now let it be

Adieu, Sister—when we meet again, it will be never to have the pain of separating again. . . .

I remain, Dear sister,

Your affectionate and ever loving Brother
Jos: Mosley

Newtown, Sept. 8th, 1758
Dear Sister,

. . . I arrived safe and sound to Maryland on the 19th of June, after a long and tedious voyage of ten weeks. I find here business enough on my hands in my Way of Trade,—I've care of above fifteen hundred souls: we stand in need here of Labourers, if more only had zeal enough to come to our assistance: for myself, I can say, that I preferred this place to any I knew, and I hope to spend my life and whole strength, I think it the happiest place in the world, and I also find it so, for one of our calling. No Prince in his Court can have more satisfaction and enjoy himself more, than I do in instructing those that are under my charge. I am daily on horseback, visiting the sick, comforting the infirm, strengthening the pusillanimous, &c. And I enjoy my health as yet as well, as if I were breathing my own native air. . . .

Newtown, 1st of Sep: 1759
Dear Sister,

You desire a short account of this part of America. The climate is very hot and sultry in summer to a great excess nay several West-Indians that lay under the very sun tell me, that they find it warmer here than there: the winter is not so cold as in England: the changes of weather is prodigious sudden—on a clear day a hurricane, or a *gust* as they call it here, rises in an instant, and will in a few minutes lay down all the houses and trees in the vein it blows. Thunder and lightning is, I believe, as dismal here as it is in any part of the world. You can't go ten yards in the woods (which composes the greatest part of the country), but you see some tree or other struck with lightning at one time or other. I've seen it myself strike the trees within very few yards of me. The country is the best laid out for trade of any in the world. The Rivers are spacious and wide. . . . Our horses are almost all natural pacers, they will easily go, as I know it by experience, a whole day without food, at the rate of 7, 8, 9 miles an hour, in a constant pace: which is a great comfort to us in our way of life. The buildings in this country are very poor and insignificant, all only one storey, commonly all the building made of wood plastered within,—a brick chimney in the better houses. You may find a brick house here and there: our Body commonly has them. The poorer people have nothing but a few boards nailed together, without plastering, or any brick about it. Very few houses have glass windows. . . .

Now I look upon myself out of the world in the desert parts of America, yet don't think that I am tired of my situation. I am here as content as a King, and never shall desire a change if I can keep my health and be of service; I allow our fatigues are very great, our journies very long, our rides constant and extensive. We have many to attend, and few to attend them. I often ride about 300 miles a week, and never a week but I ride 150, or 200: and in our way of living, we ride almost as much by night as by day, in all weathers, in heats, cold, rain, frost or snow. Several may think the colds, rains, &c, to be the worst to ride in; but, I think to ride in the heats far surpasses all, both for man and horse. But, as I've told you, our horses are well gaited and everlasters. . . .

Yr ever loving and affectionate Brother,
Joseph Mosley

New-Town, Oct: 5th, 1760

Dear Sister,

. . . I can't say that my health is at present so good as it has been; for a ride of 52 miles in the rain, and another of the same length in a warm day all in the sun, cast me into violent fevers attended with constant vomitings: but, thanks be to God, I am upon the recovering hand. . . .

This year has gone very hard with us; the rains have caused a great many diseases, and to us a great many rides. Our Hands are few, weak, and in great decay. Our rides are often twice a day: yet, I've often in a week rid between 50 & 60 miles a day. It's true, our horses in this country go so easy that a ride of 50 miles, perhaps, won't tire a man so much as 20 or 30 with your horses in England; yet, they are so frequent, that it is enough to break the strongest constitution. . . .

I recommend myself to all your good prayers in this Life I lead, banished into the remotest corner of the world, amongst Indians, Negroes and Slaves, and separated by the Atlantic from my dearest friends: yet, notwithstanding all this, perhaps the happiest man that breathes: for, if true happiness consists in a contented mind, never did it reign more truly than in this Blessed Country, Blessed, I say, but only so for one of our profession. Adieu, Dear Sister: perhaps we never shall meet again in this world, yet I always shall have the happiness of subscribing myself even at this distance,

Your ever loving and affectionate Brother,
Joseph Mosley

Portobacco, 30th July 1764
Dear Brother,[5]

　　. . . The method of our lives seems to give you some uneasiness
for us. I think you may be easy, as you reckon our deaths will be precious
in the sight of God. God send [?] they may, and I am sure that our
multitude of fatigues and oppressive labours, as you are pleased to style
them, will be abundantly rewarded. You hope, I'll be a better steward
of a life, not at my disposal: but it is at God's, and he is welcome to
it, to spend it in the service of my fellow-creatures, or Brethren in Christ.
My crown won't be the less for having laboured the longer, it's true,
if you and I can agree about the word *labour*. *Consummatus in brevi*
will sooner have your approbation than *Puer centum annorum*, or *Longam
vitam injusti.*[6] I know you have good sense, and are a great Master of
Divinity, and *argue well by means* of both in favour of prudence and
discretion: yet, to my comfort, He who came to destroy and confound
the prudence of the prudent, and the wisdom of the wise, laboured but
three years amidst indefatigable hardships and insupportable miseries and
wants for our example, and died, 'a folly to the Gentiles': and the great
Xaverious, the glory of our S[ociet]y, trod in his footsteps, in an immense
field, where he was yet much needed, died after ten years labour and
fatigue: Fr. Campion was cut off in the very first year of his great undertakings. To be numbered amongst this glorious Company is beyond
all my pretension, *et non tali me dignor honore:*[7] if I could follow them,
although *non passibus aequis,*[8] would be the very summit of all my zeal
and ambition. As to the circumstance of long fasting (which you can't
well comprehend in the details of our labours), I am afraid you never
will understand by any explication I can give: Theory will never do;
experience may convince you, to your cost, of all I said. "Have our
people we visit neither eatables nor drinkables?" "Do they live on the
air?" So much I know, as to the first demand, that I've asked, when
I've been almost fainting, for a mouthful of bread, or a glass of milk,
and I could not get it. As for bread, few or none ever use it in this
country: what they eat with their meat is a sort of hasty-pudding made
of Indian corn, which they term *Mush*, which is made out of hand when
[?] [they] eat, and so much disagrees with [the] English, that they never
pretend to offer it to us. This Indian corn they turn into different shapes,
to supply the place of bread: but, in none, does it agree with an English
constitution. As to the second demand, of living on the air, I know not;
let them answer for themselves. I know fresh air, in the heats, is as scarce
with us as bread and cheese. I've often taken with me, as you suggest
in yours, a crust of English bread, as we term it here, to support foreseen
wants. . . . As for saddlebags, it's true we have them, but they are too

incumbersome to be troubled with them, in our frequent long rides, and too apt to heat our horses, whose ease we chiefly consult, even more than our own. Here, perhaps, you'll object *prudence:* but, while I favour my horse, I think I consult my own advantage, for one night in the woods under our treacherous air, would be of worse consequence with us, than twenty without supper. . . . As for our present labours, they are more or less the same as I've acquainted you, and the accidents of life as various. Swamps, Runs, miry holes, lost in the night, as yet, and ever will in this country attend us: thank God, we are all safe as yet. Between 3 or 400 mile was my last Mass fare, on one horse; the same I blindfolded. I am just leaving Portobacco to go to Bohemia, where they tell me I am wanted. The Cong[regatio]ns are fewer, but the rides much longer. On the 1st Sunday, 50 mile, where I pass the whole week in that neighbourhood, in close business with the ignorant. On the 2nd, I go down to Chesapeake Bay, 40 mile farther, which makes me 90 mile from home: the other two Sundays are easier. the Mission has picked me out to settle a place between these two, if I can, to make it an easier Miss[io]n. Pray that I may succeed; I shall have at Bohemia a fair plantation to manage, the best, I believe, we have, and nigh Philadelphia, which is a vast advantage. . . .

Yr Loving Brother,
Jos: Mosley

Tuckahoe, Talbot County
14 Oct. 1766
Dear Sister,

I received yours of the 18th March, 1764. I am heartily sorry I could not answer it last year. But a new Mission I had undertaken, so took up all my time and leisure, that I could not steal even a few moments, either to answer yours or my Brother's, or any other. . . . It's a Mission that ought to have been settled above these 60 years past, by reason of the immense trouble and excessive rides it had given our Gentlemen that lived next to it, although within 200 miles of it: yet, till these days no one would undertake, either for want of resolution, or fear of the trouble, notwithstanding it had contributed much to the deaths of several of Ours, and had broken the constitutions of every one who went down to it, although it was but twice a year, except calls to the sick. I was deputed in August, 1764, to settle a new place in the midst of this Mission: accordingly I set off for those parts of the country; I examined the situation of every Congregation within 60 mile of it: and, before the end of that year, I came across the very spot, as Providence would have it, with land to be sold, nigh the centre of the whole that was to be tended.

I purchased the land, and took possession, in March following. On the land there were three buildings, a miserable dwelling-house, a much worse for some negroes, and a house to cure tobacco in. My dwelling-house was nothing but a few boards riven from oak trees, not sawed plank, and these nailed together to keep out the coldest air: not one brick or stone about it, no plastering, and no chimney, but a little hole in the roof to let out the smoke. In this I lived till the winter, when I got it plastered to keep off the cold, and built a brick chimney; the bricks I was obliged to buy and cart above five mile. . . . The chief Congregation is but ten mile off; 2nd 20; the 3rd, 24; 4th, 22; 5th, at home; 6th, 22. All these I visit once in two months. I have two others which I visit but twice a year—the first, 39, the other 90 mile off. This, you'll say, is still hard. It's easy, Dear Sister, to what it was. . . . I have now my cows, my sheep, hogs, turkeys, geese, and other dunghill fowl: I've my own grain, and make my own bread. In fine, I had a thousand other difficulties to go through, which at present I can't call to mind and which then took up all my time and thoughts, exclusive of all the hardships and fatigues of a very laborious mission: but, thank God, I have had and have at present my health as well as ever I had it in my life, and I think this inland situation suits my constitution better than the waterside, and if it was not for a few gray hairs on my head, you would never know by my present health, the long fasts, fatiguing rides and restless nights, that I've already undergone. My brother Mick tells you, that we need not expose ourselves to the dangers and hardships we do: it's true, he advises me himself to be careful of my health, more cautious in my rides, and more moderate in my labours. His advice is good, when it can be followed: but, in the circumstances we are in, what part of our labours can we cut off, without neglecting our duty. Must I refuse, when the sick wants me? must I neglect my Sunday Church exercise, to ease myself, by staying at home? Must I, when at the Chapel, refuse to hear half that present themselves? Must I, if called to the sick in the night, sleep till morning, and thus let the sick die without assistance? Must I, if called to a dying man in the rain, stay till it's fair weather? It's fine talking over the fireside: but, it's what I can't practise, when the circumstances occur. Poor Mick, with all his caution, care and moderation, he can't enjoy that health even at Bath, as I enjoy with all the dangers and fatigues of Maryland: don't you think he takes as much pains to preserve his little health with the waters of Bath and St. Winifred's Well, as we do to destroy it. I am really sorry to hear that he is so much indisposed; I wish him his health with all my heart. The greatest labour with health is more satisfactory, than an easy life under a sickly constitution. He, with his great patience, may probably reap more merit in his sickness than Missioners with their greatest hardships. . . .

Yr most loving and affectionate Brother,
Joseph Mosley

Tuckahoe, September 8, 1770
Dear Sister,

I have as yet the saddle you sent: it is an excellent one; I've made it groan for many a long day under my load. I believe it will last me my life with a little care. When it is present with me, in my solitary ride, it brings your frequent benevolence to me often to my mind. . . . You seem to pity me much in these my sufferings and hardships: I may suppose that really I have suffered much since I've been in America—if the motive has been only perfect, for which I did undergo them. Yes, I believe, I can say with truth, that I've suffered a great deal, especially since I undertook this new settlement. But, I am afraid that I deserved to suffer a great deal more, God be merciful to me. I would not now be willing to change the laborious suffering part of my past life, for the lives of those that have lived far more comfortably: I live in hopes that it will stand my friend on the Last Day: God only knows what of my life is yet to come: a more comfortable one seems more agreeable to flesh and blood, yet, if not granted, by experience I know that it can be endured, living in hopes that the time will come, when, "we shall rest from our labours, and our works will follow us." For, we are assured by St. Paul, that "our labour is not vain." I don't intend to extol myself: if I've suffered, I've equally sinned, and have my faults. I've often seen poor, miserable, abandoned families in poverty, want and misery, suffer far more than all I've ever suffered: we are all God's creatures: what right have I to be better off than they? If their intentions and motives were only good and conformable to God's holy will, how great would be their merit! Yes, greater than mine, if a proportion of misery will enhance our merits at the Last Day . . .

I am, ever dear Sister, your most affectionate
and ever tender loving Brother,
Jos: Mosley

Tuckahoe, 5th June, 1772
Dear Sister,

I received yr favour of 28th of Feby 1772, on 23rd of March 1772, after it had wandered thro the world for better, than a year. . . . It grieves me, Dr. Sister, to hear of the loss, you've had in Mr. Dunn, bear the cross & affliction of Widow-hood with Christian Patience & Resignation. I failed not the three next Days to offer up the whole Duty of the Altar & Day for him. Comfort yourself, blessing God, that as he is gone fearing God, so the

Mercy of our Lord is from ever & to be for ever upon them that fear him. Psalm 102, v. 17. Don't let self loss (which may crave to indulge itself in his company) to eagerly desire to invert God's Will, & wish him back into this vale of Tears, whilst his D: Goodness has placed him, as we believe, in a far better Situation. Dr. Sister, such repining, such fruitless Tears must savour more of self Love, than real affection for the Dr. Man you've lost. We believe him more happy & in better company out of this World of Misery, than in the Enjoyment of yours, while therefore, you are bewailing his Loss with Sobs, Sighs, & Tears, you would seem to begrudge him his present Happiness in his Absence from you. Would you, if in your Power, desire him to quit his present Happiness, to tarry with you & enjoy life again? You surely would not. Therefore, Dr. Sister, Comfort yourself that Life is short, the remains of it, if well employ'd, will transmit you to his Company for ever, never more to part. Carefully, therefore husband up, what remains of Life, to the End you may enjoy his Company for an Eternity whose Loss & absence for a Time you may now lament. You say, he died wholy resigned to the Will of God in leaving the World and you; follow the Example, live you wholy resigned to the Will of God in quitting him: If Resignation gives signs of a Happy Death, Resignation also must be a Token in us of a good Life. If it was the Will of God he should leave the World, it was also his D[ivine]: Will he should leave you & of Consequence if the D: Will demanded Submission to these appointments in him, the same D: Will must equally demand the same submission in you: for in both of you it would tend to one & the same End, viz, the Honour & glory of God. But why, Dear Sister, so much on this melancholly Subject? Do I doubt of your Resignation? Did I hear your Sighs & Tears? No! Dear Sister, I neither heard the one, nor do I doubt of the other. I only here prick down a few silly thoughts of my own, to comfort you in the Widow-hood & to enliven that certain Article of our Faith; that we shall all rise again; the Good to a far better Life, than what we now enjoy. In fine to avoid any farther multiplicity of Words, I conclude in heartily condoling with you for the Loss of your Husband. Bear the loss with Patience, you know God gives, & God takes away, Let his Name be blessed. As he is taken away by God's Will & Pleasure, be careful of his Remains, I mean yourself & your children. Thank God, that he has left both you & them an ample sufficiency for your finishing, & their beginning of the World. . . .

Last June, I was desired to attend at Philadelphia with all speed. Philadelphia, from my house, is 110 miles. On a Sunday, after prayers to my Congregation, I set off after one o'clock, P.M., taking at my house a light refreshment of a few dishes of tea. The day was excessive hot, and I arrived that evening at Bohemia, 50 miles, just as the Gentleman whom I was to meet there was sitting down to supper—a long afternoon's ride, and never by any of us performed before. I thought, as my horse was good, to have done it without any hurt to myself. The next day, we went to Philadelphia, 60 miles, a very sultry day, where after some necessary excursions into the country, I returned home again in two days, the weather being very warm. On my return, after a constant ride in June and July in the heats of the year of about 430 miles, I was seized with a violent fit of the gravel: I've had several small fits since, but none so violent. That particular fit held me ten days, without any respite, ease or sleep, night or day. If all the caution I now use prove unsuccessful, I must quit, and see my native country once more, which I never intended. God's will be done. If I can't ride, I should be here an unprofitable servant. Horsemen are little needed in Flanders or in England. . . .

Yr ever affectionate and loving, tho' far
distant brother,
Jos. Mosley

Tuckahoe, 5th July, 1773
Dear Sister,
    . . . I've lived entirely alone for these nine years past, not one white person with me. I wish I may have made good use of my time. I am thronged sufficiently abroad, but am a true eremite at home. . . . Captain Woolfe arrived here about the middle of June. . . . He dined at my house soon after his arrival. What small curiosities I can come across either in bird or beast, I shall send them according to directions by his return. . . . I've had as yet no violent return of the gravel, or as the physicians call it, a paroxysm of it. I am forever troubled with a heaviness about my loins and kidneys: if it is a stone, I've reason to dread the next paroxysm or motion of it. I am in all other respects as well as I ever was in my life; some few precautions I take have been of great service to me in that complaint, as well as in my health in general. Long rides, night and day, I can't avoid, to comply with my calls and duty. I know they hurt me, but God's will be done. This last winter, I was riding the whole night to the sick, three or four times, as I remember. One night in particular, in a ride of sixty-four miles, raining from the first jump of my own door till I returned, to a sick person that is as yet alive and little wanted me. It was the third ride I've had to that same man, three successive winters. He lives in a little hovel of his own. How I fared for any comforts there, you may well guess. I returned through the rain, next day, with no sleep, victuals or drink, except bad water. . . . I could tell you of a thousand other uncomfortable accidents of this kind, that happen often to us, which would make you pity us. By this one ride in the rain you see how much I wanted the boots which I've now

got; God reward you for them. It's for Him, I hope, that they shall be employed. I can't as yet hear of quitting my stand; he is a cowardly soldier that quits it. He that puts his hand to the plough and looks back is not the man for Christ's service. When I am unfit, and a burden, I'll listen then to an invalid's berth; a berth that I can never wish for.

Your loving and affectionate brother,
Jos: Mosley, S.J.

Maryland, 3rd Oct. 1774
Dear Sister,

. . . Yes, . . . I had heard before I wrote to you that our total Dissolution was much dreaded by us, yet it was not executed even at Rome when I wrote to you in July. It was little to the purpose to mention it to you, as I imagined you was an entire stranger to the cause; and to let you into it would only have given you trouble to learn how we have been used: and now I mention it, I can't do it without tears in my eyes. Yes, Dear Sister, our Body or Factory is dissolved, of which your two Brothers are members, and for myself I know I am an unworthy one, when I see so many worthy, saintly, pious, learned, laborious Miss[ionerer]s dead and alive been members of the same, thro' the two last ages. I know no fault that we are guilty off. I am convinced that our labors are pure, upright and sincere, for God's honour and our neighbour's good. What our Supreme Judge on Earth may think of our labours is a mystery to me. He has hurt his own cause, not us. It's true he has stigmatized us thro' the world with infamy, and declared us unfit for our business or his service. Our Dissolution is known thro' the world; it's in every newspaper, which makes me ashamed to show my face. Ah, I can say now, what I never before thought of: I am willing now to retire and quit my post, as I believe most of my Brethren are. A retired private life would suit me best, where I could attend only myself, after 17 years dissipation in this harvest. As we're judged unserviceable, we labour with little heart, and, what is worse, by no rule. To my great sorrow the Society is abolished; with it must die all that zeal that was founded and raised on it. Labour for our neighbour is a Jesuit's pleasure; destroy the Jesuit, and labour is painful and disagreeable. I must allow with truth, that what was my pleasure is now irksome: every fatigue I underwent caused a secret and inward satisfaction; it's now unpleasant and disagreeable: every visit to the sick was done with a good will, it's now done with as bad a one. I disregarded this unhealthy climate, and all its agues and fevers, which have really paid me to my heart's content, for the sake of my rule, the night was agreeable as the day, frost and cold as a warm fire or a soft bed, the excessive heats as welcome as a cool shade or pleasant breezes—but now the scene is changed: the Jesuit's metamorphosed into I know not what; he is a monster, a scarecrow in my ideas. With joy I impaired my health and broke my constitution in the care of my flock. It was the Jesuit's call, it was his whole aim and business. The Jesuit is no more; he now endeavours to repair his little remains of health and shattered constitution, as he has no rule calling him to expose it. In me, the Jesuit and the Missioner was always combined together; if one falls, the other must of consequence fall with it. As the Jesuit is judged unfit by his H[oli]ness for a Mission, I think that it is high time for me to retire to a private life, to spend the remains of my days in peace and quiet. I should be sorry to be quite inactive, and doing no good; but a small employ would now content my zeal. If I could hear of a vacant place in your neighbourhood for a Chaplain, I should accept of it. . . . While I was actuated with the old spirit, I could seek my neighbor's good in any corner of the world, where I could procure it; but as now that noble spirit is abolished by Authority, I don't care how soon I see my native soil, and leave my place to younger and healthier hands, which I never would have designed, while I could stand or walk, could I have remained on the same footing. We are now like dispersed sheep, or disbanded soldiers: what man could live in such a confused distracted state, without some danger to himself? . . .

Yr. ever affectionate and Loving Brother,
Jos: Mosley, S.J., for ever, as I think, and hope.

Tuckahoe, 16th Aug. 1775
Dear Sister,

. . . Times here look very gloomy and seem to threaten a stoppage of all intercourse with you: we must submit to the decrees of Providence, on Whom must depend all events of war and peace, and of consequence, our happy correspondence must hang on to the same wing. In fine, let us trust to God, write when you can, and I'll do the same. . . . As to my return to England, the present times here, and our own destruction as J[esui]ts at home, might make you think that I had sufficient reason to be serious. I am really between hawk and buzzard, I know not what step I best take. My brother Michael has at last favored me with a line, and presses my return, if I am any way discontent with my present situation: but discontent or not, I see that I am a very necessary hand in my situation, and our Gentlemen here won't hear of my departure. I can't tell you, as yet, what I shall do: it will depend upon certain events; don't be surprised, if you hear me knocking at your house door before many years are over my head. A Clergyman's call has little to do with civil broils and troubled waters; the fisherman never chooses to fish in muddy or disturbed water. In fine, to be sincere, bad times and inward trouble from our own affairs make me little content and less fit for my trust and business here. . . .

Dear Sister,

Your Affectionate and loving brother,

Jos: Mosley.

St. Joseph's, Talbot County, Maryland
4th October, 1784
Dear Sister,

Our correspondence has been long interrupted by reason of the late tedious and calamitous war. Peace is returned; I wish it may be happy in every circumstance. In this we are happy, that we can correspond again. I am yet alive, and thank God, I enjoy a middling good state of health, notwithstanding my fatigues and long frequent rides in my old age. I hear my brother Michael is dead, but I've had no certain intelligence of it. I've often prayed for him as dead. I've heard nothing concerning you or your family's health since your last letters . . . I am yet on the same farm, on which I lived, when you wrote to me last. I've informed you many years ago of my purchase of it, in what situation it was first in, and what I really suffered in settling it. I've been on it now twenty long years, and I've made it, thro' God's help, both agreeable and profitable to myself and to my successors: not knowing the length of life, my chief aim was to make it convenient, happy, and easy to my successors, that they might with some comfort continue a flourishing mission that I have begun. When I first settled, I had not one of my own Profession nigher than six or seven miles; but now, thro' God's particular blessings, I've many families joining, and all round me. The toleration here granted by the Bill of Rights has put all on the same footing, and has been of great service to us. The Methodists, who have started up chiefly since the war, have brought over to themselves chief of the former Protestants, on the Eastern Shore of Maryland, where I live. The Protestant ministers, having no fixed salary by law, as heretofore, have abandoned their flocks, which are now squandered and joined different societies. We've had some share. Since the commencement of the war, I've built on my farm a brick chapel and dwelling-house. It was a difficult and bold undertaking at that time, as every necessary, especially nails was very dear. I began it, trusting on Providence, and I've happily finished, without any assistance either from our Gentlemen or my Congregation. . . . My Chapel will hold between 2 or 300 people. It could not contain the hearers, last Easter Sunday, when I first kept Prayers in it, and every Sunday since it has been very full, when I attend at home, which is only once every month. We are all growing old, we are very weak handed, few come from England to help us. I suppose they are much wanted with you; I understand that few enter into Orders of late years, since the destruction of the Society. Here, I can assure you, the harvest is great: but the laborers are too few. where I am situated, I attend ten Counties, by myself; to have it done as it ought, it would take ten able men.[9] Pray fervently, that God may bless all our undertakings. The *Book of the History of the Church,* which you sent me, some years ago, has contributed much to our numbers; it is forever agoing from family to family of different persuasions. Be so good, if you know any books of equal force, that have appeared of late years, to contribute your mite towards our successes, by sending them to me. . . .

> I am, Dear Sister, Yr
> affectionate & loving Brother
> Jos: Mosley

St. Joseph's, Talbot County.
> *Head of Wye, Maryland, 20th of July, 1786*
Dear Sister,

 . . . I've been these 10 months several times at death's door with bilious fevers and frequent returns of the gravel. I seem to be at present upon the recovery, thro' God's blessing, for I know not what will become of my little flock, if I should be taken from them. . . . I found a few when I settled here, but thank God and his Divine Assistance, we can now count between 500 and 600 Communicants. The present incumbents are growing very old and infirm, and few come to supply our places. . . . I am yet all alone, and have but one other of my Call on the Eastern Shore of Maryland, and he lives 50 miles from me: we see one another perhaps once a year. You may pity my situation: I pity that of my poor flock, and not my own. I wish I was younger and healthier to serve them as I would. . . . I recommend myself to your good prayers. I shall never forget you in mine. I am, Dear Sister,

> Your loving and affectionate
> Brother,
> Jos: Mosley.

SERMONS[10]

On Saint Ignatius

If personal pride, in the Jesuit worldview, was a major obstacle to sharing Christ's spirit, corporate pride was not. Jesuits saw the hand of God so pow-

erfully in the life of Ignatius and his Society that to sing their glories was
to celebrate God himself. Such holy boosterism is prominent in Mosley's
sermon on Ignatius, given at Newtown in 1759 and repeated in the same
place a year later. The occasion was undoubtedly Ignatius's feast day. Despite his recent arrival, Mosley does not hesitate to rebuke them for their
failings in living up to the Ignatian tradition to which they were so indebted:
the pursuit of God's glory and the neighbor's good.

Hic iam quaeritur inter dispensatores ut fidelis quis inveniatur, ad Cor:
Cap: 4. v 2.
Here now is required amongst the Dispensers or Ministers of Xt, that
a Man be found faithful. They are the Words of St. Paul to the Corinthians,
Epis. 1st, chap: 4. Ver 2.
St. Paul writing to the Corinthians, in a few Words draws the Image
of an apostolical Man, when he says he is the Minister of Jesus Xt & Dispenser of the mysteries of God, for you know, says the apostle, when a man
acts as a Dispenser of God's mysterys, we expect of him the greatest Fidelity to his Divine Master ut *"Fidelis inveniatur."* It's not sufficient that
God is faithful to him, but likewise he must correspond, fulfil his vocation
& so prove faithful to God. A Fidelity so far necessary, that God, all powerful as he is, can't raise a Man to be a Minister of his Gospel without it;
without this Fidelity there can be neither prophet, or Saint. St. Ignatius was
called to this exalted Function of the Minister of God to be faithful in the
Defense of God's Church & zealous in saving God's People. That is, he
was to be faithful to his Ministry. Yes: D[ear] C[hristians]: if he was called
by alm[ighty] God to this exalted function, he was to be a man dead to himself, crucified to the World & flesh, zealous for the honour of God, ready
to undertake all things for his Glory & Sacrifice all to accomplish the same:
a man, to whom the salvation of souls becomes more Dear than all the
World can propose, as Ease, health & Life itself. Behold in what consists
this Fidelity of a true Minister of God, & how our Saint became faithful in
all these Points shall, I hope be clearly shown from evident passages of his
Life, wh[ich] I endeavour to lay clearly before you, begging y[ou]r favourable attention.
Ignatius is no sooner called to this high ministry, but he begins immediately to prepare himself properly for it, But what does he do? to put
himself in a condition to follow the vocation of God & to become a proper
Subject for the conversion & Sanctification of Souls? Ignatius at his calling,
was an entier Worldling, without Learning or any other knowledge, besides
that of a Souldier. But now how does he conclude? what does he design?
what does he say? Lord I know your will & willingly consent. I must become a new Man, I must cast off, what I was, to become what you desire.

There is no hope as I am of complying with your adorable Designs. I must change, I must destroy the old Man, and since that can't be done, but by violence, by continual mortification, by an entier Denial of myself, it is by this I'll begin my carrier for y[ou]r Service. These are the sentiments of Ignatius, this his Resolution, & we are all acquainted how he put it in Execution. Let us follow him to Manresa, the 1st Scene of his combats, see him hidden in this Grotto so much renowned for his Penances, abstinences & Fasts. We've heard of 'em a 100 times & can't be ignorant of 'em. He boar a mortal hatred to himself, he allow'd of no other nourishment but Bread and Water, no Bed but the baer ground, Bloody Disciplines & hair cloaths were his daily exercise to repel & beat off all attacks of the Enemy. Yes, he denyd his languid carcass all food & nourishment for eight long Days, yet in this Warfare he is all life, all vigour, his greatest Prudence, as he says himself, was not to regard the Prudence of this World. But why such Rigours? They were to make him faithful to his God, & faithful to his Neighbour. Faithful to God, because he cou'd not labour efficaciously for God's church, unless he began by an utter Destruction of himself; it's in this Light I represent Ignatius to myself coming forth from the Grot[to] of Manresa, having now consumed in the Fire of Mortification & self denial all the remains of the world, the Flesh & Sin, & now presenting himself, like I say, to alm: God, Behold Lord here I am send me, Behold Lord, here I am ready to embrace & execute your Divine Orders. You are in search of one to publish your Commands & make you known, send me; I am not now that Ignatius once in the Court of the Emperor, a slave to the world & all its vanities, all that I was, I've destroy'd, I now think of nothing else, but of hearing your Voice & obeying your commands.

But Ignatius y[ou]r virtue, without knowledge and Learning will ne'er suffice to comply with your vocation. You must be instructd to be able to instruct your Neighbour: Your Zeal, let it be never so sure & fervorous, if it is not governed by a proportionable Learning may prove dangerous to you & cast upon a 1000 Rocks. What therefore, is there to be done? Are you now, at an[11] age, to begin a course of Studies, of whose very Rudiments you are entirely Ignorant: ah D:C: let us here admire the Fidelity of Ignatius. Ignatius has learn'd to be humble,[12] he is generous, he is resolute & that's enough, nothing can come amiss. His virtue, learnt in the grot[to] of Manresa, makes him at the age of 33 begin the lowest class of his studies, to sit on the Bench with children & Infants, to submit to all the School Laws & Rigours, with Patience & assiduously to apply to the hardest difficulties of Grammar. If I consult certain Worldlings on this Resolution of Ignatius, how would they judge of it[13] according to their Worldly Notions, they would call it a Weakness, & low base Spirit, & Folly & Madness. But I can truely tell 'em that Ignatius never preform'd a more heroic action. and why?

Because he never used greater violence with himself to suppress his Worldly Sentiments & overcome the Repugnance of his Nature & haughty Spirit. Here, not like his Divine Master, a child amongst the Doctors, but a man of 33 seatd with the children in a publick School. Jesus Xt rises himself above his age to teach the Doctors, Ignatius debasses himself below himself to receive instructions. Jesus is admired as an Infant, Ignatius is contemned as an ignorant clown, as a foolish idiot. Oh D: C: what a Difference you see in the conduct of the master & the Disciple; But I am affraid, as I may say to you, what Christ said to his Parents in that occasion, don't you know, that it behooves me to be occupied in the things that belong to my Father. This Xt did as an Infant in the middle of the Doctors, this Ignatius did as an illiterate clown amongst the children of the schools and this alone makes Ignatius renew his Fervour in the lowest schools, altho' never so tedious, never so fatiguing; he begs his Bread from Door to Door to sustain himself, he cleans and sweeps the school, he denys no office altho never so minor, never so contemptible, altho lately a noble man at the Court of Spain of your greatest Distinction by his Birth & Empl[o]y[ment]s. But says he, what does it signify to what we are reduced if it is to promote & advance the greater glory of God. Let me be poor, let me be dependant, let me be a slave, let me be of the rank of the most contemptable, only God be honourd & my neighbour sanctify'd. Yes: why should it not cost as much to become a souldier of Jesus Xt, as it does to become a vain empty Wor[ld]ling? Nothing daunted me, to come to the knowledge of the sword, and must I do less to arrive to the knowledge of God & my salvation. Moved with these reflections he redoubles his love & attention, the least negligence he severely punishes on himself. and God supports him & bless[es] his undertaking in so marvelous a manner that it even surpasses our admiration. Scholar as he is, he now commences Master. Inspired from above & govern'd by the Spirit of God: he lays the 1st foundations of that Society, of wh[ich] he was to become founder & Father. Already in the University of Paris he had associated to himself nine companions: illustrious for their Learning, but more so for their Zeal & Piety. He lists 'em under the Banners of Jesus Xt as auxilierys to serve his Church, wh[ich] encreasing from year to year, were in time to spread the Universe over.

But if Ignatius proves faithful in preparing himself to be a proper minister of the Gospel, he is no less so, in the Execution of this Divine office. So judge of this, behold what is his Fervour & the Extent of his Zeal for the Glory of God & the Salvation of Souls. What a vast scene lys open before me; time will never allow me to run thru each particular. I could never lay before you those 1000 particular Examples of his Zeal & charity? I could never recount all he undertook, all he did, all he suffer'd not only for the Glory of god, but for his greater Glory, not only for the Salvation of his

Brethern but for their greatest Perfection. I'll omit that frozen lake into wh[ich] he plunged himself up to the very neck, hoping by that holy strategem to reclaim a harden'd sinner. I'll say nothing of his zealous sermons & the fruits he produced, nor of his care of the sick more to save their souls, than relieve their Bodys, nor of those fatiguing Journeys he took to visit the holy Places of Judea, or to preach the Gospel thro villeages & Burgs. I'll say nothing of his infatigable Industry in laying foundations for Convents, monasteries & collegs. All these things I must pass over in silence, altho' eternal profs of his Fidelity & Zeal for God's honour. And remain on one circumstance of his Life, wh[ich] seems the most of all to redoun'd to his honour & Glory.

I mean, D.C: the institution of the Society of Jesus, whose whole end is the Glory of God & santification of our Neighbour, whose subjects are to aim at nothing else; whose vows, whose whole interest, whose Functions, whose labours & Fatigues ought to have no other End, but the glory of God & the Sanctification of their Neighbour. A Society, not bounded within the Limits of a Province or an Empire, but must carry the glorious Name of Xt thru all Nations, yes the Universe, & preach his Gospel to all Men without Distinction, to the child as well as the advanc'd in Life, to the Poor as well as Rich, to the lowest in Life, as well as the Grandees of the World. A Society, not constrain'd to any one way, but embrasses all means to Glorify God & to help Souls, as by publick Schools, instruction of youth, the knowledge of Humanity, Philosophy & Divinity, Preaching the Word of God, the Direction of Souls, congregations[14] of Piety, Sodalitys of our Lady. A Society, publickly renouncing to all Salerys & Dignitys, in the church, to disengage itself from all Interest, but that of God & Souls bought by Xt's pretious Blood; that exposes itself to all the Miserys of Poverty, to all the horrours of a Loathsome Prison & Goal, & all the terrors of a most cruel Death. A Society, thro' the Mercy of god, from age to age, activated with the same Spirit, for laborers lost & diseased, can substitute others, that inherit their Zeal, that embrase their Labours, undergo their Fatigues, expose 'emselves to the same Dangers, engage the same Enemy, equally sacrifice their Reputation, their Ease & their Lives. . . . Behold, D:C:, what Ignatius has done, I don't say, behold, what Ignatius proposed to himself, what he talked off, what he began, but behold, what he brought to the utmost perfection. It was he, by the Fervour of his Prayer, by supernatural Lights, by a superior Genious, by his invincible Resolutions & undanted Courage; formed the Design of this Society; dictated all its Rules, lay'd out all its Functions, united all its Parts, reduced it to a Body, nurish't it, strenthen'd it, & enabled it to act to the utmost Bourders of the Earth. To say Ignatius is the founder of this Society, is to say in a Word that he was faithful to God & to his Neighbour; for it is to say, that not satisfy'd to Glorify God by himself, he glorify'd him by so many missioners sent thro' the vast Ocean to the farthest Extremitys of the Earth to publish the Gospel & destroy Infidelity, by so many Preachers employ'd the World over to teach the Faithful their Duty & reclaim 'em from their disorders, by so many learned Men as I may say spent in night watches & studies to overthrow heresies & defend Religion, by so many Martyrs, that have lost their lives by the Sword, by Fire, by Cross, or more cruel Torments for the honour of their Faith wh[ich] they have sealed with their Blood, by so many others that have extended their Conquest of souls & the Kingdom of Jesus Xt from Pole to Pole; and he not only still glorifys God in glory where God has crown'd his Labours, but thro' the whole Universe, where his children under his conduct, actuated by his spirit labour to maintain the great Work their Father began, & consecrate their Lives, therewith. For when St. Paul says of Abel & of his offering, I may lawfully here apply it [to] our Saint, sc. "defunctus adhuc loquitur." altho dead, he speakes as yet. Yes, D:C:, Ignatius, dead as he is, yet by his children of the Society of Jesus, he makes his Voice resound the whole World over, it's by those he distributes the celestial Bread of Divine Doctrine to all needy & helpless children: it's by those he penetrates into the wildest Deserts, thro' Hurricans & tempests to bring back the lost sheep of Israel, it's by this Society that so many holy Souls are directed & gouverned, so many Sinners tuch'd & brought to Penance, so many have seen the Light of the Gospel thro' the dark Shades of Idolatry & Paganism. Pardon me, D:C:, & permit me to give that society its due to wh[ich] probably we all owe our Religion & Instructions. But when I thus explain myself, I don't imagine that I aim [to] extol his children, but rather to inhance the Merit & glory of the Father, or rather, still more, the glory of God himself for[15] wh[ich] the Father did & his children ought always to labour & sacrifice their Days & Lives. No, D:C:, I may say you owe nothing to his children, if you please, but if you acknowledge any obligations for your Instructions & the pains his children have taken for your Sanctification & salvation, let 'em abundantly be pay'd unto the Father. For all is one unto the Father, since the children only act by his prescriptions & Rules, by the Spirit he inspires 'em with, & the Means he has left 'em. In fine to speak better, all you owe either to the Father or the children, return acknowledgement to God for it's to God & to God alone that all honour is due.

But notwithstanding all I've said, I must finish with some thing of the greatest Importance on wh[ich] I hope all will make a serious Reflexion. You must know it was Fidelity to alm: God that raised Ignatius to this pitch of Glory. Why D:C: are you not Saints as well as he? Examine well the true cause & reason. Why is Ignatius a man of God & you a worldling? why are all his thoughts of God & yrs on the World? why is he always glorifying his name, & you offending his Divine Majesty. Is it that God desires you not to be saved, that he desires you not to sanctify yourselves in your station

& condition? Or does he refuse you necessary Means? Perhaps indeed you persuade yourself as; to autherize your Cowardice & cloak the Disorders & irregularitys of your Life. Oh D:C: it's a grave Error. You've often heard, & I'll repeat it to you again to take away all Excuses, Providence has so ordained, that in whatsoever Station you are, he allows sufficient Means for every one's sanctification. But then if God is thus faithful to us all, as he was to Ignatius, the queue remains, are we as faithful to God, as was Ignatius? You've a mind God shou'd do all, & cost you nothing. But Ignatius has left us an other Rule, to do all with God. . . . Is this the fidelity of an Ignatius? You neglect yr love of yr Family, you neglect yr children, you see 'em do amiss & remain silent. Ah is this yr Fidelity. You neglect publick prayers in yr Family, you don't instruct yr ignorant children & servants, you scandalous 'em by yr anger & passions, you fly out into bad & undecent expressions in their presence. And this is yr Fidelity? You neglect yr Promeses to Alm. God for humane Respects, you unbecomingly approach the sacraments of the altar, nay perhaps are so far blind as to commit the most outrageous sacraleges, by false confessions & this is yr Fidelity? You pass whole Sundays & holydays in company, perhaps in singing & dancing or some thing worse: and this is yr Fidelity? Surely no one now will be surprised to find they are not Ignatiuses when they see their Fidelity to alm: God compared to his. Be therefore faithful, D:C: that you may hear those Words from your Judge, Come profitable & faithful servants. Because you've been faithful, enter into the joy of the Lord. . . .

On the Good Use of Time

This was apparently one of Mosley's favorite sermons. He notes that he delivered it nine times between 1760 and 1782. The occasion was appropriately New Year's Day, then as now a Holy Day of Obligation. Such a theme was a standard one in the spiritual manuals and sermon collections.

> Quid nobis profuit superbia? aut
> divitiarum iactantia quid contulit
> nobis? Transierunt omnia illa tamquam
> umbra. Sap. 5.v: 8.&9.

> What has Pride availed us, or our
> Riches? All those are gone & passed
> away as a shadow. Words of the Wise-Man
> in the Book of Wisdom. Chap. 5th
> Ver: 8th & 9th.

As it's a Certain Truth that[16] we advance as fast towards death as we advance in age, & perhaps may see an End of our Days, before we see the End of this very (insuing) year; it is of the utmost Importance to make good use of Time, & to labour without intermission to husband it to our advantage.[17] I shall not use[18] long Methods to persuade you; there is nothing I shall say to incomber or perplex, your memory, it is all containd under one single Thought, one single Word[19] of the Wise-Man. It's a Thought, it is a Word applicable[20] to the Dead, either Blessed in Heaven or cursed in Hell. A Thought[21] of such Power with us, that when it is well digested, is sufficient to wean us from[22] the World & all things agreable in it, to detest Sin & all things whatsoever, that ever made us love it, to seek God, in spite of all opposition[23] that may stand in our Way. A Thought[24] of the greatest Force & Significance both to the Just & Sinners. In the Just it excites a firm Hope, & solid Joy, & an unmoveable constancy in the most difficult[25] encounters. In the sinner, it causes fears, frights, horror & chagrin. It is a thought of comfort[26] to the dying just man in the state of Grace, but to the unrepenting sinner a subject[27] of grief & anguish: a Thought[28] which the Wise-Man has inculcated & we shall all remember as long as God is God; in fine it is a serious thought[29] taken from the Words of the Wise-Man, which I've chosen for my Text & for your Entertainment.[30] *Transierunt,* says he, all's gone, all has disappear'd, Like unto a shadow:[31] altho short,[32] it's more efficacious to a thinking Man than all the Eloquence of the greates orators. But, D:C:, be upon your guard, that this[33] *transierunt;* all is past & gone, be of no power with you. You must reflect on all, it means, all is past & gone, weigh it at your Leisure as an affair of the greatest Importance. It's now nigh 6000 years since the creation of the World. and since that time to the present moment, how many men have appear'd on the Theatre of this world, & have now so disappear'd that all we can say of 'em, is *transierunt* they are gone, they have past away. how many things have been said, writ, done & thought off by these great men, how many witty saings, solid Reflexions, learned Discourses, prounounced by 'em. How many Sumptuous Buildings, magnificent Palaces, & stately Structures have been finished by their Hands. How many Balls, magnificent entertainments, publick Rejoicings, & solemn Feasts have been celebrated by the greatest Monarchs. How many Towns been storm'd & capitulated, provinces conquered & subdued, Battles fought, victorys gain'd & Triumphs granted to great Generals & Captains; all these glorious performances where are they now? *Transierunt* they are all past, they've gone, they've disappeared, they are talked off no more. D:C: where is your youth, where are those youthful Days, where are those ten those twenty, those thirty years that have past over your Head? where are all your Words you've said, all your Thoughts you've had, & all the actions you've done, transierunt, they are past & gone. With what comfort do the B[elove]d in Heaven pronounce this word transierunt, all's past, all's over; But with what anguish & regrets do the damn'd in Hell say in their Confinement, transierunt, all's past, all's over. Oh glorious St. Peter where are all those torments you suffer'd for Jesus Christ upon a Cross,[34] St Stephen where are now those Bruses you receiv'd from the Stones wh[ich] at last overpowerd you?[35] oh glorious St. Laurence where are now those burning Coals with wh[ich] you was boild alive? oh great St. Sebastian where are now those arrows, that cruelly pierced your Side? oh glorious Martyrs of Jesus Xt where now are those Prisons, those Racks, those swords, those wheels, those Lions, those Flames, that were the cruel Instruments of all your Torments, Transierunt, they're all past & gone. You great Saints, that left the World, to hide yourselves in a Clositer, or follow'd in the World the most rigourous maxims of the Gospel, what is now become of your penitential Moans & Sighs, your Fasts & Watching,[36] what is become of your Sweat & toil, of your Fatigues your rigourous & innocent Cruelty inflicted upon yourselves, what is become of all your suffering, of all your afflictions that have acquired you the Glory, you profess. Transierunt, they are now all over, they're gone, &[37] past.[38] Emperors, Kings, & Princes where now is all your Glory, your honours, Scepters, Crowns & Kingdoms? where now is all that Pride & those Delights you had from the Possession of 'em? Transierunt, they're past, they're gone, they've disappeared. These unfortunate Wretches will have in their Mouths eternally those dismal Words. It's all past, it's all over with us. But those torments, to which they are now condem'd, will never pass, will never leave 'em. And the remembrance of past Pleasures, which now are all gone & past[39] like unto a shadow, will make 'em continally cry out with lamentable sighs. Transierunt, those pleasures[40] which cost us so much time & so much money have disappeared,[41] yes those very pleasures are now past; which we thought wou'd never pass, & in which we placed all our Happiness & last End. Alas they are now all gone, all past, which made us lose the grace of God, the Glory of Paradise. Yes those pleasures are gone, which were & only now remain the cause of all our miserys & misfortunes, of which we never shall see an End. Transierunt, so they are gone, they are past, they never will appear again.

Thus they deplore their Misfortune after Death, who never refused their Senses anything in time of Life. But D:C:, if you are Wise (or at Least if you have a mind to be so) consider & reflect, that as yet there is time enough left, which is not gone, nor past, which these unfortunate wretches wou'd not look into, till it was to late. Behold all that is, or ever will be in the World. Behold all that ever has been since the Creation, is now gone & past, so all that ever will be, will have the same End, & will pass as all has past before it. Behold what is present passes away like a shadow, & passes

away so fast that in few moments, we may say of the present which you
esteem so much, transierunt, they are likewise all gone & are now no
more.[42] It is of God alone & after him, of the Recompenses prepared for
the Just & of the torments that will punish the Sinner, that we never shall
be able to say, past.[43] You give alms to the poor, you bewail your sins, you
receive an affront for God, you pardon an Injury received from your Enemy,
and of these good actions we never shall be able to say transierunt, they're
gone & past. In fine in[44] the day of Wrath, & the Day of Judgment,[45] when
the Day for labouring is gone & past, or the decisive Sentence of a happily
or miserable Eternity shall be pronounced to all, to the Elect, come ye
Blessed of my Father, & to all the Reprobate Go ye cursed into eternal
Flames: Then will the Elect cry out with Sentiments of the greatest Joy &
Satisfaction. Transierunt all those afflictions we've suffer'd to gain eternal
Joys are now all past & gone. And the Reprobate overwhelm'd with Shame,
Confusion & Dispair, will pitifully cry out, Transierunt, all those pleasures,
which were so delightful in Life, & which are the deplorable Cause of our
everlasting Perdition[46] are now no more, they've gone. they are past away;
ah, D:C:, if this be the End of Pleasures & Delights, let us live that we may
say they are gone, but gone to rise again to our Eternal Comfort. This present time is a pretious present offerd you from Heaven. It is composed of
years, months, weeks, Days & Moments, but dont deceive yrselves, all this
time composed of so many moments, Days, Weeks & months, is yet short,
time is short says St. Paul. It passes like a shadow says the holy Ghost, and
if Time so quickly passes, take care to make such good use of it, that you
may never have any Reason to regrete the loss of it for all Eternity, when
time will be no more. If time passes & your Life with it, take care it passes,
so like unto the People of Israel from the Land of Egypt to the Land of
Promise, or like Jesus Xt "from this World to his Eternal Father" from
Earth to Heaven, from Men to God, from your Place of Banishment to eternal Joys,[47] What, D:C:, must be the Conclusion of all that has been said?
No other than to resolve to quit all affection to Worldly things by the Force
of your Will, which sooner or later you are certainly to quit in Effect. Employ your thoughts on nothing else but what is Eternal; for Fear of setting
your affection upon perishable things, you never run the Risk of perishing
with 'em. Take care not to deffer your Execution of so noble a Design; because remember what the Wise-Man says, the Time of a Man's Life is nothing but a shadow, a short passage from the Womb of our mother to the
Bowels of the Earth, from the Cradle to the Coffin, from Life to Death,
from a moment to an Eternity. those who are gone before us have Experienced my assertion. Those who are to follow, will find it in their Turn: and
we ourselves won't fail in time to know it by fatal Experience. Our Fore-
fathers, transierunt are gone & are no more. It will be said one Day of your

children transierunt they are gone & are no more. And of ourselves the self same will be said; we need not doubt it; & perhaps very soon. God knows, but[48] this very year perhaps this very month, in a few Days; some sooner, some later; some that heard me last year give the same notice as now I give you, are gone & are no more. And probably, now we need not doubt it, some who hear this notice given 'em will be gone & will be no more before the End of this very year. Perhaps, just Soul, it may be you, & perhaps, impenitent sinner, it may be you; as strong, as hearty & as well as you had their Turn[49] last Year, what Security have you to guard against this or the next.[50] In fine before long it will be said of us all, they are gone, they're dead, & are no more. If you are now a Drunkard, perhaps e're long you'll be in Hell, if now a Gamester, perhaps soon a Companion to the Devels, if now a Rake, a Libertine perhaps soon you'll be in eternal Torments: Drunkards, gamesters, Libertines lud & debauched transierunt are gone, are now no more; unless in Hell & torments. They were once as easy & as thoughtless as you. They thought as little of the torments they now suffer, as you think of those you're to suffer perhaps within a year. Be wise, D:C:, by their Example, for Fear you yourselves become an Example to Posterity. This moment is your own, but I can't promise that the next will be in your Power or at your Disposal. One moment longer in your Lives, may bring you the next in Hell, one moment of true & Sincere repentance may insure you God's Mercy & eternal Joys.

My God, we know and acknowledge, that our Time is short, & that everything that we here possess, will pass away like unto a shadow. We've been Silly enough to have so set our Hearts on them, as if the Enjoyment of them, was to have been eternal, but how have we been deceived? Our sinful Pleasures, our criminal Delights, our wicked Companies are all no more, they are like the Flowers of a Day, they flourish in the Morning & decay by Night. How truely have we been told, that it is but for a Moment what delights & pleases our Senses, but that it is eternal, that torments. Thus all that have gone before us, have experienced this truth,[51] & we in our Turn shall find it equally true.[52] Here then before yr alters, Dear God, we acknowledge our Folly, we detest our past silly Pleasures, that are now slipt out of our Hands, & in their Room we find nothing left with us but Sorrow, Chagrin, Remorse of conscience & Despair.[53] Thus seeing our Folly we heartily renounce it for ever. We'll seek in thee & in thy D[ivine]: Law more solid Pleasures & everlasting joys which will never leave us. Thy Love shall be our Study & Care, thy Law shall be our Rule of conduct, & thy Example shall be the object of all our aims & Endeavours, for we know that if we desire to enter into eternal Life, we must keep thy Commandments. Our[54] Follies & Pleasures will certainly pass away, but eternal Life can never pass away. Our Follies are the Desires of Flesh & Blood, eternal Happiness shall be our future aim; Reason, Duty & Religion tell us[55] that this is true Wisdom & will be our only Comfort at the hour of Death, That you may persevere in these sentiments is my hearty wish. It's a Happiness I wish you all in the name of the Father & of the Son & holy Ghost. Amen.

NOTES

1. "Response to Patrick Smyth," [1789], in Thomas O'Brien Hanley, S.J., ed., *The John Carroll Papers* (Notre Dame, 1976), I, 338.

2. Georgetown University Special Collections. Mosley Papers.

3. These letters to his sister Helen were all addressed to "Mrs. Dunn Junior at Bladon, near New-Castle upon Tyne, Northumberland."

4. The Poor Clare community at Gravelines in the Netherlands, established in 1608.

5. Mosley's brother, Michael, was also a Jesuit, and in 1760 chaplain to the Acton family at Aldenham in Shropshire.

6. Mosley is suggesting that his brother would surely prefer that he accomplish much in a short time rather than be an eternal adolescent or aged scoundrel.

7. "I am not worthy of such an honor."

8. "not at the same pace."

9. Mosley's mission stretched from the head of the Chester River to Cape Charles. It included the entire Delmarva Peninsula, with the exception of Cecil and Kent counties in Maryland.

10. GUSC, American Catholic Sermon Collection.

11. Crossed out: "yr."

12. Crossed out: "is humble."

13. Crossed out: "this resolution."

14. Crossed out: "assemblies."

15. Crossed out: "towards."

16. Crossed out: "because."

17. Crossed out: "for our salvation."

18. Crossed out: "Dont fear those."

19. Crossed out: "under the signification of one Word."

20. Crossed out: "to apply."

21. Crossed out: "a Word."

22. Crossed out: "make us love."

23. Crossed out: "things."

24. Crossed out: "a Word."

25. Crossed out: "hard."

26. Crossed out: "word of wrath."

27. Crossed out: "word."

28. Crossed out: "Word."

29. Crossed out: "Word."

30. Crossed out: "upon w[hic]h we Mortals must meditate with [illegible].

But that I may not keep you any longer in suspence, it's the Word used by the Wise-Man, wh I've taken for my text.''

31. Crossed out: ''a Word of the greatest force & signification.''

32. Crossed out: ''as it is.''

33. Crossed out: ''that.''

34. Crossed out: ''O great.''

35. Crossed out: ''that were flung at you.''

36. Crossed out: ''yr long prayers continued even half the Night.''

37. Crossed out: ''they.''

38. Crossed out: ''But you unfortunate victims of Hell, what is become of yr Joys, yr abundance, & all yr sinful pleasures? Heliogabole where are all yr Delights? Sardanapole where are all yr Pleasures? Augustus, the greatest Emperor, where now are all yr Trophies? Alexander where now are all yr conquests? Croesus where now are all yr Riches?''

39. Crossed out: ''away.''

40. Crossed out: ''are gone.''

41. Crossed out: ''They are gone.''

42. Crossed out: ''past.''

43. Crossed out: ''Transierunt, they are gone & past.''

44. Crossed out: ''when.''

45. Crossed out: ''is past.''

46. Crossed out: ''(wh will never pass).''

47. Crossed out: ''& not from Earth to Hell, from Men to Divels, from a World of Miserys to Eternal Torments.''

48. Crossed out: ''perhaps.''

49. Crossed out: ''died.''

50. Crossed out: ''why may you not come to dy also.''

51. Crossed out: ''found it true.''

52. Crossed out: ''Dr. God.''

53. Crossed out: ''Dr. God.''

54. Crossed out: ''my'' here and in other places after this where ''our'' appears.

55. Crossed out: ''me.''

IV

JOHN CARROLL AND ENLIGHTENED
CATHOLICISM

*A native of Maryland, Carroll (1735–1815) left America as a teenager in
1748 to study at St. Omers. Five years later he entered the Society of Jesus.
He likely would have spent the rest of his life in Flanders where he taught
at the colleges in Liège and Bruges, had it not been for the suppression of
the Society. How traumatic that dissolution was for Carroll, who by chance
found himself in Rome as the events built to a climax, the following letters
make clear enough. That he was apparently ready to request a return to
America on the eve of the Suppression shows how alienated he had been
by his Roman experience. When events overtook his deliberations in the
fall of 1773 in the brutal ouster of Carroll and his brethren from Liège College, he sailed for Maryland in the spring of 1774.*

LETTERS ON THE SUPPRESSION
OF THE SOCIETY OF JESUS

To Thomas Ellerker[1]

Rome Oct. 26–1772[2]

My dear Sr.   I suppose this will find you returned from England, tho
you have not yet given me any account of it. We are just arived at Rome,
viz: the 22d. of this month. My intention was to proceed the next day for
Naples before any suspicion could be formed of my character here; but certain accidents will detain us here till the 27th. I keep a close incog[nito].
during this time, not going to any of our houses. I called privately to see
Thorpe & Hothersall[3]; but they were both in yr. country: so that having had
no manner of communication with any J[esui]t, I can send you no news

concerning the affairs of the Soc[iet]y. I heard it said in some company, that such Sp[anish]: Jts, as being Europeans would not secularize themselves, would be obliged to settle in Majorca: the natives of America to be fixed in the Canaries. This will be a saving to Spain of a great sum of money, which is every year sent out of the country. . . . The immediate cause of the suppression of the Irish College [here] was a petition presented by the alumni to return to the Jts Schools. Cardl Marefoschi[4] foamed with wrath, & violently insisted on the popes taking the step, which ensued. . . .

To Thomas Ellerker

Jan 23–1772 [1773]

My dear Sir   Our catastrophe is near at hand, if we must trust to present appearances, & talk of Rome. The intelligence, which was talked of some time ago, importing that Spain had acceded at length to the Pope's plan, is greatly confirmed by universal persuasion at present; and I am assured that some of our best friends in the Sacred College, tho' not admitted to state secrets, yet now look upon the determination of our fate as entirely certain. All this notwithstanding, I am far from regarding this intelligence as infallible: to be sure, we have great reason to fear it to be true; but we have been alarmed so often during the present Pontificate with like reports, and the date of our destruction has been fixed so often without anything coming of it, that I hope this will have the same issue. Our friends however hope in nothing but the interposition of providence: and indeed by the attack made against the sacred heart, & so much encouraged here, the cause of J[esus].C[hrist]. has been so closely connected with ours, that this cannot fail of giving much confidence under the present dreadful appearances. Another very late fact may corroborate the idea you have probably formed of the spirit of the times here. On the feast of the chair of S. Peter, it is customary for a graduate of the Sapienza to make a discourse before the pope. The young man, who made it this year, proved the truth of the doctrine of the Rom: See from the constant succession of its pastors, & having occasion to introduce the mention of heresies springing from the poisoned minds of their founders, he said Ante Nestorium non fuere Nestoriani, ante Lutherum, Lutherani &c, nec *ante Jansenium fuere Jansenistae.*[5] You will not believe that at Rome this was looked upon as highly blameable, & I was astonished beyond measure, when I heared the poor ignorant Child Gastaldi, who hears all the Cardl York's[6] family discourse, wondering how the orator came to rank Jansenius amongst the sectaries, or Jansenism amongst the heresies. I am assured likewise that when printed copies of the discourse were afterwards carried to the Cardls according to custom, Marefoschi refused taking his, saying he would not have it because Jansenius [was] made in it the figure of an archheretik. . . .

To Thomas Ellerker

Feb. 3–1773

My dear Fr   You Liegois are sad correspondents. I dare say you are curious to hear news, and yet give no encouragement to your friends to write. Yet you have many particularities to communicate to us at this distance, which would give some relief to the gloom, which overspreads us here at Rome. The report of an agreement being at length settled with Spain has subsisted now so long, that it gains very much credibility. The articles of it are said to be, 1o., depriving the Jesuits of their general. 2o. subjecting them to the ordinaries, as a congregation of priests. 3o. Forbidding them (I suppose those of the Ecclesiastical State) to admit any supplies into their body. 4. Avignon to be restored. 5. The town of Aquila with its dependenceis to be ceded to the pope in lieu of Benevento. 6. Castro & Ronciglione to be recognised formally as belonging to the Holy See. This agreement with Spain will be published, 'tis said, about Easter. It is likewise stipulated (tho not expressed in the paper which circulates about Rome) that the Jesuits are all to be sent at least 20 miles from hence, that they may not keep up a spirit of fanaticism and blind zeal amongst the cardinals and prelates.
    . . . Another very serious affair here is, that the presses swarm with writings against the devotion to the sacred heart. What a revolution of ideas do all these proceedings produce in a mind accustomed to regard this city as the seat of Religion, and the bulwark against the incroachments of irreligion and impiety? Some of the most understanding as well as virtuous men here are persuaded entirely that the Jts will be expelled [from] Rome, that they will lose the Roman College, Jesu, &c, but still that no essential alteration will be made in the Institute: but for the ground of their hopes, they can only alledge their trust in providence. . . .

To Daniel Carroll[7]

Bruges, September 11, 1773[8]

. . . After spending part of the autumn of 1772 at Naples, and its environs, we returned to pass the winter at Rome, where I stayed till near the end of March, from thence came to Florence, Genoa, Tunis, Lyons, Paris, and so to Liege and Bruges. I was willing to accept of the vacant post of prefect of the sodality here . . . that I might enjoy some retirement, and consider well in the presence of God the disposition I found myself in of going to join my relatives in Maryland, and in case that disposition continues, to get out next spring. But now all room for deliberation seems to be over. The enemies of the society, and above all the unrelenting perseverance of the Spanish and Portuguese Ministries, with the passiveness of the court of Vienna, has at length obtained their ends: and our so long persecuted, and I must add, holy society is no more. God's holy will be done, and may his name be blessed forever and ever! This fatal stroke was struck on the 21st of July, but was kept secret at Rome till the 16th of August, and was only made known to us on the 5th of September. I am not, and perhaps never shall be, recovered from the shock of this dreadful intelligence. The greatest blessing which in my estimation I could receive from God, would be immediate death: but if he deny me this, may his holy and adorable designs on me be wholly fulfilled. Is it possible that Divine Providence should permit to such an end, a body wholly devoted, and I will still aver, with the most disinterested charity, in procuring every comfort and advantage to their neighbors, whether by preaching, teaching, catechizing, missions, visitng hospitals, prisons, and every other function of spiritual and corporal mercy? Such I have beheld it, in every part of my travels, the first of all ecclesiatical bodies in the esteem and confidence of the faithful, and certainly the most laborious. What will become of our flourishing congregations with you, and those cultivated by the German fathers?[9] These reflections crowd so fast upon me that I almost lose my senses. But I will endeavor to suppress them for a few moments. You see that I am now my own master, and left to my own direction. In returning to Maryland I shall have the comfort of not only being with you, but of being farther out of the reach of scandal and defamation, and removed from the scenes of distress of many of my dearest friends, whom God knows, I shall not be able to relieve. I shall therefore most certainly sail for Maryland early next spring, if I possibly can.

SERMONS

[The Christian and the World][10]

Carroll's continuing use of the Jesuit motto at the head of his sermons was no mere inertia but a symbol of the persistent influence of Ignatian principles upon him. The world is not to be shunned but transformed into God's kingdom by men and women guided by the Ignatian spirituality of ordered affections. One of Carroll's recurring images for the Church is the Mystical Body of Christ. In the republic of the Spirit Christian "projectors" build up the body of believers by their actions in the world.

Ad majorem Dei gloriam
*Love not the world, nor the things which are in the world: if any man loves
the world, the charity of the Father is not in him.* 1 John 2:15.

We cannot open the gospel, without finding in every page the sentence
of reprobation pronounced by our B[lesse]d Lord against the world. Its doctrines and maxims are placed continually in opposition to those of eternal
wisdom and holiness: its conduct is represented as subversive of that worship of God in spirit and truth, which is essential to real religion. *Whosoever,* says St. James, will be a friend of this world, *becometh an enemy
of God.* James 4. *The world hates me* (these are the words of our Bd. Lord),
because I give testimony, that its works are evil. John 7. *If any man love
the world, the charity of the F[athe]r is not in him.* 1 John 2.v.15. When
we were made members of[11] Christ's mystical body, that is, when we were
incorporated into his church by the regenerating waters of baptism, we were
prepared for this sublime dignity by renouncing the world and all its pomps.
From which it results, that we are bound to keep in abhorrence the world,
spoken of in these & other passages of holy writ,[12] and in our baptismal
vows—But tho you have often heard this doctrine inculcated[13] by inspired
writers and the ministers of religion, yet many are at a loss to understand
what that world is,[14] so reprobated by J. Christ; or if understood, what precautions should be used to guard ourselves against being fascinated by its
love, & deluded by its errors. To render therefore this[15] discourse on the
dangers of the world useful & salutary to you, my Dr. B., I will endeavour[16]
in the first place to trace its character and distinguishing features that you
may see the evil which you are bound to avoid, and 2ly to assign the means
& precautions to be used that you may never[17] be misled by its errors, or
seduced by[18] the deceitfulness of its pretended enjoyments.

What then is this world so hateful to Christ, & represented as so fatal
to mankind? Surely not the material frame of this universe, of which God
is the author, & in which we discover so many evidences of his Almighty
power, and infinite beneficence: nor does this world so severely reproved
consist of all[19] men, who live in it; for even God's best & chosen servants
have here their earthly habitation. No, my Xtian Brethren, these are not the
objects of the condemnation pronounced by our divine Lord & Master: But
his curses are uttered 1st against the seductions, which[20] continually flatter
& strengthen our intemperate[21] passions; 2ly against those immoral maxims, which pervert & lead the understanding far from the paths of truth; &
3ly against those irreligious[22] &[23] imposing examples, which spread the
contagion of impiety, and impress the sanction of authority & prescription
on the boldest violations of the law and the Gospel. Such is the world, which
is at enmity with God.

I say in the first place, that whatever tends to flatter & strengthen, instead of moderating & governing our intemperate passions, appertains to that sinful world already spoken of. . . .

[Independence of Church in America][24]

During his episcopacy parishes from Boston to Charleston experienced factionalism. This sermon may possibly have been given to the Boston congregation in May of 1791, when Carroll visited the city to reconcile the ethnically divided Catholics.

God has visited you in particular by a signal instance of his mercy in removing the obstacles which heretofore cramped the free exercise of our religious functions. Our meeting together in this place to perform our public worship; that cross, the signal of our faith and monument of its triumphs over the powers of idolatry & infidelity; that altar, erected to perpetuate the great sacrifice of the law of grace, and continued oblation of Xts body & blood, as a propitiation for sin; these, Dr. Brethren, are objects calculated to renew the memory of events, in which is displayed the eternal wisdom,[25] reaching from end to end, embracing all space and ages under its comprehensive arrangements, and harmoniously disposing all things. In the events, to which I allude, they, who attribute nothing in the affairs of mankind to the government of providence, will only discover the result of human counsels & passions; but they, whose enlightened faith[26] beholds in the history of mankind the traces of a divine and overruling wisdom, will acknowledge the power of God continually exerted for the preservation of religion. We particularly, Dr. Brethren, must feel a tender sentiment of gratitude towards the bestower of every good gift for the favours, we now enjoy, whenever we recall to our remembrance the vicissitudes, which have filled up the destinies of our Church since her first establishment by her head and founder Christ Jesus, down to this present day. Divine providence has so directed the course of human affairs; the Holy Ghost has so worked upon & tutored the minds of men, that now, agreeably to the dictates of our own consciences, we may sing canticles of praise to the Lord, in a country no longer foreign or unfriendly to us, but in a country now become our own, & taking us into her protection. In return for so great a blessing, your first duty was, and I trust, that you forgot it not, to render to Alm: God the tribute of thankfulness due, above all to Him; and next, to bear in your hearts gratitude, respect & veneration for them, whose benevolence was the instrument of Gods favour & mercy towards us. Let your earnest[27] applications be addressed to the throne of grace, that every blessing, temporal & eternal, may descend on your fellow citizens, your Brethren in J. Christ. Be sollicitous to extend, by your example and encouragement, the prevalence of Xtian

virtues; to recommend your religion by the innocence of your manners &
the sanctity of yr. lives, and especially by cultivating the first of Xtain duties, that, which is dearest to our B[lesse]d and charitable Redeemer, a spirit
of peacefulness, & mutual love, one for the other. Your particular circumstances call upon you for uncommon watchfulness over yourselves, and unusual exertions in all the exercises of a Xtian life. The impressions made
by your conduct will be lasting impressions; and the opinion, favorable or
unfavourable to our holy religion, which shall result from observing your
manners, will have consequences extending down to the remotest times. I
cannot therefore but lament, that some untoward circumstances have disturbed that tranquillity & harmony, the preservation of which[28] would have
encreased[29] your happiness & been singularly[30] advantageous to the promotion of piety and truth. Of the causes and circumstances of past misun-
derstandings I wish to be entirely silent; and may the memory of them never
be revived. May the blessed spirit be shed into your hearts, that divine
spirit, which drew & held the first Xtians together in the bonds of perfect
unity. They buried all distinctions of birth and Country in the happy & comfortable character of disciples of Jesus. Of Medes of Parthians, of Jews &
Proselytes, of Elamites & the natives of Mesopotamia it was said, that their
heart was one, and their soul was one. To this heavenly disposition of mind
and affection God now calls you. J.C., the Prince of peace, sollicits you by
his grace to forego all jealousies and contentions; and each one to have no
other views in the service of God, but the advancement of his glory, & the
salvation of his own, & every one of his neighbours souls.

    Thus will you correspond with the visitation of mercy, of which I have
spoken.

    Again, God has visited us[31] by affliction, by poverty, by infirmity, &c.
In time of prosperity, we turned our backs to him, forgetting our continual
dependence &c.

Confess Our Religion Exteriorly[32]

*If the credibility of religion in America depended on the tests of reason and
experience, Catholics assumed a great responsibility for their public behavior. For Carroll religion in a republic could never be a private affair. In
this instruction he shows the importance of Catholics making "a just and
reasonable homage" to their religion by their actions.*

Credidit ejus et domus ejus tota—He himself and all his family believed—
S. John c.4

    The Gospel proposes to us this day the example of the master of a fam-
ily, who being moved by the miracle, which our divine Redeemer had

worked in his favor, embraced the faith of Jesus, & brought his whole family to the same resolution. He did not effect this by using violence, or drawing from them a forced confession; in matters of faith everything must be free & voluntary; and God would reject a worship in which the heart had no share. If then this happy family became attached to the doctrine of J. Xt, it was because they were encouraged by the example of their chief, & indeed thereunto by the weight of his reasoning, his prudent advice and salutary remonstrances,[33] For these undoubtedly conveyed to them an instruction that enlightened & convinced them. They were the outward[34] means[35] which God employed,[36] whilst he inwardly acted on their hearts & diffused in their souls[37] the rays of his heavenly light. If the master of the family had not believed, or had kept his belief[38] smothered in his own breast, the rest of his household[39] would have remained perhaps for ever in the darkness of infidelity: but because he[40] contented not himself with inwardly believing, but both in words & actions publickly professed & recommended his faith in J. Xt. by his virtuous life & good example, he became next to[41] God the cause of the conversion of all the rest. Now Dr. Xtians it is this holy zeal which I wish to enkindle in your hearts;[42] that your lives corresponding with the purity of your faith & sanctity of it the innumerable scandals may be prevented, which hurt and discredit our Religion. We are under a natural & indispensable obligation of honouring it, as we are of honouring Alm: God: for God is our last end, to which we are obliged to refer our lives & actions; & Religion is the means which connects and unites us with our end; as it is therefore impossible to arrive at[43] the end, without embracing the means of coming to it;[44] so it is impossible to honour God without honouring Religion. This is the noble zeal, which can ever animate us, & that to which we must be the most invariably engaged, for to honour God, which can only be done thro' the mean of Religion is the first & principal of all duties.[45] The conjugal alliances,[46] the duty of children to their parents, the ties of gratitude[47] considered merely as the dictates of reason, are all of them the foundation of strict obligations; but[48] these are of an inferior order[49] to the important[50] obligations of Religion[51] w[hi]ch result originally from our entire dependence on God, as our 1st beginning and last end, qualities which we, as Xtians, must acknowledge it [sic] immediately, from those qualities wch. Religion derives from its Divine Author, truth & holiness: truth in doctrine, & holiness in its preceptial morality. From which I draw the two consequences, which shall divide the discourse. The first; our Religion is true; therefore we must honour it by the profession of our faith: second; our Religion is holy, therefore we must honour it by the sanctity of our lives.

To acquire Xtian righteousness and salvation two things are necessary, to believe with the heart and outwardly to profess our beliefs.[52] For with the heart, says the Apostle, we believe unto justice; but with the mouth confession is made unto Salvation. Rom. c.10. It is therefore the essential duty of every Christian to honour his Religion by subjecting[53] his understanding to its doctrines & confessing them openly, when the interests of truth require it. It was by complying with this twofold duty, that the first Xtians contributed so much not only to the honour, but the propagation of our holy Religion. When, after the passion of our Saviour & the first spreading of his Gospel, all the powers of earth combined to persecute it, & exert the utmost rage of cruelty & torment against its followers, what arms did they oppose to the violence of its enemeies? No others, Dr. Christians, but the arms of an inward steady faith, & a generous open profession of their belief. These, joined to the efficacy of a virtuous life, brought at length their persecutors themselves to respect & then to embrace doctrines, which could raise men to such invincible fortitude. These[54] were the effects of the glorious testimony they bore to the truth of their Religion. The times of persecution are now no more:[55] Thru Gods mercy, you are not now liable to be carried before Pagan tribunals to be punished for the profession of Xtianity. But if you have not an opportunity of giving this testimony to your Religion, there are still remaining many occasions of honouring it, less splendid, but perhaps not much less difficult, & meritorious than those of the primitive martyrs of Gods church: and it happens, by neglecting those[56] occasions of paying[57] a just and reasonable homage to your Religion, that you discredit & dishonour it.

For when it pleased God to institute a Religion here on earth he surely did not intend that it should remain hidden in darkness & sequestered from the eyes of mankind. As it is[58] to serve to glorify him, it cannot be sufficient for it to remain shut up in the secret of mens hearts: it must be visible & by its splendor contribute to raise in us ideas worthy of the greatness of the master to whom it subjects us, & proposes as the object of our worship. For this purpose were ordained the publick ceremonies of Religion; the solemn celebration of our august misteries;[59] & in a word all the outward duties which accompany the service of God. If then we purpose merely to confine ourselves to a pretended Religion of the heart;[60] without drawing any outward appearances of it, we betray a disposition[61] so severely condemned by J. Xt in these remarkable words (Luke 9.26.) He that is ashamed of me, & of my words, of him likewise will the son of God be ashamed, him will he disavow on the great day of judgment, in the presence of his Fr. and the angels, in the face of heaven and earth.

But the evil proceeds farther by our withholding from God our publick & apparent testimony to his holy Religion; & we transgress another important obligation, namely that of the example which every believer owes to the Society of which he is a member. For we are all but one body in

Christ, & that which strengthens & gives vigor to this mystical body, is the common edification mutually given & received, and resulting from the outward functions of Religion, which make the greater impression, as we are naturally more encouraged to imitate what we see. But if, on the other hand, this[62] outward worship begins to be neglected, all languishes with it: the idea of Religion itself begins to fade away in our minds; impiety[63] avails itself of this neglect[64] & introduces not only a disgust, but even a contempt of all publick & every private worship. If the seats fall into disuse; if attendance on mass is failing &c—if [unintelligible]. . . .

From hence may be concluded how important the duty is, to which I now exhort you, the duty of honouring your Religion. A duty extending itself to all of us, but particularly to Parents; to the Masters of families, and those who by their talents or any accidental circumstances have acquired a weight & influence amongst their neighbours & acquaintance. Their example, a word from them will often have more efficacy, than all the endeavours of the ministers of God's church to confirm[65] their children, their serv[an]ts, their acquaintances in a zealous regard to the divine worship. For when we announce the great truths of religion many of you consider all we say more as the duty of our office &c. The Royal prophet comprehended this important duty when he said, I believed; therefore did I speak—ps. 115—I did not seek thro a cowardly condescension to be silent & dissemble, when Gods honour required of me to bear[66] testimony to truth, & vindicate his dispensations from the blasphemies of ignorance & impiety; I believed, therefore did I speak.

Such was the fidelity of this holy King. But what on the contrary is the general behaviour of Xtians? would to God I were able to lay before[67] your eyes the full extent & fatal consequences of it! Instead of honouring our faith by professing it according to the rules of a holy and unspotted Religion, we dishonour Xtianity[68] by the scandalous excess of barefaced and avowed irreligion[69] or a cold indifference & mean submission to human respect in matters relating to the service of God.

Let[70] each one here examine himself whether he does not endeavour to bring disrepute on practices of piety, and[71] aim at applause & a certain dishonorable renown by a false display of[72] wit, or indications of a mind superior to what he thinks vulgar prejudices. Do you[73] not affect to ridicule fervent & tender conscienced[74] Xtians; & thereby[75] prevent the weak & irresolute from pursuing the ways of[76] piety? Do you not endeavour[77] to bring into contempt the ministers of the Gospel & counteract their services for the promotion of Gods hon[ou]r[78] by their ministry? Do you not despise openly[79] the religious offices[80] of the church, as founded on[81] credulity, ignorance & superstition; & does not this turn to the prejudice of the Church itself, w[hi]ch authorizes them? Do you not ridicule[82] the frequentation of the Sacraments, and do not thereby those fountains of grace & salutary remedies for sin become neglected?

You will observe, Dr. Xtians, that the scandals I here speak of, are only those which tend to the prejudice & dishonour of Religion & many remain to be added to the catalogue I have just begun. For what must I call that rashness so common & yet so unpardonable, with which persons destitute of all sacred knowledge . . .

[Necessity of Revelation][83]

Infidelity, the denial of the necessity of revelation, was the bête noire *of orthodox Christians, both in Europe and America, in the wake of the radical claims about human autonomy and perfectibility emerging from the French Revolution. Carroll, who condemned Voltaire and Rousseau as much as any New England Calvinist, makes his case in this sermon for a Christian order in which faith saves reason from itself.*

Ad Majorem Dei Gloriam
Moses indeed said: a prophet shall the Lord your God raise up unto you out of your brethren, like unto me: him you shall hear, according to all things whatsoever he shall speak to you; and it shall be, that every soul that shall not hear that prophet, shall be destroyed from among the people.— Acts iii.22, et seq.

Hitherto the chief object of those religious instructions, which it has been my duty to deliver to you, dear brethren, was to imprint deeply in your minds the principles, and to recommend to your esteem, love and practice, the precepts of christian morality. Little has been said by me, to convince you of the truth of your divine religion; because I hoped and thought that all, or very nearly all of you, not only professed outwardly, but likewise inwardly believed the doctrines of the Christian Catholic Church. With this conviction on my mind, when any deviated unfortunately into the ways of sinfulness, I imputed their transgressions to human frailty, and ungoverned passions, and not to the disastrous lessons of infidelity. But shall I now disclose my fears, and openly express the suspicions laboring in my breast? The last time of discoursing to you from this place, my subject led me to make a few observations on the imperfection of the human understanding, and its insufficiency to guide us, not only in all points concerning the doctrines and precepts of religion, but even in those which form, as it were, the very elements and first principles of faith and morality. Reflecting farther on that subject, I have thought it advisable and likely to produce many beneficial effects, to treat it more particularly, that you may be more convinced of the imperfections of the human understanding, and the need it has of being informed and enlightened by the splendor of divine revelation. For I cannot dissemble my fears, that many of my hearers are intoxicated with that spirit of presumptive infidelity, which inspires a daring confidence in themselves, and a bold assurance that they need no other direction besides that which their own reason suggests to them. After seeing with anxiety and grief, that the many powerful means employed by God's merciful Providence (over you) are far from having produced an universal reformation, or begotten an attention so general, and such a solicitude for salvation, as your best interests require; may I not reasonably fear, that the minds of some are poisoned with error, and have imbibed the doctrines of irreligion, especially when I consider the close alliance subsisting between licentiousness of manners, and a contemptuous disregard for the most sacred institutions, derived mediately or immediately from the revealed word of god; when daring unbelievers by advancing propositions, more blasphemous, if possible, than they are extravagant, assume in society a preponderence and authority, of which they avail themselves, to infuse into others an impious ambition of becoming accomplices in their guilt? What ever effect these vain and ostentatious enemies of truth and morality may have produced in you, it cannot be amiss to put you on your guard against the shafts of their profaneness and impiety. I therefore in my text address you, in the language adopted by the prince of the apostles, St. Peter, when in the very birth of christianity, he explained to the Jews the evidences of its truth. He reminds them, that their own legislator Moses, bore testimony in favor of Jesus Christ, of whom it was foretold in the law, that he should be endowed with the powers and all means necessary for authenticating his divine commission, to teach and reform mankind, that it should be the duty of all *to hear him in the things, whatever he should speak to them; and that every soul refusing to hear him should be destroyed.* These are momentous points, and highly deserving your utmost attention; for unless you be intimately convinced of the existence of religion, and your obligation to believe it, and submit to its laws, the lessons of morality can have no hold on your hearts. I purpose, therefore, with God's assistance, to prove that divine revelation is necessary to make known to mankind, with sufficient clearness, and establish upon sufficient authority, even some of the first principles of the law of nature, and secondly, that the law of nature, as far as it is discoverable by the powers of human reason alone, leaves us ignorant of, and uncertain in many points of our duty to God, on which our happiness essentially depends. These propositions being proved, the result must be this: if a Divine revelation be necessary for purposes so highly important, to deny that God has favored mankind with it, is an impious denial of his goodness and sincere good will to bestow happiness on his rational creatures, the works of his own hands. True religion lays a perpetual restraint on every inordinate passion, and inflexibly condemns all injustice, pride, oppression and intemperate sensualities. This is the cause of the opposition it meets with, and of the hatred with which it has been calumniated and insulted in every age and country, by men abandoned to their lusts, and puffed up with pride and a vain conceit of the eminence of their own understandings. Various are their devices to free themselves from the yoke, the restraints and the terrors imposed on them by religion. Sometimes they attempt to discard it altogether by impiously denying the existence of that supreme Being, who is its only author and object. But the language of these infidels is regarded by the royal prophet, as proceeding not so much from the persuasion of their minds, as the corruption of their hearts, and from the folly and blindness generated by shameful and disorderly lusts and passions. The *fool,* as it is expressed by the royal prophet, *said in his heart, there is no God.*

Other enemies of religion, equally impatient of its control over their haughty minds and unruly desires, suggest different means of withdrawing themselves from a subjection to its precepts. Instead of denying that we know any thing of God and his perfections, of our obligations to honor him, and of our relative duties to our fellow-creatures, they pretend on the contrary, that we know every thing necessary in these respects, by the exercise alone of those natural faculties and that portion of reason, which are granted to every man; that by employing these, we may learn the few principles to which they reduce all religion, and which, therefore, is called *natural religion.* Of this they proclaim the sufficiency for all the purposes of worship and morality; they celebrate its praises, and set themselves up for its most zealous advocates and champions; and under this mask, they insinuate the poison of their tenets into incautious minds. For while they extol the merit and dignity of natural religion, their zeal and malicious purpose is, to inculcate a persuasion that any other manifestation of god's being and providence, any other injunctions of his will, are useless and unnecessary, consequently that there is no revealed religion, and that all pretensions to it are false and interested impositions. After enumerating the few articles comprehended in this all-sufficient religion, *behold,* says one of the principals of this sect (Rousseau) *the only true religion, which is not liable to be preverted by impiety or fanaticism. Besides this, every thing else is foreign to us.*

This is that first capital error against which, with the Divine Assistance, I am to warn you this day.

Allowing then to infidelity more advantages than she has a right to claim, I will suppose for the present (though this will be proved false in the sequel of our enquiries,) that the only principles of knowledge and morality necessary to our happiness are these: that there is a Supreme Being, the arbiter and disposer of all human things, who commands justice, truth and mutual love of one for the other; and that there is a state of existence after this life, in which the Supreme Being will dispense rewards and punishments, according to each man's deserts. Religion cannot surely be reduced into a narrower compass than this, and with respect to the necessity of believing these articles, St. Paul agrees with the enemies of revelation. But they think and assert that these points are sufficiently known and enforced by the natural lights of reason alone; whereas the apostle teaches, and you, my dear brethren, will be convinced, I hope, that unless the additional authority of God's word come in aid of the weakness of our understandings, mankind, in general, cannot acquire such a certainty of these fundamental articles of religion, as will be sufficient to insure their obedience and support their hopes.

I am far from deprecating that precious gift of God, human reason; or from asserting, that it must always be involved in error and uncertainty. But it is so liable to be blinded by passion, to be warped by prejudices, to be bewildered by the subtleties and contradictions amongst mankind, that it cannot teach with sufficient evidence, or prescribe with sufficient authority the necessary truths and duties just now enumerated. The proofs of this are to be found in the weaknesses, the passions, and the history of mankind; for though we should grant that some, endowed with superior talents, and favored with the advantages of leisure and education, are able to discover the existence, unity, power and wisdom of god; his providential superintendence over the works of his creation, and the convincing reasons for believing in a future state of rewards and punishments, yet is it not evident at the same time, that, comparatively speaking, few will be able to investigate these important truths? and consequently that with respect to all others, that is, to the great bulk of mankind, their reason will be a most defective guide? For many things concur to render them incapable of and unfit for that application of mind, without which the very fundamental points of religion and morality, cannot be investigated and understood sufficiently, to command our belief and practice. Many are incapable through bodily indisposition, many more are rendered so by the necessity of providing for the subsistence of their families, and by unavoidable occupations incident to their conditions of life, and have neither time nor opportunity to make those deep researches, without which they must remain ignorant, in a great degree, of the things most needful to be known, respecting God, their own duties and the end of their creation. I mention no other obstacles, to prevent the researches and discoveries of the human understanding when left to its own natural powers, besides these, which extend to so large a portion of mankind, as evidently to demonstrate the necessity of other means of information, than those of reason alone. Can any judicious and reflecting mind persuade itself, that the multitude, who have to struggle with these obstacles, whose progress in knowledge must be retarded by them at every step, will be able to discover sufficiently, not only the existence, but the nature and providence of God, and our accountability to him?

A further proof of the necessity of a superior direction is this: that these comparatively few persons, to whom leisure, education and supereminent talents, are not wanting to explore the essential truths of natural religion, cannot nevertheless succeed in their enquiries, without much and long investigation; during the whole period of which, as their understanding is in a perpetual state of fluctuation, so their moral conduct must be without any invariable rule and direction. For in the first place, even the brightest and most penetrating geniuses, must meditate long on God's nature and attributes; on the qualities of the human soul; on the powers of our mind, on the differences of virtue and vice, and the future condition of the good and wicked, before they can be fully satisfied (if ever they are satisfied) of the truth of their speculations. In the meantime, that is, during a great part of their lives, they would be floating on the waves of doubt and uncertainty, without sufficient motives to cherish virtue or fly from vice, unless God enlightened them, and by his divine revelation, compensated the imperfections and slow progress of human reason.

Again; no time of life requires to be governed and restrained by fixed and indubitable principles and precepts, so much as that of our youthful years, when all our passions are in a state of ferment, and agitated by the tempests of most boisterous and tumultuous desires. Is this period of our existence adapted to the cool, unbiassed and elaborate enquiries and meditation, necessary to discover and demonstrate the essential truths of natural religion? Experience teaches on the contrary, that however favorable the season of youth may be to the cultivation of those sciences and those literary pursuits, which please and embellish the imagination, it is nevertheless the most unfit for the study of that sacred morality, that divine philosophy which requires stability of thought and maturity of reflection. To gain their entire belief, and obtain their obedience, truth must be manifested, and come recommended to them by an irrefragable, a much higher authority, and more persuasive influence than the dubious and controverted opinions of men, distrustful themselves, if they be truly learned and modest; or disgustful by their rash confidence, if they be presumptuous. Behold then another convincing proof of the necessity of a Divine revlation, to supply the defects of the mere natural powers of human reason.

To evince more fully this necessity, the best argument which I shall now draw from the imperfection of the human mind, is this: if some, after much investigation, come at length to a demonstration of the first principles of religion and morality, yet they are never able to form any regular and consistent system of either; the reason is, because they mix and disfigure the truth with many fatal errors, as will be shown not only by the history of the most eminent sages of antiquity, who were not enlightened by the torch of revelation, but like wise by the example of modern unbelievers, who extinguish it in their hearts and vainly undertake to find their way without its direction. St. Paul speaks of such in his first chapter to the Romans, *who from the creation of the world— . . . when they had known God, glorified him, not as God . . . but became vain in their thoughts, and their foolish hearts were darkened. . . . who changed the truth of God into a lie.*

If any doubts can yet remain on our minds of the necessity of a Divine revelation, these must vanish, when we consider the endless uncertainties, and inconceivable errors of the wisest amongst the ancients, who were not favored with the knowledge of it, and of those most celebrated wits of our own times, who rejected the truths which God in his mercy has displayed before them. To begin with the ancients: Socrates universally esteemed as the wisest of the heathen world, after having discovered by the acuteness of his mind, and the penetration of his intellectual powers, the existence and many of the perfections of the one, only God, affords us nevertheless a memorable instance of the darkness in which human reason, unassisted by revelation, leaves the mind involved. For this eminent sage, after all his researches into, and discoveries of God's nature and attributes, being at the point of death, had the weakness, and thought it his duty to comply with the popular superstition of his country, and command a sacrifice to one of its false divinities; nor was this all; for after many sublime speculations and discourses on the nature and immortality of the human soul, his very last words are expressive of the greatest uncertainty respecting this very point— I mean a state of future existence; without the firm belief of which, it is evident there can be no religion; none at least to deter us from the commision of vice, or encourage us in the practice of virtue.

If such were the errors and uncertainties of so great a master in the faculty and art of reasoning as Socrates, we can be less surprised that other eminent philosophers of Greece and Rome blended so many grievous errors with the few religious truths discovered by them; not only speculative but practical errors, pregnant with the greatest corruption of manners. The splendid talents and unrivalled elegance of Plato, could not preserve him from such astonishing blindness of understanding, that he recommended and advocated the practice of the most execrable and unnatural vices; such vices, as every christian, blessed with the light of revelation, not only trembles to commit, but even blushes to hear mentioned.

Let us now turn our eyes from ancient philosophers and sages, to contemplate the infidels of a later date, and those of our own times. Here we shall meet a still more sensible demonstration of the insufficiency of human reason. To evidence this, I will select for your information a few examples from the history and writings of those men whom the tribe of deists venerate as preeminent in talents and wisdom. In the first place, it appears evident to the christian, and I may say further, that if the light of nature alone makes evident any one principle of morality, it is this, that human liberty is necessary to the morality of human actions; that it is incompatible with the divine justice, to make man accountable and liable to punishment for doing or omitting those things which it is impossible for him to avoid doing or omitting; and to which he is compelled by the necessity of his nature and circumstances attending him, or by the decrees and ordering of God himself: that if man enjoy no power of self-determination, he cannot be a moral agent, and those things which always have been deemed the greatest enormities, as murders, parricides, incests, would be, in the estimation of right reason, no crimes at all, if he who committed them was compelled by commanding and irresistible necessity. What a dreadful perversion of order, what an inundation of the most horrible excesses would break in upon the world, if these opinions had general prevalence? But fatal as is their tendency, these are the doctines of many of the most famous modern enemies of revelation. None amongst them have surpassed Hume in subtlety of argument and acuteness of understanding. Yet having discarded revelation, and disdaining to follow any other guide than his own reasoning faculty, he not only asserts without ambiguity, but employs all his talents to prove, that mankind act continually under the influence of necessity; that they really enjoy no freedom of determination, and that they are always under a delusion, while they imagine themselves to enjoy perfect liberty.

Again, vice in this world is generally so elevated and virtue so depressed; so many are the enjoyments of the wicked, whom no considerations of conscience restrain, and so continual are the self-denials which a sense of duty imposes on the good, that there would be no consolation for the latter, if the belief of a future state and of the immortality of their souls did not support their hopes, and certify to them, that all the seeming disorders and irregularities of this life, would be rectified by a just and righteous God in the life to come. but what do we learn on this important point from modern infidelity? If we consult another of its greatest lights; one, whose brilliant talents have been celebrated with the most exalted encomiums, we find nothing but uncertainty and discouragement respecting a tenet so necessary to morality, so essential to the encouragement of virtue. This great man's reason could discover no sufficient proof of a future state. Ah! my brethren, who sees not in this acknowledgement the necessity of Divine revelation? Nor does Bolingbroke[84] alone betray the state of uncertainty and doubt in so capital an article. Almost all other advocates for the sufficiency of natural reason, hold the same language. The unbelieving Voltaire, he, whose writings are so widely diffused to the destruction of religion and manners, endeavors continually to raise doubts to obscure the doctrine of immortality. His numerous disciples have caught his spirit, and sometimes lament, with hypocritical concern, that a doctrine so full of comfort, remains so full of doubt; whereas in their hearts they wish nothing so much, as that it may be false, having all to fear from its truth. You remember, my christian brethren, to have read with horror some years ago, a particular account of the deaths of more than twenty of these apostates to anti-christian philosophy, who were sacrificed at the same time to the vengeance of a faction, more powerful and sanguinary than themselves; when they were at the instant of their execution, when their heads were just ready to be laid under the fatal instrument, instead of disposing themselves for reconciliation with the great judge of mankind, they affected to discuss the reasons for and against a future state, and closed their existence here with expressions of the utmost uncertainty respecting any existence hereafter. Yet, by all accounts, these men had great endowments from nature, and had cultivated them by the study of every human science. After these memorable examples, who will be bold enough to assert the sufficiency of human reason for all the purposes of morality and religion? Indeed, so many evidences have occurred in these our times, not only of the advantages, but absolute necessity of revelation, that the sincere friend of religion feels one comfort amidst all his disasters. He consoles himself with this reflection, that perhaps Divine Providence has permitted some of the first geniuses of the age to pursue without restraint, their own systems and speculations, that we might take instruction from their fatal and monstrous errors, and learn how deeply we are interested in having for our guide in the way of salvation, a more sturdy rule than the natural lights of the most famed philosophers. To give this lesson was worthy of divine wisdom; especially in an age when infidelity and a contemptuous disregard for the revelation and gospel of Jesus Christ, were laying waste his kingdom on earth, his glorious inheritance, and threatening to extirpate from the world all respect for his law and most holy name. And we may hope that infinite wisdom, drawing good out of evil, will make the delusions themselves of anti-christian skepticism, and the extravagance of its errors, the very means of its total overthrow, by discovering to all men the depth of misery into which we should be plunged without the cheering light of revelation.

However demonstrative of this truth, the examples hitherto adduced are, yet I must beg leave to trespass on your patience, by alleging one more, which places this point, if possible, in a still stronger light. Accustomed, as we are from our infancy, to consider and honor God as the source of goodness and justice, and experiencing many effects of these divine attributes in the providence exercised over ourselves and others, we naturally conclude that every human creature must confess, that justice and goodness are inseparable from the Supreme Being; and that we need consult no other light than natural reason to be firmly convinced of it, and certainly without a firm persuasion that god is possessed of these perfections, the whole race of mankind would be exposed to the most outrageous violence, all peace would be banished, all confidence destroyed, and life itself, instead of being a blessing, would be our most grievous misfortune. All this, notwithstanding, if we turn to those luminaries of the modern world, who are said to have diffused a splendor over the present age, greater than ever enlightened any other, do we find that their writings illustrate this fundamental doctrine of morality, this consolatory truth, the great Master and Lord of the universe, is infinitely *good,* and infinitely *just?* No, my christian brethren, I am sure that you will hear me with astonishment. Almost all these famed philosophers spread doubts and uncertainty respecting this subject, and employ the subtlety of their understandings, to prove that there is no sufficient evidence of wisdom and justice appertaining to the All-powerful God. This they expressly teach, and make this doctrine the basis of many other impious opinions, tending to remove every barrier against vice, and to damp all ardor for improvement, or perseverance in virtue. After exhibiting these almost incredible and pernicious errors of the great leaders in the cause of infidelity, I need insist no farther on the manifest insufficiency of reason alone, to teach us all the necessary points of even the law and religion of nature.

From the observations already made, may I not hope, that you both feel, and will testify the most sincere gratitude and reverence to that Divine Person, *who enlighteneth every man coming into this world?* (John i.9) who has spread the effulgence of revelation over the face of the earth, and has not left us to grope in darkness, or afforded only the dim light of reason to search into the ways of truth and life, *but the grace of God, our Saviour, has appeared to all men, instructing us, that renouncing impiety and worldly desires, we should live soberly, and piously, and justly in this world, waiting for the blessed hope, and coming of the glory of the great God, and our Saviour, Jesus Christ.* Titus ii. 7, *et seq.* With this impression on your minds, you will not only be prepared to resist the insidious and poisonous lessons of infidelity, but you will even refuse to hear them. Expose not yourselves to the artful seduction of books destined to weaken and extinguish your faith. Be not misled by that miserable sophistry, which pretends that none should be afraid of reading works, however hostile to religion, that to be convinced of its truth, they should know the objections raised against it. What? is there no other way of being acquainted with the malignity of poison, but by drinking it up? Are not the evidences of divine revelation so many and convincing, that we may safely and firmly believe it without searching to know whatever pride and licentiousness have devised to oppose it? Let it be your duty to fly from danger, which many of you are not prepared to encounter. Let humility of faith be your shelter and safe-guard. In this most important concern, bear in your mind these words of my text: *it shall be, that every soul which will not hear that Prophet whom the Lord God hath sent, shall be destroyed from among the people:* that is, they who reject his doctrines shall not belong to the chosen race, destined to the possession of an everlasting inheritance of glory. May God vouchsafe to rescue us, at least, from that fatal destruction, and save us in his mercy, through the merits of Jesus Christ. Amen.

Deo Gratias.

Two Sermons on Confirmation[85]

The first of these sermons would seem to have been given in the winter of 1784–1785. In November Rome had appointed Carroll superior of the church in the United States. Certain faculties were given him, including that of administering confirmation. On this occasion the privileges of the Jubilee year which Pope Pius VI had declared were extended to American Catholics.

1. Building yourselves upon your most holy faith, praying in the holy Ghost, keep yourselves in the love of God, waiting for the mercy of our Lord Jesus Christ unto life everlasting. Jude v. 20–21.

Christian virtue must be[86] established on the foundation of faith; must be reared[87] and increased by prayer; must be compleated[88] by the love of God; and rewarded[89] with mercy in life everlasting. Such is the comprehensive instruction delivered in the words of my text. We see[90] the root, from which our sanctification springs, *building yourselves upon your most holy faith:* We see the means of preserving & increasing it, *praying in the holy Ghost:* We see the excellency, to which it must arrive, *keep yourselves in the love of God:* and finally we are presented with the motive, which is always to be kept in view,[91] & to encourage[92] us in our struggles thro this time of[93] trial & temptation; to wit the *mercy of our Lord Jesus Christ unto life everlasting.* The foundation of our spiritual building, the means principally to be used in raising it, the summit of perfection, to which it is to be carried, and the recompence of our labours in[94] erecting it; that is, faith, prayer, the love of God, & heavenly happiness should be the frequent employment of our meditation, and either the object, or incitement[95] of our zeal in the service of God. They deserve each to be treated of in particular, & I appropriate the first to this day's entertainment, that is faith, as being the foundation of the rest, *building yourselves upon your most holy faith.* I chuse moreover to give the preference to this subject, because you are now going to receive the Sacrament, which is emphatically called the seal of our faith. For the Sacrament of Confirmation is, according[96] to the import of the word, the making of that strong, which already had a being. In the Sacrament of Baptism, you were introduced into the Church of Christ; you received, with other virtues, the heavenly gift of faith. But this divine gift being that, on which the superstructure of Xtian perfection[97] is to be raised, & without which, according to St. Paul, *it is impossible to please God.* Heb. 11.v.6, our divine Redeemer was pleased to institute a Sacrament of peculiar efficacy to secure, to strengthen, to enliven it,[98] that it may neither be shaken with the storms of persecution, or bewildered[99] by the sophistry of worldly wisdom; or seduced by the still more dangerous insinuation[100] of sensuality and licentiousness. This Sacrament is that of Confirmation. Baptism[101] by communicating to us the gift of faith, made us Christians:[102] but Confirmation, perfecting this gift, renders us perfect Christians.[103] Before I proceed upon my subject,[104] I will in a few words recall to yr. remembrance the nature & properties of faith. This divine virtue is a homage we pay to one of God's noblest attributes, &c. Holy Scripture informs us repeatedly, that, after baptism, the Apostles were used to lay their hands on the faithful, & that the immediate effect of this imposition, was the coming down of the holy Ghost upon them. He came in a visible & miraculous manner, & manifested his presence by the signs, which he performed; by the gift of tongues, of prophecy, & other wonderful tokens. These were either necessary in the beginning of the Church; or at least, greatly conducive to the speedier spreading of the gospel truths throughout the world. But now tho' these miraculous gifts & outward manifestations of the presence of the divine spirit have ceased; yet &c. . . .

Allow me, Dr. Christians, to congratulate you on the mercies, which God Alm: has graciously shewn you, & the many favours bestowed on you, more than were shewn to your fathers—Free enjoyment & exercise [of your religion]—an extensive Jubilee &c an opportunity of receiving a Sacrament the benefit of which was never extended this Country before. Almighty God has now right to say, what more could I do to my vineyard, & have not done it? But, heaven forbid, that our gracious Lord, after all these mercies shewn us, should have cause to reproach us, as he did the Jews, I expected that my vineyard would produce grapes, but it has brought forth nothing but brambles—Dr. Christians, from you I will hope better things—Henceforward you will *walk—not in rioting and drunkenness, not in chambering & impurities, not in contention & envy, but you will put on the Ld. Jesus Christ,* & make not provision for the flesh in its concupiscences. Above all, you, who are young, will derive from this Sacrament that firmness[105] & liveliness of faith, which will make you resolute to withstand the seducing voice of wicked companions, the allurements of evil example, & the importunity of your own passions, that building on the foundation of faith, you may be rewarded by that mercy, which is in Christ J. our Lord.

2. This is the victory, which overcometh the world, our faith, First [letter] of John, ch.5—

The beloved apostle of our Lord was not only full of confidence in the promises of his heavenly Master, but likewise endowed with the Spirit of prophecy when he announced with so much assurance the victory of Christian faith over a world fortified against its doctrines by inveterate prejudices, & read to come forward with all the means of resistance[106] & force to support its antient establishments of superstition and idolatry. What the apostle foretold, came to pass. The faith of Christ overcame the world. The doctrine of the Gospel enlightened mankind; the darkness[107] and delusions of false religions faded before the resplendent light of Xtianity; the Church of God rose conspicuous on their ruins, and has always remained in the public profession of the same faith, in the teaching of the same doctrines, in the administration of the same Sacraments, in the possession of the same ministry uninterruptedly derived from Christ & his Apostles, in the offering of the same one holy[108] & adorable sacrifice to the Eternal Father, and in retaining its distinguishing & characteristic title of Catholic, tho it has been contested by so many sects, which from the earliest & thro all successive ages, have endeavoured to wrest it from her and appropriate it to themselves.

I begin with these observations, because one of the special duties imposed on me at the visitations of[109] the congregations committed to my charge, is to instruct & confirm them in their faith, & to inculcate the lessons of religion, which you have received from those, who have more constant opportunities of recommending them to you. Some few[110] of you, my Dr. B., & children in Xt, are to be admitted to day to that Sacrament, which was specially instituted by our Bd. Lord, that thro it & by it you may receive into your souls that Holy Spirit, who with his other gifts brings with him the gift of fortitude & magnanimous[111] faith, of which the Apostle speaks, when he saith, that it overcomes the world. But tho the Sacrament will be now administered only to a few, yet almost all of you have been made heretofore partakers of it: and the grace, then conferred on you, may be stirred up & re[vi]ved even in your souls this day, tho it should have become extinct by your infidelity to it, after it was first bestowed on you. St. Paul writing to his beloved son in J.C., Timothy, whom he had ordained to the ministry of the Church, exhorts him to reanimate the grace received by the laying of his hands—In the same manner, I now intreat you, my dear Brethren in God, to revive in your souls the grace of confirmation, the grace which was infused into them by the coming of the Holy Ghost. . . .

NOTES

1. An English Jesuit who was a colleague of Carroll at the College at Liège.

2. This and the following letters are all in the manuscript collections of Stonyhurst College, and published in Thomas O'Brien Hanley, S.J., *The John Carroll Papers* (Notre Dame, 1976), I, 26–31.

3. John Thorpe was a member of the English College in Rome.

4. Mario Cardinal Marefoschi (1714–1780), former Secretary of the Congregation for the Propagation of the Faith (1759–1770).

5. "Before Nestor there were no Nestorians, before Luther, Lutherans, nor before Jansenius, Jansenists."

6. Henry Benedict Maria Clement (1725–1807), the last of the Stuart Pretenders and the Cardinal-Bishop of Frascati.

7. Carroll's older brother Daniel (1730–1796) was a wealthy merchant planter in Maryland who served in state and national governments during the Revolutionary and federal eras and was a member of the Constitutional Convention in Philadelphia.

8. Printed in John Carroll Brent, *Biographical Sketch of the Most Rev. John Carroll* (Baltimore, 1843), 25–27.

9. Since the 1740s German Jesuits had been serving immigrant communities in Philadelphia and southeastern Pennsylvania.

10. GUSC, American Catholic Sermon Collection.

11. Crossed out: "the church of C."

12. Crossed out: "testimonies of the word."

13. Crossed out: "both in the language of the."

14. Crossed out: "what is meant by that world."

15. Crossed out: "following."

16. Crossed out: "I will describe."

17. Crossed out: "be (become) the victims to its."

18. Crossed out: "intoxicated with."

19. Crossed out: "those."

20. Crossed out: "are."

21. Crossed out: "unruly."

22. Crossed out: "vicious."

23. Crossed out: "detes."

24. GUSC, American Catholic Sermon Collection.

25. Crossed out: "which."

26. Crossed out: "minds."

27. Crossed out: "frequent."

28. Crossed out: "which to preserve."

29. Crossed out: "been."

30. Crossed out: "great."

31. Crossed out: "you."

32. GUSC, American Catholic Sermon Collection.

33. Crossed out: "Aided & supported by grace operating on their souls."

34. Crossed out: "preventing and."
35. Crossed out: "graces."
36. Crossed out: "availed himself."
37. Crossed out: "there."
38. Crossed out: "it."
39. Crossed out: "so many persons subject to his authority."
40. Crossed out: "as he."
41. Crossed out: "he was under."
42. Crossed out: "& thereby prevent."
43. Crossed out: "come to."
44. Crossed out: "obtaining it."
45. Crossed out: "The love of our fellow creatures, our submission to the Law."
46. Crossed out: "fidelity."
47. Crossed out: "links of intimate friendships."
48. Crossed out: "all."
49. Crossed out: "most necessary, give way."
50. Crossed out: "great."
51. Crossed out: "and these are chiefly deducible from the two essential."
52. Crossed out: "with the mouth."
53. Crossed out: "by joining to the subject."
54. Crossed out: "Such."
55. Crossed out: "Dr. Xtians:".
56. Crossed out: "just."
57. Crossed out: "doing."
58. Crossed out: "was."
59. Crossed out: "publ."
60. Crossed out: "& despoil it of all its."
61. Crossed out: "we betray a shameful neglect of God's service" also: "are deficient in a material part of our duty."
62. Crossed out: "if."
63. Crossed out: "irreligion."
64. Crossed out: "of it."
65. Crossed out: "& attach."
66. Crossed out: "give."
67. Crossed out: "the."
68. Crossed out: "it."
69. Crossed out: "impiety."
70. Crossed out: "I say scandalous exesses of barefaced and avowed irreligion: for not to insist upon some shocking acts of this kind, which tho' too common in places, have not yet, I hope, found access amongst you, not to insist, I say, upon these."
71. Crossed out: "ridicule holy things, & seek to gain."
72. Crossed out: "his."
73. Crossed out: "Does he."

74. Crossed out: "pious & holy pers."
75. Crossed out: "does not this."
76. Crossed out: "embracing."
77. Crossed out: "ridicule."
78. Crossed out: "thereby hinder them from glorifying God."
79. Crossed out: "ridicule & laugh at."
80. Crossed out: "devotions."
81. Crossed out: "& under prete."
82. Crossed out: "condemn."
83. Printed in John Carroll Brent, ed., *Biographical Sketch of the Most Rev. John Carroll, First Archbishop of Baltimore: With Select Portions of His Writings* (Baltimore, 1843), 278–301.
84. Henry St. John Bolingbroke (1678–1751), English deist.
85. GUSC, American Catholic Sermon Collection.
86. Crossed out: "is to."
87. Crossed out: "to be raised."
88. Crossed out: "and perfected."
89. Crossed out: "to be crowned."
90. Crossed out: "It discovers."
91. Crossed out: "must animate us to obtain so excell sublime a have."
92. Crossed out: "& support."
93. Crossed out: "way of virtue, waiting for."
94. Crossed out: "the."
95. Crossed out: "encouragement."
96. Crossed out: "because I trust, that when you have the happiness to be admitted to it."
97. Crossed out: "life was."
98. Crossed out: "our faith."
99. Crossed out: "seduced" and "deluded."
100. Crossed out: "delusions."
101. Crossed out: "made us the children of God."
102. Crossed out: "the children of God."
103. Crossed out: "strong & perfect men resolute in the profession of our faith."
104. Crossed out: "allow me."
105. Crossed out: "of belief."
106. Crossed out: "instruments of physical force."
107. Crossed out: "errors."
108. Crossed out: "sacred."
109. Crossed out: "which."
110. Crossed out: "very."
111. Crossed out: "Xtian magnanimity."

V

THE EX-JESUITS AND THE TRADITION

THE PIOUS GUIDE TO PRAYER AND DEVOTION (1792)

Containing Various Practices of Piety Calculated to Answer the Various Demands of the Different Devout Members of the Roman Catholic Church (1792)[1]

The Devotion of the Sacred Heart of Jesus

Although explicit evidence of this devotion dates only from the 1760s, it almost certainly had a much longer history in the Maryland Catholic spiritual life. John Carroll, when requesting general permission from Rome in 1793 for the Mass and Office of the Sacred Heart on the Friday after the octave of Corpus Christi, noted that it had "enjoyed great favor here for many years."[2]

The Nature and Excellence of this Devotion

THE devotion to the sacred Heart of Jesus has Jesus Christ himself for its author; it is he that planned the project thereof, he explained the nature of it and foretold its future progress. The Church has at all times considered the sacred Heart of Jesus as an object worthy her veneration; for whilst she honoured, as she ever did, his sacred humanity, doubtless the heart which is the principal part thereof, must have deserved her adoration. However this devotion (tho' ever holy in itself) has not always been solemnized alike. It is only in these latter days, that the time appointed by the eternal decrees of Providence being come, Almighty God was pleased to disclose to the whole world the inestimable treasures of the sacred Heart of his divine Son. Such ever was the conduct of God over his Church; from time to time in order to rouse and stir up the piety of the faithful, he sets up devotions, which tho' not new in themselves as to the substance and groundwork, are yet so in their solemnity and respective circumstances. Thus has he established the devotion to the most adorable Sacrament of the Altar; thus again the devotion to his sacred Name, to his sacred Wounds, &c.

But to give a more clear idea of this devotion, let us trace it back quite up to its source, and see on what occasion it came forth.

In the year 1680, there lived in the Diocess of Autun, in the town called Paroi le Monial, in the monastary of the Visitation, a young woman unknown to the world, but favoured with the most strict communications with Almighty God, a worthy spouse of the spotless lamb. Her life was a series of the most eminent virtues, and her soul was filled with the most distinguished graces. For many years, this devout soul had been incessantly engaged in the meditation of the immense riches of the adorable Heart of Jesus Christ: For many years, she glowed with the holy extasies of a divine and uninterrupted love at the sight of its perfections; she had long sighed after that happy moment, when she might see this amiable Heart known, honoured and loved throughout the whole world. She then little knew that she was to be the happy person chosen by Almighty God to bring about this great work. On a certain day, within the Octave of Corpus Christi, finding herself more than ordinarily burning with this ardent desire, Jesus Christ appeared, and spoke thus to her.[3] "You cannot,["] says he, ["] testify your love for me better, than by doing what I have so often asked at your hands;" and disclosing his sacred Heart, he said: "Behold this Heart, which has loved mankind so tenderly, and spared nothing even to the wasting and consuming itself in testimony of its love, and yet in return I generally meet with nothing but ingratitude, contempt, sacrileges, irreverences and coldness, even in the very sacrament of my love; and still what more sensibly affects me, is, that I receive this usage from hearts peculiarly consecrated to my service. Wherefore I demand of thee, that the first Friday after the Octave of the blessed Sacrament, be consecrated to a special feast in honour of my Heart, that a solemn reparation of honour and a public act of atonement be offered to it on that day, and holy communion received, with an intent to repair by it, as far as possible, all the injuries and affronts it has received, when exposed on the altars, and I promise it shall delate itself, to pour profusely the gifts of its divine love on all such persons, as shall pay to it this homage, and induce others to the performance of the same religious office."

These are the words of Jesus Christ himself, and from them duly weighed, as from a most copious spring, flow such truths, as most properly belong to this devotion, and are the fittest to convey a distinct notion of the nature of it. They will be more fully unfolded in the following queries.

FIRST QUERY

What is the Object of this Devotion?

A. THE object thereof is the heart of Jesus Christ, an object of all others evidently the noblest, the holiest, the greatest, the most divine and altogether the most sweet and most amiable that can possibly be conceived. Hence it follows, that a devotion relating to it, bears with it that particular mark of sanctity, dignity, grandeur, sweetness and loveliness, which no other can come up to. The dignity of this adorable Heart arises 1. From its union with the most perfect and most compleat soul that ever was, whereof this divine heart has been the organ in the production of its sensible affections. From this close union of the heart with the soul, that universal notion among all polite nations is sprung, whereby they are induced to pay to the hearts of great men, after their death, honours suitable to the merits of the soul they were united to. If so, what shall we say of the sacred Heart of Jesus, since it was united to such a soul? 2. To what a pitch of grandeur and infinite merit, is it not raised by its union with the second person of the blessed Trinity? Whatever belongs to the adorable person of Jesus Christ, claims all our veneration in an infinite degree; the least part of his sacred body, a drop of his blood, a hair of his head deserves our utmost adoration. Every thing that has but touched his sacred body, becomes thereby venerable, as the cross, the nails, the lance, the thorns. If the lance, which pierced the Heart of Jesus, is by that very touch become an object of veneration to the whole church, what shall we say of the Heart itself, which has imparted so much dignity to the contemptible steel?

3. A farther proof of the dignity of the Heart of Jesus is taken from the divine function it was formed for, I mean that of burning incessantly with the purest and most ardent flames of the love of God. From the very first instant of its production, it glowed with that divine and uninterrupted fire to the last instant of its mortal life, and will ever thus burn for all eternity. By one single act of the love of God produced by it, the divine Majesty is infinitely more honoured, than it could possibly be by the united love of all creatures even possible during a whole eternity. How noble then must that Heart be, the function whereof is to receive continually the impressions of this sacred love, and produce the highest acts therof uninterruptedly for all eternity? Hence the complacency of the eternal father for this divine object, since nothing can be more acceptable in his eyes, than the never ceasing love of his only Son.

It is plain from all this, that we do not mean to honour the sacred Heart of Jesus barely as an inanimate and lifeless Heart, but we consider it as united to the divine person and as the chief instrument of the most holy soul that ever was. This undoubtedly was not sufficiently attended to by those who at first seemed to attack this devotion. They considered the sacred Heart merely as an inanimate and lifeless Heart, but we consider it as united to the divine person and as the chief instrument of the operations of the most holy soul that ever was. They considered the sacred Heart, merely as an inanimate piece of flesh without life or feeling, as a holy relick purely material, without paying any attention its union with the divinity, and to such spiritual and divine riches, as are annexed to it, and which impart to it life and motion.

SECOND QUERY

What is the End of this Devotion?

A. WE are to consider the sacred Heart of Jesus under two different aspects; on one side, as a Heart full of love and breathing nothing but the salvation of mankind; on the other side, as a heart that is offended, insulted and despised by unthinking man, by sinners void of all sense of gratitude and unaffected by his love. The inclination of this adorable Heart to reconcile man to god, and Earth to Heaven, must raise in us sentiments of the most ardent love and feelings of the greatest sorrow, to dispose of us for a reparation of the wrongs and outrages it daily suffers. The end therefore proposed by this devotion, to which the faithful are earnestly invited, is in the first place to honour by frequent acts of love and adoration, and by all manner of submission and homage the unbounded love of Jesus for us throughout the whole course of his mortal life, but chiefly in the Sacrament of the holy Eucharist, the sum and abridgement of all his wonders, where he still burns with the love of us. In the next place it is to share in his grief and to make amends on our part for those many insults his love for us exposed him to during his mortal life, and still now exposes him to every day in the blessed Sacrament, where he is so little loved by men, so little known, and oftentimes so outrageously abused even by those, who know him.

THIRD QUERY

What are the advantages of this Devotion?

A. THEY are numberless, and unspeakable. We need but look about us, and we shall immediately discover the many singular blessings it produces in all hearts. What more beneficial, than a devotion, which so far from being confined to some barren and outward practices chiefly consists in a constant study of the interior dispositions of this adorable Heart, and in an uninterrupted endeavour to model ourselves on it, and transcribe its virtues into our own lives; so that in all things, as far as we can, we should keep an eye on this divine object, as the model we are to copy after in each of our actions.

Do you desire, pious souls, to attain the very summit of perfection? Behold here a safe and easy road to it. I say a safe road: in matters of devotion nothing is so much to be feared as illusion. Whatever is uncommon and singular, is deservedly to be mistrusted. Now this devotion steers clear of any such danger; the object it honours is of all objects the most worthy, the Heart of a Man-God; the end it proposes, is quite divine; the practical duties performed therein, are agreeable to the spirit of the church; and since Jesus Christ speaking of himself, says, that he is the way, that leads to life, and the gate, thro' which we must enter heaven, how can we fear being misled by penetrating into the most august Sanctuary of his sacred Heart in order to partake of that fullness of grace and sanctity, abiding therein as in its centre? O! how noble, and precious a sight, how worthy of the divine Majesty must the Heart be, which is modelled on this divine original! Hence that uncommon recollection, and that modesty so conspicuous in the whole comportment of many fervent clients of this devotion, that spirit of mildness and peace, that odour of sanctity, I may say, which charms, invites and edifies every body. Again, by this means the heart is imperceptibly weaned from itself, and from all creatures; self-love abates, the empire of sin ceases, faults are diminished, imperfections redressed, the soul fills with God, the inward man is renewed, and acquires every day an additional degree of strength.

It is therefore a most safe and unerring road to perfection. But as a farther matter of comfort, I must add, that it is also a most sweet, easy and pleasant road, attended by an uncommon salutary unction, such as must inspire the love of virtue, and an answerable degree of fortitude to practise it. For if a solid devotion to this sacred Heart is ever inseparable from an unfeigned love for our divine Saviour, it is scarce possible to have this warm and tender love, without finding in it an admirable store of interior and quite divine consolation. And whereas the bare sight of our Saviour's sacred wounds, naturally calls up in our hearts an unspeakable confidence in his mercies, so the remembrance, the least thought of his sacred heart, creates a certain degree of joy, which is easier felt than described. I appeal to your testimony, devout souls consecrated in a special manner to this devotion, what sweets have you not felt in those happy moments, when Jesus Christ has admitted you into his sacred heart? What delights, what comforts, what extasies! Were they not a kind of foretaste of the joys of Heaven?

There is still another benefit entailed on this devotion, and it is this. It is not confined merely to some select and privileged souls, more versed in spiritual matters, and more enlightened than the common. No: it lies within the reach of all degrees of people, the unlearned as well as the most learned. The great ones and the rich of the world have here no superior advantage over the poor, and those of the common sort, because it rests wholly on the dispositions of the heart, and all have a heart to give to God, and may find one in Jesus Christ, ever ready to receive their gift. Cheer up therefore, ye afflicted souls, narrow geniuses, indigent and forlorn creatures. If you be not allowed to enjoy, in this world, neither the pleasures of life, the splendours of honours, nor the treasures of wealth, yet you may be admitted into the sacred Heart of Jesus Christ, and therein you will find abundantly, whatever the world has denied you: happy, if you but know, how to improve this great treasure, where you may provide yourselves with riches for time and eternity itself.

What then remains, but that we enter into the adorable Heart of Jesus Christ! He came down on earth chiefly for this end, to bring with him the sacred flames of divine love, which ought to fire all hearts. Let us then throw ourselves into that burning furnace, to glow with its heavenly heat; repair into that sacred asylum, to be under shelter from all the dangers of salvation; to that spring of living water, to find comfort in our troubles; to that model of all virtues, to transcribe them into our lives; in a word to that place of delights, to commence there our heaven on earth.

FOURTH QUERY

What are the Obstacles to this Devotion?

A. 1. TEPIDITY, which as scripture teaches, bears hard on the Heart of Jesus.

2. Secret pride, ever opposite to humility the essential virtue of this Heart.

3. Self-love, the capital enemy to this devotion.

4. Unmortified passions; these stifle the love of Jesus towards us, and destroy the inward peace and quiet of the mind.

FIFTH QUERY

Which are the Means of acquiring it?

A. 1. TO petition often for it, and that with fervour, because it is the gift of God, who bestows his blessings on such, as ask with perseverance.

2. To communicate frequently. Fire carried in the bosom must warm, as the Holy Ghost assures us.

3. To visit diligently the most blessed Eucharist. This is the furnace of divine love, this the sacrament of the Heart of Jesus. Love is preserved and entertained by visits.

4. To persevere with fidelity in our devotions to the Heart of Jesus. Perseverance is crowned and love is the reward of fidelity.

5. To have a filial confidence in our blessed Lady, and a tender devotion to her and the Saints.

6. To procure a great interior recollection. A heart opened on all sides and exposed to a thousand distractions, can never receive or preserve the love of Jesus, who is only pleased with the solitude and retirement of the heart.

7. To entertain a strong desire of loving Jesus Christ.

SIXTH QUERY

What is the Difference between the Devotion to the Sacred Heart, and that which is paid to the blessed Sacrament?

A. 1. IT is very great. They differ in their object, motive and end. The first is directed wholly to the adorable Heart of Jesus Christ in the blessed Eucharist, without any relation to the other parts of his body: in the latter, the Body of Jesus Christ whole and entire, as hidden under the sacramental species, is proposed to our adoration, without any special reference to his sacred Heart. Again, the motive of our devotion to the sacred heart of Jesus is 1. the infinite love he bears us in that sacred Heart, united personally to the Divinity, and 2. the many injuries, affronts and indignities, it receives still in return from ungrateful Man, especially in the blessed Eucharist: whereas, the motive of our devotion to the blessed Sacrament, is the infinite dignity of the adorable body and blood of Christ, united to the divinity, and worthy of the adoration of Men and Angels.

The end proposed in the devotion to the sacred Heart, is to excite us to a special honour, and love for that sacred Heart, and to make an atonement and compensation, as far as in us lies, for the many injuries and affronts offered to the divine love at all times, but principally in the abuse and profanation of the most blessed Sacrament. This reparation of honour, is directed to the adorable Heart, as to the source and principle of this Divine and Eucharistic love. Now, the devotion to the blessed Sacrament, is absolutely independent of the sacrilegious indignities, committed against the real presence; and it would equally subsist in all its parts, if Almighty God had always been worthily served in the blessed Sacrament, since it would still ever be just to pay to the sacred humanity, under the sacramental veils, an infinite honour, love, devotion and gratitude.

The Practice of this Devotion

IN general, by the practice of this devotion, nothing more is meant, than the use of such means, as are best calculated to render us true adorers and faithful imitators of the sacred Heart of Jesus Christ. Now, this practice is both interior and exterior. The interior practice consists in the inward acts of faith, adoration, love, hope, confidence, gratitude and the like. The exterior practice consists in outward and visible acts, such as are meant to denote outwardly the inward devotion. Of this sort are prayers, novenas, confessions, visits to Jesus Christ in the blessed Sacrament, associations, confraternities, fasting, penances and generally all pious and edifying acts, which are performed to honour the adorable Heart of our blessed Redeemer. Whereupon, it is not amiss to observe, that we must not so rest and depend on these outward practices, as to persuade ourselves, that if we have but performed them, we have thereby fulfilled all justice. This would be confining the whole system of devotion to bare and empty ceremonies. Much less ought they to be considered as a claim to impunity for one's faults, or as a security of a future conversion after having long slighted almighty God's grace. This would be a gross illusion and a fatal abuse, ever disavowed by all true devotion. But on the other hand, because devotion is misused, it is no reason why it should be condemned or suppressed; for the best things are liable to be misused. The abuse indeed ought to be checked, but the devotion itself, wholly saintly and solid, should ever be preserved.

These general notions being once premised, let us now consider in particular, the devotions to be practised in honour of the sacred Heart of Jesus. Among them, some are to be performed every year, some every month, some every week, and some every day.

EVERY YEAR

THE solemn festival of this devotion, is fixed on the first Friday after the Octave of Corpus Christi. This day must be sanctified and consecrated to the love of our blessed Saviour by prayer, pious reading, visits to the blessed Sacrament, and every other good work; and therefore from the very eve, prepare for this solemn day, by some act of penance or charity, in order to prepare your heart for the divine grace. On the festival itself, repair to the sacraments of penance and holy communion. In your confession on that day accuse yourself, and detest in a special manner your many infidelities and acts of disrespect towards the blessed Sacrament. Your communion ought to be performed with so much the more fervour, as it is intended as a reparation of honour and supplement for the many negligences and defects in former communions. In the afternoon, you shall make a special visit to the blessed Sacrament, and there make a solemn act of atonement to the sacred Heart, to make amends, as much as possible, for all the indignities it receives every day in the blessed Eucharist, and for such, as we ourselves have perhaps been guilty of.

E V E R Y   M O N T H

BESIDES the principal feast, which happens but once a year, the first Friday of every month, has been consecrated to the sacred Heart. On that day, the clients endeavour to perform anew, either wholly or in part, the religious duties practised on the feast itself, as for instance, confession, communion, visits to the blessed Sacrament, the reparation of honour, &c.

They consider the first Friday of the month, as a special festival proper for them. They are not however thereby debarred from attending to their own respective employments, provided they offer their work to God for that end.

E V E R Y   W E E K

THE warm and fervorous clients of this devotion, who endeavour to procure for themselves a more plentiful flow of heavenly graces, are not satisfied with honouring this divine Heart once a month: they have moreover consecrated the Friday of every week, to its honor. On that day they perform some acts of devotion, some good works, or small mortifications, either interior or exterior in this view, and with this motive, to testify their gratitude, and repair by their love, the ingratitude of man to Jesus Christ. Thus we find, that in other devotions, besides the principal festival, particular and privileged days are kept every week. Tuesday, for instance, is consecrated to the Guardian Angels throughout the whole year, Thursday, to the blessed Sacrament, Saturday, to our Blessed Lady, &c.

E V E R Y   D A Y

THE following practices are so much the more valuable, as they are more frequent, and lie within the reach of every body. They are reduced mostly to this: to perform all our daily actions, in union with the sacred Heart; so that, when we pray, we pray with it; when we love, we love with it; when we act, we act with and in it; when we suffer, we suffer in and for it. This is an admirable art to heap up treasures of merits, graces and glory. for as there is nothing so noble in the eyes of the Divine Majesty, as the sacred Heart of his Son, so there is nothing more acceptable to him than the union of our actions with that adorable Heart. The infinitely holy dispositions of it, make up for the deficiency of our very imperfect actions, which thro' this union, are in some measure divinized. Think therefore often, devout souls, on Jesus Christ, and repair to him, in all your wants; advise with him, in your doubts and anxieties; speak to him, of your troubles and afflictions, give him an account of your thoughts, designs and schemes, lay before him, your faults, temptations and passions. Beg of him, to remedy all your evils, live in him, breathe for him alone. He will stand you in lieu of every thing else, if you but know how to seek all things in him.

Besides these methods annexed to certain particular times, there are others that may be used at all times. Such are the reparation of honour, the act of consecration to the sacred Heart, communions, visits to the blessed Sacrament, &c. Such again are the outward signs, the clients of this devotion wear about them, as Pictures, Medals and Scapulars; such in short are the Beads, the Litanies and other prayers, consecrated to the honour of this divine Heart.

The Act of Consecration to the Sacred Heart of Jesus.

O MOST amiable Heart of my divine redeemer! considering thy infinite love for all men, and for me in particular; in view of the oppressing grief and other pains, thou has endur'd for my sins, in view of the most precious blood, thou hast been pleased to shed for my redemption; in view of the excessive love, thou hast shewn us in the institution of the most blessed Sacrament of the altar, and in view of those infinite perfections which make thee so amiable; I, N.N. do this day consecrate myself to thee without reserve for all the remainder of my life. I consecrate to thee, my body, my soul, my thoughts, my desires, my words, my actions and my sufferings, desiring thereby to contribute to thy greater glory. In particular, I consecrate to thee, my heart, with all its motions, desiring it may love thee only, rejoice in thee only, and not breathe but for thee alone; and however unworthy the offering be, thou canst not refuse it, since thou hast asked it of me.

Receive it then, O divine Heart of Jesus; purify it, sanctify it, and inflame it with thy most pure love, that it may not act, but by the motion of thy love, nor suffer, but for thy love, grieve only, that it loves thee so little; have its only joy in loving thee much; desire nothing, but the continual increase of that love, and fear nothing, but to let that holy love relent and be consumed; in a word, make my heart like to thee, that by thee, and with thee, and like thee, it may eternally love the Father, the Son, and the Holy Ghost. Amen.

THE MANNER OF PERFORMING THE NOVENA;
OR THE NINE DAYS DEVOTION
TO S. FRANCIS XAVERIUS[4]

There is no evidence that the Novena was a part of colonial Catholic spirituality. This particular set of instructions and prayers was taken from a Flemish manual of 1765. Here too, however, was a very distinctive Jesuit devotion to which the compilers of The Pious Guide *gave prominent attention in a foreshadowing of its role in American Catholic devotionalism of the next two centuries.*

This *Novena* commences on the fourth of March, and continues nine days, that is, till the twelfth of March, upon which day in the year 1622, Pope Gregory the XV, canonized S. Francis Xaverius. The persons, who perform this *Novena,* are to be employed upon each of the nine days in prayer and good works to the glory of Almighty God, and in honor of his servant S. Francis Xaverius; always endeavouring to repose an entire confidence in the merits of this apostle, and hoping through his means to obtain from God, whatsoever they shall ask, provided it be conducing to their salvation and the good of their souls; or that other wise, instead of that blessing, which they beg, and which is not for their benefit, this Saint will obtain for them of God some other grace they do not ask, and which tends more to their eternal felicity.

For the exact performance of this *Novena,* they are to take for their advocates the nine choirs of heavenly spirits, making particular mention of the principal virtues of S. Francis Xaverius, and they are to observe other directions which shall be given hereafter. It will be convenient to confess and communicate the first day, that so the soul being cleansed from sin and honored with the sacred Eucharist, all the works we perform in the state of grace, may be meritorious of eternal life, and the more efficacious towards obtaining the benefit we ask. Those who do not confess, must at least, begin every day with an Act of Contrition, to cleanse their souls from sin and to secure themselves of obtaining their petition.

When this *Novena* is not performed in the Church with the general concourse of the people, it were convenient, that if it be done in a private house, all the family should join in performing it all together, begging that of God for everyone, which each apart begs for himself.

For the conveniency of such as stand in need of farther direction, we will here set down those prayers, that are proper to be said every day; nevertheless such as are more devout, may beg the same thing of the Saint in such terms and language, as their devotion shall dictate, and may direct their prayer as they think fit: When many together perform the *Novena,* one of them may read the prayers, changing the singular number into the plural, and saying: *we desire, we beg, etc.* The others may repeat the prayer after him, or else only hear it with attention, inwardly desiring and begging that which is asked in it.

Instructions for the Exact Performing of the Novena

Those who perform the *Novena* are to observe these instructions upon all, and each of the nine days. *First,* they are to endeavour to imitate some one of this saint's virtues by practising some exterior act, or acts thereof; as for instance, his zeal, humility, patience, &c. *Secondly,* they are to do some work of mercy either spiritual or corporal for the benefit of their neighbour; as giving of alms, visiting the sick, or those that are in prison, comforting the afflicted, praying for the souls in purgatory, or for those that are in the state of mortal sin, &c. *Thirdly,* They are to offer up for this end some particular mortification, as fasting, wearing of haircloth, disciplining, using themselves with less tenderness, &c. *Fourthly,* They are to curb their senses, their eyes, their ears and their tongue, endeavouring to avoid even the least of sins. *Fifthly,* They are to read some chapter or page of the life of this saint; or meditate while upon some one of his virtues with an earnest desire to imitate them. *Sixthly,* They are to endeavour, for the glory of God to excite some person to bear devotion to this saint. *Seventhly,* It will be convenient they every day invoke the intercession of some one rank of the saints, as they do of the choir of Angels, to the end, that their advocates and intercessors being multiplied (as the church expresses it) they may the more readily obtain what they ask. The classes of saints may be divided into patriarchs, prophets, apostles, martyrs, bishops, doctors, priests, religious, confessors, virgins, and other saints in Heaven. For the more effectual prevailing with S. Francis Xaverius, it will be convenient every day, to make a special commemoration of S. Ignatius of Loyola, whom S. Francis Xaverius honoured, respected and loved, as his father, master and superior.

Upon one of the nine days, the person performing this devotion must confess and communicate, making a most diligent preparation to please God and S. Francis Xaverius, for the more ready obtaining of the thing desired.

Such as cannot read, may cause another to read these prayers to them, they giving great attention to them, and offering them up to S. Francis; or instead thereof they may say ten times the *Lord's Prayer,* ten *Hail Mary's,* and ten times *Glory be to the Father*, &c in memory of the ten years that S. Francis Xaverius spent in preaching in the Indies; begging of the Saint whatsoever they desire, and praying as he did for the conversion of Infidels.

Tho' the properest time for performing this Novena be from the fourth of *March* to the twelfth, which is the day of the Canonization of S. Francis Xaverius; yet it may be performed at any other time of the year.

How much the devotion of this *Novena* daily spreads, is well known: on this account S. Francis has obtained favours for several persons as they themselves testify. In the year 1688, it was performed at Madrid with extrordinary solemnity, in the royal chapel of the palace, their Catholic Majesties being every day there present.

The First Day of the Novena

The person performing this devotion kneeling before an altar, or the image of S. Francis Xaverius, shall lift up his heart to God, and profoundly humbling himself in spirit, and offering up all his prayers, thoughts, and words to his glory in honour of the blessed Virgin Mary, S. Francis Xaverius, and all the Angels and Saints in Heaven, he shall make the sign of the Cross, and say the following prayer:

O LORD Jesus Christ, true God and true man, my creator and redeemer, for thy sake alone and because I love thee above all things, I am sorry from the bottom of my heart for having offended thee; and I do firmly purpose never to fall into sin again, to shun all occasions of offending thee, to confess my sins, and perform the penance that shall be enjoined me, and to make restitution and satisfaction, wherever it shall be due from me. For the love of thee I forgive all my enemies; to thee I offer up my life, actions and sufferings in satisfaction for my sins; and since I humbly beg it of thee, I trust in thy goodness and infinite mercy, that thou wilt forgive me them through the merits of thy precious blood and passion, and wilt give me grace to amend my life, and to persevere in thy service unto my death. Amen.

MOST Glorious S. Francis Xaverius, Apostle of the Indies, if it be for the glory of god and to thy honor, that I obtain what I desire and beg by performing this *Novena;* obtain for me this grace of our Lord; if not, guide my petition, and beg of our Lord for me, that which is most proper for his glory, and the benefit of my soul.

A Prayer for the first day of the Novena. This prayer changes on each day of the Novena as noted. . . .

O GOD and Lord of the Angels, whom thou dost instruct with the guardianship of men; I make thee an offering of all the merits of these heavenly spirits, and those of thy servant S. Francis Xaverius, who was called an Angel for his purity; and because he preserved men from many spiritual and corporal dangers. I beseech thee, grant me that purity of soul and body, which thou didst confer on this thy holy apostle, and that particular grace, which I beg in this *Novena* to thy greater honor and glory. Amen.

Here say *thrice the Lord's Prayer,* and three *Hail Mary's,* and then the following prayer to *S. Francis Xaverius.*

MOST holy father, S. Francis Xaverius, who receivest thy praises from the mouths of innocent children; I most humbly implore thy bountiful charity for the sake of the most precious blood of Jesus, and of the immaculate conception of our blessed Lady mother of God; to the end thou mayest obtain of God's infinite goodness, that at the approach of my last hour, my heart may be separated and withdrawn from all worldly thoughts and distractions, and be fixed in the most ardent love of him and a vehement desire of a happy eternity; so that laying aside the multiplicity of earthly things, which hitherto have perplexed me, I may most diligently seek, and perfectly find that one thing which is necessary, which is to die and rest in peace under the protection of the most holy Virgin Mary, in the wounds of Jesus her most blessed son, in the sweet embraces of my God, and in thy presence, holy Saint, through whose intercession I hope to obtain this mercy. But yet, whilst it shall please the divine providence to preserve my life, I beseech thee, my most loving protector and most affectionate father, to obtain for me of his divine Majesty, that I may live, as I would wish to have lived at the hour of my death; ever imitating thy virtues, and fulfilling the most holy will of God; that so my temporal death may be to me a passage into life everlasting; I also beseech thee to obtain for me, that which I ask in this *Novena,* if it be for the glory of God and good of my soul. Amen.

In the next place, you are to ask of S. Francis Xaverius, the particular favour you desire to obtain, heightening as much as in you is, your confidence in him, with such words as your affectionate thoughts shall suggest, or with such aspirations, as your devotion shall dictate.

Then the more to please this holy Apostle, in imitation of him, say that Prayer, which he himself composed and used to say every day for the conversion of Infidels, which is as follows:

ETERNAL God, creator of all things, remember that thou alone didst create the souls of infidels, framing them to thy own image and likeness: Behold, O Lord, how to thy dishonor hell daily is replenished with them: Remember, O Lord, thy only Son Jesus Christ who suffered for them, most bountifully shedding his most precious blood: Suffer not, O Lord, thy Son and our Lord to be any longer despised by infidels; but rather, being appeased by the intreaties and prayers of thy elect the Saints, and of the Church the most blessed spouse of thy Son, vouchsafe to be mindful of thy mercy, and forgetting their idolatry and infidelity, cause them also to know him thou didst send, Jesus Christ thy son and our Lord, who is our health, life and resurrection, through whom we are made free and saved, to whom be all glory for ever. Amen.

Then conclude with the Prayer proper to this Saint.

Antiph. Well fare thee, good and faithful servant; because thou hast been faithful over a few things, I will place thee over many things; enter into the joy of thy Lord.

V. Our Lord hath guided the just man by right ways.

R. And hath shewed him the kingdom of God.

The Prayer.

O GOD who wert pleased to reduce to the bosom of thy church, the nations of the Indies, thro' the preaching and miracles of S. Francis Xaverius, mercifully grant us, that we may imitate his virtues, whose glorious merits we hold in veneration. thro' Jesus Christ our Lord. amen.

A COMMEMORATION OF S. IGNATIUS OF LOYOLA

Antiph.

THIS Man despising the world, and triumphing over earthly things, heaped up riches in Heaven by word and work.

V. The Lord loved and adorned him.

R. A garment of glory he hath put on him.

The Prayer.

O GOD, who for the propagation of the greater glory of thy name, hast by blessed Ignatius strengthened the church militant with new auxiliaries; graciously vouchsafe, that we by his assistance and imitation, solicitiously combating upon earth, may obtain with him an everlasting crown in Heaven.

A COMMEMORATION OF S. GREGORY

The Great, Apostle of England

Antiph.

O MOST excellent doctor, light of the holy church, blessed Gregory, lover of God's law, supplicate the Son of God for us.

V. Thou art a Priest for ever.

R. According to the Order of Melchisedech.

The Prayer.

O GOD, who hast bestowed the rewards of eternal blessedness on the soul of thy servant Gregory, grant mercifully that we, who are deprest with the weight of our sins, may by his prayers be delivered. Thro' our Lord. Amen.

For the second Day, begin

O Lord Jesus Christ, true God and man, &c. as before on the first Day. . . .

Most glorious S. Francis Xaverius, &c. as the first Day, and so on all the following Days.

A Prayer for the second Day.

LORD God of the Archangels, whom thou dost instruct with the most weighty concerns of thy glory, and the benefit of men; I offer up to thee the merits of these most diligent spirits, and those of thy great servant S. Francis Xaverius, whom thou madest the Minister of thy glory, and to whom thou recommendedst [sic] the spiritual welfare of innumerable souls. I beseech thee grant, that I may perform those duties, which thy most holy and divine will hath imposed upon me, and also that I may obtain that particular grace, which I beg of thee in this *Novena,* to thy greater honour and glory. Amen.

The third Day.

LORD God of the Principalities, who according to the disposition of thy divine will, by means of angels and Archangels, takes care of the welfare of mankind, enlightning, instructing, and governing them; I offer up to thee the merits of these most zealous spirits, and those of thy servant S. Francis Xaverius, who enlightened and converted many kingdoms and provinces and in them unnumerable souls not only by himself, but by his disciples and followers, instructing, teaching and commanding. I beseech thee, grant me the zeal of this holy Apostle, and the particular petition I tender in this *Novena,* to thy greater honour and glory. Amen.

The fourth Day.

LORD god of the Powers, who have a special prerogative to curb the infernal spirits: I offer up to thee the merits of these most potent spirits, and those of thy servant S. Francis Xaverius, to whom thou gavest singular power of expelling devils from bodies and souls. I beseech thee, grant me the grace to overcome all the temptations of the devil, and that which I beg of thee in this *Novena* to thy greater honour and glory. Amen.

The fifth Day.

LORD God of the Virtues, by whose means thou workest miracles and prodigies peculiar to thy sovereign power: I offer up to thee the merits of these most stupendous spirits, and those of thy servant S. Francis Xaverius, whom thou madest a new Thaumaturgus, or worker of new and prodigious miracles, renewing in him the signs and wonders of thy blessed Apostles, that he might discover the gospel to new nations. I beseech thee, grant me that profound humility, wherewith S. Francis

Xaverius, amidst so many miracles sought thy glory and not his own honour, as also that, which I beg in this *Novena,* to thy greater honour and glory. Amen.

The sixth Day.

LORD God of the Dominations, which preside over all inferior spirits as ministers of thy providence, and submit themselves to thy will, being ever ready to fulfil it: I offer up to thee the merits of these excellent spirits, and those of S. Francis Xaverius, who tho' superior to many, yet humbly submitted to all Superiors, in them acknowledging thy Majesty, and readily fulfilling their commands. I beseech thee, grant me a ready and perfect obedience to all my Superiors, and that special petition which I make in this *Novena,* to thy greater honour and glory. Amen.

The seventh Day.

LORD God of the Thrones, on whom thou reposest as on the seat of thy glory, and chair of thy Majesty: I offer up to thee the merits of these supreme spirits, and those of S. Francis Xaverius, that throne of thy glory, that vessel of election to convey thy name to new nations, who denied himself to himself and to all worldly things, casting them out of his Heart, that thou alone might possess it. I beseech thee, grant that I may despise all worldly things, and rest in thee alone; grant me also the petition I make in this *Novena* to thy greater honour and Glory. Amen.

The eighth Day.

LORD God of the Cherubims, who are adorned with most perfect wisdom: I offer up to thee the merits of these most knowing spirits, and those of thy servant S. Francis Xaverius, whom thou didst grace with supereminent wisdom, and to whom thou didst reveal most profound secrets that he might teach thy law to many people and nations. I beseech thee, grant that I may learn to fear and please thee which is true wisdom, and that by word and example I may teach others to keep thy Commandments, and that thou wilt also grant me the favour I beg in this *Novena,* to thy greater honour and glory. Amen.

The ninth Day.

LORD God of the Seraphims, who are inflamed with the most ardent love of thee: I offer up to thee the merits of these most fervent spirits, and those of thy servant S. Francis Xaverius, who like a Seraphim, was inflamed with thy love, conquering innumerable hardships and dangers of his life, to please thee, and to make those know and love thee, who before offended thee and knew thee not. I beseech thee, grant that I may love thee my only God, and my Lord, and endeavour to bring all men to the knowledge and love of thee; and also that thou wilt grant me that which I ask in this *Novena,* to thy greater honour and glory. Amen.

NOTES

1. Georgetown, 13–29, 160–172.

2. Carroll to Leonardo Antonelli, June 17, 1793, in Hanley, *Carroll Papers*, II, 96.

3. As the Church does not pronounce on the authenticity of this revelation or the sanctity of the person to whom it was made, in order to conform as we ought, to the wise regulations of the Holy See, we only relate this as an historical fact, yet so certain and so averred as to challenge deservedly our belief and adherence. We speak here as formerly the faithful spoke of the revelation of S. Juliana, which gave rise to the solemnity of the feast of Corpus Christi [the Editors].

4. This appears in *The Devotion to the Sacred Heart of Jesus with other pious practices, devout prayers, and instructions for the use and convenience of Christians in general* (Bruges, 1765), 216–235. It apparently was reprinted from Levinius Brown's translation from the Italian of *The Manner of Performing the Novena, and the Devotion of the Fridays in honour of St. Francis Xavier* (Liège, 1741). See Carlos Sommervogel, S.J., *Bibliothèque de La Compagnie de Jésus, Bibliographie*, II (Brussels, 1891), 224; Foley, *Records*, 7, 94; ibid., 3, 541.

Part II

THE NINETEENTH CENTURY:
NATIVES, IMMIGRANTS, AND CONVERTS

VI

BENEDICT JOSEPH FENWICK
AND THE MARYLAND TRADITION

"I love Bishop Fenwick as a father," Isaac Hecker wrote to Orestes Brownson shortly after he had decided to enter the Roman Catholic Church in
1844. *"He [is the] best man I ever knew. He comes the nearest to being a
saint and no man can do more for his diocese than he is doing."*[1] Given the
decidedly low opinion that Hecker had of the spirituality of American Jesuits in general, his appraisal of Fenwick is all the more notable.

Fenwick (1782–1846) was the descendant of one of the first families
of Maryland. A native of St. Mary's County, he had studied at Georgetown
College and St. Mary's Seminary before entering the Society in 1806 as one
of the original novices of the restored Mission. Immediately after his ordination in 1808, he was sent to New York City with Father Anthony Kohlmann. There his pastoral work included the conversion of an Episcopalian
priest and his wife, Virgil and Jerusha Barber, and an abortive attempt to
bring Thomas Paine into the Church on his deathbed. When the New York
mission was closed in 1817, Fenwick became rector of Georgetown. A year
later Ambrose Marechal, the new Archbishop of Baltimore, sent him to
Charleston as a peacemaker for a congregation long divided by trusteeism.
After preparing the way for John England in Charleston, Fenwick returned
to the Chesapeake region where he divided his time between Georgetown
College and the Carmelite Monastery in Charles County, Maryland. Then
in 1825 he was named the second Bishop of Boston.

MOUNT CARMEL

The relationship of the American Carmelites and Jesuits reached back to
Europe. Andrew White had been chaplain to the Carmelites in Antwerp before volunteering for Maryland. From 1780 to 1790 Charles Neale, one of

seven brothers to join the Society of Jesus, served as chaplain in the same monastery. In that latter year he and another former Jesuit, Robert Plunkett, led four Carmelites to Charles County, Maryland to establish at Portobacco near Neale's ancestral home the first community of religious women in the United States. Neale continued as their chaplain until his death in 1823. Although Fenwick succeeded Neale for a very short time before being recalled to Georgetown, the following selections make clear how fully he had entered into their life and why his own brief chaplaincy left such a deep impression on the communal memory of the monastery.

A SONG FOR THE REV[EREN]D MOTHER[2]

To the tune of "Hortentia"
Lucius at a distance pointing to Mount Carmel and describing its beauties to an inquiring friend.

	See yon delightful blooming Mount
	Which bound th' adjacent fields;
	Around whose Base sweet flows a Fount
	Which purest water yields—
	'Tis Carmel lovely, sweet abode,
	Where heavenly Virtue dwells;
Thrice	Fair Daughters of Teresa's mode
	Of life adorn it's [sic] Cells.

2.

	Not more melodious Philomele
	Queen Songstress of the Spring
	Her warbling notes does Smoothly swell,
	Or greater raptures bring;
	Than the bright Virgins of yon Seat:
	You'd think that Angels sing,
Thrice	When they in heav'nly strains repeat
	The praises of their King.

3.

Ah Carmel! much as thou dost soar
Above the Meads beneath;
So much doest thou excell and more
All other Hills in health.
Enchanting Spot! Sweet Paradise

Of innocence and ease!
Thrice   Where care is never known nor vice,
Nor aught that does not please.

4.

Sweet are the Flow'ers that bloom around
So pleasing to the eye!
Not sweeter fruits than there are found.
You ask the reason why?
Th' Almighty is the God they love
His will is all their care—
Thrice   Hence flow all blessings from above
Upon those who are there.

5.

Vain, bustling, treach'rous, lying world!
Thy pleasure is but pain:
Thou drivest on with Sails unfurl'd
But ah! tis all in vain.
Nor happiness in thee is found,
Nor true and real joy;
Thrice   'Tis vanity all—nothing's sound—
All, all is but a Toy.

6.

The Soul immortal in her birth
Created for above
Must look beyond this passing Earth
for happiness and love.
No sublune object yields content
To her who is divine;
Thrice   'Twas God alone her hither sent—
For God she'll ever pine.

7.

There in that far sequester'd Spot
Those Angels pass the day
Most happy in their blessed lot,
Joyful and ever gay.
Nor frightful dreams disturb their rest,
When Night invites respose;

Thrice   Nor rankling care lurks in their breast,
The hours they sweetly dose.

8.

A Reverend Mother, kind and good
With ev'ry virtue crown'd
Supplies their wants with choicest food
With which her Stores abound
Are any sick and want relief?
She feels a Parent's care;
Thrice   She sooths their pain, and o'er their grief
She drops a tender tear.

9.

Happy Children! you feel her worth.
Else why that deep concern?
Those anxious cares about her health?
The cause one need not learn.
Yes;—to you she is a treasure
Of price and value great—
Thrice   Her virtues, ah! none can measure
When known 'twill be too late.

10.

Their Father . . . . . . But here, let me stop—
Once dear, once honour'd name![3]
See'st thou yon weeping Willow droop?—
'Tis th' Emblem of their pain.
The tears which still abundant flow
Announce their poignant grief;
Thrice   Long on his Grave the grass shall grow
'Ere they obtain relief.

11.

A better greater one than he
More learned, prudent, wise,
Society does seldome see
For Providence denies.
But now he's gone—God will'd it so;
His Name be ever bless'd!

Thrice   Great is his loss; this well we know
           And long 'twill be confess'd.
                    FINIS

                              Composed by Revd. Father B. Fenwick
                              and presented to Revd Mother on her
                              Cloathing Day May 1, 1823.

                    RETREAT[4]

As missions began to be popular with clergy and laity, traditional retreats continued to be annual occasions for spiritual renewal for religious. The following excerpts of a retreat given by Fenwick to the community at Mount Carmel, presumably in 1823, adhere closely to the Spiritual Exercises of Saint Ignatius. *In each Ignatian meditation or contemplation three points or themes are outlined. Each day of the retreat the director would also be expected to give some instruction on the spiritual or religious life.*

                    Second Day
                    First Meditation
On the esteem we should have for Creatures.
                    1st Point.
     God having created us to serve him and to render us happy, has furnished us with all the necessary means to arrive at this end. Some are supernatural, such as grace: others natural as are all the goods and evils of this life which are destined to conduct us to heaven.
                    2nd Point.
     It follows from this truth:
1st   That we must never become attached to creatures, because they are only means to arrive at our end and it is not lawful to seek repose anywhere but in that end.
2nd   That we must esteem the evils and goods of this life but inasmuch as they are conducive to our salvation: just as we attach importance to a medicine but inasmuch as it is calculated to restore health. Therefore we ought to be indifferent with regard either to glory or to contempt, to riches or poverty, to pleasure or pain, to health or sickness; since it is the judgment of God that should regulate our judgments, & his will that should regulate ours: and inasmuch as all that humbles & afflicts nature, conducts us more securely to God, than what elevates or flatters this

same nature, so we ought to have far more esteem & far more affection for things that are contrary to our natural inclinations, than for those which are agreeable to them.

3rd   It follows that we ought to look upon all creatures with indifference, & love in them only the good pleasure of God. When this is wanting, we must hate & dispise them.

3rd Point.

Look back into your life, & see what afflicts you: you will find that it is the resistence of your will to the will of God. You wish what that does not wish & you wish not what [it] wishes. Well, which of the two ought [you] to obey? Is it not just that God should be Master? Shall we be always miserable? Shall we never enjoy peace? Never if we do not make the will of God ours. We must therefore make it; by keeping his commandments, & abandoning ourselves to all the orders of his providence.

Second Day
Second Meditation

On the evil of one's own will.

Prelude.

Represent to yourself Lucifer wishing to put himself on a level with God and ascend his throne. It is what they do who wish to do their own will.

1st Point.

Consider the evil which a person does who prefers his own will to the will of God.

1st   He withdraws himself from the direction and jurisdiction of God wishing to be his own master and independent like him.

2nd   He rises even above God wishing that God should yield to his caprice and subserve his passion.

3rd   He wishes to deprive him of his crown to put it on his own head; for as it belongs but to a King to wear a crown, so it belongs but to God to do his own will. In fine he annihilates as much as in him lies the Divinity, desiring that God should not know his sin, or should not wish to punish it or should not have power to punish it: and thus that God should be without wisdom, without power and without justice.

Behold what you have done since you have been in the world. You have surpassed the pride of Lucifer, for he pretended only to be equal to God, whereas you wish to be above him, since you desire that he should obey you & should do your will. . . .

Fifth Day
Consideration

On one's particular employ.——

As you belong not to yourself but to God, you ought not to labour for yourself, but for God. You never manage your own concerns better, than when you manage those of God: You manage the concerns of God, when you act well in your employment considering it as one given you by him, and which you acquit yourself of with all the strength, vigilince [sic] & fidelity of which you are capable.

Make no distinction between the concerns of God & yours. You have but one affair in hand, & that is to save your soul; And your Salvation is the only affair of God as well as your. On this affair he has thought from all Eternity; for this affair he has laboured from the beginning of the world; it was this affair that caused him to descend from Heaven, that caused him to be born in a poor stable & finally to die on a cross. Do you think on this? Does it not at least merit your attention? Be fully persuaded that you labour effectually towards your salvation & perfection when occupied with your particular employment. Your salvation is attached to the accomplishment of the will of God, & God wishes you to discharge faithfully the employ-ment he has given you. We are all servants of this great Master, each one labours in his vineyard, & each one has received talents which he must turn to advantage. In what do you employ yours? Are you ready to render an account of them?

There is a certain description of people who wish always to do what they ought not to do, & who never do what they ought to do. It is enough for them to know that they are obliged to do a thing to conceive an utter aversion for it. Offices are a torment to them, & rules & regulations a tyr-anny. All that they can do is to bear with God, because they cannot hinder him from being; but they cannot submit to his dominion, nor to the jurisdic-tion of men. They work when they please & because they please & as soon as any coertion [sic] is used, labour becomes an insupportable burden to them. Such souls are without rule & without discipline, without order & without laws, without subjection & without obedience, who do nothing but trouble the peace of every community & are a burden to every one. Are you not of this class? There is another description [of those] who wish to do exactly that which they are unable to do, & will never do that which they can do. They refuse those offices which God has given them talents for, & seek with avidity those for which they are not at all calculated. They mea-sure their abilities by their desires, and not their desires by their abilities. Passion cause[s] them to think that they are capable of every thing, except that very thing for which only they are capable. These people labour much,

& gain nothing. They bury the talents which God has given them, & becomes [sic] guilty of two crimes; the one of not having done what they ought to have done; the other of having done what they ought not to have done. Are you not one of these rebellious children? Do you leave to your Superiors the entire disposal of yourself?

To have much ambition is a great cross: it is prodigious folly for one to think himself capable of every thing. Our capacity & abilities are limited: God, says St. Paul, divides his graces. When he sends us to labour in his vineyard; he gives us precisely what is necessary for us. When he places us in any office, he assigns us that portion of grace requisite for us to discharge it well. Thus to speak correctly we possess talents only to do what God commands us to do; in any other thing, we are as incapable of succeeding as a bird is of flying without wings. Take away the blessing of God, & of what avail will your talents be? And what is it that gives this blessing, but obedience? If you do not succeed in your office there is reason to believe that it is not the one God has laid out for you; that you intruded yourself into it; that ambition prompted you to seek it; that favour thrust you into it; at least that you did not beg of God his grace & blessing, & that you secretly sought your own satisfaction in it rather than his.

Whatever the case may be it is certain that is the ordinary course of divine Providence. And if one succeed not in the office God has laid out, it is to be ascribed to a very rare & extraordinary conduct. You should always ascribe to your sins rather than to any other cause, the ill success of your labours. Live without choice, destine yourself for nothing, say always with the Prophet: Lord, behold me, what wilt thou have me do? I am ready to go whithersoever thou pleasest. Happy the individual who is capable of doing any thing, & who is equally ready to do nothing; who keeps himself hid under a bushel, until God is pleased to put him on the candlestick. Never intrude yourself into an office to which you have not been called, and never refuse any one that is given you. By following this rule, you will enjoy wonderful peace. God will bless all your exertions & the success with which your labours are crowned will not anywise diminish your merit. The world is a stage where each one has to perform his particular part: one performs the part of a Captain, another that of a soldier, another that of a merchant, another that of a judge, another that of a King, another that of a Bishop. Does it belong to a Bishop to perform the part of a Captain? Does it belong to a Captain to perform the part of a bishop? You possess grace to do one thing, but you do not possess it to do another. If you enter upon the stage at a wrong time, & out of your order, you will make there but a poor figure. If you do not acquit yourself as becomes you of your duty, you will disturb the beautiful order of the Universe, you will offend God & the Angels who are spectators of your actions, and in the end you will become an object of ridicule, of contempt and indignation to all creatures.

Do then what you wish, but bear this in mind that your labour will be in vain if you do not do what you ought. Your duty, once more I repeat it, is to do what God wishes, & to acquit yourself faithfully in the office he gives you. You will discharge it well if you receive it from his hand, if you enter upon it by his orders, if you rely upon his grace, if you implore his blessing, if you covet not another office, if you perform your labour with gaiety, quietly, courageously, constantly: with gaiety, without ill-humour; quietly, without uneasiness; courageously, without baseness; constantly, without disgust and without relaxation. What is your defect?

God wishes not that all should fill honourable situations & brilliant employments. There are some who in the body of the church are destined to see, as the eyes; others to hear, as the ears; others to speak as the tongue; others to labour, as the hands; others to walk and to bear the burden of the whole body, as the feet. Take a member out of its proper place, & there will be no longer any peace, any repose, any life, any motion; it will immediately incommode the others, it troubles the harmony of nature, you must therefore cut & lop it off. If one should wish to be in the place of another and perform his office, it is evident he would lose his labour, and would not succeed. Are you where you ought to be? Do you do what you ought to do, & as you ought to do it? Do not imagine that your office is not a fit one for you because it does not please you. Inclination is in reality a mark of vocation, but it must be pure, quiet, obedient, disinterested, divested of all human respect & disengaged from all ambition. Distrust that inclination which is turbulent, impetuous, rebellious & impatient. A good religious ought to live without any inclination, or should make it subservient to obedience.

Never separate the service of God from the duty belonging to your office: do not think it allowable to be in the Guire [sic] when you should be in your cell, or to say your particular prayers when you ought to be at your work. The most acceptable devotion is to do what you ought to do. Work without prayer is a vain occupation; prayer without work is a false devotion. Satisfy your devotion after having first satisfied your obligation. What is of command is preferable to what is of counsel, & duty, to acts that are free.

Do you wish to succeed in your work? If so, take care never to separate it from prayer. Pray before you begin to work, pray whilst you are at work, & prayer after having finished your work. The spiritual is to the temporal what the soul is to the body. What can a body do separated from the soul? Seek first the kingdom of God and all other things will be added unto you; take care of the principal thing & the accessary will be sure not to fail.

For whom do you labour? Are your intentions pure? These are the marks of a pure intention: When you labour with a composed mind: when you are ready to leave or to continue the action which you have begun: when you love interruptions as well as the end provided they do not proceed from you: when you would rejoice to see others succeed better than you: when you take no voluntary complacency in your work after it is done: when you labour as if there were only God[5] & you in the world: when you are pleased at experiencing no sensible & natural satisfaction: when want of success does not dishearten you, nor afflict you, then it is a sign that your intention is pure.

But if you labour with a disturbed mind, disquietude & overeagerness; when crossed or when you do not succeed; if you feel & show displeasure when others succeed better than you, if you experience a secret pain when they make a greater progress in virtue, or when they draw on themselves more esteem, more attention and a greater degree of approbation; if you make continual reflections on yourself; if you seek your own satisfaction, & if you omit the duties of your office, when troublesome to you, it is a sign that your intention is not pure & that it is not solely for God that you work.

Consider all the good & all the evil you are capable of doing in your office, the one that you may practice it, the other that you may avoid it. Beg pardon of God for having so badly acquitted yourself of it till now. Endeavour henceforth to conduct yourself better in it, as an officer of divine providence who has given you this commission, who has put you in this office, who gives you graces to exercise it properly, who will make you render him a[n] account of it at your death, & who stores up a rich reward in return for your services.

Observe exactly all the rules of your office. It is a claim which the public has upon your liberty, & you cannot exempt yourself from it without an injustice. The practice[6] of those who have discharged it well before you should be a rule for your direction. Conform yourself to their example in the exercise of your office. Never abuse your authority. Remember that God will do justice to every body. In the discussions that may arise between you & those under you, take always their part against yourself, & presume that they are in the right, except the contrary should evidently & manifestly appear. Never take advantage of your authority, & of their inferiority. Remember that you are put in place but for the benefit of others, & that God who is your Superior will treat you as you shall have treated your Inferiors.

Eighth Day
Third Meditation
On the happiness of possessing God.

Prelude.

Represent to yourself God in your heart as on his Throne, in his temple, his palace & his paradise. Beg grace to know and to love.

1st Point.

Consider that God is the plenitude of all good and that he is sufficient in himself: because he stands in need of none of his creatures, & possesses every kind of good, that all that is in him is perfect, and can receive neither diminution nor augmentation.

2nd Point.

Consider that God is not only sufficient in himself, but is likewise sufficient for all his creatures, & that we shall find in him all the glory, all the goods and the consolations we can desire.

3rd Point.

Consider that all creatures are not sufficient for our heart, because they are limited and our heart is not. They are made for us, but we are not made for them. As God alone is our last end, God alone must be the centre of our repose. Why then seek this repose in creatures? O my God and my all! Thou shalt ever be my all, and creatures shall henceforth be nothing to me.

THE ADIEU[7]

To the Tune of "Hail Virtue"

Farewell Carmel! Dear sweet abode, adieu!
Mansion of worth, to ev'ry virtue true!
Peace to thy lovely humble cells,
Where naught but purest virtue dwells!
Accept this slight tribute—'tis all
A grateful heart its own can call.

June 5th 1823   Lucius[8]

BOSTON

Fenwick's memoirs, composed in 1836, reflect his post Charlestown attitude. Written in spare moments over a three month period, the memoirs borrow heavily from other writers. But there is enough of Fenwick in his diary excerpts and hurried reflections to make one appreciate why he so impressed Brownson and Hecker. Nearly 120 pages dealt with John Thayer's controversies with Protestant Boston in the 1790s, even though this converted minister spent less than four years in the city as a Catholic priest. To Benedict Fenwick, looking backward from the Boston of the 1830s, John Thayer must have seemed a proleptic figure.

THE CONVERSION OF JOHN THAYER[9]

The Rev. John Thayer arrived in Boston on the 4th of January 1790. This excellent clergyman was a native of this City. He had been a Congregational Minister, and had officiated as such in Boston during two years when he felt a great desire to visit Europe, to learn some of the languages spoken there, and to make himself acquainted with the constitution of the different governments, their laws, the manners and customs of the people, in order that he might be more highly considered in his country, and render himself more useful to it. With this view he left Boston and sailed for France at the end of the year 1781. He immediately on his arrival set himself to read the best authors, and to study the principles of government. He was shortly after taken sick: and fearing that it might prove fatal, gave orders that no Catholic Priest should be admitted into his room, so strongly was he attached to his Sect. Upon his recovery he passed over into England where he spent three months. He was here asked to preach, which invitation he accepted; but his doctrine was found not to be conformable to that of the country where he was. He remarked, in reply, that he had drawn it from the Holy Scriptures. It is here that all Protestants find their different doctrines. He returned to France for the purpose of travelling to Rome, having his mind bent on the same objects and greatly *prepossessed against the Cath[olic] religion and the people of Italy who had been always represented to him under the most odious light. He had,* however, during his stay in France conceived a somewhat more favourable *opinion of Cath[olic] Doctrine, and his intercourse with the Italians* tended also much to correct his former preventions against them. In his passage from Marseils to Rome, he was obliged, for want of wind, to remain several days in a small harbour, called *Port Ercolé.* The Marquis D'Elmoro, a respectable old Gentleman, Mayor of the place, without his having any recommendation to him received him politely and treated him with paternal affection and kindness. His house, his table, his library, all were at his service. On his departure he made him promise to keep up a correspondence with him by letter. He had every where, he tells us in the account which he afterwards published of his conversion, the happiness to meet with Italians of the same character: and all those with whom he had any conversation testified the same readiness to oblige him, especially in the decent and virtuous house in which he took up his lodgings at Rome, and in which he was treated as in the bosom of his own family. So much kindness and cordiality towards a stranger, and a Protestant known as such, both moved and surprised him. "This religion then," said he to *himself, "is not so unsociable, as it has been represented to me; nor does it inspire sentiments of intolerance and hatred towards those who* are out of its pale." Thus was he led to condemn from day to day those unjust prejudices with which his mind had been filled against it, and thus did God prepare things from afar to lead him insensibly to the happy term at which he at length arrived. As soon as he entered Rome, his first desire was to go and visit some of the principal Monuments of Antiquity which are *so attractive to strangers, especiale [sic] the rotunda or the Pantheon, a temple formerly consecrated to the worship of heathen Divinities, but now* dedicated to the honour of the Blessed Virgin and the Saints.

At the sight of this superb edifice, he was struck with an idea which seemed to him lofty, and which would be very proper, said he to himself, to furnish matter for a fine discourse, if the Catholic religion were the true one. The following is the substance of what suggested itself to his mind: This temple formerly consecrated to the worship of false Gods, become now a Temple of the only true God, the cross of Jesus Christ elevated upon the ruins of all the Idols united, in order to form, as it were, a more beautiful trophy, and thence exhibited to the whole world: this City, formerly mistress of the Universe and Capital of the pagan World, become now the Capital of the Christian world: here are speaking and ever subsisting monuments of the triumph of Jesus Christ over the *Strong one armed,* and the establishment of his Empire upon the ruins of the empire of true religion: the first city of the world the Capital of his kingdom: in fine, of that great school of the arts, of that celebrated City, which attracts all eyes and which draws the curious to it, and strangers from all parts of the world, the School of truth and the common centre of Union among all the faithful who believe in Jesus Christ. Then nothing would be wanting to the external glory of his religion and the visibility of his Church, which he doubtless wished to place under the eyes of all his people, then she would prove to be that City truly built on a mountain and exposed to the sight of all nations, in such a manner as not to be concealed.—"This idea pleased me *much," said he, "and as I was fond of Pulpit eloquence, I almost wished that she was the true Church in order that I might handle so* beautiful a subject." This first ray of light was calculated to lead him farther: but as yet it was only a Chimera abounding in pleasant thoughts, and he left it there to occupy himself with matters which he had first proposed to himself.

He acquired the Italian, in a much shorter time, and more easily, than the French, and was soon able to read the best authors in that language. He

studied, at the same time, agreably to his project, the constitution and actual
state of Rome.

Nevertheless, the Cath[olic] religion came frequently into his mind;
although it did not enter into the plan of his studies, still he wished to study
it profoundly, as long as he remained in the city, as he would have wished
to know the Mahometan religion, had he been at Constantinople: besides,
he was far from suspecting that his own was false, or at least of thinking to
embrace another; his only object was to learn the Catholic doctrine from the
mouths of Catholics, that he might not impute to them what they would
disavow. He addressed himself for this purpose to several Ecclesiasticks,
and, according to his usual manner, to cause each one to speak of his particular profession, he put them upon the topick of religion: but they had
more piety than light. Beholding a determined Protestant, they condemned
without enlightening him, and they separated mutually discontented, they
with his attachment to his errors, and he with their zeal which did not appear
to him conformable to science; besides, he wished to know only their opinions and not to be undeceived with regard to his own: he did not experience
the necessity of being enlightened, but only desired to satisfy his curiosity.
Thanks, however, to that admirable Providence that makes all things serve
for a good end, as the desire of travelling had conducted him to the centre
of light, without his knowing it, so the desire of being informed equally
carried him on to the knowledge of truth without his thinking of it.

After having often sought occasion to have conversation with a well
in*formed man who should be able to acquaint him with the Catholick doc-*
trine and at the same [time] who should be willing to undertake to give him
his knowledge, he met with two ecclesiastics in a place he was in the habit
of frequenting: he there entered into conversation with them, declaring at
the same time what he was and what he desired. His ideas, at that time of
the Jesuits, corresponded with the opinion which Protestants generally entertained of them; nevertheless, he was anxious to become acquainted with
some of them,—''I am not ignorant,'' said he to himself, of their cunning,
and political craft, but they are considered by all as men of great learning;
I shall know how to profit by their learning and at the same time to be on
my guard against their subtilties'': It was precisely to two Jesuits he was at
this time conversing: his candour was not displeasing to them; they acknowledged that they belonged to the Society: but would not undertake to
give him the information he required, themselves, but promised to introduce him to one who was in every respect qualified to satisfy him.[10] They
accordingly introduced him to one of their lecturers, well known at Rome,
and highly considered both for his learning and virtue. ''Sir,'' said he to
him, ''it may be that I entertain false notions of your religion, having had
no opportunity to ascertain it except from its enemies. If that be the fact,

my intention is to undeceive myself, for I have no wish to entertain prejudices against any denomination. Do not, however, believe, that you will
convert me; for, surely you will not succeed." This abrupt manner of ad-
dressing him, did not prevent him from receiving M. Thayer, with a mildness and affability which could only be the effect of charity: he consented
to his request to be allowed to have conversation with him on the subject
of religion. He began by expounding to him, one by one, all the articles of
catholic faith. This exposition lasted many days. He listened to him attentively, and without ever interrupting him. But on his return to his lodgings,
he took care to commit to writing the objections which occurred to his mind
and the arguments which seemed to combat each of these articles and dog-
mas. Although many difficulties presented themselves to him, he could not
forbear, nevertheless, remarking that wonderful agreement *which was to be
found in the whole body of catholic doctrine, and which seemed to bespeak
a wisdom nearly divine. After he had ended his* exposition, M. Thayer pro-
pounded his difficulties and doubts; in this way three months were spent in
discussing all the different articles. He found himself often at fault and without having anything to reply, because he saw the fairness with which the
discussion had been conducted, and he was sincerely disposed to be instructed and not to waste time in mere chicanery. Nevertheless, his mind
was still greatly clouded, and he felt much embarrassed about several things
upon which he was anxious to be informed; and as this respectable gentleman could not spare from his other avocations more than a few hours, at a
time, and this at intervals on some days, he sought to fill up the space that
intervened, by having recourse to another Jesuit equally learned and zealous. This gentleman's manner, at his first interview, appeared to him not a
little singular: "We shall not enter," said he, "upon the matter today, go,
and first recite the *Lord's Prayer* three times, and return on such a day."
He could not help smiling at this commencement. "What," said M.
Thayer. "I am not yet a member of your Church, and already you impose
a penance on me." He left him after this: however, on his return home, he
reflected that prayer far from leading him astray, could not but be useful to
him, and that a religion which teaches to begin with prayer, before examining into it, was, to all appearances very sure of itself. He executed, accordingly what had been prescribed him, and on the day appointed he went
to see him. He already was in possession of what the Catholic doctrine was;
he now only wished to have certain points cleared up upon which he still
entertained some doubts. In proportion as he proposed these points to him
with his objections, he pointed out to him the places in the works of the best
Theologians and Controversial writers, in which they were treated at great
length, and at the same time procured them for him. M. Thayer studied
them attentively: this study led him to examine at bottom each of the articles

contested between Protestants and Catholics, and to weigh the reasons which these *adduce in support of their sentiments. He derived also considerable assistance from an Augustinian Friar, to whom he addressed himself at the* same time. He confined himself altogether to the pointing out to him the necessary distinction to be drawn between what is of faith among Catholics, and the private opinions which the Church allows to be treated in schools, without either adopting or rejecting them. This distinction threw much light upon the matter, and contributed to give him a clearer conception of things; for Protestants are in the habit of confounding these two objects, and thus of throwing every thing into confusion. There exists a perfect unity in things belonging to faith, the difference relates only to opinion; by blending these two things together, they take occasion to ascribe to faith what appertains solely to free and indifferent opinions.

The care which he took to consult in this manner different learned men, was doubly useful to him; he always profited by their particular lights, and was thereby enabled to observe their perfect agreement in faith, which, in fact, should be but one, as truth is one. This uniformity of sentiments, which has prevailed, in all ages among Catholics, caused a sensible impression in him, because he had never seen any thing like it among Protestants. . . .

M. Thayer had been on terms of intimacy with the leading Ministers of the different Protestant Sects; he had often conversed with them; he knew well their sentiments; there never were two of them that agreed even upon the most essential articles; and what is more there never was one of them that had not himself varied in his doctrine. . . .

This instability on the part of the leading Ministers of his communion gave him uneasiness. He saw in it a necessary consequence of the fundamental principle of Protestants, according to which each one is to be judge of his faith; according to this principle, there is no fixed rule of faith:— hence, that everlasting contradiction of Ministers among themselves:— hence, the frequent variation of each of them in his doctrine. M. Thayer had often tried to bring them to an agreement, and he had found that it could be only done by adopting the principle, that it was sufficient to believe in Jesus Christ, and to have the intention of honouring his Divinity; but with this system, which pleased him much, he would have united all Sects, even the most opposite; thus he went on, proceeding farther and *farther daily, and at len[g]th set no bounds to his liberty of thinking. He had friends among the Quakers, and Anabaptists, the Arminians and* others: he, in a short time, would have adopted toleration in its most extended sense. It is idle for Protestants to say, that they admit the Scripture as their rule of faith; as soon as they acknowledge no living authority to determine the sense; as soon as they leave the interpretation of it to every particular individual, there exists no longer any means of convincing them of error; and, if it should please the Socinian, for example, to say that he finds nothing in the Scripture which proves the Divinity of Jesus Christ, no one has any right to require of him the belief of this dogma or to condemn him, if he reject it. This principle leads still farther: it conducts a man, who reasons justly, on to indifference [with] respect [to] all religion, and it overthrows the very foundation of Christianity, by allowing the reason of each individual, as supreme judge of his belief. This reflection, and a thousand others which occurred to his mind, had not, at that time, all the effect which they might have produced, but they disposed and prepared him to open one day his eyes to the truth. Already had his researches conducted him much farther than he had thought; he had, at first, only intended to obtain an exact knowledge of the Catholic Doctrine, and he was insensibly led on to discover nothing in it but what was perfectly reasonable. He had, at the commencement of this examination, entertained no suspicion that his particular Sect was wrong; and now he perceived distinctly all the weak points in it, and even entertained serious doubts; but he was nevertheless far from having made up his mind to renounce it.

The prejudices of his education had yet a strong hold upon his mind; neither was his heart disposed as yet for such a sacrifice as this change would require of him; he thought it much to have taken the resolution to bring with him, on his return to America, the best controversial works, composed by Catholic writers, and to read them at his leisure, determined then to change his religion, when he should be no longer able to answer the arguments contained in them, after due reflection; for, he had made up his mind, whatever proofs might be adduced him, not, by any means, to make his abjuration at Rome, lest he might take an over-hasty step; but Divine Providence, which watched continually over him, would not allow him to use a delay, which might have proved fatal to him; it made different events serve to hasten his conversion. There fell into his hand a work of Father Seignery upon Guardian Angels.[11] This pious belief, that each one of us has a tutelar angel as a witness to all his actions, was not new to him; he had been taught it from his childhood; but it had not had until then any effect upon him, or very inconsiderable. The reading of this work awakened in his breast those early impressions of piety which he had received from his parents. He reflected upon his life past,—he reproached himself with having often failed in the respect which he owed to his Angel-Guardian, and he took the resolution to watch henceforth over himself with the view of avoiding whatever could displease him. This attention to keep himself from sin, contributed without doubt, to his conversion to the faith; it was, at least, one obstacle less to the grace which God wished to bestow upon him. Such was the state of things when the death of the Venerable *Labre* and the miracles reported to have been wrought through his intercession began to make a noise at Rome, and to become the subject of almost every conversation.[12] In spite of the instructions he had received, and the lights which these instructions had procured him, he was by no means disposed to believe all that was said of them. Of all his prejudices against Catholics, the most deeply rooted was a formal incredulity in regard to the miraculous events said to have happened among them. He had been brought up in this belief like all Protestants, who far from admitting the gift of miracles, disdain it, and take upon themselves to deny it positively. He not only denied absolutely those which were published at this time, he went so far as to turn them into ridicule; he even allowed himself to utter indecent jokes in the different Coffy-Houses, upon the Servant of God, whose poverty and apparent filth had disgusted him, and upon this subject he went even much farther than his friends who were also Protestants. However, the number and weight of testimony increasing daily, he thought it was incumbent on him to examine into the thing itself; he held frequent conversations with the Confessor of the deceased from whom he was made acquainted with a part of his life. He went to see four of the persons said to have been miraculously cured; he became assured of their actual state, and of that in which they had been before; he took information of the kind and duration of the disease with which they had been attacked, and of the circumstances of their cure which had been wrought in an instant; he collected the testimony of those who knew them, and after all this information taken with the greatest care, he became quite convinced that the reality of each of these miracles had been better proved than the best established facts ordinarily are. One of these persons, a *religious* of the Convent of St. Appollonia, had a bloodvessel broken in her breast; for the period of eighteen months she had fallen into a state of languor which had daily increased; her weakness had been such, that she could with difficulty endure the slightest nourishment; she invoked the Venerable *Labre,* she took, with faith, a little liquor into which had been dipped one of his Relicks, and she found herself in an instant perfectly cured. The same day she went down to the Choir with the other *Religious,* she eat [sic] with them without being in the least incommoded, and performed with great ease the most irksome labours of the house. This was attested by the Superiour of the house and six of the religious of the same Community. He himself saw repeatedly the religious Lady who had been healed; spoke to her and found her in the enjoyment of the best of health. He did not stop here; he paid a visit to the Physician who had attended her during the whole time of her illness; he confirmed all that the Community had stated in her regard, and he added, moreover, that he was ready to swear upon the holy Gospel that the infirmity she laboured under was naturally incurable. M. Thayer continued his visits to the good Lady during the whole time he remained at Rome, that is to say, during the space of six months; he accordingly had abundance of time to satisfy himself that her cure was effectual, and at his departure left her in perfect health. Persuaded, as he was, that these cures had something supernatural in them, he could [not] help reflecting within himself upon the danger he exposed himself to by remaining in a false religion. These reflections threw him into a strange perplexity; it would be difficult to express the violent situation in which he then found himself. Truth displayed herself to him on every side, but she was combatted by all the prejudices which he had sucked in with the milk of his mother. He felt the force of the reasons which were opposed to the doctrine of Protestants; he had not, however, the courage to yield; . . . in a word, his understanding was perfectly convinced, but his heart was not changed. It was while he was thus wavering and irresolute, that a small book was put into his hands, intitled *Manifesto d'un Cavaliere Christiano convertico alla religione Catholica.* . . . The author gives historically an account of his conversion and briefly discusses all the points which are controverted between Catholics and Protestants. He places at the beginning a Prayer which was communicated to him by a Catholic, to implore light of the Holy-Ghost. . . .

He felt, on receiving this book, a kind of presentiment that it was to give him the finishing stroke; consequently it was with extreme difficulty that he could resolve to read it; his soul was, as it were, torn by two contrary movements: what combats, what terrible assaults had he not to sustain at this time! He ran his eyes over this prayer, but could not prevail upon himself to utter it; he desired to be enlightened, and yet feared to be too much so; his temporal interests and a thousand other motives presented themselves, in crowds, to his mind, and kept in balance the salutary impressions of grace; in short, the interest of eternal salvation at last triumphed. He threw himself upon his knees, and endeavoured to recite this prayer with all the sincerity he was able; and the violent agitation of his soul, added to the struggle which he had just experienced, produced abundance of tears; he then set about reading this book, which was a short exposition of the principal proofs of the Catholic religion. The united collection of these different proofs, which until then he had only seen separately; so many rays of light brought, as it were, into a focus, struck him sensibly. He now no longer offered the same resistance to grace; God spoke to his heart at the same time that he enlightened his understanding, and gave him strength to surmount the obstacles which had stopped him until then. He had not yet finished reading the book when he cried out: My God, I promise thee to become a Catholic. The same day, he announced his determination to the family with whom he lived, they were overjoyed at it, because they were truly and sincerely pious. He went the same evening to the Coffee-house, where he communicated to all his friends his change of religion, the most of whom were Protestants; and, to repair, as far as he was able, the scandal which he had given, he boldly defended the sanctity of the venerable *Labre,* and furthermore declared that he had found more proofs of the truth of his miracles than he would have required for any fact whatever. Moreover, not to be ashamed of Jesus Christ, he invited a great number of friends to assist at his abjuration; many of them pitied his weakness, while others mocked; but God, who had called him to the faith, supported him and he had the firmest confidence that he would support him until death. . . . M. Thayer observes[:] . . . How different is my condition from what it then was! My thoughts, my inclinations, my pursuits, all are changed; I do not know myself any longer; from the moment that I took my determination I renounced all profane studies which had until this time occupied my attention; I left my books half read; I distrusted those which belonged to me; from that time the passions have had but little *influence over me; my views of ambition and worldly promotion have entirely left me; I have bid adieu to them; I have now no other pleasure* than what is derived from the service of God; I experience in my soul a peace which I had never known before. It is no longer now the deceitful security of a slumbering conscience that presumes upon the mercy of God, and sees not the danger to which she is exposed; it is the sweet confidence of a child, who finds himself in the arms of his Father, and who has reason to hope that nothing will ever sever him from him in spite of the dangers which encompass him; Yes, this religion is made for the heart; however strong, however solid the proofs are, which have convinced me of the truth of the Catholic religion, the content of mind, the pure joy which follows it, is, as it were, a new proof equally persuasive. The truths, which gave me most trouble to believe, are those which afford me now most consolation. The mystery of the Eucharist which had appeared to me so incredible, is now become a perennial source of spiritual delights. Confession, which I had regarded as an intolerable burden, appears now to me infinitely attractive in consequence of the tranquility which it produces in my soul. Ah! if hereticks and unbelievers could only experience the delights, which are experienced at the foot of the altar, they would soon cease to [be] either one or the other! Oh! that I could make myself heard by all! I would cry out to them: taste and see by your own experience, how sweet is the Lord, how good he is to those who serve him in the holy society which he himself has formed, and which he vivifies by his Spirit. . . .

M. Thayer pronounced his abjuration, at Rome, on the 25th of May, 1783. . . . He shortly after concluded to embrace the ecclesiastical state being fully persuaded that he was called to it by God for his greater glory and the sanctification of his own soul as well as that of his neighbour. . . .

NOTES

1. September, 1844, in Joseph F. Gower and Richard M. Leliaert, eds., *The Brownson-Hecker Correspondence* (Notre Dame, 1979), 115. The acerbic Brownson also thought highly of Fenwick, but characteristically was most impressed with his "varied and profound learning" (Orestes Brownson, "The Right Reverend Benedict Joseph Fenwick, Second Bishop of the Diocese of Boston," *Brownson's Quarterly Review,* III [Oct., 1846], 526 f. Quoted in Robert H. Lord, *et al., History of the Archdiocese of Boston In the Various Stages of Its Development, 1604 to 1943* [Boston, 1945], II, 275, as cited in Joseph M. McCarthy, ed., *Memoirs to Serve For the Future* [Yonkers, N.Y., 1978], viii).

2. Archives of the Carmelite Monastery of Baltimore (hereafter ACMB). The Mother Superior was Clare Joseph Dickinson (1755–1830), one of the original band of four and the second superior.

3. Charles Neale who had died four days earlier at the monastery.

4. ACMB

5. Crossed out: "in view."

6. Crossed out: "custom."

7. ACMB

8. Eight years later the Carmelites themselves left Mount Carmel in Portobacco for Baltimore. By the late twenties the poor state of the economy and two lengthy lawsuits combined to reduce the monastery to such a state of delapidation and destitution that Archbishop James Whitefield urged them to relocate in Washington or Baltimore where they might more adequately support themselves by conducting school. In September 1831 the Carmelites moved to Aisquith Street in East Baltimore.

9. Joseph M. McCarthy, ed., Benedict Joseph Fenwick, S.J., *Memoirs to Serve For the Future* (Yonkers, 1978), 26-38. For this narrative Fenwick was very dependent upon Thayer's own apologetic, *An Account of the Conversion of the Rev. Mr. John Thayer.* It is possible that Fenwick was using a French translation, which would explain the peculiar title he gives Thayer and his paraphrasing of direct quotations of the convert. Thayer's pamphlet was widely published, including editions in French, Spanish, and Portuguese. The first known English edition was printed in London in 1787. The earliest American printing was in the following year; it continued to be reprinted decades into the nineteenth century. See Wilfred Parson, *Early Catholic Americana, 1729–1830* (New York, 1939), 19.

John Thayer (1758–1815), after his conversion and ordination to the priesthood, served in Boston, New York, and Kentucky. Controversy plagued his ministry in New England and Kentucky. Anti-slavery views and allegations of scandalous conduct led Bishop Carroll to remove him from Kentucky in 1802. Thayer went to England in 1804 and eventually settled in Ireland. Ironically he willed his entire estate toward the establishment of an Ursuline convent and school in Boston.

10. Since the Society of Jesus was suppressed at this time, Thayer's con-

tacts, presumably, were with former members of the order. In his account he does not name the priests who proved to be instrumental in his discovery of Catholicism.

11. The Jesuit Paolo Segneri (1624–1694), writer and itinerant preacher.

12. Benedict Joseph Labre (1748–1783), the French pilgrim who became known as "the beggar of Rome" after he settled there in 1776. Proclaimed a saint by the people immediately after his death, he was canonized a century later by Leo XIII.

VII

JOHN McELROY AND CATHOLIC REVIVALISM

No American Jesuit in the first half of the nineteenth century left a greater mark on the religious landscape than did John McElroy. The founder of colleges, builder of churches, Army chaplain during the Mexican-American War, itinerant preacher of missions from Canada to Mexico—McElroy from the 1820s to the 1860s seemed to be everywhere.

An immigrant from northern Ireland in 1803, John McElroy worked as a clerk at stores in Baltimore and Georgetown before joining the Society of Jesus in 1806 as a temporal coadjutor or brother. Even before he applied to the Jesuits he was practicing the Spiritual Exercises of Saint Ignatius and had acquired a spiritual library that ranged from Augustine's Confessions *through a Kempis'* Imitation of Christ *to Bishop Challoner's* Garden of the Soul.[1] *As a Jesuit brother at Georgetown his duties included the instruction of the younger boys. Apparently his talents for teaching and preaching caught the eye of superiors and his status was changed from temporal coadjutor to scholastic. Ordained in 1817, he continued to work at Georgetown until 1822 when he was appointed pastor of St. John's Church in Frederick, Maryland.*

From Frederick, McElroy served congregations from Rockville to Taneytown. During his 23 years there it has been estimated that he traveled some 10,000 miles on horseback and carriage in the circuit-riding tradition that had marked Jesuit ministry in America since the seventeenth century. But McElroy was concerned about more than keeping alive the faith of established Catholic communities. He was vitally interested in poor Catholics, whether they were Irish immigrants constructing the Baltimore and Ohio railroad east of Frederick or those trapped in the north end of Boston. One of his first acts at Frederick was to eliminate pew rents in certain portions of the church to accommodate blacks and "strangers." When he

started a college in Frederick in 1829, it was to provide education for the
children of the Catholic poor.

REFLECTIONS AND RESOLUTIONS[2] (1806–1851)

In 1805 McElroy began to keep a spiritual commonplace book and diary
in which he recorded "Instructions, from Spiritual Directors, Sermons,
Pious Books, Mental Prayer &&c." By the 1820s he limited it to re-
flections occasioned by his annual retreats. He faithfully recorded them
into the 1860s.

June 26 [1806] Of the knowledge of one's self the source of humility

Let us consider O my soul what we have been, What we are, and what
we will be. 1. What have we been a few years ago. Infinitely less than the
smallest atom in the air. The world subsisted for upwards of five thousand
years and there was no word of me all this time until the infinite love of
God for me call'd me out of this abyss. May all honor and Glory be given
to God alone. 2nd. What am I at present but a sink of Corruption, out of
which comes so much vile excrements and filth as is sufficient to make me
detest this mortal Body which heretofore has been cause of so many sins
and particularly pride.—ah let me detest this body as my greatest enemy.
3rd. What I will be in a few Years, a moments reflection will ans[wer] . . .
nothing but dust & ashes and food for worms . . .

June 27th

O my Lord & my God too late have I known thee, too late have I loved
thee, who has loved me so much. Thou hast called me to thy beloved Society, to the School of Virtue in preference to so many millions of others.
O my good God, how should I repay you for this so great & incomprehensible a benefit? I have nothing that is worthy of offering to thee, it is true.
I have a heart which thou demandest, a heart which has been so often defiled
with sin, O most Bountiful God how much hast thou loved me. O that I had
never offended thee, O that I had ne'er defiled that heart, which thou hast
so often asked of me, that heart which thou so often made thy Tabernacle,
O Incomprehensible Love of my dearest Jesus, how powerful thou art. was
it not enough for thee O God, of my Soul to suffer the most bitter torments
that have ever been or ever will be inflicted on Man. Was not this enough
to satiate that incomparable Love which burned in thy most Sacred Heart.
ah no my soul! he lov'd thee too much and this his love would continue

until the end, and for this reason he invented that admirable Sacrament wherein he gives thee himself to be thy real food lest in this pilgrimage *you should faint and fall by the way;* Oh my Lord and my god what is there you could do for me and hast not done it, O my dearest Jesus thou God of my heart and the life of my Soul why did I ever offend thee, why did I ever seek any thing out of thee, O my Lord and my God have pity on this hard and stony heart of mine, cleanse it & purify it O my God from all terrene affections, and from the vicious habits which was the cause of my offending thee, O Infinite Purity! Thou seest how often these old customs separate my heart from being closely united to thee, thou dost knowest o searcher of all hearts those passions which prevail over thy unworthy servant, and to whom shall I apply for relief, in whom shall I place my Confidence, but in thee who art my only Hope my Lord, my Father and my Redeemer. Teach me O my God to hate myself that I may love thee, that I may love nothing else beside thee. O teach me in all my actions, by thy Holy Grace that I may be united to thee, that I may walk in thy divine presence and always keep my heart united to thee.

(This is the exercise which thy Minister, my Superior has commended so much to my practice.)[3] *Thy grace is sufficient for me,* O my God, and since it is thou (in the person of my[4] Superior) who has commended this practice so much I trust in thy goodness which is infinite that thou will enable me to perform[5] it. *Teach me O my God* by thy divine Spirit *to do what thou commandest and command what thou pleasest.* But O my God such is my weakness & such is my misery, that instead of advancing in the practice of this virtue, I rather feel myself go back; and from whence comes this O my God but from a want of a more strict guard over my heart, permitting it to wander on so many diff[eren]t objects, &c. Ah then my soul for the future be more on thy guard, watch over the avenues of y[ou]r heart that Sin may not enter, but that it may entirely be taken up in Conversing with her Lord & her God. Oh! how happy might we spend the Day my Soul in this Holy conversation.

Ah then my dear Lord according to the advice of my director this day I will endeavor to retire at least some time in the day into my Interior and unite my heart with thee my God and my All, I will offer thee my actions thro the Sacred heart of my dearest Jesus and in union with his most precious merits, and as all I can do O my God is nothing I will offer thee more frequently the Glory which thou possesseth in thyself, that Love with which thou Loveth thyself &c. This O my dearest Jesus I will beg most earnestly of thee in Holy C[ommunion]. Tomorrow with the assistance of thy D[ivine] grace that I may keep my heart always united with thee and walk in thy sacred presence, O my most merciful God, in thee I put my trust in order to obtain this for of myself I can do nothing—

Retreat
Before Renovation of Vows Jany. 1st 1810
Faults to overcome &c &c

1st. Never go to prayer (as heretofore) without duly preparing the subject of y[ou]r Med[itation] the night before also next morning because to keep the presence of God before you during this time, always take a view before hand of the fruit you want to draw from it, and particularly to mortify y[ou]rself in some thing that day—If you experience dryness &c you may still persevere reflecting that it is your own sins that is the cause of it, and you must rem[embe]r the saying of a Holy Man, "Such as you will be out of prayer such will you be in prayer, how can you expect to be recollected &c in prayer, when your mind is entirely taken up all the day, without thinking once seriously on the presence of God.["]

This neglect of the presence of God must be corrected, it has been recommended to me constantly for 3 years past, and now to my confusion I must confess that I practice it but very little which shows the little fruit I have gathered from my Med[itation]s Examins &c. If you were at this time call'd before the tribunal of A[lmighty] God what acc[oun]t could you give for this time? O my Soul if your Saviour & Judge would say to you now, what hus[ban]d of his vine I have planted you[6] in my beloved Society. I have watered you with many graces. how many Communions, Confessions, Instructions & what is there I could do for you and have not done it, and will you still remain unprofitable, bringing forth no fruit what shall I now do with you? Spare me O my God for these ensuing six months and I resolve now to begin to reform those many failings I have been guilty of this time past[7]. . . . I am now persuaded that a small omission in my spiritual duties is not recovered without great labor, and by omitting the ordinary visits to the B[lessed]. S[acrament] Examin S[piritual] Lecture &c &c for sometime (as I found by experience) I do it then without much scruple, why then could I expect to walk in the presence of God, to enjoy Spiritual consolation in my prayer, when I have been so deficient in my Spi[ritual] duties [with thy] assistance O my God. I resolve to begin a new life this new Year, and to spend the ensuing 6 Months with more care and diligence. I will make my med[itation] in the best manner I can one hour each morning in the Chapel on my knees, be it ever so cold unless prevented by obedience. I will call to mind often in the day those resolutions I make in med[itation]. I will not neglect (as I have often done heretofore) to make my ordinary visit to the B[lessed]. S[acrament]. after Breakfast & Dinner & before Supper as I have beads to say after Supper.

My particular examen I have been very deficient in this I must correct and (with leave) will inflict some penance on myself for omissions therein.[8] I must in future read some each day in Theo[logy] a Kempis & reflect on it the remaining part of the day.

I must be more particular in what regards my own[9] office never to seek employment in any other until my[10] own is done, then with leave I will[11] employ myself, in some (if my choice) of the meaner offices of the house——————— I must not lose so much time in future in talking with seculars without necessity as such discourse tends to distractions in time of prayer &c.

Remember how often that a small neglect in the observance of y[ou]r rules &c. is the cause[12] why you receive so few consolations Inspirations, &c—If you are liberal to God, God will be liberal to you. On the contrary if you neglect small things he is displeased with you and will not give those extraordinary favors he would otherwise do, reflect often how sorry you c[oul]d be now if you were going to die for having so often broken your rules &c. &c.

A.M.D.G.

Retreat commenced at the Sem[inary] of Washington preparatory to my last vows in the Soc[iety]—commenced Jany 25, 1821 & ended Feby 2—
Somewhat moved in meditating on the benefit of Creation, vocation, &. In this the infinite goodness of God appears very manifest[ly] to have elected [illegible] us from all eternity, to be his chosen people—and for me in particular—the special favors rec[eive]d—from his bounty viz. my call to the Soc[iety] of Jesus, to the Priesthood, and the inmemorable benefits contained therein—What ought I to render to God for all things he has done for me—O Religious, O Priest of the most high never degenerate from the exalted State in which you are placed

A faithful and exact compliance
with our holy Rules—
A.M.D.G.
2d Day

In Medit[ation]s on Mortal Sin, conceived faintly, the great injury done to the divine Majesty by the commission of it—A God infinitely holy—pure, good, &c &c to be offended by a vile creature, a worm of the earth—O how detestable, how ungrateful does not the Sinner act—I am that person—I must be confounded—always walk with fear & trembling in the sight of God—Even *Venial Sin* is to be avoided more than all imaginable evils better that all the creation, men, angels, Saints &c were annihilated than one venial Sin to be committed—nay to redeem all the damned and place them in Heaven, a venial sin ought not be committed so contrary it is

to the infinite perfections of God, and so displeasing to him—Keep this
always present to y[ou]r mind—

3d Day

In my exercises this day, conceived a great horror of Tepidity and a dread
of its fatal effects—

It destroys all merit in Jesus Xt, it converts good actions into sins, it
merits from God, that he sh[oul]d *vomit the Religious* out & it prevents that
interior comm[unicatio]n the soul should have with her God—and if per-
severed in will finally lead him to distruction—Preserve me my God in future from falling again into this Vice—I now see in some measure its
dangers—I now see how much I have offended you by it—my God, O that
I may now keep inviolate the Resolution made of performing my Religious
duties—as is becoming I sh[oul]d do—To avoid that curse pronounc'd
against those who *do God's work neglig[ent]ly.*

4th Day

In meditating this day on Eternity was more particularly moved at the
sentiment of the infinite goodness of God in preparing so great rewards for
his creatures—his incomprehensible patience in bearing with the Sinner in
expecting his conversion in order that he may make him partake of his eternal joys—

A great desire of promoting Gods honor—having nothing else in view
in all my actions—to promote this by every means—and in treating with
my Neighbor to have this particularly at heart that God alone deserves all
honor—praise—love &c

O that I could always act with these sentiments—O that no other way
can find place in my heart!

This is reward enough for me O God to be permitted to serve thee here,
to love thee here regardless of future rewards—

5th Day

The meditations of this day tended to excite in the Soul a great fear of
the inscrutable judgments of God—

The innumerable benefits rec[eive]d, the abuse of so many graces—
wo be to thee Corozain & Bethsaida—wo be to thee O Religious if you
do not comply with your obligations—The name alone will not save
you—The virtues of worldlings will not save you—you have rec[eive]d
much—much will be required from you—The Servant was condemned
for not improving his talent—he did not squander it, he only concealed
it—Have you done even as much—O Religious—O Jesuit your obligations are great—the graces you have rec[eive]d are invaluable, were it
only that [h]our, your call to Religion—O begin now at least to act gen-

erously for your God—to observe exactly your holy Rules & the duties of y[ou]r Office—

6th Day

In meditating this day on the Kingdom of Christ, the two Standards[13] &—conceived an ardent desire of imitating the most holy life of our D[ivine] Captain and leader C. J.—a sentiment of my unworthiness to be ranked with so many great Souls—as have been in our Soc[iety].

I wish O my God to become little in my own eyes, to place myself entirely in your hands, that your holy Will may be accomplished in all things—I have hiterto rely'd too much on myself, attributed success in some things to myself, for which I now grieve—O that I may esteem myself as I ought in future—and that I may always have a feeling [sic] sentiment of my own nothingness—

Unusual anxiety, a desolation[?] of spirit—a privation of all comfort &c &c—

7th Day

Exercises on the Sufferings of Xt and his B. Mother—moved to imitate them. Heroic examples of self-abnegation in my Saviour, of his extreme poverty—not having wherewith to [illegible] but to appear naked, his entire & most perfect obedience, to death even so ignominious a one—O Religious, O companion of Jesus, are you worthy the name, in what do you imitate y[ou]r divine model, in what do you deny y[our]self—when or where do you carry y[ou]r Cross—do you not rather seek y[ou]r own comfort too much—your ease—your vanity alas! how unworthy am I of that title *companion of Jesus,* Grant me grace O God now to begin for all I have done is nothing

8th Day

Practices to be punctually observed in future

Towards your God

1. A great Rever[ence] and respect at all times for his D[ivine] Presence, impressing this sentiment deeply in y[ou]r heart, that he is every where present, and at all times requires the affections of y[ou]r heart. Do therefore, all things purely for him—
2. At your prayer, Examins, H[oly] Mass and Divine Office—place y[ou]rself in a particular manner in this D[ivine] presence & acquit y[ou]rself of these ex[ercise]s as it is becoming you should—
3. To have a great desire to promote the honor of God, by every means in y[ou]r power—chiefly by an exact observance of all Religious duties— by an ardent zeal for souls and y[ou]r utmost endeavors to prevent Sin & & &

Towards your Brethren

1. To esteem them all as my superior and to pay them that deference—even in the exterior. I am now convinced that this is no exaggeration, that I am infinitely beneath (in the sight of God) all the Religious of the house—

2. To be extremely kind to my Br[ethre]n to oblige them whenever I can—and never to speak of their faults—seeing that I have so many—and that they have to bear with me in all my faults.

3. To esteem myself as in reality I am the most abject of the house to insist in this in my prayer and examens and never to admit any thought to the contrary much less to speak in my own praise—as I have often done.
    To speak well of all my Breth[re]n on all occasions.

Towards Seculars

1. Treat them with Charity, with mildness and always a modest exterior[;] enter not into unnecessary conversation with them—such as their temporal affairs—state affairs &.—

2. To avoid all familiarity with Seculars, especially females—think often how our Holy Father acted in such occasions—the more reserved (without affectation) you keep y[ou]rself the greater edification you will give—

3. Let your Visits to such be very seldom and never without a view of their spiritual profit—and take care that you imbibe no part of the spirit of the world—whilst you endeavor to draw them to God—

4. You must also be convinced that much time spent with seculars, is very detrimental to that interior peace which you should always aim at—and moreover that it is far from giving edification to them—

5. To be of real service to your Neig[hbor] you must keep your Room, as much as possible, attend there exactly to the duties assigned you—well ordered charity begins at home—and what will it profit you to gain &.

6. In the discharge of external duties give always the first place to those of your office, it is that God & the Soc[iety] require from you—the other business you may be required to do, does not properly belong to you—nor are you responsible for it.

Conclusion

1. In concluding these holy exercises I must be convinced that I am now about to contract as it were a new obligation by being admitted to my grade in the Soc. as one of its members[14]—that I ought consequently to comport myself as is becoming a companion of Jesus, that I am, to observe exactly our H[oly] R[ule] and consti[tution]s that I am to endeavor all in my power to advance in the way of perfection—chiefly by the Practice of Self denial & union with God, with these two virtues I must

continually arm myself—and be convinced that without exercising them I shall not correspond with the designs of God over me—To be a true companion of Jesus *you must deny y[ou]rself* and to be perfect *you must walk before him.*

A.M.D.G.

Retreat commenced Wednesday night the 20th Janu[ar]y 1836—at St. Joseph's near Emmits[bur]g, having made my last here also, thirteen months ago (Dec. 1835)

All my exercises reproach me of the neglect of Prayer-Recollection, and Mortification—to the neglect of them may be traced all my sins & my little proficiency in virtue—Infidelity, Sloth and indevotion [sic] are the unhappy consequences—By thy grace O my God I hope to correct in future, convinced as I am now, of my misery, of my entire want of spirit, of my extreme poverty in spirituals—I will from such conviction go to my prayer with debasing myself in the presence of my God, and of exercising myself for a certain space of time in the knowledge of my sins & miseries—begging fervently light and grace to know myself—I will resolve always in conclusion to practice recollection in my ordinary duties—to think often on God's Holy presence—this will help me to practice acts of Self denial—especially by restraining my eyes & avoiding idleness—

Recollection—

I conceive this to be especially necessary to preserve the Religious spirit—to live at home, to hear the Divine whisper, to speak interiorly to God, whilst exteriorly employ'd, is the duty of every Religious, but particularly one employ'd in the Sacred Ministry—who is compared to *Salt* & a *light* &c &c &c

I find to my great confusion, the little pains I have taken to please my God, to make some return for his love—O Ingratitude! that persons of the world will do & suffer so much to please the object of their affections (a poor miserable sinner) and I do almost nothing to show my love for the infinite majesty of my God—to whom I have bound myself by the most Sacred ties—my vows & by them obliging myself to a union with him by Love-doing & suffering all for love of him—2. I find also that I have not only given no proofs of my love but that I have often, very often offended my best beloved—by idleness—by sloth—by distractions—by self Love &.

Retreat commenced the eve of St. Fr[ancis] Borgia's feast 1837 at St. Joseph's Emmits[burg] it being twenty one months since my last—

The necessary preparation for consecrating the new church—after that a visit of three weeks to the canal, to collect in aid of the s[ai]d Church—&.&.&c—were the reasons for deferring this important duty.[15]

1. From various reflections I find it essential to be exact in future in the performance of ordinary duties—which have been hitherto often omitted.
2. I shall endeavor uniformly so to rise as to make the hour's prayer before Mass—as also a short time for preparation before going to the Altar—
3. After Mass at least one quarter [of an hour] by the watch then to the confessional.
4. My particular examen which I have omitted for a time I will resume and persevere I hope faithfully in it, never neglecting it at noon—
5. My visits to the B[lessed] S[acrament]. must be resumed—I can make two every evening at 2 oC & before 7—
6. My instructions both for the morning & evening on Sundays I intend to prepare with more pains than formerly, making notes & a synopsis of my plan—
7. —I feel the great necessity of the practice of humility interiorly & exteriorly—for some months I shall take this for my particular examen— the interior acts of this virtue—the sight of my sins and great infidelities to grace will aid much in this practice.
8. Sloth has been my predominant failing—I must endeavor to cancel from this time—to rise promptly—to make my prayer, and all other duties with a true desire to honor God—who is so much dishonor'd by men— never to idle my time, as I find I have done—in my room, by useless visits &c.—
9. To read over these [resolutions] every Sunday evening and examen how they have been observed, this may be the last time you will have an opportunity of shewing your fidelity to God—
10. I must be more exact in performing the accustomed penances than formerly—my sins require much of satisfactory works—*In thee O Lord do I hope & . . .*

1840

Retreat commenced the 10 July at St. Josep[h's] Emmits[burg] giving at the same time the exercises to the sisters of Charity 97 in number—it is one year and two months since my last.

    I foresaw that unless I availed myself of this opportunity I could not easily find another—and still it is not so profitable—having to speak three times a day to the community and of course to prepare it.—I have found alas! in reviewing the past year, & the state of my interior the same failings to predominate, all proceeding from sloth—I find this has vitiated every act especially my prayer—O my God what ingratitude on my part—

1. I must resolve anew, what I see I have down in 1837, to be faithful above all in meditation preparing the subject over night—thinking of it at waking and spending the whole hour in it before Mass—

2. Next in importance—my particular examen—I shall apply it for a time to my ordinary duties, so as to perform them with fervor and exactitude—*In all my work, I must remember thee O Lord.*

3. My vocal prayers have not been exactly attended to—to the B[lessed]. V[irgin]., to the passion of our Lord &c&—I hope to resume them and also my visits to the B[lessed]. S[acrament].

4. I find that a neglect of spiritual reading has been injurious, in as much as it helps essentially to my instructions—I have also neglected to prepare according to the opportunities I had—I hope to correct this also.

A.M.D.G.

Retreat commenced Dec. 14 1841 Geo[rge]: T[own] College being 17 months since my last—

I used the book of exercises for the first time, the first days, and find it very profitable—I have a great desire to make a general confession of my whole life, and did so, to Fr. Grivel, Spiritual Father of the house[16]—I divided it in three parts—1st from use of reason till I arrived in America—2 till I went to Frederick—3d Until this time—I was somewhat consoled by so doing & grateful to our Lord, for the opportunity, as this *may* be the last I shall ever make, and even the last retreat. I must be careful not to lose the graces of either—A trifling with grace or not seeking it with fervor has been among my numerous faults. With the assistance of our Lord I hope in future to remedy this—

To this end I resolve on nothing new—our Institute & holy rules point out all that is necessary—fidelity, on my part is all that is wanting[17] to persevere—I must give the whole time without interruption to my Med[itatio]n if possible—also to be exact in my particular & gen[eral] examen—not so hurried in retiring at night—but to acquit myself of my prescribed practices to the B[lessed]. V[irgin]. the Souls in purgatory and for a happy death—Alas! how deficient do I find myself in solid virtue on its practice—so easily discouraged—troubled from very slight causes—not guarded in my conversation.

In thee O Lord I trust—do aid & assist me for thy honor and Glory—This I hope to keep steadily in view, thy *honor*—to renounce to all self-seeking or approbation of men and to aim only to please & glorify thee—

A.M.D.G.

Retreat commenced at the Noviceship Monday morning feby 27th 1843—the last I made in Geo. Town, December 1841 - 14 mo[nth]s

Made use of the Meditations of Father Shedler S.J.[18]—Made my confession for the past year to Fr. Mulledy on the 4th day of the exercises[19]—felt a little, the effects of too close application on the third day—continued, with little interruption—*took* more exercise—

I find much to correct especially faults against humility—I fear most of my actions have been deprived of their merit & efficacy on others—by self love, vain glory—self esteem &c—I have, thank God, seen more clearly my duty to my God & to myself than in any former occasion—How evident does it now appear that, I am nothing, have nothing, *but sin,* this alone is mine, where is there room for vanity—In the order of nature I am indebted to God for all things—equally so for those of Grace—I cannot move hand or foot (even) or utter a word, without the divine assistance, the use of reason is his pure gift—he can deprive me of it at any moment—how unreasonable, and opposite to truth to attribute any thing to myself!!

In the order of grace, how much more unbecoming to imagine for a moment, that I can do any thing to merit it—or to procure it for others without the divine assistance—*without me you can do nothing, says our Lord*—aided by thy light O Lord I will act in conformity in future, and take this subject in its divisions for my particular ex[ame]n, aided by thy grace O my God I hope to profit by it this year.

When I meditate the insults, affronts & Contempts rec[eive]d by my divine redeemer, how debased must I appear in my own estimation—he loves humiliations, contempts &c whilst I seek to be esteemed loved & admired—he loves these because it is the will of his heavenly father, that by them he should atone for our love of the Contrary—O inconceivable mystery, the inflicting on the innocent the portion of the guilty—and the guilty refuse the small potions dealt out by the same divine Justice—such is my case, O God, be propitious to me a sinner—

Retreat commenced in Bohemia on Saturday even[ing] Aug[us]t 30 1845[20]—

Having left Fred[eric]k to return no more, I was very desirous to make my retreat before going to Geo. Town College, my future residence in this Prov[ince]. Fr. Visitor[21] acceded to my wishes.

1. I have to bemoan my great sloth and tepidity in the service of God and trace to this all my defects.

2. To remedy this, I must in future, exercise myself in acts of interior humility, acknowledging my great unworthiness for the post and confounding myself as I have done in these exercises—

3. To walk in the presence of my God at all times raising my heart to him frequently by ejaculatory prayer.

4. To make my intention, and renew it more frequently of doing all for the honor of the divine Majesty, and thus avoid idleness or doing what might be unprofitable.

5. To resume the holy practice of allotting a day in each month for the

prep[aratio]n for death, at least some thing more than usual to be done on that day—

6. From a desire of the Salvation of souls, to pray more frequently for them, especially for those who make retreats, and my former congregation of Frederick.—

7. Ended my exercises this morning and left for George Town in the Cars— Sep. 8—1845

L[aus]. D[eo]. S[emper].

Retreat commenced in Phila[delphia] Sept. 13th in the even[in]g 1847 it having been two years and a few days since my last—made the exerc[ise]s in the house of the Bishop, a very retired and quiet place—

I

A great dryness and tepidity in all my exercises made me very desirous to make the exercises, in the first days treated more particularly on my own miseries and nothingness—

II

Felt some courage to imitate our D[ivine] Lord and Master in the practice of his humiliations and contempts in his sufferings—what a treasure, to those to whom our Lord imparts it—alas! I find myself a stranger to it in practice—so easily disturbed in mind so much afraid of contradictions or reprehensions—still I hope O Lord with thy grace to amend—prayer and self denial are the best way to effect so desirable an object—

III

I find my greatest difficulty in the practice of religious virtues, is inconstancy of mind, not persevering in my good purposes faithfully—hence omissions—negligence almost habitual in my spiritual exercises—May the Lord have mercy on me—

IV—The means of perservering in future 1. To be *exact* in all my duties performing them with *fervor, perserveringly*—inconstancy of mind has been my great obstacle—with God's grace assisting I hope this year to correct—particularly as my future occupations will not place much impediment in the way—Help me O God without thee I can do nothing—

V—To labor assiduously for the souls committed to my charge, in the various ways duty points out—recommending them often to our Lord by his blessed Mother—I must attach great importance to the catechism of the children—to the confessional and to prepare my Instructions for Sundays & other occasions.

Retreat commenced in St. John's College *Fordham* Jany. 29th 1850. My *last was in Salem for 5 days last Feby.*

In reading over the foregoing I find the sentiments equally applicable as they were two years ago. I have only to adopt them and reduce my *resolutions* to practice.

I feel rather more impress'd with the necessity of exercising faith in the presence of God & of performing my actions in accordance—May I not trace all my distractions at the Altar in reciting the Divine Office, want of zeal, in the confessional in the pulpit & the dissipated mind through the day to this neglect?—If I could but have our Lord present to my mind in all my actions, it would remedy many of the imperfections & faults committed in them—above all a want of purity of intention and true zeal for the honor of God and good of Souls—

Retreat begun at St. Fr[anci]s. Xavier's College, *New York City*—Jany. 12th, 1851—I anticipate the time to be free for Jubilee &c
God *alone* is *good,* as well as *great*—what would become of me, if his clemency was not without bounds, so patient, so forbearing—I resolve, it seems to me only to prove my infidelity in violating them, when I read over the reflections & resolutions of past retreats. I am confounded and filled with shame and confusion.

In the first *week*[22] I have discovered the necessity of being practically convinced of two inferences or fruits from the exercises of these three days, namely a knowledge of myself—my miseries with a view to a hatred of self—the other, to suppress pride & the love of esteem—looking upon all as superior to me in every respect—To conceive a sovereign hatred and detestation for all sin both mortal & venial—the latter in those occasions you are most accustomed to fall into them—reflect on the sorrow you felt for them when writing this—

In the second week discovered how little resemblance my life bears to that of Jesus Xt.—so little generosity, so little enamored of his love—and so little zeal for his imitation—I *have resolved* to correct this, but alas! I have not put it in execution—

The last week conceived more than usual the importance of aiming at the perfection my state requires—in this I shall be encouraged—and strengthened I hope by the example of our Divine Master—made use of Bellecius[23] for the first time during this retreat—
Deo Gratias.

Decem[be]r 24, 1851
Commenced my retreat this evening at St. Fr. X[avier's] College it being a little over 11 months since I made my last in this College—presumed I could absent myself better at this time & anticipated my usual time—
Have discovered more than usual my great miseries and want of all

consolation, on acc[oun]t of my sloth & little zeal for my perfection—I see that my actions have been done generally from mere custom—not with that purity of motive they ought [to have]

Losing sight of my obligation, to aim at perfection, in the practice of Evan[gelica]l virtues, has been a fruitful source . . . whence sloth & indifference proceeds—Having our Lord always before my eyes, I must with his divine assistance, be more careful in the practice of all my religious obligations—as they now appear to me—

Ended my retreat this morning feast of St. Fr. Xavier Dec. 3d— 1851—*Deo Gratias*—

LETTERS TO JAN ROOTHAAN[24] (1840)

No instructions or meditations of McElroy survive. We know that he carefully prepared notes. His daily schedule included an hour of preparation for his next mission. His diary and correspondence indicate that his missions were something between the Ignatian Exercises and the missions that Jesuits, Redemptorists, Paulists, and others made such an institution of American Catholicism later in the century. In the following letters to Father General Roothaan he describes his activity on the mission circuit in 1840.

Frederick Jun. 4 1840

Very Revd D[ea]r Father in Xt.

Since my last of August 1838 I take the liberty of communicating to your paternity the following details, connected with my several duties—1. at the date of the last, I was busily engaged in Philadelphia with the new church of St. Joseph, which was completed and consecrated to the service of God, Feb[ruar]y 1839 by Bishop Kendrick; Bishop Hughes preached on the occasion the clergy of the City assisting—the Provincial (Mulledy) was also present—having changed the duties assigned me there, I left in April same year and returned to my post where I found all things succeeding under Father Young.[25] During the last year I gave the exercises at the usual places: 1) In St. John's Church—2) In St. Joseph's for the Sisters of Charity; 3) at Mt. St. Mary's college for the Students, 4) for the Boarding School of St. Joseph's, 5) George Town College for the Students. Lastly at the Visitation Convent for the Boarders. 2. This year our infant college continues to be blessed with peace and good order throughout—there are now attending the school 114 students in the respective classes from Rudiments to Rhetoric. This sample of a public school, founded as near as can be on the institute, has now been tested for eleven years, and found to be well adapted to this country. In *Philadelphia* one on the same plan, would succeed very well, provided we had competent members to open it—3. At the urgent request of the Bishop of Cincinnati,[26] Father Prov. (McSherry) consented that I should give the exercises to the Clergy of that Diocese, and to the laity of his Cathedral—I arrived in Cincinn[at]i Ash Wednesday, and commenced the exercises on Friday following—there were 25 priests present, *strict silence* was observed, and the whole deportment of the Gentlemen very edifying during the ten days, and I have reason to think our Lord helped his own work, in a particular manner on the last day of the retreat, the Bishop officiated pontifically (it being the 2d Sunday in Lent) and the Clergy received the holy Comm[unio]n at his hands, together with the Seminarians. . . . On the same day at Vespers, I opened the *Retreat for the Laity*, the Cathedral was quite crowded—The faithful continued to attend the exercises during the whole week, spending 6 hours daily, in the Church; I have never witness'd more attention and devotion to the exercises than these good people manifested. On the 3rd Sunday in Lent we had again a solemn high Mass, at which I preached, as also at Vespers, the conclusion of the Retreat—on this day 300 persons approached the Holy table, and during the week 200[,] making 500 which was a greater number, than ever approached here on any former occasion.

From my little experience in the happy effects of these retreats both for clergy and Laity, I am convinced, it is the *most profitable part* of our Ministry, and *to form a band exclusively for such,* say 3 or 4, would deserve almost any sacrifice, this would be *the means under God, of laying solidly, the foundations of our holy religion in this new world [,]* of renovating the Clergy, and through them the Laity—the Bishops would gladly invite us to their respective dioceses, and thus by the powerful means, bequeathed us by our Holy Father, would the Salvation of many souls be affected—if your Paternity could aid *us, with two, even one father, knowing the language of this country,* and having some facility for such functions; I w[oul]d willingly offer myself as the last & the least, to labor with them in this glorious enterprize—by such a band it is not only a single city or village, that would profit by our labors; but *the whole United States!* What an immense good & to a people well disposed and well affected towards us!! pardon me very R[everen]d F[athe]r if I urge this too much, it is a matter near my heart, and of which I made mention in former letters—this function [Missions] and our colleges would not only be more in the Spirit of our vocation—but much more secure for us, than our dispersed congregations—where our fathers are sometimes quite alone— . . .

5. After my labors in Cincinnati I visited our fathers at *St. Mary's College Kentucky.* I was much edified with their charity and union—also their extreme kindness towards us—their College, all things considered, seems

prosperous, and their students very orderly—I visited also the good Bishop Flaget, who was very kind indeed, he wishes very much that I sh[oul]d return there in Sep[tembe]r to give the exercises to his clergy. I do not know what Fr. Prov[incia]l will decide as yet—On my way home I delayed 3 days at Wheeling Virginia, to give the exercises to the Cath[olic]s of that city, at the request of the Pastor—they were well attended, and I hope with much fruit—I got home on Wednesday in Holy Week, having travelled nearly 2000 miles, and preached about 70 times[.] Thanks to God my health is still good and busily occupied at my former post—I commend myself to y[ou]r H[oly] S[acrifice]S - Your devoted B[rothe]r in Xt.

John McElroy, S.J.

New York, Nov. 23, 1840[27]

Very Rev. Dr. Fr. Gen[era]l in Christ,

As I did not write to your Paternity last year I take the liberty of writing twice this present year[28]— . . . last month I gave the spiritual exercises to the nuns of the carmelite convent Baltimore, to the students of St. Mary's College, Emmitsburg—to the Scholars of St. Joseph's female boarding school Emmits[bur]g & to the students of St. John's College Fred[eric]k.— the latter ended on the feast of all Saints, fifty one of our boys received Holy communion on that occasion—the next day the 2nd I left home for this city at the request of Bishop Hughes to give the exercises to the clergy of his diocese. 44 were present with Bishops Hughes & [illegible]—the place selected was twelve miles from the City at the New College[29] (which the Bishop intends opening next year, at present occupied by his Seminarians) and very suitable for a retreat. The Bishops & Clergy performed the exercises with great edification. Strict silence and retirement all the time. I never witnessed more order and regularity, and I hope the fruit was very great— this was the first retreat for the Clergy in the diocese of N. York—on the last day of the exercises (Sunday 15th) all came to the City for the High & Solemn Pontifical Mass, in the Cathedral, at which the Clergy communicated—it was a very interesting & novel sight in New York, to see three Bishops and forty eight Priests' in the Sanctuary; the Cathedral which is large was crowded by the faithful. I preached on the occasion and thus concluded the Retreat of the Clergy. At the same time I announced at the Bishop's request that a Retreat would be given also to the Laity in the Cathedral to commence the next day—this was very well attended through the week— the usual confessors for the Cathedral are three, sometimes only two, but during the week, the Bishop invited others to assist, on this occasion, so that eight daily, the last day ten confessors, were employed and could not suffice for the number who presented themselves at the tribunal—The Zeal & piety of these good people, consoled us very much—On yesterday morning (Sunday) it is said 1000 persons approached the Holy Table in the Cathedral, the greatest number ever known to approach on one occasion in this City. This is additional proof of the great good of Retreats, given throughout this Country—your paternity was kind enough to approve of my suggestion to have two or three fathers associated as Missionaries, as I have been informed by Father Provincial, but Alas! he has no one to spare for that purpose[;] if I could be relieved from Frederick with even one other, we could render (with God's help) great good to souls, to religion & to the credit of our Society—the Bishop of this City wishes very much that I should remain to give retreats in all the churches, of the City but my post being vacant at home, I must return tomorrow. There are 90,000 Catholics in this City!! what a field for the Zeal of the Missionary, and what abundance of fruit to be reaped—at the late retreat, persons advanced in years, were seen going to Comm[unio]n for the first time in this city—others who had not been for 50 years &&—

Two missionaries set apart for this purpose would do more good for our holy religion, than ten could do in their respective congregations—if your Paternity approves of it, be pleased to recommend it again to Fr. Prov[incial]. I have reason to think our Lord would be pleased to have me labor in this way the remainder of my life, and thus aid, in the establishment of retreats for the clergy & laity in the different dioceses—this year a beginning has been happily made, in Cincinnati & New York, and the Bishops of both places are resolved to keep them up annually—the good effects produced in the Clergy, of both places, were very visible, and I am sure will extend them to the laity—With these few words I commit the whole to the Sweet Providence of our Lord and to your paternity, fearing that perhaps on account of my unworthiness, our Lord may frustrate our desires, *may his will be done.* . . . I recommend myself to your H[oly] S[acrifice]S & prayers—

Yrs. devoted[ly] in Xt.
John McElroy, S.J.

A MISSION BAND'S SPRING CAMPAIGN (1851)

Although lack of men prevented the formation of a permanent mission band, a more resourceful provincial, Ignatius Brocard, found a means to begin this apostolate that promised so much. In 1851 he sent the six young priests completing their formation at Frederick in bands of two through parts of Maryland and southeastern Pennsylvania to give a series of missions at the Jesuit parishes. Among the six were the future provincials Charles

Stonestreet and Angelo Paresce. The following was their report of their evangelical itinerary.

Missions of the Tertians for 1851[30]

As an experiment the Fathers in third probation[31] were sent to give missions, some into southern Maryland, some into Northern Maryland, and some into stations in Pennsylvania. . . . They followed the schedule below:

9 am they gave points for a meditation followed by a sung or said Mass; then after a reading similar to a meditation the psalm *miserere* was sung in chorus. Thence followed an instruction and the exercises of the morning consisting of the examination of conscience. At 2 o'clock in the afternoon the first part was devoted to the public recitation of the Rosary, then another instruction, then the litany of the Blessed Mother was sung, followed by a meditation: then Benediction of the Blessed Sacrament closed the daily program at 4 p.m. Each day four hours were given to the exercises. Nearly all the exercises were from the first week, instructions were on the use of confession and of communion, in all things however, they tried to stress the mercy and love of the Eternal Father even in his punishment of the damned. For the people from a variety of fears were in dread of the confessional, that tribunal of God's overflowing love. . . . Sinners who had fallen into the ways of iniquity for twenty or thirty years or even more were brought back to the bosom of the church and many who had begun to waver in their faith were confirmed and strengthened. Concubines were separated or brought through marriage into a good state, . . . old hatreds of many years standing were dissolved; bad confessions were made good, marriages were validated in the Church; infidels, heretics and protestants were converted, these were the fruits of our labors. Many were not happy to have heard the saving truth in their own churches, but followed the fathers to a second or third mission twelve or twenty miles away, and when the end had come [there] they were sad that they were forced to say goodby to us so soon.

The services were aimed at Catholics; scarcely anything was said about controversial matters, and whenever reasons for believing were proposed we found not only that the faithful were strengthened, but that protestants sought further enlightenment in the Catholic faith that they had discovered through what they had seen and heard. But let us describe the individual missions.

For the mission at *Saint Inigoes*[32] there were two sites, one at St. Inigoes itself, where Ours live, the other at St. Nicholas, to which one of Ours goes on Sundays. In the former approximately 500 came to confession and communion. Ten Methodists or other Protestants converted. If the weather had been better, more would have come.

At *St. Nicholas* 600 were reconciled and received Holy Communion. Six Protestants converted and many Catholics who might just as well have been protestants returned to Mother Church. Often our whole day was taken up in hearing confessions, excepting for the times of meditations and instructions, when the one giving the talk was free from hearing confessions. . . . Often it happened that we distributed communion at three o'clock to those who had come twenty miles on foot. The faithful were so filled with spiritual joy that at times they seemed out of their heads, especially the negroes who for eighteen years or even more had been away from confession because of some vague fear instilled in them through the severity of the priests. I could hear them exclaiming out of joy: "I am in the Church, I have profited from the jubilee."[33] Five days we remained in each station for confirming the good and with such fruit that there were scarcely ten who had not approached the sacraments.

At *Leonardtown*[34] we stayed 7 days. More than 600 confessed and received communion. There were only three left in the town who had not come and of them two followed us into other missions to surrender their souls at last to divine grace. Many who besides their baptism had no religion, although they were thirty or forty years old, came to confession surrounded by their sons and sought instruction. This happened in other missions as well. Two Protestants sought instruction. What was particularly consoling to us was the young doctors, lawyers and persons from other professions who came together as a body to confession and communion and gave witness to the happy state of Catholics.

At *Saint Joseph*[35] about 800 . . . confessed and received communion. Here we remained five days, following the same schedule as in the previous places. As in the others, people abandoned the working of the fields that they might have time for the exercises of the Jubilee.

At *Sacred Heart of Jesus*[36] we found few prepared, but this obstacle and the foul weather, which reduced the exercises to two days, did not prevent us from drawing 364 persons. We baptized one adult who had been vacillating for a long time, and many other protestants sought instruction.

At *St. Thomas*[37] there were more than 300 confessions and communions. Many persons because of the cold weather turned their backs on the grace of the Jubilee. The exception was the negroes who from the first day flocked to the exercises and the sacraments. You might say that the masters were reserving for themselves this earth, while their slaves were laying claim on heaven.

Although the number of the faithful is small at *Pomfret*,[38] and the time was not favorable, the crowd was large and the fruit good. Nearly 300 confessed and communicated. One adult Protestant was baptized and another few sought instruction.

About *Cornwallis-neck*[39] the same must be said, where with a smaller number of Catholics nearly two hundred confessed and communicated. Six adults were baptized among whom was one over 70 years old [and] negroes well instructed by their fellow slaves.

At *Cobb-Neck*[40] nearly 500 were reconciled with God and received communion. Only one Catholic did not do so. Five Protestants asked to be instructed.

At *Newport*[41] some out of curiosity came to the church but even before they had heard the instruction, impelled by divine grace, they threw themselves tearfully at the feet of the Confessor. . . . More than 600 confessed and communicated. One Protestant and many Catholics who had been away from the sacraments for many years were converted.

About the mission at *Bryantown*[42] one must say that the good effects were even better, that the faithful were more fervent. They are served by a secular priest, a good friend of the Society. The good tree has produced good fruits. Four hundred came to confession and communion; a few prodigal sons. Here indeed an individual who had followed us for 60 miles and seemed to be almost seeking to be forced to confess, finally came to the confessional and being questioned at last brought his quest to an end by such singular signs of grace that even the confessor marveled. Reconciled to God he returned home full of joy.

At *Petersville*[43] 200 received communion among whom were many prodigal sons and one who had been away for sixty years. One Methodist was baptized . . .

At *Liberty*[44] about a hundred communicated among whom were some who had not done so for a long time. Two Protestants sought instruction.

At *Frederick* more than 200 communicated. Many prodigal sons returned. Cold.

Gettysburg is the seat of the Lutherans in Pennsylvania and there our fathers went full of fear that from the prejudices of Protestants and severe cold little good would be done for Catholicism. God was pleased however to give us the fruit of 40 persons brought back to the faith, . . . and many who had denied the faith were converted, twelve adult protestants were baptized, and many others were given instructions, five marriages were validated and three who were a public scandal were reconciled. It is estimated that there were two hundred communicants at this mission . . .

The Fathers having spent two months giving missions returned to the tertianship full of consolations. May God make the good a lasting one.

NOTES

1. Other books in his library were the Douay New Testament, Butler's *Lives of the Saints, Elevation of the Soul to God, Pious Christian, Key of Paradise, Vade Mecum, Spiritual Combat,* Hubey's *Spiritual Retreat, The Cross in its True Light.* See Louis Berkeley Kines, S.J., "Lincoln in a Cassock: The Life of Father John McElroy, S. J. From 1782 to 1847," Georgetown University Master's Thesis, 1960, pp. 5-6.

2. GUSC, McElroy Papers

3. This would seem to have been Francis Neale, then pastor of Holy Trinity Church in Georgetown and the first novice master of the restored Maryland Mission in 1806.

4. Crossed out: "thy."

5. Crossed out: "practice."

6. Crossed out: ",planted you."

7. In the Society of Jesus those without final vows made a devotional renewal of their vows every six months.

8. The particular examen was one of the spiritual exercises recommended by Ignatius for those who were seeking to reform their lives. It consisted of concentrating on the elimination of one vice or fault at a time by examining twice daily one's behavior in this regard in order systematically to reorder one's life.

9. Crossed out: "particular."

10. Crossed out: "your."

11. Crossed out: "you may."

12. Crossed out: "reason."

13. The meditations on the Kingdom of Christ and the Two Standards of Christ and Satan (poverty, humiliation, humility, versus riches, honor, pride) are pivotal exercises in the Ignatian retreat goal of producing within the retreatant the commitment to imitate Christ in continuing his mission. See introduction.

14. At the time of a Jesuit's final vows, he receives his permanent grade within the Society; either that of profession, spiritual coadjutorship, or temporal coadjutorship. The first designates priests who take the fourth vow of special obedience to the pope; the second denotes priests without the fourth vow; the third includes all brothers. McElroy, because of his limited education in philosophy and theology (he lacked, for one thing, any training in Latin, a prerequisite for such studies), became a spiritual coadjutor.

15. McElroy regularly ministered to the Irish immigrants constructing the Chesapeake and Ohio Canal along the Potomac River in central and western Maryland. The new church was St. John's in Frederick.

16. Fidèle de Grivel (1769–1842), had entered the Fathers of the Sacred Heart in 1794, then joined the Society in Russia in 1803. After teaching theology in France and England, he came to Maryland in 1831 to be novicemaster.

17. Crossed out: "necessary."

18. Anthony Schedler (1742–1794), German Jesuit who rejoined the Society in Russia after the suppression. He published two collections of meditations, *Col-*

lectatio meditationum pro octiduana recollectione in exercitiis S.P. Ignatii (Polociae, 1793), and *Collectio meditationum pro octiduana recollectione in exercitiis S. P. Ignatii, pro scholasticis Soc. Jesu* (Polociae, 1794).

19. Samuel Mulledy (1811–1866), at that time master of novices in Frederick.

20. Bohemia, the mission and plantation established in 1703 in Cecil County on the Eastern Shore of Maryland.

21. Peter Verhaegen (1800–1868), a Belgian who had come to the United States in 1821 to work with the Indians. He was the first president of St. Louis University and superior of the Missouri Mission of the Society of Jesus. In 1845 he was appointed both Provincial of the Maryland Province and official visitor for Father General Roothaan.

22. Ignatius divides his *Spiritual Exercises* into four parts, which he designates as weeks, although even in the full month long retreat they do not correspond to seven day periods. Roughly the first week concerns one's origin and nature as well as sin and its consequences; the second focuses on Christ through his early life and public ministry; the third dwells on Christ's passion; the fourth concludes with his resurrection and call to action for the exercitant in response to God's love.

23. Aloysius Bellicius (1704–1757), theologian and missionary, was a prolific writer on ethics and asceticism. His *Exercitia Spiritualia S.P. Ignatii Loyola* went through many editions and translations. The first English translation, however, was not published until 1876. It is not certain what edition McElroy used, perhaps the Latin edition published at Turin in 1835. See Sommervogel, I, 1260–1265.

24. Roman Archives of the Society of Jesus (hereafter ARSI), Maryland Province (hereafter MP) 7 V 6-7, John McElroy to Jan Roothaan, Superior General of the Society.

25. Aloysius Young (1798–1844), one of the first American Jesuits to study in Rome, was then Prefect of Studies at St. John's College in Frederick.

26. John Baptist Purcell (1800–1883), second Bishop of Cincinnati and first archbishop of that city when it became an archdiocese in 1850.

27. ARSI Maryland Province 7 V 7.

28. As superior of St. John's parish and college, McElroy was obliged to make an annual report to the superior general.

29. St. John's College, later Fordham College, which Bishop Hughes turned over to French Jesuits from Kentucky in 1846.

30. ARSI MP, 9 XI 64, Missiones PP 3ae Probationis sub anno 1851.

31. In the Jesuit course of training three years are set aside for spiritual formation. The novitiate constitutes two of these years; the third comes at the end of the course of studies and/or shortly before the taking of final vows. During this "tertian" or third year the Jesuit, among other things, makes for a second time the full Spiritual Exercises of Ignatius and is sent on various pastoral assignments.

32. The oldest mission of the Maryland Jesuits, located in St. Mary's County approximately a mile south of St. Mary's City.

33. 1851 was a Jubilee year proclaimed for the universal Church by Pope Pius IX, with special indulgences for those who fulfilled the requisites of confession and

communion. One can only speculate how the southern Maryland blacks, mostly slaves, understood this within their own mythology related to the Year of Jubilee.

34. The county seat of St. Mary's.

35. At Morganza in St. Mary's County.

36. At La Plata in Charles County, Maryland.

37. St. Thomas Manor in Charles County, one of the Jesuit plantations, and the site of St. Ignatius Church.

38. A mission of St. Thomas Manor, located in northwestern Charles County.

39. Another mission of St. Thomas Manor, in southwestern Charles County.

40. Still another mission of St. Thomas Manor, in southern Charles County on the neck between the Wicomico and Potomac Rivers.

41. A mission of St. Thomas Manor in southeastern Charles County.

42. St. Mary's Church, Bryantown, in eastern Charles County.

43. A mission attended from St. John's, Frederick, in southwestern Frederick County.

44. A mission of St. John's, Frederick, in eastern Frederick County.

VIII

BETWEEN TWO WORLDS I:
STEPHEN DUBUISSON

Stephen Dubuisson (1786–1864), a native of Santo Domingo, fled during the revolution there with his parents to France. In 1809 he entered the army and held several positions in the Treasury until 1815. Always a pious believer, Dubuisson, while at prayer after confession in 1814, experienced a sudden spiritual "revolution" in which he felt an immense attraction for the spiritual life. Family opposition forced him to defer for a year, but he eventually took refuge with the Sulpicians in Paris. "My first idea," he later wrote, "was to bury myself in a Trappist monastery," but a spiritual director persuaded him that the Church could not afford strict contemplatives in its struggle with the forces of infidelity. After exposure to a commentary on Ignatius' Constitutions and other Jesuit spiritual works, his "affections were all for the Society." Lured by the enormous possibilities he saw for the Church in the United States, he entered the novitiate of the Society of Jesus in White Marsh, Maryland.[1] The gentle, scrupulous Dubuisson was early noted for his unworldly ways. Students took advantage of him. Fellow Jesuits scorned his pious strivings. He was painfully aware of his limitations. When there was a possibility of his being made president of Georgetown College in 1825, he pleaded with Father General Jan Roothaan: "How could any body have ever got such an idea into his mind? I have no head to govern, no talents to make an impression, no secret for winning the confidence of my brethren in religion. The mere thought of such a responsibility crushes me."[1a] Despite his plea, he was appointed president, but lasted scarcely a year before superiors freed him from the torment of office. He spent the next three years in Rome where his intelligence and saintliness made a deep impression on the general. Returning to the United States in 1829, he spent the next decade in parish work in Philadelphia and Alexandria. In Philadelphia his gentle, saintly manner

217

won many converts among the Quakers. A boy who later became a Jesuit claimed to have seen him levitating one day while at prayer.[2] *But declining health, which had been frail from injuries sustained in the Napoleonic Wars, forced him to return to Europe in 1842.*

Spiritual Diary
    From 1818, while he was still in formation at Georgetown, until his appointment to parish work in Philadelphia in 1833, he kept a diary of his spiritual life. From the very beginning, even though his command of the language was slight, Dubuisson kept the diary in English.

SPIRITUAL DIARY (1818–1830)[2a]

[1818]

A.M. + D.G.
&
B.V.M.J.C.[?]

November 8th
    . . . I am positively now beginning a new Diary (spiritual), let it be an omen, o my sweet master Jesus, of the renewing of my spirit! Drive away I earnestly beseech you, all those importune thoughts which are in me the ordinary attendants, nay the very cause of sloth! Teach me that noble confidence in your help, which argues a lively faith, and is so acceptable to you!

November 9—
    A branch of that vice of natural laziness, is procrastination, to which unfortunately, I have ever been subject. O my God! here do I want the most efficacious assistance of your graces! I am perfectly convinced how ungenerous, how fatal such a disposition is; I have at several epochs tried to retrieve [sic] from its influence, yet I am far as yet from having fully succeeded in that point. Domine, ad adjurandum me festina![3]
    Never put off to another day that which you can perform on the present one—. . . .

November 13
    O Heart of my Jesus, that it were given me to feel the smart of some of those thorns which surrounded & were pressed on you, when you appeared to the Blessed Margaret Alacoqua![4] O Jesus, let me suffer something

for your love, I beseech you! But then, grant me the same love in such a plenitude that I may be enabled to stand all trials! Oh! vita hujusmodi expers dulcedinis, mors et magis quam vita![5]

O my Love! Communion to-day! Friday!! Feast of St. Stanislaus![6]— oh! give me a burning Heart!—

November 15

What more salutary subjects of reflection would I have? a great confidence in the care which almighty God takes of the church and all religious orders, and the useful apprehension of forfeiting my share of divine grace to see it reversed upon another!. . . . Thy grace, o my God, thy grace I most earnestly beseech! Grant thy blessing upon this beginning of new efforts towards the attainment of my end, the perfection of a religious life! . . .

November 17

O Teacher of all that is good, Holy Ghost, come to me! and first inspire me with a true desire of receiving thee! I am entering as it were upon a new course of life; eased from an office which prevented my practicing sincere particulars conducive to perfection in a religious life, for instance forbearing from all unnecessary looks, I can now apply with eagerness to these particulars: oh! so grant me that Blessed success, of coming to some degree of perfection! Jesus! Mary![7]

November 18

Is it possible, O Divine Comforter, all-Powerful advocate; most amiable of all Patrons,[8] is it possible, that I have not always been inflamed with the desire of possessing thee? Ah! at least now I feel in what need I stand of thy assistance; come into this little world of my heart, come and show what is pleasing to my God that I may do it! and most especially do not abandon me after inspiring me with good resolves, but stay with me until I have come to the execution; nay, never, never forsake me entirely, o spirit of Love!—

November 19

Yes, o Donum Dei Altissimi, God omnipotent who yourself are the gift & the giver, the chief presents which I crave from you, are 1: the spirit of charity towards you, my adorable maker, and Redeemer, and comforter; toward the Blessed and most pure creature from whom you, o Divine Word, would derive your human frame; as also towards all the heavenly inhabitants; towards my own soul, and in fine towards all my fellow-creatures upon earth, nor do I forget such as are now expiating in purging flames those faults which still shut them from the Blessed abode; 2: the spirit of *Humility*, o Jesus! o Holy Ghost! grant me true Humility! and the fire also of mortification—3: Lastly the spirit of science, which is necessary for my progress in those acquirements which my beloved call requires, especially as my rule prescribes I should pray for such a progress— . . .

November 22

What benevolent communication of my God! Eternal thanks, o most amiable Lord! How comforting! I must not be apprehensive because I do not feel the effects in my *interior world* of that burning zeal to which I aspired: when it is there, the Holy Ghost will come down and suggest to me both sentiments and actions. In the mean while, my duty is to wait for him in peace . . . and study myself in the calm of Recollection & Humility— Tho' indeed, o sancifier, I am surely allowed to pray and long for your heavenly visit!— . . .

November 26—

Oh! do continue, Holy Ghost, to excite me, to spur me on! Let never my fainting heart entirely sink oppressed by the weight of nature and my sins! Tell me the way to make some little reparation for these sins, and teach me how to conquer, to rule nature! I wished I could do nothing but what yourself would have me do! I wished every word of mine were conformable to your suggestions! For the last purpose, govern also my imagination; replenish it with proper ideas when it is my duty to converse! Jube quod vis, sed da mihi quod jubes—[9]. . . .

November 28

Fraternal Union! Oh! that I might prove a means of preserving it, tho' at the expense of my own outward character! Good God! is there not something strange in what happened to me in this regard! So desirous of contributing to such an union, wishing so earnestly whilst a Prefect to gain and create friendship, laudable affection: and yet!—I kiss thy chastising hand! O supreme Ruler of my fate!—Let me never forget, however, that any way of creating mutual affection, that would not be consistent with *Perseverantia in doctrina apostolorum,* that is with the spirit of the Society; & *in fractione panis,* [10] with an unremitting punctuality in the performance of all my duties; lastly, & *in orationibus,* with a love and continual practice of prayer, yielding to no kind of purely human consideration! that any such way, I say, is not lawful, and would create sentiments not only of short duration, but also rather calculated to disturb our internal peace.

November 29th

Strange indeed! It seems to me, that I sincerely wish to behave in such a manner, as to establish, as far as lies in my power, that sweet fraternal union: yet I can't help again observing it; it appears to be a very difficult thing. Your finger is here, o God! However it doubtless depends a great deal upon my ways; oh! let me then strive to mend them. Mildness, humility, Deference to the sentiments of my Brethren! Com[munio]n of this day to the obtaining of these qualities . . .

November 30

It is your holy will, o my God, that I should be tried and deprived of interior comfort in this moment; give me the necessary virtue to derive my perfection from such trials!—

December 2

O my Dearest Lord! My God! What a felicity, if my will was really no other but your own! grant me, force upon me that generosity of love which is so pleasing to you! . . .

December 6

O Providence! what then are you preparing for me? My God! quid me vis facere?[11] Not that I wish with an eye of distrust to pry into your adorable secrets: no, I abandon myself without any wilful reserve, to your conduct. Holy Ghost! be my guide; I will do my best to be faithful—Should I spill some of my blood for my Religion directly or indirectly, what a noble fate!—O Glorious Stephen my Patron, where death has so much contributed to the propagation of the Faith and the spreading of Almighty God's eternal glory, impetrate [sic] for me, the signal grace first sincerely to wish, and then to obtain, that I may die for my Dear Lord Jesus! . . .

December 10

The gift of Piety makes us love & respect our Superiors, and bear a maternal affection for our Inferiors! Force concerns ourselves, against each one's personal weakness of nature—Fear is with regard to Alm God— Counsel shines most eminent, as it is essential both for the contemplative and active life—

December 11

3 things in order to derive fruits from the meditation on the gifts of the Holy Ghost: 1: a great confidence in Alm. God's infinite goodness, 2: an earnest application to pious reading, prayer & contemplation, as the ordinary channels through which grace is bestowed upon us; 3 a warm gratitude for all favours received and fidelity to correspond.

My Good God! continue to support and animate me. Thanks for the victory which you have enabled me to gain over myself with regard to fra-

ternal charity. Oh! let it be the dawn of a new day! the beginning for me of
a new life of mildness, humility, & obedience!—

December 12

Great Stephen! you had drawn on yourself the choice of the almighty;
why could I not also attract his eye so as to be marked for a noble victim
like you? Have I not a heart? Is not the Holy Ghost ready to pour in his
graces, if I but oppose no resistance? oh! what an exalted thought! to die
for my Dear Saviour. You already, Holy Inspirer, have therefore suggested
me *something:* keep on, I beseech you; keep on, and be not disgusted at[12]
my tardiness!

December 13

It is dangerous to pray for extraordinary favours from above; yet it is
very laudable to act so as to deserve them. Chiefly men of prayer and contemplation obtain them.

Frequently at least such favours are not granted us for us only; but also
for the sake of promoting God's glory among our fellow-creatures, and then
we must publish them.[13]

Abstain from all useless or unseasonable thoughts.

December 15

When Alm. God grants us some extraordinary favours, we must expect
soon to have some great trial to undergo!—

December 16

Let us never forget, that well ordained charity must begin with our own
reformation!—what fruit can we produce in others, if we ourselves are ster-
ile in good works?

December 17

Alm. God suffered Paul's violence & persecutions against the Christians, because he wanted to make him a great saint, and thus to let him lay
up for himself a treasure of future *sentiments of humility!* O inscrutable
Providence of our God!—Behold, the fruit which we can derive from our
very sins!

December 18

I had to declare a few days ago to a certain person, that were the house
to crumble down, or were all my friends in this country to fail me, I would
still invariably persist in Religion, and go to the other end of the world if
necessary in order to meet again with Brethren—It was the spontaneous,

the candid expression of my feelings. . . . Yet alas! as soon as some cloud darken our horizon I am immediately seized with anxiety! Would to my God, it were a mere temptation, and that in reality I had a little of Ignatius's admirable fortitude in this point; but miserable I! Poor worm of the earth, who know but to crawl along in a path where my models ran freely and joyfully! O Jesus, you have called me; support and perfect me!— . . .

December 31

What thanks do I not owe you, my God, for the strength which you grant me at a time when I am in so great a need of it! Dearest Society, I consider it a choice blessing, that my love for thee augments by those very occurences which might seemingly be apt to produce a diminution in such a sentiment.

[1819]

January 1

A new year opening! Good God, let it be a year of great progress for me in thy service! Jesus, my dear Captain, I sincerely wish to follow thee; help me with thy all-powerful assistance, make me a true Hero of the cross. Mary, most Dear Mother, I have long determined upon it, I am your son by adoption for ever; take a tender care of my soul, obtain for me all the graces which I want to continue in those comforting desires lately revived in my heart by the Holy Ghost—And, let me insert here this particular request, do, I beseech you, do obtain that signal favour which I am petitioning from the Almighty for one of my Brethren. Mary! Mary! every person placed under your special protection has been manifestly favoured by Divine Providence: I know, that so ungrateful a servant, so inveterate a sinner as I am, is a very unfit Patron to present you with a new child; but consider Him, and since notwithstanding my continual infidelity to the grace of God, you have not ceased to be for me a kind mother, give me a new proof that you are more generous & powerful of intercession than we are weak and self-interested.

St. Joseph, my Patron for modesty and Recollection of mind, in a word for interiour life; in this new beginning year grant me a most peculiar protection. One of the great obstacles to my improvement in virtue is that I do not sufficiently center my thoughts upon the proper object of observation or study. Now it is precisely your province to obtain for me the contrary blessed habit; do then show me this year, that it is not in vain a person should go by that advice of the Holy Inspiration of the Scriptures: "Ite ad Joseph."

St. Stephen, Hero of faith, and zeal for the glory of our God, glorious Patron of mine! Pardon me, for having neglected you for so many years, and now that the thought of your illustrious tho' short life, and so admirable death, warms my breast, intercede with all vehemence with the arbiter of my fate, that I may receive some of those choice inspirations and occurences . . . —

Ye all, Saints of our Dearest Society, look down, you especially Great and Holy Ignatius, Xavier furnace of love & zeal, and Aloysius[14] my model, look down on your weakly follower, and impetrate for him some strength and constancy—

Nor do I forget you, the Protectors of my first steps toward Religion, Francis of Sales, & Sulpicians! Patrons of mildness and patience and humility, do not refuse me your continued intercession—

Teresa, fond spouse of the Sacred Heart of Jesus! in spite of my levity, of my preoccupations, of my innumerable defects, send down to me, Thy Spouse cannot refuse thee, send of those burning coals which made thy own heart whilst upon earth turn a real fire of love and zeal— . . .

January 5

What help of grace! how grateful I ought to be!

January 6

How good the Lord is to those that wish to love him! for an inward movement of hatred against human respect and warm offering of my whole self to his glory, what sweet comfort did I not receive for the rest of the day—But, not in this world we are to look for our recompense, let me never forget it, and consider such favours of Alm. God as drops of milk granted to the cries of a child in spiritual ways!

January 7

How admirable your conduct of me, o my God! For I know not how many times I had remarked that previous to some great trial I always received some great spiritual comfort: a new opportunity of observing it has occurred—I certainly have been put to the test today on a very delicate point; great efforts were wanting to keep my mind within bounds; but my good friend had fortified me, and my heart is at peace! . . .

January 13

It is too true, this is a home thrust upon me. I am especially too apt to feel exceeding grief when I see any failings, in my Brethren, and to harbour great apprehension that the intended work shall not succeed! . . .

January 16

What trials! What interior motions! I am indeed in the furnace . . . but I cannot but kiss your chastising hand, o my God, when I find that in the midst of these interiour disquiets my love & zeal for the Society increase, and also my desire of acquiring those virtues which are properly Jesuitical, mortification, debasement of ourselves, fortitude in our Lord, mildness with regard to the neighbour, and tender, most tender affection of piety, oh! that I could indeed see you daily growing to greater power & influence in my heart! . . .

January 26

My dearest of Friends! to what internal trials I am destined! It is beyond my power to stifle that poignant grief which grasps upon my heart when I see the rule contemned, or obedience overlooked! I know that I myself were more than any one apt to transgress, but it is precisely that which increases my disquiet: I should want to have edifying, encouraging examples before my eyes, and now I have as it were to set the example to others! oh! support me, since you thus situate me!

I must, tho', yes I must acknowledge your favour—It really seems to me, that the less I meet with what I would wish, the more directly I am led to the end of my blessed vocation. My love and zeal for the Society daily increases, I believe; human respect I more than ever trample under foot; my desire of advancing is also increasing; and I was so happy as to enjoy today an internal glow of delight at the idea of suffering for the sake of our Lord! . . .

February 1st

I consider it a great favour, that I am allowed to entertain a peculiar devotion to St. Aloysius. I always had a great veneration for him, but especially these few months, and more particularly during my present blessed retirement, I felt extremely desirous of acquiring some degree of those virtues for which he was so eminent, and my being allowed to take him for my Patron in the summit of those virtues, fills my heart with hopes & joy.

Not, O my Jesus, that I forget the devotion to your Sacred Heart, to which I was so strongly excited in my retreat of last year. No, I am too deeply persuaded of the immense spiritual riches that flow from that admirable source, ever to become altogether neglectful of making there an earnest application. but my present condition of a student in divinity naturally places me under the peculiar patronage of Aloysius, nor is it contrary to your intentions, that we should thus take along with us a helper, as it were, to keep alive our desires and resolution.

. . . I hope I shall be granted the object of my desires, first because it is the very desire also of that most loving Leader of ours, Jesus, the support of the weak; then because I am certain of having for my warm advocates

his glorious Mother and Yourself [Aloysius]; lastly, because for these last
months, I have experienced the most comforting motions of grace, acting
in my interior, and reviving that fervency that inflamed ardor of wishes for[15]
religious perfection, with which I was blessed on my being called so suddenly and so extraordinarily from the sinful world. . . .

Recollection is what I most particularly want, now more than ever. A
great many of my imperfections proceed from this, that I suffer too easily
my mind to be tossed to and fro by unseasonable solicitude or reflections.
Besides this virtue of recollection, which is nothing but a continual sense
of the presence of God, is the best, a necessary, and most natural preparation to prayer; if I am recollected, I shall be a man of prayer, and if I am
a man of prayer, I shall obtain numerous favours from the Almighty. Let
this, therefore be my first pursuit, with your assistance, O Aloysius! Recollection, Golden Recollection in God!— . . .

February 4th

It is beyond my power to suppress the emotion of grief which thrills
thro' me when I behold something which I conceive to be injurious to God.
In fact, such a feeling is only to be kept within reasonable limits, for it is
evidently praiseworthy in itself—But alas! here I am deficient! I know not
as yet how to master myself, how to moderate the effect of either exterior
objects or internal movements of my soul. I am at school indeed! (most
happy school!) I cannot expect to be far advanced—Nonetheless, o God,
give me that dominion, that sway over myself as quick as possible—. . . .

Feb. 11

Always disposed to harbour excessive solicitude! Why do I not seriously apply to the practice of those truths, which I know perfectly? I am
thoroughly convinced that it is necessary I should keep my mind in peace
and confidence in the sight of God; and yet as often as occasions of disquiet
offer, I am sure to trespass the limits of a reasonable solicitude! Heu! me
miserum! . . .

Feby-14 (Recollection)

I have again undergone pretty hard interior trials this week—I indeed
experience the truth of this observation, that when a person begins to live
with more fervor, then the Devil redoubles his efforts and abominable suggestions. But not all his guile will be able to make me fall entirely; I know
I will not, because I have for me the promise of my God! My care must be
therefore to redouble on my part the vigilant watch necessary over the motions of my carnal heart, and also over the roving of my imagination, so as
to shut up all avenues as much as I possibly can. And not to rest contented

with such cautions, but to carry on with unrelenting activity the work of my perfection by the means pointed out in our blessed Institute—I must especially, situated as I am whether with respect to my interior conflicts or in point of behavior towards my Brethren, I must then particularly make Humility the object of my continual pursuit. I have long wished & tried to get possessed of so desirable an acquirement, but the prize is of greater value than to be carried with little endeavouring & toiling. It will undoubtedly be one day my reward, I feel the sweet confidence that it will, yet I also easily conceive that since it is a recompense, it must be given me only after I have fulfilled the task, which is here to put into practice those resolutions of humbling myself suggested to me by divine grace with so constant benignity—
. . . .

Feby. 27th

Faith, all powerful virtue!—But to obtain it in a high degree, it must be petitioned with great perseverance, and with effectual prayers, that is, not with mere motions of the heart, but with a generous practice of what actions those motions of the heart excited by divine grace, will suggest most assuredly. It must be in some degree merited by sincere endeavours on our part! Aloysius help me!— . . .

March 3

Oh! that I could say indeed, I share in the bitter cup of my Jesus! an exquisite anguish was, I confess, granted me to-day, but did I take it as was proper? You, my God! Holy Ghost, who drew most mercifully my mind to such reflections, who excite in my sinful heart so many desires of amendment, do, then, set a finishing hand to your work, lead me on to . . . sanctity! Yes to Sanctity, that is the aim which I am prescribed to bear in view, whatever may my sense be of the immense distance which still separates me from the blessed goal!—Mortification both interior and exterior, humility, obedience, perfect charity; those are the steps, I know; and unless grossly mistaken I joyfully will set my foot on them. Begone, ye weaknesses of puerile nature; do not any more disgrace the work of the grace of the Most High! . . .

March 7

Recollection
(reading over the notes of my triduum of 7br, 1818)
Tepidity! Abominable Monster! that I might crush thy head, and destroy at least for all of us in this house thy hateful, fatal; detestable influence! What could I do to this purpose? Inspire me, o my God! Holy Ghost, impart to my soul those salutary incitements by which you frequently make

us sensible of your desires! Immense goodness of our God! always acting as with free and reasonable creatures! and what return is made to that kindness? alas! alas! We sinners, we beseech thee to hear and change us!—

O Xavier, Aloysius! Some one is speaking already of having me ordained, when I am at so immense a distance from the requisite degree of both holiness of life and solidity of doctrine! Pray for me! obtain of our God that my Superior may not be so situated as to have to hasten my ordination! Present before that tremendous majesty my earnest, my warm desires of serving him well! Or at least obtain that I may continue studying after being ordained—Sweet, melting, transforming flame of zeal, come and revive my desponding soul!— . . .

March 10

Blessed are they that suffer persecutions! Is it applicable to me already in some small degree? or at least has it been so?—I will not examine, Dear Lord! but earnestly beg to taste of your bitter cup, confident that you will not bring it up to my lips, without confirming my resolution—

March 11

Salt of the earth! What an honor for me! Is it possible, o God, that you intend me for one of your apostles, one of your ambassadors with man—? Oh! therefore let me then first acquire and preserve the true savour of Christ in myself, so as to impart it to others!

March 12

Light of the world! City on the top of a hill! I, an apostle!—*Make* me so, then, o Lord! Change and reform every thing in me, so that I may become exemplary—

Ignatius, Xavier, Aloysius!

March 13

How delightful the study of Sacred Scripture! Poor petty heads of the world! You imagine, that we are groaning under the heavy burthen of a religious life!

March 20

Happy burning of my heart! Yes, my God, I am truly thirsty after fulfilling your will, and actually working my own and others' sanctity—May I become really thirsty also after anguish and sufferings, since it is the very path my Jesus has trod in, and that the disciple must not fare better than the master—Sweet Recollection! Contemplation! . . .

May 11

O God, since you send new trials upon me, bestow also new strength upon my poor soul!—I know that I am nothing by myself, I knew it from the first moment when you vouchsafed to call me to your service; but I know, on the other hand, and I likewise was persuaded of this from that happy hour, that I would find my faculties multiplied by your grace! O my sweet Master! Imprint this persuasion deeper and deeper on my mind; be lavish in my regard with that kind of grace, which renders a soul unshaken in confidence thro' reliance on you, and at once over cautious and fearful thro' a knowledge of human frailty!—Most glorious Mary, admirable Steven; amiable Aloysius, mild Francis & Sulpitius, you undoubtedly obtained of our common Father those precious flames which I felt and feel again with unspeakable delight, burning in my breast! Continue your work of commiseration; help, efficaciously assist a poor heart and poorer head, which yet wishes to do and suffer something for God!— . . .

June 26

On the 22 of this month, June 1819, I spent the night in Mr. De-Longueville's room.[16] He was then in a desperate state, and it was thro' an invitation of Dr. Warfield, that some person of the College sat up to wait upon him—I poured forth to God some prayers as ardent as my natural sloth would allow; I had chiefly in view that the Patient should worthily accept whatever dispensation divine Providence had decreed, yet I was not without hopes of his recovery, and I prayed for it, because I thought it might prove to the greater glory of God. I particularly recommended him to glorious Aloysius of Gonzaga, inviting him at the same time to take spiritually his refuge in the protection of the Blessed Virgin and that great Aloysius. On the next morning, I was strongly excited to invite him to take a vow in case he should recover, consisting in this, that he would have an altar built in his house dedicated to B. Aloysius. I was prevented from seeing him during that same day. In the course of it, I heard that there was a favorable change observed in his state, and that the Doctor, who, before imagined he had a few days only to live, then entertained hopes of his recovery. I do not pretend to boast of my application to our Angelic Aloysius; yet it seems to me that Saint has obtained the man's recovery—Dear Patron! obtain now of Alm. God, that I may know how to act to his greater glory, and your own honour. . . .

July 4th

Nearly two whole weeks have elapsed since I had the immense advantage of placing myself more than before under the protection of St. Aloysius! were I to inquire with myself whither I have already laid to profit so precious moments, what could be my answer, but that of an indolent soul? Yet, I think that my inward sense of my unworthiness has increased, which shows some little progress in humility. . . . I feel very desirous of living an interior life, of offering myself an entire holocaust to God in the obscurity & silence of my heart. Confirm Dear Lord, these comforting marks of thy operating grace! Aloysius, help me! help me, glorious Aloysius!

July 5th

Poor M. DeLongueville died this day! Let your will be done, o God! Blessed Aloysius, I hope this will not cause any alteration in my confidence! It was no doubt better for the poor man that he should leave this earth at this time, and I am besides more[17] unworthy a soul than to obtain extraordinary favours. Yes, I acknowledge, that to my sins is to be imputed the non compliance.

July 8

O God, do not abandon me in this difficult juncture! I am ready to sink under the painful impression; my heart fades away on believing that you are entirely neglected! but excite in me such sentiments as you wish me to entertain in that regard! Let me know what I am to think & do—Meanwhile I make bold to offer you the real doleurs which I have to bear. Happy, were I allowed to look upon them as a share that I have in my Redeemer's cup!—
. . .

July 21

O Aloysius, obtain for me a heart like yours! Almighty God loves all creatures, but he loves *me* in all of them and those irrational creatures being not capable of knowing and loving him, the return of so infinite a love, both of benevolence & beneficence is incumbent upon me! Oh! indeed, that I could discharge so grand an obligation! that I could not too unworthily, repay our God's Love for myself, for other men who are not faithful; and for all insensible creatures! . . .
N.B. In the last days of July I was seized with violent sickness—disintery— and when convalescent, went to Conowago.[18]

Instruction by F. Kohlmann[19]

8ber 15—1819

Nothing can excuse us in the sight of God for being willing, of our own accord & determinations to leave the Soc[iety]. Whatever may be our feelings, we must not trust them if they incline and will that way, it was by indulging such feelings, that all apostasies & heresies originated.

All the reasons which the spirit of darkness may suggest, will if analysed come to these two viz. that our Pride cannot bear controul or that we are determined to yield to the dictates of our immortification, —and will such motions justify in the eyes of God so glaring a violation of our oath to that All-seeing, all-wise, Almighty Being?

It is shocking but too undeniable, that apostasy & reprobation are synonymous expressions!— . . .

October 27—1819

What a medley of joy & grief, comfort & anxiety, this life of ours is! At least, let me lay up a great deal of spiritual strength in the sweet refreshment of the visits of my God, that I may be proof against all anguish & toils I shall have to bear for his love & service. Oh! that my heart were really a burning furnace of love! Who shall give me such feelings! Aloysius help me with your warmest intercession. . . .

[1820]

Octiduum of September 1820
begun on the 3rd at night—

O what a noble call! what a sublime part I am chosen to perform! to labour with God for the salvation of souls, a work which has so much affinity with the grand act of man's creation, & redemption, and receiving the Holy Ghost!

And this is to be done equally by any of the means which Religion may afford. I would grossly mistake, were I to think that one is in itself better than another! All, all that our omnipotent Lord requests, is that I should give my whole heart to the exalted object.

No reserve, therefore!—O let me deeply imprint this on my mind, in order successfully to resist despondency!!—(O Jesus! how bitter thy chalice must have been!)

Yes, O my God! for ever I will serve you! In all circumstances, whatever my condition may be, yours will be all my thoughts, words, & actions! Some way or other I will always devote to you my whole self and all that I shall be able to do! Greater Glory of God! Salvation of souls! . . .

Stanislaus   O admirable youth, obtain for me Patience, Obedience, & Love!

Ven. Fr. de Hieronyme[20]   Am I not owing to him for the bettering of my state of health, nay perhaps for a prolongation of life, which enables me to do penance for my past sins—The truth is, that we made a novena to Ven. Fr. de Hier., four of us at the White Marsh[21] & that all four recovered if not completely, at least in great measure!—All honour be to God and his Saints.

7ber 12

I came out of the retreat, and already so much inclined to vague thoughts & apprehensions!—Oh! then think first of the kingdom of heaven and all the rest will be added to thee: think first of thy spiritual advancement, and God will direct the rest.

7ber 17

What an agitation of mind! and for ever the same cause of it, that apprehension respecting future offices! Oh! so desirous to acquire confidence, and so very little successful in the pursuit of it! My Jesus, if this uneasiness of my mind be the will of your Eternal Father, I readily submit and accept the tribulation; but if it were only because I do not sufficiently . . . [entry ends abruptly]

7ber 18

Diffidence   I am really guilty of diffidence in God, when I undertake some labour, or when I am enjoined something by the Superiors, which I judge to be untimely or likely to be attended with evil consequences. . . .

1821—Feby—9

Yes, o Jesus, I will try to give by means of love some value to every little action of mind. O searcher of hearts, and support of souls, enlighten me, excite me, support me!

Feby 10—

At home family concerns, petty jealousy, animosity; attentions which parents insist upon; the very comforts & conveniences which they endeavour to procure you; and an intercourse with people who have witnessed your former life: all these generally prove great obstacles to the fruits of the sacred ministry—

Country people are generally far better disposed to receive the gospel, and more docile to its precepts & counsels.[22] Their actions, for the most part, only want motives to be acts of virtue—What immense good could be done perhaps amont [sic] the blacks of Virginia!!! O God, shew me thy will, and propose me to make it the only rule of my conduct! . . .

Feb 13

If Jesus Christ were oftener the subject of our conversation and reflections, he would be more known and loved!!!—

Feb 14

O my God, I willingly accept of my present tribulation! only give me strength to beat down every obstacle to my holy call! . . .

Feby. 20

O Jesus, who lie hidden on our altars, because the brightness of your glory would keep your faithful servants at too much distance, and the wicked would adore you only thro' fear, give me that lively faith and ever increasing love!!!

Feby. 21

It is not enough for me, not to blush at the Gospel: if I do not faithfully correspond to the suggestions of the Holy Ghost, I shall be covered with confusion on the last day! O my God! da quod jubes & jube quod vis!—[23]
. . .

Feby—28

The favours which Alm God grants us in this life are only transient, so as not to let us consider this earth as a place of enjoyment! . . .

April 23–24

Seek first the Kingdom of God and his justice, and all those things shall be added unto you (Matt. 6.39), may also be applied for the good discharge of a temporal office (Rodr. 1 Tr. ch. 1)[24] What a folly, therefore, for me to indulge such anxiety concerning my incapacity, my being inadequate to the task imposed or apprehended to be imposed on me! Let me strenuously exert myself to act in all things as a good Religious, and God will, if it agree with his designs, enable me to act also as a good Procurator or teacher, or preacher, or confessor—. . . .

May 17

. . . we live in a continual expectation of every thing except Jesus! Wealth, promotion, news, changes, we eagerly wait for! and Jesus perhaps will, before, knock by means of a disease or some accident! Let, then, all our pursuits, wishes, expectations, and exertions, have a tendency to the attainment of our blessed end!

June 3

How severely tried on the approach of my ordination! The evil spirits how perseverant in magnifying difficulties in my eyes! O Jesus, thou hast called me; support me to the end!

June 6

Let us always act with candor & simplicity; whether successful or not, intrigue reduces man, in the sight of God, to the condition of a brute prone to craftiness by instinct— . . .

June 28

O gracious Lord! into what an abyss I was on the point of being pushed! I know, now I know what that kind of hellish allurement is, by which we get disaffected to our Blessed call—Too wanton imagination, woefully but truly the crazy one of home, who will give me such chains to shackle thee down, which thou mayst never break? Thine, o God of infinite mercy! thine it is to fit me out for thy work, thine it was to call me up: let not thy grace be refused to my wretched heart, tho' ever so undeserving of any such favour—To work miracles is for thee nothing more than *to will:* Keep me up, and it will be a true wonder!—

July 7—

Whatever you may intend for me, my God, give me a most copious supply of grace, for I am frightened indeed at my extreme misery. The least difficulties, the least obstacle, the most indifferent, the contrary occurrence will dishearten me and something then banefully whispers in my ear, that all hopes of success are gone; that I will never be able to produce any fruit of edification, that I am good for nothing but to create trouble—Oh! change my heart & head!

July 10

Is it the dawn of a clearer day, which is opening before me? Thy will, my God, thy will, and nothing else! But give strength and persever-ance!— . . .

[1822]

May 29th

Jesus! O Jesus! how prone I am to be softened by communications with the world! Is it possible, that such a danger almost found me fascinated. Good God, how easily clouds gather together around our mind and we hardly observe them! Oh! let it be my hourly effort to call myself back again to the true spirit of the Society!— . . .

[1823]

February 18

My God, I cannot admit of any other object of my wishes and of my labour, but thy glory and the salvation of souls—Vainly have the most furious gales of temptations assaulted the bark of my vocation, it has continued afloat, and tight—Thanks, thrice thanks to thee, o my Lord, for the wickedness and cowardice of my own heart is not unknown to myself! . . .

Feb 20

Union, sweet union with my Jesus, with my God; the object of his own views, of his own desires, of his own ardent desires! O goodness divine! and upon whom? a wretch, a worm—worse than that—a sinner! Who will give tears to my eyes? oh! who will give me a contrite heart, a heart of flesh instead of one as hard as rock? . . .

Feby 27

Strange, but admirable thy conduct, o Wisdom of my God!—and how clearly I now conceive, that the least degree of infidelity or merely non correspondence to the grace of Christ, throws me back, and brings into my soul trouble, discontent, sadness, fear—Jesus, Jesus! let it never bring giving up the pursuit after thy prize! . . .

April 9

Wonderful indeed are thy ways!—Shall I harbour surprise at not enjoying certain sweetness of devotion as upon leaving the world? alas! what have I done what now am I doing, to deserve that reward? Let us go on!—Deus est benignitas, Deus est misericordia! . . .

[1824]

June 21—St. Aloysius

Perhaps after wading long and painfully through a marshy extensive tract of land, I shall come to some solid pleasing ground, where advances will be much less impeded.

June 23

I am determined to try it. . . . For thee, o my god, I will work, think, live!—Let me not deceive myself! there can be no true comfort, in seeking for self . . . in the violation of our rules—What were they given us for? . . . If we could gain our object without them, why should S. Ignatius have been heavenly prompted to frame them? . . . Suppose S. Ignatius were to appear before us, could we presume to tell him, that we need not be so very particular in observing his rules? and is not that Holy Master of ours constantly occupied with the care of his family? incessantly watching from the sky over his struggling brethren on earth? Oh! wo[e is] me if he find me a sluggish one!—

June 24

A friend of Jesus Christ . . . should follow him in the high way of the Cross! . . . and, there can be finally no true peace, but in the love of the cross! . . .

June 29th (S.S. Peter & Paul)
Renovation of vows!

O my God! again, and solemnly (at least solemnly for me) and with new happiness I have given myself to thee, with all that I am, know, and can do. Accept of the offering, tho so little deserving of thy regard, and give, oh! give & make it good! I am delighted in taking it as a favorable omen, that i have experienced, thru the whole of this regenerating period, an unusual tranquillity of soul—a kind of sweet peace in my inmost faculties: nothing vehement, nothing extraordinary, —but a reliance on the protecting arm of Jesus, which casts a mild most consoling tinge on all my thoughts. What a favor, after so enormous sins! . . . Good God!

An awful reflection! I cannot dissemble it to myself, there is in my being matter for God's service. Nothing is wanting by my faithfully corresponding to God's aid and call—and what proof have I not had of his fidelity in standing by me in cases of exigency? I shall, therefore, be put to a severe account, if I do not lay those *talents* to profit, . . . for the Master— for the Lord!!!— . . .

November 8th

. . . My great struggle for these past weeks has been to oppose the continually rising effects of an over-anxious foresight of what may happen to me or to the Society, and of an unconquerable dread of being appointed to any government. My all-bountiful Maker favored me, however, with glimpses of a nature to encourage me very much. Oh! what a state it would be, to view every thing with the calmness of a Christian eye, to preserve on every occasion the coolness of reflection, and above all . . . to rejoice at adversity, contradiction the most bitter, prosecution the most unjust!

November 15

Consideration made in Mrs. Mattingly's room, during her trip to the lower counties. O Faith in Jesus Christ! My God, what a favor to myself! And I would become insensible! I would become ungrateful! I would return to my vomit! No! no; no! . . .

[1825]

Feby 9th

Time, time, how fast gliding along! My life . . . alas! O God, let thy holy will be done! Don't I wish to procure your glory, O Lord? Don't I constantly think of it? Am I not incessantly urged by the desire of promoting the happiness, especially the spiritual advantage of my fellow beings? Yes but . . . how far I am from answering the divine call. . . .

[1833]

Feb 23

God of mercy! and I would yet be slow in throwing myself into thy arms with unbounded confidence!

Feb 27

My God! I am in straights for time & thou hast so often made me almost preter-naturally emerge out of difficulties: ah! help me, Lord of mercy! For thee, for thee! for thy honor and glory!

CURES

His desire for the hidden life notwithstanding, Dubuisson within a short time of his ordination in 1821 found himself in the public eye with the sensational cure of Ann Mattingly in the late winter of 1824. He had keenly followed the cult that had developed in the 1820s around the European wonder-working priest, Alexander Leopold Francis Emeric, Prince Hohenlohe-Waldenbourg-Schillingfürst. No one in the United States did more to promote the prince's charism than Dubuisson. He made the arrangements for the prince's prayers in behalf of Mattingly, one of his parishioners at St. Patrick's where he was an assistant pastor. He gathered the affidavits for the pamphlet that was published about her cure. He was involved in at least three cures that took place at the Georgetown Visitation Convent between 1825 and 1838. He was intent on gaining recognition, both in the United States and in Europe, of the "digitus Dei" that he felt had so singularly touched the American Catholic community.

Deposition on the Cure of Mrs. Ann Mattingly[25]

I have had the honor of Mrs. Mattingly's acquaintance, (a sister of Captain Thomas Carbery, the present Mayor of Washington) for more than two years. I habitually visited her, and always found her a prey to an inward illness, with which I was told, that she had been taken about six years ago. The symptoms which I witnessed, or frequently heard herself state, were the following:

She constantly felt excruciating pains in her chest, on the left side. It seemed as if her inside frame, in that part, were corroded by a cancer. She usually threw up blood and a mixture of corrupt matter, in such quantity, that it may well be said to have been by full bowls. Owing, no doubt, to that internal ulcer, her breath was extremely offensive, oftentimes she spoke to me of a red and hard spot, below her left breast, which at intervals threatened to break open. From the violence of the pains in her breast, she had lost the use of her left arm, so far as to have been unable to lift it up, or to use it in dressing, without assistance, for about six years. In her worst paroxisms, which lasted, not merely a few days, but whole weeks, and returned several times each year, it was impossible for her to take any substantial food whatever. She has spent so long as four weeks together, literally without swallowing any thing else than a few cups of tea or coffee. She then used to be reduced to that state of weakness, that she could not stir from her bed; and it was a subject of astonishment to all her friends, that she lived. Towards the last period, she experienced an increase of malady. She was taken about six months ago with a cough, which became worse and worse, and for the last six weeks was such, as to place her in imminent danger of expiring in the height of the fits. I do not recollect ever witnessing any thing like it, both for violence and the puking of blood with which it was attended. Finally she was taken a few weeks since, with chills and fevers. In short, so continual was the state of suffering of Mrs. Mattingly, that I remember only one period when she enjoyed some relief, and that but a temporary and very incomplete one; particularly for the few weeks immediately proceeding her cure, she was in a sort of agony, which, I found, almost every body judged must have been the precursor of her departure from this world.

The physicians consulted on the case, or who attended, had declared that it was evidently out of the reach of medicine. . . .

In the beginning of February last, Mr. [Anthony] Kohlmann, returning from Baltimore, reported that the Rev. John Tessier, a Vicar General, of the diocese of Baltimore, had received a letter from Prince Hohenlohe, stating that his Highness would offer up his prayers, on the 10th day of every month, at 9 o'clock A.M. for the benefit of those persons, living out of Europe, who wished to unite in prayer with him. . . . the Prince recommended a nine days' devotion, in honor of the *Name of Jesus:* . . . Meanwhile, impressed with a kind of awe, by the nature of the proceeding, I determined to act with the utmost circumspection. Accordingly, I wrote to the Rev. Mr. W. Beschter, in Baltimore, to obtain some more positive information. His answer fully satisfied me with regard to the existence of the letter on the part of the Prince, received in Baltimore, and likewise respecting several late striking cures in Holland. Not contented with those precautions, I *would* have the approbation of the head Pastor of the Diocese,

Archbishop Marechal, before taking upon myself to direct the infirm persons alluded to, in their devotions, in such a step, as an application for their cure from Heaven, through the efficacy of the prayers of Prince Hohenlohe, a Roman Catholic priest, residing upwards of 4000 miles from this place, and at the precise time of prayers in union with him. I consequently wrote to Archbishop Marechal, whose answer confirmed the information which I had already received, communicated various directions on the mode of proceeding, and graciously promised his joining in prayer with us, on the appointed day, 10th of March instant.

I owe it to the truth, to say, that I then should have been unjustifiable to my own eyes, had I not directed, assisted, countenanced, Mrs. Mattingly and a few more persons similarly situated, in their call upon Heaven; and that, if I had delayed so long, it had by no means been from distrust, for I had not the least doubt left on my mind, concerning the miraculous cures obtained by Prince Hohenlohe's prayer in Europe, and I entertained a lively hope, that Heaven would grant us also some favor of that kind. . . .

The novena, i.e. nine days devotion, in honor of the *Name of Jesus,* began on the 1st day of March, so as to be concluded previously to the 10th. It consisted of the Litany of the holy *Name of Jesus,* with some other prayers, such as the Acts of Faith, Hope, Charity, and Contrition, and the short ejaculation: *Lord Jesus! may thy name be glorified!*

. . . I imagine, that the number of those who, in this country, thus implored Heaven, for the favor alluded to, in union with Prince Hohenlohe and his own friends in Germany, was nearly two hundred.

During the course of the novena, Mrs. Mattingly was desperately ill; I saw her on the 29th of February, and 7th and 9th of March, always confined to bed, and frequently in those fits of coughing and vomiting of blood, which looked very much like her last struggles with death. When I left her, on the 9th, at about half past 10 o'clock at night, she was worse than ever, and there was an expression of gloom upon all . . . the family. . . .

I celebrated mass, in St. Patrick's church at half past 2 o'clock, and afterwards carried the Blessed Sacrament to Mrs. Mattingly, at her brother Capt. Carbery's house. On my arrival, she was in the same state of extreme weakness and suffering, and a paroxism of her cough, which came on, made me almost apprehensive lest she might be prevented from receiving communion, but it proved of very short duration. This was the hour of expectation.

I dispose every thing according to the rites of our church. A small towel was to be put under her chin; she would help to fix it, but finds herself unable to lift up her arm. I address her with very few words of encouragement—telling her, that the best possible exhortation for her, was the very

letter of Prince Hohenlohe's directions, which I read to her. I then give her
the Holy Communion. There were some consecrated hosts left in my pix.
I shut and wrap up the whole—give the usual blessing to the family (there
were five persons in the room, relatives or friends)—and kneel down before
the Blessed Eucharist, previous to taking it with me on retiring: when, behold! Mrs. Mattingly fetches a deep sigh—rises slowly to the sitting position—stretches her arms forward—joins her hands—and exclaims, with a
firm, tho' somewhat weak, voice: "Lord Jesus! what have I done to deserve
so great a favor[?]" The emotion, the affright of the persons in the room,
is betrayed by sobs and tears, and half suppressed shrieks. —I rise, with a
thrill through my whole frame—step to the bed side—she grasps my hand:
—"Ghostly Father!" she cries out, "what can I do, to acknowledge such
a Blessing. My first, my spontaneous expressions are: "Glory be to God!
—we may say so! oh! what a day for us!" I then, bid her say what she felt:
"Not the least pain left." —"None there," said I pointing to her breast?
—"not the least—only some weakness." I ask her how she has come to be
relieved. She had felt as if she were dying from excess of pain—had offered
up a short prayer of the heart to *Jesus Christ*—and instantly had found herself freed from all sufferings whatever.

"I wish to get up," she exclaims "and give thanks to God on my
knees." "But" I replied, "can you?" "I can, if you will give me leave."
Her sisters immediately look for her stockings (she used to lie in bed, nearly
dressed)—but upon my observing that our very first occupation should be
to give thanks, we kneel down, she remains sitting in her bed—and all recite
three times *the Lord's prayer,* with the *Hail Mary,* and *Glory be to the Father, and to the Son, and to the Holy Ghost,* as also the short ejaculatory
prayer, *Lord Jesus may thy name be glorified!* She joins with continued
firmness of voice—(I then looked at my watch. It was 22 minutes after four.
I accordingly estimated that the cure had been effected at about 15 minutes
after 4). Directly after, her stockings are brought—she is surrounded by her
friends—gets up, and walks, unassisted, and with steady deportment, to the
table, dressed in the shape of an altar, on which the Blessed Eucharist lay—
there bends her knees, and remains for a while lost in an act of adoration.

I confess that the impression upon my soul was so profound at the sight
of the whole scene, but particularly of this last circumstance, that I do not
think it could have been more so, had I seen Mrs. Mattingly dead and raised
to life again. In the habit of finding her perpetually in bed or on a sopha
[sic], racked with pains, spitting—vomiting blood—when, at once, in the
sudden transition of one minute to another, I saw her rise up, stand, walk,
kneel down, and speak with words, and a tone of voice which denoted
soundness of mind as well as of body—I underwent I believe, the very same
sensation, as if I had seen her rise out of the coffin. There was especially

in her look and features, something, which I shall not undertake to depict—
an expression of firmness, and of earnest awful feelings, the recollection of
which it will be my consolation to preserve through life: O Faith in Jesus
Christ! those are thy effects[.]

As I had to hurry on to another sick person's house, I left Mrs. Mattingly about 10 minutes after her cure. I immediately determined upon
going on the same day, to Baltimore, to be myself the bearer of the important news to our venerable prelate, Archbishop Marechal. But multiplied
engagements detained me until eleven o'clock. Then, on the point of leaving Washington, I went down in company with the Rev. Mr. Matthews to
see Mrs. Mattingly again. she came and met us at the door, knelt down to
receive her pastor's blessing; in short, looked and acted as one perfectly
restored to health, who has only more strength and flesh to recover.

We are now, on the 17th of March, seven days, therefore have elapsed
since her cure. She is daily acquiring strength, as is witnessed, I may say,
by the whole city, which flocks to Capt. Carbery's house in order to see
her. Doctor Jones, her physician, has examined her, and found no vestige
of the species of red tumor which she had on her side, nor any sign whatever
of ill health; a very remarkable trait; as also the following, which several
of her friends have been able to ascertain. Previous to her so sudden recovery, her breath, as I mentioned before, was extremely offensive—from that
moment, all kinds of unpleasant effluvia from her stomach have been dispelled; and she declares that she constantly has a taste like that of loaf sugar
in her mouth.

Whilst in Baltimore, on the 11th, I hastily drew up, in French, a pro-
visional account of this glorious event for Prince Hohenlohe, and left it with
the Rev. W. Beschter, Pastor of St. John's Church, to be forwarded by the
first opportunity. I deemed that step a duty of gratitude to the truly blessed
man, whom the Almighty thus makes the instrument of his wonders for the
benefit of mankind; as I now feel it a sacred part incumbent upon me to
procure authenticity and notoriety to this deposition, in order that God may
be praised in his works; a deposition to which I swear on the Holy Gospel
of our Lord Jesus Christ, with full certitude of accuracy, and which, I trust,
I would subscribe with my own blood.

*Narrative of the Wonderful Cure of Sister Mary Eugenia Millard, a Nun in
the Convent of the Visitation, in Georgetown, District of Columbia, on the
10th February 1838.*[26]

The church of Christ, in these United States of North America, has
been favoured of late years with [extraordinary] events . . . : some [cures]
were deemed destined only for private edification; whilst, there seemed to

be a loud voice calling for the publication of others. Not only the U.S. but Europe also . . . rung with the report of Mrs. Ann Mattingly's cure, wrought in the city of Washington, on the 10th March, 1824: and although that of Sister Apollonia Digges, of the convent of the Visitation, in George-town . . . on the 20th of January, 1831, did not create the same sensation, still the knowledge of it was also widely spread.

One more cure of the same wonderful case has just occurred, in that favoured house, the Georgetown Monastery, and amidst those circum-stances which, unquestionably, have at once stamped the event with the supernatural impress. No one, so far, presumes to dogmatically pronounce it a miracle; but, with regard to many, —particularly those who have been intimately acquainted with the case—as well speak of severing their spirits from their clayish forms, as of making them ascribe the result to any thing else but the touch of the divine hand. . . .

Sister Mary Eugenia (Catherine Clare Millard, of Washington) entered the Novitiate of the Visitation, in Georgetown, in March, 1835. She was, then, nearly seventeen years of age, and enjoyed good health, although nat-urally of a delicate constitution. After six months, her health became dis-ordered and created great alarm. . . . At first, a strong tendency of the blood to the head, obstinate and violent head-aches, —then a pain settling in her right side . . . The liver seemed to be affected; but Dr. Magruder . . . thought that the case would terminate in a consumption: the Sister, at that period, would spit blood frequently, —indeed on the least occasion of ex-citement. Bleeding, cupping, blistering, dieting, every means was resorted to, but proved ineffectual. . . .

About a year elapsed in this manner. In the autumn of 1836, the disease took another form: the swelling of the jugular glands, or rather hard tumors that appeared on the throat. . . . For three or four months, all efforts to disperse those tumours were vain. Finally, they broke—but inside: the throat, far back, and even the root of the tongue, became ulcerated, and exhaled the most offensive effluvia. . . . The patient . . . grew exceedingly weak, —could no longer swallow any thing but liquids, —could not speak, could not even breathe, without increased suffering: . . .

At last, after remaining a long time in the fearful state just now de-puted, Sister Eugenia was relieved; she recovered from that illness, —but it was to fall into another: the radical cause of disorder in her had not been removed; no remedy, it seemed, could reach it. About summer last year (1837), a pain which she had felt for some time in her back proved to be the beginning of a spinal affection. In spite of all attempts to check it, the pain went on increasing. The spinal nerves became contracted; a protusion of the stomach was quite apparent in the month of October. The bend was decidedly of the upper parts backwards, —the Sister could no longer bend forward, —felt perfectly stiff: she could not lie down nor sit, without experiencing a great increase of suffering. . . . That there was such a distortion of the spine as to have caused some displacement of it, may be considered as certain. . . . Emaciated, pale, disfigured by a contraction which drew up her mouth on the right side, so agonizing and ghastly was her aspect, that she could not be looked at without feelings of the most painful interest, —and some of her friends said they *could not* look at her, others that she appeared like one in the agony of death, —others again, that she was dying on her feet, walking to her grave! . . .

The new year, 1838 . . . her suffering increased considerable. She had experienced fevers, head-aches, bleeding at the nose, through the course of her complex disease. Her sister-Nuns, . . . observing that from all appearances . . . all hope was lost of curing her by medicines, by any natural means, began to look up to a higher source for hopes of her preservation.

To many who may chance to read this, it will appear passing strange, chimerical, perhaps visionary, —but to the faith of the inmates of the Convent, enlivened by even late wonderful occurrences, it was by no means illusory, to apply extraordinarily to heaven for the recovery of the beloved young Sister.— . . .

The Ladies of the Visitation formed the project of resorting to . . . [Prince Hohenlohe], on the 10th February [for] the cure of Sister Eugenia. . . .

The Ladies of the convent, however, about the middle of January, considering the very alarming state of Sister Eugenia, conceived the desire of not waiting so late as the 10th of the next month, to solicit heaven for some extraordinary interference. Such interference of heaven in behalf of suffering members of their community, they had already obtained, and once in particular, not long ago, through the intercession of the ever Blessed Virgin Mary, by means of what is called the miraculous medal, that is by paying a special homage to her as conceived without the stain of original sin. They resolved upon petitioning in this mode, without delay, and actually commenced a nine days devotion for this purpose, in which they desired Mr. Dubuisson to join, when he called at the Convent. . . . At the termination of the novena, Sister Eugenia received the holy communion, but was not cured.

. . . A favour was asked of God by means of the medal of the B.V.M. and not obtained. Soon after, the same favour is asked by a communion of prayers with Prince Hohenlohe, and it is obtained. This, surely, can be considered as a marked, fresh sanction from heaven of the devotions performed in union with Prince Hohenlohe. And why would it not be a peculiar trait of heavenly regard for that Prince? . . . Did [Jesus] not say to his Disciples: *He that believeth in me, the works that I do, he shall do also, and greater than these shall he do?* (John 14.12)—. . . .

The state of Sister Eugenia, during this last period, was worse than ever. . . . On Friday, 9th, about noon, she was compelled to go to bed with a high fever, although the position, lying down, was painful to her. . . .

Sister Eugenia appeared as usual, calm and resigned in the midst of her trials. She had attained that self-renunciation, which made her only desire the accomplishment of the divine will, whether it were to be cured—to remain in the crucible of suffering—or to die. Her fever, high on the day before, continued so all night, and although unable to sleep, yet she did not leave her bed until helped to the choir, in order to attend mass. The feeling of her mind she described as having been awful, —as though she were near her grave. . . .

At half after three o'clock, on the morning of the 10th, the Rev. Mr. Dubuisson commenced the mass, so that the communion might be, as exactly as possible, at the time when Prince Hohenlohe himself celebrates Mass in Hungary. At this moment, therefore, at the communion, —at 4 o'clock, on the morning of the 10th of February, 1828, —the Georgetown convent of the Visitation witnessed within its walls one more of those prodigies, which no pen can describe, but which thousands of faithful hearts have hailed and acknowledged: the moment the Blessed Eucharist was dropped on Sister Eugenia's tongue, an awful sensation pervaded her whole frame; —the moment she had swallowed it, she felt herself totally, perfectly relieved from all her ailments, which had continued to that very instant; she now was a new person, well and strong! . . . —O Jesus-Christ! Thus is thy presence felt, to this day, as it was at the time mentioned by the inspired penman, when *virtue went out from him, and healed all!* (Luke 6.19)—

Sister Eugenia thus instantaneously freed from all her maladies and their consequences, —now restored to the full use of all her physical faculties, rose up herself, unaided, from the communion table, and walked back to her place in the choir, she says, as though she had been gliding along, without touching the floor. She knelt down and remained silent, — or rather would have remained silent, till the end of mass, but she was heard many times repeating to herself the divinely sweet appellation, "My Jesus! My Jesus!" . . .

It is now three months since Sister Eugenia thus instantaneously passed from a state of desperate, incurable illness, to one of perfect health, and this state of perfect health has been uninterrupted. But the bodily strength with which she has been since gifted, calls for special attention. The sudden transition from such a state of illness as hers was, to one of perfect well-being, and that transition, particularly, attended with the circumstances of previous prayer and the reception of the holy Eucharist, would, assuredly, be sufficient to denote something mysterious, something naturally inexplicable, something prodigous in the event. But when a look is carried further; — when it is observed, that the person has not only been brought back to integrity of health, but is now found to possess physical, bodily forces which she never had before, —forces far surpassing what is ordinarily possessed by individuals of the same sex and complexion, —forces that endure, that bear any test, —then indeed, the mind, overwhelmed, cannot resist the inference, *Digitus Dei est hic. . . .* (Exod. 8.19)

And . . . what is the *commencing* wonderful state of Sister Eugenia, has been the *permanent* wonderful state of Sister Apollonia, of the same Convent, these seven years, and of Mrs. Ann Mattingly, of Washington, these fourteen! . . . *Thine, O Lord, is magnificence, and power, and glory . . . : and to thee is praise. . . .*

NOTES

1. ARSI MD 3 VIII, Dubuisson to Luigi Fortes, Georgetown, April 22, 1826.

1a. Roman Archives of the Society of Jesus, Maryland 3 IV, Dubuisson to Roothaan, 26 January 1825.

2. R. Emmett Curran, S.J., ed., "Reminiscences of Father Patrick Duddy, S.J.," *Woodstock Letters* 96 (1967), 391.

2a. GUSC, Feiner-Dubuisson Papers.

3. "Lord, make haste to help me!"

4. Margaret Mary Alacoque (1647–1690), Visitandine nun whose revelations played a central role in the establishment of the Sacred Heart devotion.

5. "Oh that I may experience a life of such sweetness, a death sweeter than life."

6. Stanislaus Koska (1550–1568), Polish nobleman who died as a novice in the Society of Jesus.

7. Dubuisson had been teaching French in the College and serving as a prefect for the students.

8. Crossed out: "consolations."

9. Order what you will but give to me what you order.

10. The breaking of the bread, the eucharist.

11. What do you wish me to do?

12. Crossed out: "by."

13. The annotation on the side of this entry lists as his source "Duponte, p. 5, med. 28 on St. Stephen—2d pt." Louis de la Puente, S.J. (1554–1624), Spanish spiritual writer.

14. Aloysius Gonzaga (1568–1591), at the time of his death, a scholastic in the Society and later declared the patron of students.

15. Crossed out: "after."

16. Severe Charles De Longueville of St. Lucia, West Indies. Mr. De Longueville had two sons, Henri and Severe De Longueville, in the college from 1817 to 1821.

17. Crossed out: "too."

18. Conewago, in the southeastern part of Pennsylvania, was the site of a Jesuit mission and 550 acre farm. Founded in the 1740s to minister to German immigrants, the Conewago mission was considered to be on the healthiest and most productive land that the Jesuits in the United States possessed.

19. Anthony Kohlmann.

20. Francis de Hieronyme.

21. White Marsh, mid-way between Annapolis and Washington, was the largest of the Jesuit plantations and housed the novitiate.

22. In margin: "Ev[ening] med[itatio]n—89th med[itatio]n.

23. "Give what you order and order what you wish."

24. Alfonso Rodriguez, S.J. (1538–1616). The reference is to his *Practice of Perfection and Christian Virtues* (1609), which became a centerpiece of Jesuit training in the spiritual life.

25. *A Collection of Affidavits and Certificates Relative to the Wonderful Cure of Mrs. Ann Mattingly, Which took place in the City of Washington, D.C. on the tenth of March, 1824* (Washington, 1824), 36–40.

26. ARSI, Maryland 7 XI 6.

IX

BETWEEN TWO WORLDS II:
THOMAS MULLEDY

Thomas Mulledy, the provincial who was forced to resign in 1839, was a native Virginian who was among the first group of Jesuit scholastics sent to Rome for studies in 1820. In 1828 at the completion of his studies he made the Spiritual Exercises, *during which he was impelled to volunteer to work among the Indians in the West, an impulse he had been fighting for some years. Father General Fortis granted him permission to do so, so long as the Maryland Mission Superior, Francis Dzierozynski, was also favorable. The latter, however, needed men too desperately to relinquish a person of Mulledy's talent and training. It is easy to imagine that the enormously energetic and large-hearted Mulledy would have made a very effective missionary with the Indians. In Maryland he became a major force over the next three decades in shaping the new province that was formed in 1833. Besides being provincial, he was president of three colleges in the province: Georgetown, Holy Cross, and St. John's, Frederick. He played a central role in shifting the focus and resources of the Maryland Jesuits from the farms and rural ministries to the cities and colleges.*

Impulsive and tendentious, Mulledy alienated many Americans by his imperious manner while his fondness for the manorial lifestyle of Chesapeake society seemed in the eyes of the Europeans to be unbecoming a religious. They found him too lax as a superior, too absorbed in brick and mortar concerns. He was lukewarm, at best, about the mission movement. The week-long exercises, he felt, produced very ephemeral zeal in its participants.[1] He apparently shared the skepticism of many native Jesuits about the Hohenlohe cures.

POETRY[1a]

As part of their classical education Jesuits traditionally composed poetry, in both Latin and English, if not Greek as well, on secular and sacred themes. Mulledy continued to compose occasional poetry long after his ordination in 1824. The epic models he strained to imitate are obvious enough. Most of his poetry was secular, much of it patriotic. Even in the ode to Father General Fortis, Mulledy could not suppress his patriotism. Such praise of liberty and scorn for monarchy was little appreciated in Roman circles in the nineteenth century. It tended to confirm the worst suspicions of the American Jesuits.

For Christmas 1818

1.

It is not mine, with living lyre
Or with the Poet's raging fire
  To sweep a mortal lay
But ply my verse & loud proclaim
To distant worlds with deathless fame
  The wonders of this day.

2.

Where am I? Tis enchanted ground
Yes; more than wonders wrap me 'round
  And lock each silent sense
Is it a dream that round me plays?
Or is it truth's life darting rays
  Tis something, God! immense!

3.

Oh humble every living string
Leap into life ye notes & sing,
  Enraptured, rapturing lays
And ye astonished heavens quake
Earth tremble, to thy centre shake
  Be fixd in wondrous gaze.

4.

Bow down, ye mounts your heads of snow
And check ye floods, your thundering flow
  Suspended hang & hear;
Be mute, ye roaring winds, as Death
Let all creation cease to breathe
  Let silence rule the sphere.

5.

Are ye then still? oh come & hear
Astonish'd list, with awe & fear
    Draw near the wondrous sight,
Here crowded into time see! see
Contracted lies Eternity
    Veil hev'n's your head in night!

6.

To space confin'd, dwindl'd, condens'd,
Here lies immensity's immense
    Surpasses mortal ken
Pierc'd by the fierce winds roaring breath
Bends immortality to Death
    Eternal God is man;

7.

Draw near ye Pompous things of earth
And view your God's neglected birth
    Degraded, here he lies
Admire with fear & dread, adore
The God that stays the tempests' roar
    That rules the vaulted skies.

8.

What numbers float along the sky
Hark! Hark! they peal again more high
    Oh hear them whilst you may
Hark! Glory be to God above
Peace on Earth to men that love
    To tread fair virtue's way

9.

Yes Glory to the God of light
He here has shewn his matchless might
    Eternal force of love!
And Peace to ye ye Sons of Earth
that rise unto a second birth
    & pierce the realms above.

10.

To Bethlahem. O! with me come!
What do I see? Oh Angels Gloom
    Your brows in deepest night!
Here lies a God! omnipotence!
Here lies a babe, & impotence
    Oh what a wondrous sight!

11.

Is this the God, whom Prophet said
On finger-ends the globe he weigh'd
    And held it balanced there
That check'd the jarring Chaos' strife
That bade a nothing leap to life
    And breathe a living ear.

12.

Why so neglected now & how
Or why do sorrows veil his brow
    Who can the mystery tell
Why dost thou ask thou worm of Earth
Wilst thou ne'er know a Saviour's worth
    So low wilst e'er thou dwell?

13.

For thee, vile wretch aside he threw
The mantle of his might & drew
    O'er him sad mis'ry's veil
That thou might own the realms above
To Earth he flew with wings of love
    This is the wondrous tale!

14.

That thou might be thus magnified
That thou mighst be e'en Deified
He form'd[2] th'astonish'd plan
That thou mightst raise thy form on high
And claim the glories of the sky
    He cloth'd himself a man!

15.

O sight that tears from Angels drew!
Eternal God what couldst thou do!
    And hast not done for me.
Oh shall I e'er ungrateful prove
Oh shall I e'er forget thy love
    And thoughtless ever be

16.

Sooner, my tongue, cleave to my jaws,
My voice forget all nature's laws
    Hang cold in silence's chain,
My hand to strike the warbling wire
My soul to feel the Poets fire
    Than God forget again.

To Saint Ignatius a hymn.

> Against me Satan rears his haughty head on high,
> By one sole man I wish to thwart his wily schemes.
> My Angel, hear my voice: and where that hero gleams
> Bright in his arms, and red with blood, quick to him fly,
> Ignatius I choose, light up in his ardent soul

Ref: Courage sublime heedless of toil, heedless of pain,
>   Conquer'd by him, Satan shall roll
>   Back to his own abyss again.

> God spoke: the Angel from the azure vault descends
> And in the warrior's ear he breathes these words of flame:
> Arise, prepare for battles new, be now thy aim
> To serve the king of heav'n, and all his views and ends;
> For God has chosen thee, and kindled in thy soul
> Refrain:

> Bright in his soul these words in all their vigor shine,
> And to his God who calls, he answers and he yields;
> He goes; as useless arms of his new glory's fields,
> His blood-stained sword suspends at Mary's hallowed shrine.
> Ignatius God chose, and lit in his ardent soul
> Refrain:

> Conq'ring himself, each rebel sense is prostrate laid,
> For noble deeds his soul in silence he prepares,
> Unfurls the cross, and high the glorious standard rears,
> Onward he goes, and fights and conquers 'neath its shade.
> Ignatius God chose, and lit in his ardent soul
> Refrain:

> Come haste to join the standard of the sacred war,
> Ye soldiers of the living God, march in his path,
> Triumph o'er hell, and all its rage, and all its wrath,
> Ignatius leads, the palm is won without a scar.
> Ignatius God chose, and lit in his ardent soul
> Refrain:

> With virtue and with faith he feeds the youthful age,
> From him, you'll learn, subject to his paternal sway,

To form the altar's hope, your country's brightest stay,
To form at once, the zealous Christian and the Sage.
Ignatius God chose, and lit in his ardent soul
Refrain:

In God the Saviour's name let every knee bow down,
Glory to God! this is the cry that conquer's hell,
Go, and loud o'er the world let deeds this glory tell,
Ignatius is your help, where e'er war's heroes frown.
Ignatius God chose, and lit in his ardent soul.
Refrain:

A thousand foes they face, and stem the tempests tide,
They go, with men of every race to people heaven
And harvests rich to their laborious toils are given,
In vain proud Satan roars, Ignatius is their guide.
Ignatius God chose, and lit in his ardent soul
Refrain:

Great Saint, so many virtues, which all hearts engage,
Make them shine forth again, with equal glory bright,
To make the waning torch of faith resume its light,
Console the mourning church, and bless her heritage.
For God has chosen thee, and kindled in thy soul
Refrain:

[To Aloysius Fortis][3]

While every tongue pours forth its classic praise,
And greets, you Father, with a filial love,
Columbia too, presents her feeble lays,
Throws in a mite—tis all,—her joy to prove.

She who ne'er felt the tyrant's galling rod,
Or snuff'd the poison of a Regal breath;
Joyful accepts th' anointed of her God;
And twines around his brow the freeman's wreath.

Receive this tribute of a western muse—
For there—a world lies prostrate at your feet!
Wide o'er its realms your bounteous deeds diffuse
And teach her tawny sons your name to greet.

How can a silver'd age forget that land,
Whose glories[5] in youthful days he sung,
Although the harp hangs lifeless on his hand,
Its notes neglected & its chords unstrung?

No! watchful of its good his care shall be,
His willing sons unto its aid shall fly,
Morality shall spread from sea to sea,
And Fortis' name shall ring through every sky.

SERMONS[5a]

Mulledy's sermons were carefully prepared, with liberal references to scripture and the Fathers (Mulledy had taught the Old Testament at Georgetown), and long, averaging about 14 pages of closely written script and taking at least an hour to deliver. Many were repeated several times over the course of Mulledy's three decades of priestly ministry (although he continued to compose sermons until his death).

The Dying Sinner (1832)

One of Mulledy's most repeated sermons, "Sinner" was given 17 times from 1832 to 1860. It was a timeless topic for him, not only in years but in seasons as well, serving as an appropriate topic in Advent, Lent, and Pentecost.

You shall seek me, and you shall die in your sin. John 8.21
Is it then possible, that in the course of the life of a sinner, a day shall come so dreadful for him, in which he will go in search of the Lord & not find him; in which he will ask for pity & not obtain it, in which he will sue for mercy, & die in his sins? Such however is the meaning of that formidable threat which God this day announces[7] to you, O sinner, if any such be here & which ought to freeze every drop of blood in your veins: you shall seek me, and you shall die in your sin. You ask me, perhaps, what day will this fatal day be? I answer you, if you have not heard it before, or at least guessed it, that it will be the last of your days the day of your death. You shall seek me and you shall die in your sin. Nor must you believe that this text alludes solely to him who has an express & determined will of not seeking God[8]—but in that last day—flattering himself in the mean time by saying—on my deathbed I will think of it; a good confession—nay even an act

of contrition is sufficient to save me in the moment of death. Very few, I know too would in such a case be struck with this dreadful thunderbolt.

We must understand it as alluding to those also who far from making such a mad resolution are on the contrary resolved, if you believe what they say; to seek God before their deaths, & in the mean time frequent the sacraments now & then—but quickly fall again; they form good resolutions of changing their lives—but they never amend, & putting off their sincere conversion to God, they find themselves finally reduced to the last extremity without being really converted at least in their hearts. How many are there of this sort? Let them listen. although it may be true that you do not expressly wish it, the fact is you will reduce yourselves to the necessity of turning to the Lord on the day of your death. Is it not the case? You shall seek me, therefore, & you shall die in your sins. In the mean time young men who can never resolve to overcome that wicked habit of iniquity, to abandon those licentious companions—women who wait until you are older before you will agree to throw off that unbecoming finery—quit certain conversations & stop certain practices ill becoming your sex or your religion—men who defer to restore that unlawfully acquired property, ah, let me entreat you Seek the Lord whilst he can be found; otherwise what an unhappy, miserable death awaits you! You shall die in your sin. Perhaps you do not sufficiently understand the horror of such a death.

I am now about to present before you a faithful picture of it by showing to you that the death of the sinner as the Scripture says is very bad. Mors peccatorum pessima. To do this let us make with St. Bernard the three noted divisions—to consider this death in the first place—bad—then worse—in order to consider it finally as very bad—To which perhaps the prophet alluded when with trembling he exclaimed: "The sorrows of death surrounded me, & the torrents of iniquity troubled me . . . the perils of hell have found me.["] Uniting these words with the above words of St. Bernard will give us a motive of arranging the whole subject in the following manner. Bad in the first place is the death of a sinner on account of what he leaves; there are the sorrows of death—the sorrows of death surrounded me—The death of the sinner is in the second place worse on account of what he retains—these are the torrents of iniquity—the torrents of iniquity troubled me—Very bad in the third place is the death of the sinner on account of what he expects—behold the perils of hell—the perils of hell have found me. Let no one expect any thing new from me to day—I shall say nothing but what has been a thousand times said—but all true—all dreadful—[9] to abandon that all & that only thing that one loves, to abandon it all of a sudden, to abandon it by force, to abandon it without the hope of ever again being able to recover it. This is what renders the abandonment of any thing most excruciating—& this is what renders the death of the sinners tormenting & bitter. The things in which you placed, unhappy beings, your whole hearts, to which you sacrificed your thoughts, & your affections— were honours you proud ones;—were riches you avaricious, eating & drinking you gluttons, were impure & dissolute abominations you libertines— were you pleasing spirits of the world's pasttimes, diversions & lone adventures, Of all this death will despoil you—& that in a moment—leaving you a naked cold carcass destined to the solitude & corruption of the grave. Hence with a propriety altogether divine it has been compared to a thief, to an active dextrous thief, who in the night time throws himself unexpected into a house buried in sleep, & ransacks & robs every thing. "It will come as a thief in the night." But alas! what sort of a violent & greedy robber that at one haul takes away every thing—You have a fine custom of using in your wills the term I leave on bequest—& you call these instruments your last wills. Are they really your wills, & not on the contrary dispositions forcibly extorted from you by death? Do you indeed leave, & do you of your own free wills leave, or rather is not what you have taken from you by force? Like a thief in the night it will come.

Which the holy Job, wishing to express by another noble figure, said the impious man would breath out his soul in the midst of the tumult of an insuperable tempest. Their soul shall die in a storm. What a misfortune for a merchant who on board of a ship laden with rich merchandise is in the midst of the sea assaulted with a dread & furious storm! The timbers broken & disjointed, the sails torn—the masts aboard—the yards shivered—the heavens black above him & pouring down a flood of rain—& the unhappy ship ready to sink beneath the foaming waves. The cold wind that howls around, the impetuous hail that beats her sides—the bellowing air—the black whirlwinds, & the discord and storm dash on her deck those hostile waves that are about to swallow her. What then does the unhappy merchant? Seeing the danger[10] increase beyond measure & looking upon a wreck as inevitable, he resolves at length to lighten his money chest & pressing it for the last time to his disconsolate breast—& throwing a last look on each one—he consigns all to the rapacity of the infuriated sea, exclaiming, I leave you—hastily retiring below to bewail his misfortune. In a similar excruciating dread will your soul o sinner be, when overwhelmed as it were by the angry waves of the sorrows of death you[11] will be constrained to make a universal cast of all your possessions—commodities & conveniences until then adhered to with so much anxiety. I leave you, you will say, companions adieu—adieu my relations—farewell theatres, farewell gay companies, farewell pleasures, farewell riches—world farewell. A displeasing departure & a tormenting adieu! for if as St. A[ug]ustin says—the grief of losing is proportionate[12] to the love of having, & if you have never loved anything but your frail & transitory possessions—whence entirely forgetting the future the present alone spurred you on—& you turned your whole attention & solicitude to augment & increase your fortune to grow rich, to your pleasures, to comply with the genius of your passions & beastly appetites. what will become of you miserable beings in seeing the whole snatched from you in an instant without remedy? what will become of a wealthy man of the world who has placed all his peace in his riches? what of a dissolute voluptuous man who has placed it in the pleasures of the flesh & beastly sensuality? What will become of the flippant worldly woman, who could find no peace but in the vanity & fashions, in an idle effeminate life, in pride & the pomp of appearance? Is it thus in a moment will be lost all ones treasures scraped together with the toil & anxiety of so many years? Is it thus in an instant will end in smoke all the pretensions, employments, honours, dignities, titles & preeminences? & the grand ideas, grand conceptions & grand designs—twists & turns of policy punctilios must they all thus terminate in a moment? And thus too you may add vain woman—thus are to be torn from my body all the fashionable finery & splendor of dress—& thus will disappear in a moment all my grovelling admirers? So it is my friends. To remain with them there is no time; to take them with you impossible—you must then abandon them; but this is too hard. Oh what a cruel & furious tempest. Their soul shall die in a storm.

It is still worse for you infortunate sinners—than it is for that miserable man assailed by the waves of a tempest. For in the act of throwing his merchandize into the greedy sea, he may hope to pick up some things after the storm ceases; whereas in the dreadful stormy tempest that assails you—& in which you yourself must be swallowed down—you are sure to make a doleful[,] total[,] irreparable wreck. Oh the tremendous mournful news for you which the minister of God approaching your bedside shall bring in the words of Isaiah. ''Set thy house in order sir thou shalt die & not live.''

In the total loss of every thing which the unhappy sinner undergoes by his death, & which renders his death so bad, one thing he retains—his own sins—which make his death still worse.
The torrents of iniquity troubled me.

There is a sin, says St. John which is called a sin unto death, nor must we believe says St. Gregory that it is any other but the sin which is maintained & kept until death. Peccatur ad mortem est peccatum usque ad mortem. I know that no one is sooner advised of the danger of death (for I do not wish to suppose the physicians so adulatory, friends, so faithless, your family so inhuman, as to conceal it from you; nor do I suppose that you are attacked by so dreadful a disease—that you have not your understanding sufficiently clear to know your danger) I know, I say, that no one is sooner advised of the danger of death than he begins to prepare himself or rather according to the words of the royal Prophet interpreted by St. Bernard, he is in the greatest hurry to prepare himself properly for the great journey, *"Their infirmities were multiplied afterwards they made haste."* At what ever time he receives[11] this news—he sends here & there for a confessor—he distributes perhaps alms—he calls priests & religious persons to his bedside to comfort and console him: When death comes upon them—says St. Chrysostom speaking of his own times—& he has described our own to the life, when death comes upon them, they are in a hurry, —they are solicitous, they call the priests, they wish to do penance, the saint however adds—when there is no longer time for penance.

In fact is not this sudden & extraordinary change enough to give a little suspicion? One who before lived entire years far off from the sacraments, is at present in such a hurry[12] to receive them? So desirous at present to see religious persons around his bed—who a little before could not bear their very sight? so liberal in giving alms who heretofore was so hardened towards the poor? I would not wish to say that he hopes by these means to gain the health of the body—that it was a desire to gain a good opinion among the people so that if he should die his memory might not be execrated & pass as it were into a proverb; that it was an ambition to appear in death what he always disdained to appear during his life—I would not wish to say that these were the motives of his extraordinary change. To discover the sincere sentiments of his soul—let us do so my friends—let us approach the fatal side of that bed which in a few moments will be the sorrowful bed of his death, let us approach & let us obeserve. Oh with what tears he deposits in the hands of the sacred Minister his sins! Father, says he sighing, I am a great sinner, & my life has been nothing but a continued tissue of iniquities—*"My ways are filthy at all times"* I began from my very youth to taste sin—and I have never left it off; seduced by one—I myself became the seducer of many of my companions—teaching them evil & drawing them into the most dangerous occasions of sin—Being a little more advanced in years without abandoning dissoluteness—I fell into jealousies, hatreds, blasphemy, & rivalry—Increasing in years, I increased in dissoluteness, to dissoluteness I joined injustice, to injustice overbearing power, to this I added open injuries, I have defiled my neighbour's bed, I destroyed my neighbour's reputation, I have enriched myself with my neighbour's property. My ways are filthy at all times; He protests that he is sorry from the bottom of his heart, that he is resolved never to sin any more & asks absolution, and in fact receives it; after which he earnestly demands the viaticum which is piously brought to him—Is it not a contamination for the god of purity to pass through those halls—which were lately the scenes of gambling—indecent balls—more indecent conversations & dissoluteness—& which perhaps are adorned with indecent representations on the pictured walls—& to approach that bed which was the conscious witness to so many of the sick man's abominations. Still he composes himself to receive it with the air of the most tender devotion, giving every exterior proof of fervent christian piety. What more do you wish, my friends, to be fully convinced of the excellent dispositions of his heart?

But let me ask you in the first place: do you frequently see among you worldlings such deaths—accompanied by such a sincere grief—hearty sorrow & fervent acts of humility & contrition? If you answer in the affirmative, tell me in the second place: Are you sure, that these signs are not mere external appearances—an outward devout glass of a man, who affects to die as a Christian? Oh no—tis, that is no time for mockery—people then fear too much. This is precisely what I most fear—to see him fear so much—without knowing for what. For observe well—I pass over in silence, that, in the supposition that these tears flowed from his heart, & that these sighs are rooted in his heart, still it might not be sufficient to save him. There are too many & too mournful misfortunes of similar dying persons, who, even after the most exact confessions, the most intense acts of grief, after the strongest protestations never more to offend God—assailed in that last conflict by violent temptations miserably fell & were damned. I only wish you to assure me that this grief does not arise from the sickness or danger—but for sorrow for his sins? And if it arises from a sorrow for sin—how are we sure that he is not rather sorry because he can commit no more—than because he has so often committed it? Are you sure that it is not a grief more arising from the fear of punishment than sorrow for his guilt. You fear to burn—said St. Austin to certain persons who were thus weeping—You fear to burn you do not fear to sin.

What repentance was more exteriorly perfect than that of Judas? He openly & clearly confesses his evil action: I have sinned peccavi: he declares the innocence of him whom he betrayed. I have sinned in betraying innocent blood: he brings back with the greatest grief the price of his treachery: "brought back the thirty pieces of silver"; and not finding any one willing to receive them—he threw them away. Still Judas was damned. What repentance exteriorly more perfect than that of Antiochus? He acknowledged in his sickness the hand of God who struck him, & he humbles himself; he remembers the iniquity perpetrated in Jerusalem—& he weeps for it. He recollects the injuries inflicted upon widows & orphans, those done to the Temple—& he promises to repair them—he reflects upon the scandals given to his whole kingdom & in [the] presence of the whole court loudly condemns them; he turns with a mournful heart to God & pitifully supplicates him for mercy; Still Antiochus was damned. Ah, my friends, instructed by these examples I fear—yes I fear—for the death of this sinner, though in appearance so Christian. I fear for that perverse will, & I can too easily comprehend how from the late excessive love of sin—it has so suddenly passed to the most profound detestation of it, I fear for that hardened heart & it seems to me almost impossible—that it should be so quickly softened. I fear what St Austin said, that he who does not remember God during his life—deserves that he should not remember himself at the point of death—I fear what St. Gregory says, that he who does not now, whilst he can, correct his faults will then ask pardon in vain. I fear the just & ever tremendous judgements of God—I fear for his own fear—& his sins, although he laments them. I here behold him more than ever arrived at that difficult passage—already indicated by the royal Prophet—where two things are joined & united each one of which is horribly dreadful; the sorrows of death & the torrents of iniquity. Oh how these will roll before his eyes! what a horrible appearance will they assume! & so many sins which he at present well knows—& so many others maliciously unknown dissembled excused by him—that will come forth by the light of the candle, precisely as the psalmist says, like cruel savage wild beasts, that during the whole day are hidden in their lairs & dens—but at night—all rush suddenly forth—scour the whole forest & fill it with their frightful howlings. Facta est nox in ipsa pertransibunt omnes istae sylvae. It is night[;] in it shall all the beasts of the woods go about—now this bitter recollection—is it not of itself enough to cast him into blackest despair? We have a proof of it in Saul.

That fatal day, in which his army was routed by the Philistines—& himself was flying through the mountains of Gelboe, fearing lest he might fall alive into the hands of his enemies, he drew his sword as that Amalecite relates, furiously plunged it into his breast. Thus pierced but not yet dead— he saw one of his soldiers passing, to whom he turned his distorted eyes now quivering in the shades of death & said—for mercy's sake come here & finish my life—for I am oppressed with such anguish that I can bear it no longer: Stand over me & kill me for anguish is come upon me. Abelensis & others interpret it—for the priests have come upon me—But what Priests? Those very eighty five Priests whom Saul himself, reply the above authors, in a mad fury of cruel revenge barbarously murdered by the hand of Doeg. *"He slew eighty five men that wore the linen ephod"* In that last day of his life, in his painful agony came those vulnerable & sacred shades—& straitened him with anguish; & they surrounded him each one pointing out at the same time, his bloody frightful wounds—& upbraided Saul for the crimes he committed—Behold the tormenting anguish, to which he was reduced—whence he finally dispaired—For anguish has come upon me—for the priests have come upon me. A similar frightful spectacle will also present itself to the astonished looks of the dying sinner. All the abominations of his past years will unite in a mass & will come & surround the bed of his death, those oppressed orphans, those despoiled widows—those seduced virgins, those evil reports spread abroad, those cheats, those impurities, those acts of injustice; & in the words of St. Bernard will exclaim, Do you know us? we are the works of thy hands, doubt not we will quickly follow you to the Tribunal of Christ, opera tua omnia sequimur ad tribunal Christi. The wretch will throw here & there his wide stretched eyes—in order not to see them: but in vain, for wherever he throws them he will meet the odious sight. "My iniquities have overtaken me—and I was not able to see. Like the man says the holy Ghost—who flying a lion, falls in with a bear— & flying this—is met by the venomous teeth of a serpent. . . . Hence those struggles & contritions of the dying man—that smacking of lip to lip— hence he is never satisfied with his confession—& turns from time to time to his confessor & says—Father I have confessed did I not? those scandals which I gave, those bad confessions & those sacrilegious communions. Yes, yes, don't trouble yourself, you have buried them all in the wounds of this God crucified for you—look at him, place in him your hope. Here the poor creature raises his hollow eyes to heaven, presses his parched lips & is silent—But stung again with the pangs of his accusing conscience— oh how I am afflicted with this wicked habit continued until death. my confessors told me that it would accompany me to death. I fear that it will drag me to hell. . . . & on hell he fixes his immovable stupefied looks. Be quiet I have absolved you of all. . . . Oh Father! that obligation which I never satisfied—that reputation which I never repaired—those just debts which I never paid . . . Your relations will satisfy them: be quiet. . . . Oh no listen, how I am afflicted for having contaminated so many churches with impure looks—with so many scandalous irreverences & conversations . . . Have you not already asked pardon—be quiet. . . . I cannot Father—so many bad actions you know—so much freedom in speaking—so many indecent confidences & friendships, which I once wished to excuse—now I know that they were sins. . . . I understand—think no more about them—Ego te absolvo—Ah no Father—it seems that I am dying a reprobate. . . . The Confessor bears it more than the penitent, still covering his fear with a prudent dissimulation—keeps up until he fulfils the duty of his ministry.

In compliance with which—as he sees the palpitations of the man increase—his respirations grow longer, his eyes turn over & waver in his head, he thinks proper to delay no longer to arm him with those last consolations & helps—which the holy church keeps ready for her dying children when in the act of dismissing them from this world—& in her tender & affecting prayers the sacred minister prays for this sinner a happy passage to the next world. Depart o Christian soul from this world: recommending him at the same time to God in the doubtful dangerous passage, & resigning him to those hands from which he came. I recommend thee dear brother to Almighty God, and commit thee to his mercy whose creature thou art. Behold the time o Lord to incline the ears of thy ineffable mercy to the mournful & devout supplications of one of thy afflicted ministers, & by using mercy to this unhappy man to exhibit at the same time thy mercy & power in saving him. On the contrary this is the time, in which God maintains the force & credit of those tremendous threats repeatedly thundered forth in the sacred scriptures—this is the time in which he is resolved to maintain the word that he has given—to laugh bitterly & to exult in the death of those, who deaf, obstinate & inflexible—proudly mocked his advice—did not answer his call, abused his graces. Quia vocavi & remistis, extendi manum meam & non fuit qui aspiceret. . . . ego quoque in interitu vestro ridebo & subsannabo.[sic] Because I called & you refused. I stretched out my hand, and there was none that regarded. . . . I also will laugh in your destruction & will mock. Now is the time. Still the pious priest commences accompanied by those present, some of whom hold the sick man's head on the pillow—others with swimming eyes—& others in convulsions of grief—he begins to pray aloud—Deus misericordiae Deus qui secundum multitudinem miserationum tuarum peccata paenitentium deles. God of clemency, God of goodness! O God, who, according to the multitude of thy mercies, forgivest the sins of such as repent. Mercifully regard this thy servant and grant him a full discharge from all his sins, who most earnestly begs it of thee. Respice propitius[13] super hunc familum tuum & remissionem peccatorum suorum tota cordis confessione poscentium deprecatus exaudi—And God? God hears & laughs. Have compassion o Lord—prays the sacred minister with more fervor—Have compassion o Lord on his sighs have pity on his tears—Let o Lord these tears that flow from his eyes melt thee to pity—Let the sighs sent forth from his afflicted soul touch thy heart; & as he has no hope but in thee admit him to the sacrament of thy reconciliation—ad tuae sacramentum reconciliationis admitti. And God? God hears & laughs—but finally continues the minister—Remember o Lord that he is thy creature, not made by strange Gods, but by thee, the only true & loving God. . . . For although he has sinned—still he has not denied thee & thy son & Holy Ghost—but believed—& God the creator of all things faithfully adored—Deum qui fecit omnia fideliter adoraverit. And God? God hears & laughs. Let thy place, concludes the priest, be this day in peace, and thy abode in holy Sion, & habitatio tua in Sion. And God? God hears & laughs—

What a tremendous scene of shuddering horror is presented whenever in imagination I enter the room of a dying sinner! I see there a man stretched on a bed—dying—prostrate at the side of the bed a pious priest praying—on high an indignant God—laughing & scoffing. Ego quoque in interitu vestro ridebo & subsannabo—I also will laugh in your destruction & mock—Is it then true—that this God who suffered so much—who shed every drop of his blood—in order that this wretch might not be damned—

now that he is in imminent danger of damnation will laugh? Ridebo? Ah frightful laugh the certain harbinger of eternal inconsolable weeping.

If the unhappy sinner of whom we speak, in seeing death violently snatch from him all his possessions, could nourish in his heart a founded hope that he could by this means procure the possession of better & more lasting goods in heaven; if by considering on one hand with holy Job—that he must descend naked into the grave—as he came naked from his mother's womb; Naked came I from my mother's womb & naked shall I return thither, he could also say with the royal prophet, now that I am freed from all earthly encumbrance, what remains for me to expect, but my God. "And now what is my hope? is it not the Lord?" His grief would thus be sufficiently comforted, or rather it would be changed into the liveliest exultations of joy. But here is the difficulty. *"The perils of hell have found me."* Wherefore says St. Austin—this is precisely the worst & most notable point in the death of a sinner; because being obliged in spite of himself to abandon the false & apparent good till now enjoyed, he cannot foundedly hope to obtain real & true good—he cannot hope by losing earth to gain heaven; listen to the Saint's words—when they shall have lost their life what will they possess? without nothing—within nothing—an empty chest—an empty conscience, where is there salvation, where is there hope?

This is the case, my friends, where is there hope? where? In his heart perhaps? Let him then hope, if his heart be strong enough, let him hope for eternal repose, eternal felicity; but let them in the mean time prepare to defend his hope from the fierce assault which will be made against it by nothing less than his very faith. For observe, my friends, into what difficulties he is thrown. He must on the one hand believe that there is a God a severe judge even of the good, & an inexorable punisher of the wicked. on the other hand he must hope, although he is conscious that he is wicked, to meet with the favourable lot of the good? He must believe, that the road that leads to heaven is rough & narrow; & he must still hope to arrive thither—although he has always walked in the smooth wide road that leads to hell? He must believe that he who habitually lives in sin, ordinarily dies in sin; & he must hope not to die in sin although he has habitually lived in it? He must believe that it is not enough to obtain heaven—to ask for it in any fashion whatever. Not every one that saith to me, Lord, Lord, shall enter into the kingdom of heaven; he must not withstanding hope to obtain it, although perhaps—he has never even asked it? He must believe that presumptuous sinners are not saved; & he can not hope for salvation without a kind of presumption. Now in this fierce & dangerous combat, how can he sustain himself, how guard himself? on[14] what side shall he turn? with what unite himself? With Faith? a little more & he would die an infidel. With hope? a little more & he would die in despair. Ah—the unfortunate creature who in the black melancholy & horrid palpitations of his heart, rolling his eyes around will find himself immersed in three frightful abysses, from which he has no means to escape, an abyss of inscrutable judgements above him, an abyss of continual hideous sins within him, an abyss of eternal irreparable damnation beneath him: Abyssus judiciorum, it is the meditation of St. Bernard, supra me; abyssus peccatorum intra me; abyssus inferorum subter me. In this state of afflicting desolation he extends his cold limbs & stretches on his bed—moves his lips a little &—expires.

He who has ever been present at such a scene has easily observed—to say nothing of other circumstances—has easily observed the terror which after the death of sinners—is spread in the hearts of the bystanders; some of whom cover the body &c with their heads down &c to weep for their sins—some with better resolutions have even abandoned the world entirely—Beloved sinner, then your death will be beneficial to all but to you? Your damnation will be the beginning of the salvation of others? Others will be saved at your expense? That they may fatten on the spoils of your house, occupy your farms, succeed to your honourable posts here on earth, patience. But that they may place on their heads the crown prepared for you in heaven—this o this I would never suffer—Arise then, whilst your heart is softened—your strength vigorous, your mind free, your head clear, now whilst you have plenty of time—while the grace of God incites you—while God himself calls you—fall here a victim at the feet of your crucified Jesus, & sacrificing in the true fire of sorrow & perfect charity all your sins, all your affections—exclaim in the words of the holy Job *"Suffer me that I may lament my sorrows a little. Before I go & return no more."* otherwise— great & eternal God! I already foresee, more a great deal than the loss of your possessions here on earth, more than the very remembrance of your sins, will pierce you with grief. The remembrance of this day—the remembrance of this miserable preacher. I heard, you will then exclaim, I heard that sermon it was a prophecy for me; I was even moved with sorrow for my sins—but I did not change my life—And in the mean time *"the harvest is past the summer is ended & we are not saved—*

Duty of Promoting the Glory of God (1857)

This is a late sermon of Mulledy, composed in 1857, for the feast of St. Ignatius, when he was stationed at Holy Trinity Church in Georgetown.

"The harvest indeed is great but the laborers are few." St. Luke c.10 v.2.
     To form in a few words a great panegyric of holy Job, Tertullian with his energetic pen entitled him: "The worker of the glory of God." I do not refuse to subscribe the very just sentiment of the ingenious panegyrist; but

if I may express an opinion, it seems to me that a title so magnificent is precisely the very one, that expresses the appropriate character of that great soul, whose merit we this day venerate, whose memory we solemnize. Such information of him from the old world & from the new, from him who dwells in remote regions, & from him who dwells in neighbouring countries, no one among the many to whom fame has carried the name of Ignatius, there will be no one found who does not attest that he was an indefatigable worker of the divine glory. And why not, if he never had any thing else in view, but the glory of God! Upon this he solely thought, for this he laboured, this he promoted. If he spoke, if he laboured, if he suffered, this was the burden of his discourse; this was the soul of his sufferings; this was the rule of his actions: and as in an idea he wished neither measure, nor term, he was not satisfied to seek only & always the glory of God, but he sought the greater glory of God: *"Ad majorem Dei gloriam"* If this be so, what better plan can I this day adopt to unite the good of an audience so dear to me with the genius of my great father, what I say, what better can I do, than to take the subject of the present discourse from the generous ideas of St. Ignatius, and animate you too to be zealous promoters of the glory of God! Ah it is too true that the number of similar promoters is indeed small: whilst the harvest to be hoped from it is nothing less, than a death filled with benedictions: *"The harvest is great: but the workmen are few."* Let us at least enter into the number of these few; and let us strive after the imitation of our Saint to seek in every thing the glory of God, and the glory of God alone, and the greater glory of God, particularly as we owe it to God for three reasons: in the first place as to the creator who formed us, in the second place, as to the Sovereign who governs us; in the third place, as to the father who loves & caresses us: As the work of his hands we ought in every thing seek his glory through a duty of subjection: As his subjects we ought in every thing seek his glory through a duty of fidelity: As his children we ought in every thing seek his glory through a duty of love.

As the creatures of God we ought in everything seek his glory through a duty of subjection. Although God be without us infinitely glorious, because he is of himself infinitely happy; still he wishes that we too should concur to give him glory; and we can no more refuse to give it to him, than we can deny to be his works. What more proper, what more just, than to praise, than to honor that hand which formed us? Look—in fact at those heavens, which so brightly shine, look at those fields which wave in golden abundance; look at those flowers so beautiful, which recreate you, see how many fishes glide through the water, how many birds sport in the leafy groves, how many wild beasts run through the woods, in a word how many creatures are counted in the world, all with a silent but expressive eloquence give glory to that God from whose hands they issued; and of all in general may be said, what the psalmist says of the heavens in particular, *"The heavens show forth the glory of God."* Now if creatures destitute of feeling, not only of reason, give glory to God, who gave them being, how much more shall man be obliged to do it, who of all visible creatures, if he be not the first born, is certainly the most noble, the most perfect, the most expressive of his maker?

God himself leaves no room to doubt of it, who by the mouth of Isaiah protests to have drawn him from nothing for this very purpose: *"I have created him for my glory."* to have for this end formed him with his hand *"for my glory I have formed him;"* to have for this purpose distinguished him from all other works by a beautiful mixture of frail flesh, and incorruptible spirit: *"I have made him for my glory;"* so that as the work, as he is of God, he is as much bound to give him glory, as he is in duty bound to labour for that end, for which he was made. You now understand, my friends, under what a strict obligation you are to God to give him glory; in the same manner as a tree is bound to produce fruit, because the industrious gardener cultivates it for this purpose; just as a soldier is in duty bound to bear arms, because for this end government pays him; just as a servant is bound to obey, because for this purpose his master supports him; so you are in duty bound to seek in everything to promote always the glory of God, because for this purpose he has drawn you out of the deep abyss of nothing, in which you lay buried for so many ages.[15] Be your state high & sublime, be it low & humble; be your life in its bloom, or in the decrepitude of age; be fortune avaricious, or liberal with you, God wishes to be glorified by you; nor ought a syllable issue from your mouth, nor a work from your hands, which has not the glory of God in view: *"Whether you eat or drink, or whatever else you do; do all to the glory of God."*

Now I ask, my friends, do we satisfy a duty so precise; is that glory given to God, which he requires of us, and to obtain which he has made us what we are? If we throw a look around us, ah how few are perceived, who aim at that end for which they were made! Does that distinguished man aim at it, who renders subservient to pride that position to which God has elevated him above the common run of his fellow citizens? Does that literary man aim at it, who promotes his ambition by that knowledge, with which God renders him illustrious in the world? Does that merchant aim at it, who foments avarice more & more with those gains with which God has prospered his trade? Does that woman aim at it, who the more she sees herself endowed by God with wit, with vivacity, with beauty, the vainer she grows? Ah, my friends, are we placed by God in this world, to acquire a great name on earth! Are we made to live the slaves of fleeting pleasures, of frivolous vanities, of vile interests, so that these must occupy all our thoughts, and

be the moving principle of all our solicitudes? Ah, my friends, if unfortunately we have lost sight of our end, . . . let us follow the examples of
Ignatius, and let us imitate the generous resolution which he made.

He too had at one time employed his affections more for the glory of
the world, than the glory of God. A Cavalier of a noble race, and a captain
of tried valour, he thought of nothing but winning renown, and of illus-
trating with heroic deeds his name; but when touched by God in the heart
he began to know things by the rays of a better light, how did he immediately commence to reform his conduct, how did he lament his wanderings
from his appropriate end! Farewell camps, farewell courts, farewell worldly
greatness; Ignatius no longer thinks upon you! He solely thinks upon repairing his errors of the glory not given to God, and how to prepare himself
to give it to him for the rest of his days. Fortunate grotto of Manresa! You
who received him barefooted, emaciated, a beggar, clothed with a ragged
sack, and girdled with a rough rope, you alone can tell us how Ignatius
determined to belong to that God, who created him, commenced to punish
that Ignatius, who once belonged to the world: You know the harsh treatment, which he gave his body, with the chains with which he tormented his
sides, with the fasts with which he macerated [sic] his flesh, the scourges,
with which three & five times a day he lacerated his shoulders. You know
the entire knights [sic] which he watched without repose, you know the
days, nay the weeks, which in fasting without nourishment, you know the
sighs, the seeking, you know the tears with which he gave vent to his sor-
rowed heart.

Hence what wonder if among the horrors of this grotto undertaking to
write the golden book of the spiritual exercises the first maxim which he
proposes as the first principle of the science of salvation, is that of the end
for which God has created us! And oh how often thinking upon it, and thinking upon it again; in the silence of that penitent solitude, he must have repeated to himself: Do you understand it, Ignatius? do you understand it?
God has created you for no other end, but to serve him, to praise him, but
to glorify him; for no other end, no for no other end. And by the light of
this truth, deploring the past, and providing for the future, he started in the
great career. Behold, my friends, what we too have to do; Let us too enter
into ourselves, for what end, let us say, for what end am I created? In order
that I may amuse myself from morning till night? no: In order that I may
lose myself in the chase of worldly affairs? no: In order that I may think of
becoming rich, of making a display, of growing great? no, my soul, no.
God has created me to love him, to serve him, to glorify him: have I thus
far done so? Have I lived according to my end? What glory have I thus far
given to God? By making these reflections, how many among us shall find
a subject of weeping, how many, how many!

As subjects of God we ought in everything seek his glory alone through a duty of fidelity. Joab being sent to the siege of Rabbath, after having arranged things in such a manner that the besieged city could no longer defend itself, he wished that David should be present at the storming of the city, and this for no other purpose, but that not to him, but to his prince should be attributed the glory of that enterprize: *"Lest the victory be ascribed to my name."* Behold, observe upon this fact the sacred interpreters, behold the fidelity, which the Christian owes to the king of kings: Let him be as much as you please adorned with merits, embellished with virtues, rich in talents, always in as much as is in his power, he ought to seek nothing but the glory of that God, whose subject he is. On this he must think, if he be occupied with his family, upon this if he be employed in commerce; on this if engaged in public affairs; on this the literary man must make his study; in this the military man must place his point of honor; in this the politician the aim of his views; in this the ecclesiastic the scope of his zeal. Are children to be educated? Let the glory of God prescribe the rule of education, and let this alone suggest its precepts: is an employment to be embraced? Let counsel be taken of the glory of God, and let the approbation of this alone be followed. This, my friends, this is the fidelity which as subjects, we owe to our God, to seek in every thing his glory, and if in our actions we prefix any other end to ourselves, we cannot avoid the imputation of unfaithful subjects, as it is a kind of rebellion against God not to seek him alone.

O how faithful was Ignatius in never seeking any thing but the glory of God. He had this so entirely in view, that he never undertook any thing, which did not immediately regard this. See him among little children at the age of thirty four years, to learn in a school of grammar the first elements of the Latin language; what urged him to do it? nothing but the glory of god which he thinks of promoting by knowledge & science. Behold him a pilgrim in the holy land where he supports himself with what he begs from door to door; what has lead him thither? the glory of God which he hopes to increase by the conversion of infidels. Only think if he any longer care anything about his convenience, his honor, his health, or his life. The glory of God, & nothing else, is the whole soul of his soul; does the glory of God require that he should travel? neither the roughness of mountains, nor the danger of precipices, nor the rigors of winter, nor the length of journeys terrify him; does the glory of God require that he should face the scandalous and extirpate scandals? persecutions, threats, snares, blows do not withhold him! is his name dishonoured with malignant reports? is his body ill treated with cruel beatings? is his name blackened by the most atrocious calumnies? no matter: It is too sweet to him to suffer for the glory of God; he is only displeased that for the good which he does, for the deeds which he performs, for the virtues which he practises, for the graces which he obtains, there should be anyone, who should give praise & the glory of them to him: o here indeed, he is disturbed, he blushes, he is confounded: What praise to me? to me glory? to me, who am destitute of all good? to me, who am the most ungrateful heart that God has ever tolerated, ah no, be all the glory to God. So always solicitous to correspond to that fidelity which he owed to God, to be sure to seek God alone, he did not think upon himself, or he thought upon himself to confound himself to vilify himself.

Now why, my friends, after examples so heroic shall not we too seek as far as our respective states of life permit, the sole glory of God? And what? Shall we therefore be less fortunate in business, less glorious in enterprizes, less prosperous in our families? On the contrary, my friends, on the contrary the art of inducing God to think upon you, is for you to think upon him alone. Law suits will have a most successful issue, if before instituting them, you shall examine, if the glory of God requires it: Contracts will be advantageous if the glory of God shall urge you to conclude them; The family will be prosperous, if masters, and servants, parents & children shall have at heart the glory of God: *"Whosoever shall glorify me, him will I glorify"* This is an oracle which issued from the mouth of God himself. God is pledged to exalt the man who exalts him, and to render glory for glory. I would, my friends, adduce Ignatius himself as an example of this, who was glorified by God in proportion, as God was glorified by him: but I wish to take from the sacred pages a more convincing proof. Was there ever a family that equalled in prosperity the family of Sem, the son of Noe? A family that had as an inheritance the best part of the world; A family, which numbered among its posterity the God man himself? You will say, that this was the fruit of the blessing which the patriarch his father gave him: Very true: but do you know what this blessing was? It was a benediction given to the God of Sem, and not to Sem: *"Blessed be the Lord God of Sem:"* But the blessing given to the God of Sem brought upon Sem all the blessings of God. A beautiful & holy device, says here St. John Chrysostom. Do you wish that your fields, your houses, your offspring should be blessed by God, do you bless the God of your fields, the God of your families, the God of your offspring? *"For when God is blessed, then a more abundant benediction is usually given to those, on account of whom he is blessed:"* So true is it, that no one more surely finds his own advantage, than he who seeks God alone. And why then, my friends, shall not we too animate ourselves to seek in every thing nothing but God? Why in all our works shall we not turn all our views to the honor, to the glory of our divine Sovereign? Ah let us finally conceive sentiments worthy of a true subject of the king of heaven; Let us swear to him that fidelity which he merits, and which is due to him. O my God, frequently exclaimed Ignatius, o lyre of my heart! If men only knew you! If men only knew you, there would not be one among us all who before the whole world not profess to seek nothing but God. No, no, he would say, let others seek what they please, I wish nothing else but God; I love nothing else but God; I have no other desire, no other thought, but to procure the glory of God.

As children of God we ought in every thing seek his greater glory, through a duty of love. A son of good sense and of a good heart desires nothing more, than what redounds to the honor of his father, the more he loves him, the more glory does he desire for him. Behold therefore the third duty which we owe to God; he is our father, and as a father he wishes us to acknowledge him as a father, to honor him as a father: And he himself[,] what does he not do, to give us indubitable proofs, that he has for us the heart of a father? It is just therefore that we should act towards him as children, and as children that we should show for his honor, for his glory as much solicitude as we can. In two ways a son can give to the advantage of his father clear proofs of ardent zeal: the first is by honoring him himself in the best manner that he can; the second is by desiring that he be honored by others as much as can be. And these are precisely the two ways, in which a duty of love obliges us to honor our divine father: We must in the first place omit nothing on our part, by which God may be glorified; we must prevent, as much as we can his offences; we must promote as much as we can his service; we must adore his majesty, admire his power, fear his justice; we must exalt his mercy, magnify his greatness, praise his providence, thank his liberality. but because in comparison with the merits of so great a father, will always be very little all that we can do, we must in the second place desire, that others also concur to give him glory! That the priests may concur from their altars, that the princes may concur from their thrones, that the judges may concur from their tribunals, that the just may concur with their perseverance, sinners with their compunction, heretics with their repentance, pagans with their conversion. And is not this the very thing? which Christ has taught us to ask where having invoked God as a father, we ask him that his name should be sanctified: If we well understand what is said, is not this to ask that God be glorified as much as can be, and by as many as can be?

Let us now come to ourselves, my friends; do we do, what we ask to be done? do we conduct ourselves with God as good children? do we go in search of his greater glory? do we desire that to his greater exaltation every creature should honor him? Let us see a little, what Ignatius [does] to give to God proofs of a loving son: had he ever any other intention than to promote the greater glory of his heavenly father? what did he not do to glorify him, the most that he could in himself by the practice of the most heroic virtues? With humility, and he studies the most profound; with purity, and he loves the most stainless; with charity, and he practises the most fervent; with mortification, and he wishes the most continual; with zeal and he procures the most ample, the most unwearied, the most ardent. In order then that he might be glorified by others, what did he not desire, what did he not dare, what did he not attempt? Is there a condition, is there a state, is there an age, to which he has not extended the flames of his love? He is in the hospitals, and he there consoles those who suffer; he is in prisons, and he there succours those who groan, he is [in] the pest house, and he there assists those who are agonizing: he is even in brothels and thence withdraws those who sin. The greater glory of God would wish, that there should be seen greater decorum in the temples, and he introduces it; that the sacraments should be more frequented, and he promotes it; that a stricter observance should flourish in monasteries, and he obtains it. Seminaries are required to bring up youth in piety, and in letters, and he erects them. Asylums are required for virginity which is in danger, and he finds them. And because the amplitude of his wishes cannot be contained in Rome alone, he embraces all Europe, and where the necessity is most urgent he sends messengers to extirpate abuses, to combat errors, to reprove vices, and even to the remotest Indies how many apostles does he send in Xavier alone? But this is little; not satisfied with thinking on distant countries, he thinks also on future times, and distilling, if I may say so, into holy constitutions his spirit, he founds a religious order, which in the variety of its employments for the benefit of the neighbour, looks at nothing else but the glory of God. And here even does not end his filial affection for his heavenly father. He protests, that if it were proposed to him, either to die certain of his salvation, but with less glory of God, or to live to the greater glory of God, but uncertain of his salvation; he would prefer the first to the second, & would choose the greater glory of God, although united with the uncertainty of his salvation, rather than the certainty of his salvation, but coupled with a lesser glory of God:[16] O this indeed, is to speak, this is to conduct himself as a most loving son! to what higher point can filial love reach than to sacrifice with pleasure its own glory, only to increase the glory of the father.

And we my friends, what signs of love do we give to our divine father? What anxiety do we show to increase his glory? is he not one & the same father, the father of Ignatius, and our father. And yet how after the imitation of Ignatius do we promote, both in ourselves, and in others his honor? Ah, my friends, how much I fear, that God on hearing himself called by us father, may give to us that reproof, which he formerly gave to Israel? *"If I be a father, where is my honor?"* If I be what you call me your father, where is that glory, which as a duty of love you ought to procure for me? worse still if he should have to complain to receive from us instead of glory, dishonor, & contempt: *"I have brought up children and exalted them: but they have despised me.''* But let us not dwell on a day solemn upon reflections so bitter. Let us ponder, my friends, whose children we are, and let us think upon the obligation which filial love imposes upon us of procuring as much as we possibly can the greater glory of a father so great. We have before our eyes the examples of Ignatius, let us imitate them: Let the greater glory of God be the end of our works, the scope of our thoughts, the soul of our affections, and if for the past we have failed, let us console ourselves that we have a father so good, who in this moment pardons us, if in this moment we be determined to conduct ourselves as dutiful children.

Yes, my Jesus, we are determined, and it is highly displeasing to us not to have fulfilled the duties of loving children; but we promise thee that henceforward the greater glory of a father so dear shall always be near to our hearts. Ah by the most holy wound of thy sacred side, which we piously adore, receive us with a paternal heart & grant us, to conduct ourselves for the future as zealous sons of thy honor. And thou most fervent promoter of the divine glory St. Ignatius obtain for us from God the imitation of thy zeal, so that by glorifying God as much as we can, after thy example here on earth, we may also one day glorify it in thy company in heaven.

NOTES

1. ARSI, MD 8 I 14, Peter Verhaegen to Roothaan, Georgetown, November 12, 1845.

1a. GUSC, Mulledy Papers.

2. Crossed out: "made."

3. Luigi Fortis (1748–1829), general of the Society from 1820 to 1829 and the first to be elected after its restoration.

4. Crossed out: "shrines," "victories."

5. Crossed out: "intimates."

5a. GUSC, Mulledy Papers.

6. Crossed out: "needing."

7. Crossed out: "To abandon every thing & that thing above that one loves."

8. Crossed out: "storm."

9. Crossed out: "it."

10. Crossed out: "correspondant."

11. Crossed out: "they."

12. Crossed out: "desirous."

13. Crossed out: "quominus."

14. Crossed out: "on."

15. Crossed out: "for an eternity."

16. Mulledy obviously meant to say the opposite here, that is, Ignatius would have preferred "the second to the first."

X

BENEDICT SESTINI AND THE MESSENGER OF THE SACRED HEART

Sestini (1816–1890) was a native of Florence, Italy. At the Scuolo Pia he had early shown his extraordinary aptitude for mathematics and astronomy. After he entered the Society of Jesus in 1836 he studied mathematics and physics with the renowned Andrea Carraffa at the Roman College. Assistant Director of the college's observatory when the Revolution of 1848 reached Rome, Sestini along with many of his colleagues found refuge in the United States. At Georgetown College he continued his astronomical work, conducting an extensive study of sun spots that was published by the United States government in 1851. He also published a series of textbooks on mathematics and served as the architect of St. Aloysius Church in Washington and Woodstock College in Maryland.

In 1866 he founded at Georgetown The Messenger of the Sacred Heart *to promote the spread of that traditional Jesuit devotion in response to the forces of darkness that Sestini saw threatening Christian civilization in the West. By a killing work schedule that began at 3 a.m., Sestini somehow managed to edit the monthly journal while meeting his many other scholarly and pastoral commitments. Many of the articles were translated or adapted from other sources, especially* Le Messager du Sacré-Coeur de Jésus, *which had been founded in 1861. But much of the material was Sestini's own contributions. He continued to edit the magazine until 1885 when declining health forced his retirement to the novitiate at Frederick.*

INTRODUCTION[1] (1866)

The Rev. F. H. Ramière,[2] Director General of the Apostolate [of Prayer], remarks that there are two kinds of Apostolates of which the Man-

God left an example to his followers, viz., the apostolate of action—especially of preaching—and that of prayer. That both of these apostolates, or rather these two parts of the same apostolate, are of equal merit and efficacy, is well understood from the words of the Apostles (Acts, vi,2,4). "It is not fit that we should leave the Word of God. . . . But we will give ourselves continually to prayer, and to the ministry of the Word." The same clearly appears from the constant practice of the Church, and if any preference should be given to one of these parts, it would seem to be in favor of prayer. It is well known that our Divine Lord prayed during his entire life upon earth, and that he ceases not still to pray for us; while his preaching and his public acts were confined within the narrow period of three years, during which time, also, he never omitted to unite prayer with the Word of God. The apostolate of action was entrusted by the Founder and Head of the Church to his Apostles and their legitimate successors, the Bishops, united to the visible head of the Church, assisted in this ministry by the subordinate members of the ecclesiastical hierarchy, and especially by Priests. The rest of the faithful, composing the flock of Christ, cannot, without arrogance and danger, intermeddle with their office. They are not, however, excluded from the exercise of the Apostolate, or deprived of the merit attached to it; for prayer, which is its best part, is common to all. The child, even of the most most tender age, the workman, the sick, the prisoner, the soldier, though unlearned, can exercise the Apostolate of prayer with no less merit and advantage, nay, with even more than the Priest or the Bishop. St. Paul excludes women from the ministry of the word (1 Tim., ii, 11, 12). "Let the women learn in silence with all subjection. But I permit not a woman to teach." And in another place he says (1 Cor., xiv, 34): "Let women keep silence in the churches, for it is not permitted them to speak." But she is not for the same reason debarred from the apostolic ministry of prayer, which she may exercise with even greater efficacy than man, especially when her prayer ascends from a heart that is humble and has been purified in the fire of tribulation. For our prayers are efficacious in proportion to their resemblance to those of Jesus, our Leader, who during his mortal life united prayer with sacrifice, and who, though now in a state of glory, continues to unite prayer with the sacrifice which he constantly offers his Eternal Father.

But what is the object of the Apostolate? It has in view the completion of that work which, more than any other, gives glory to God, namely, the work of the Redemption; it has in view the extension of the mystical temple of God, which is His holy Church; it has in view the union under one Head, who is the Eternal Shepherd, of the souls created and redeemed by Him, without regard to tongue, to time, or condition; it has in view the fructification of the blood which the word of God made man, poured forth on the cross for love of us; or, in other words, it has in view the giving of life and abundant life to the souls of men. Not only is it the object of the Apostolate to obtain these fruits of eternal life, but with the assistance of the Holy Spirit, it obtains them in reality. Such is the glory given to God in the work of the Redemption effected by his Beloved Son, through the Apostolate of action as well as of prayer; the latter, like the former, extending the mystical Body of Christ, gaining souls to God, and multiplying in the souls of the faithful the gifts of grace. A sick person, confined to his bed of pain for years, may by prayer obtain what the zealous missionary effects by his labors, fatigues, and privations amidst savages in the forests, or in assisting the infected in the hospitals, or devoting himself to voluntary exile in a deadly climate, or in enduring his martyrdom of patience in the tribunal of penance. A holy religieuse [sic] known only to the few companions of her solitude, and occupied with naught but the humble duties of her community, may, by means of her prayers, contribute as much to the salvation of souls as a zealous and laborious preacher of the Word of God does by his writings and discourses. These are the fruits of benediction intended and obtained by the Apostolate of Prayer, and which it is the object of the pages of this periodical to promote. This is an invitation to all the faithful to enter the vineyard of the Father of the household and gather the fruits of the Sacred Blood poured forth by the God-Man; it is an appeal to him, who has at heart the honor of his Heavenly Leader, to rush to arms and combat valiantly under the standard of the cross; it is likewise an incentive to devotion towards the adorable Heart of Jesus, and hence it is appropriately called the "Messenger of the Sacred Heart." Indeed that Sacred Heart is the nursery where springs up the choicest flower of charity, and where the most inflamed zeal of the apostle is enkindled.

Devotion is an efficacious promptness of will in favor of the object to which one is devoted; hence, the devotion to the Sacred Heart of Jesus renders our will efficaciously prompt in pleasing the Divine Heart. But what are the pleasures of this Sacred Heart?

"In the head of the book," says the word of God, "it is written of me that I should do thy will: O my God, I have desired it, and Thy law in the midst of my heart." (Psalms, xxxix, 9, 10) The perfect accomplishment of the will of His Father is the compendium of the pleasures of the Heart of His only son made man. Now, what is the will of the Father? It is that His name be glorified. God is jealous of His glory. "I, the Lord; I will not give my glory to another;" (Isaiah, xlii, 8) and the Incarnate Word repeats, "O my God, I have desired it—I seek not my own glory; but I honor my Father." (John, viii, 49, 50) The Father wills the salvation of mankind, and that all should come to the knowledge of the truth. "God will have all men to be saved, and to come to the knowledge of the truth;" (1 Timothy, ii, 4) and the Heart of the God-Man has the same desire: "I am come," he says of himself, "that men may have life, and may have it more abundantly;" (John, x) and so ardent is this desire of the Divine Heart that the Man-God subjoins: "I lay down my life for my sheep;" (John, x) that is, I sacrifice my life, I subject myself to the torments and insults of my passion, all my blood is poured forth on this account. He moreover adds, "Other sheep I have which are not of this fold; them, also, I must bring, and they shall hear my voice, and they shall be one fold and one shepherd." (John, x) Hence, true devotion to the Sacred Heart of Jesus consists in using every effort to cause the name of God to be glorified as much as possible; in employing every means, at the cost of every sacrifice, to lead as many souls as possible to the flock of Christ, and to preserve and augment the life of grace in those who already belong to his fold. Devotion to the Sacred Heart of Jesus is, therefore, identical with Apostolic zeal, whether exercised in action or in prayer; nay, more, zeal itself receives life and vigor from this devotion. Devotion to the Sacred Heart of Jesus is the root of the Apostolate, and apostolic zeal its fruit. To promote, therefore, the devotion to the Sacred Heart of Jesus, is to promote the Apostolate.

The institution of the devotion to the Sacred Heart of Jesus, as manifested by the Divine Saviour Himself to His servant, B. Margaret Alacoque, has for its object to repair the indifference, ingratitude, insults, and sacrileges committed by men against His Divine Person, in the most august Sacrament of the Altar. But this reparation cannot be made except by the contrary acts of love, gratitude, honor, and service. It was, therefore, the desire of our Divine Saviour that these acts should be multiplied in the worship of His Sacred Heart, and that without measure; for the reparation should be, as far as possible, equal to the offence. If such reparation be not in our power, it ought, at least, to be as great as we are able to make it. But to offer the Divine Heart a reparation equal to the offences daily committed against it is infinitely beyond the power of man. All the blood shed by the martyrs; all the mortifications performed by the anchorets; all the labors undergone by the Apostles; in a word, the exercise of virtues practised by millions of saints, and whatever good works have adorned, and will adorn, the church, until the consummation of the world, are not sufficient to make reparation for a single insult against the Divine Person of the word. Yet this Divine Person wishes that reparation be made by men, which, though inadequate, must necessarily be all that men are capable of offering. The true client of the Sacred Heart cannot, therefore, be satisfied with the little which he, unaided, can do in repairing the offences against the Divine Word, but strives to associate as many as possible with him in the same work. He cannot help wishing, as far as depends upon him, that want of faith in the Real Presence may be compensated by at least as many acts of faith, and as many acts of desire to give blood and life for the same faith. He cannot help wishing that the innumerable irreverences even of the faithful, and the coldness and indifference of so many millions of men towards the adorable Sacrament of the Altar, should be repaired, if possible, by as many acts of homage, and by the liveliest gratitude and charity of as many millions of men. He cannot help wishing that the too numerous sacrileges and blasphemies against this august mystery should be compensated by innumerable praises, and, so far as may be, by the service and homage of all men.

The client of the Sacred Heart in conformity with the spirit in which that devotion was established in the Church, is necessarily an Apostle, and can have no other wish than that her prodigal children should return to the arms of the Father whom they have abandoned, and that those who have wandered from the fold should find repose in her bosom. True it is that the client of the Sacred Heart is not always able, by means of the apostolate of *action,* to bring back the prodigal to the embraces of his Father, nor to lead to the ark of salvation those who are wandering in unbelief; but nothing prevents him from employing the Apostolate of *Prayer,* especially in the easy exercise of offering to God daily his good works, his sufferings, and privations, as so many supplications united with those of the Divine Heart in the blessed Sacrament; in which acts is substantially contained that which is required of its members by the Association of the Apostolate of Prayer.

We would call the attention of our readers to one consideration. Many are deterred from entering into this Association by a groundless fear of overcharging themselves with burdensome practices. Now the Apostleship of Prayer does not of itself impose any new obligation. Its aim is simply to animate with its spirit all our actions, prayers, sufferings, and privations, that thus, according to the measure of Divine grace imparted to each individual member, his every action, prayer, suffering, and privation, may be rendered more acceptable to God, more profitable to himself, and, especially, more conducive to the salvation of others. Hence this Association aims rather at perfecting and sanctifying in a more particular manner any practice of devotion, than at imposing additional obligations. . . .

Let us briefly speak of the progress which it has made in few months in the United states. Besides about two hundred religious communities, seminaries, colleges, and sodalities, which have applied for and received the diploma of the Association of the Apostolate, letters have been sent us from different States, informing us not only that the work has been hailed with joy, but that there is every prospect of its constantly increasing diffusion, with the consoling assurances of abundant fruits of eternal life. The tickets of the Association have been distributed by thousands in every part of the country, and especially in the West. Many prelates and superiors of religious communities have been pleased, by approval and encouragement, to sanction the promotion of the work; and finally, the desire to see the book and manual of the Apostolate published, together with the present periodical, has been repeatedly, and in different ways, manifested by the promoters of the Association. In the course of this publication, we hope to be able to give proofs more explicit and in detail of the apostolic zeal which the Almighty designs to infuse into the hearts of the faithful in this country. . . .

But, independently of the preceding circumstances, every time is opportune for promoting the Association of the apostolate; for at all times there is a world to combat, there are temptations to overcome, dangers to avoid, inclinations to restrain; at all times does the Church of God invite every soul to enter the fold; at all times is it true that *the harvest is great, the laborers are few;* at all times does our Lord direct us to ask *the Lord of the harvest that He would send laborers;* that is to say, apostles of action and of prayer. If we seek for another motive which may convince us of the opportuneness of furthering this work, we may find it in the spirit of association which prevails in every class of society, as it is at present constituted, and especially in the fact that not a small number of these associations have for their object, under the guise of philanthropy, not the salvation, but the perdition of the souls; not the well-being, but the utter subversion and ruin of the world. Indeed, never did the world manifest its tendencies to paganism by efforts more formidable and gigantic than at the present time, when, to effect its object, it employs every means, and especially the blasphemous, infamous, and licentious publications which are poured forth from the press. The principles of our age tend to precipitate the world into the darkness of error, and the frightful abyss of pagan life; and that portion of mankind, by no means small, which has suffered itself to be carried away by these principles, has, to a great extent, assumed a pagan attitude, as the cold egotism and materialism which prevail to such an extent in the world leave no room to doubt. Now, the devotion to the Sacred Heart and the Apostolate are diametrically opposed to the tendencies and principles manifested by the world, and hence it is most expedient at the present time to promote the Association of the Apostolate. Devotion to the Sacred Heart of Jesus has, among other effects, the salutary one of assimilating the heart of the client to that of his Lord. It strips the hearts of the faithful of all selfishness, replenishes them—not with false friendship, which the world calls philanthropy—but with true charity, which is the charity of Christ, rendering it prompt to sacrifice fortune and life itself for the eternal salvation of men. The spirit of prayer, especially of that prayer which has for its object the glory of God, the exaltation of His Church, and the salvation of the world, is a spirit of union with God; a spirit, consequently, which elevates the mind and the heart above everything created, and therefore detaches man from terrestrial and material things. It is a spirit which looks to the eternal, and cannot, therefore, content itself with the perishable things of time. Earthly riches, pleasures, and glory, are consumed in the fire of charity, which is the origin and fruit of prayer. This spirit is likewise the source of truth and light, which discover and destroy the false principles of the world, and hence it is not only a barrier to the progress of pagan tendencies, but, as the latter stand in need of falsehood and darkness for their maintenance and advancement, it eliminates these very means themselves.

May the Sacred Heart grant that this heavenly fire and light may replenish the minds and hearts of our associates; and not only of those who are members of this Association, but of all who, through their means, shall participate in the fruits of the Apostolate of Prayer.

THE LOVE OF JESUS, STUDIED IN HIS SACRED HEART[3] (1868)

"Zeal for the glory of God, for the triumph of the Church, and for the salvation of souls," Sestini had written in the January, 1867 issue of The Messenger, *"is intimately connected with the devotion to the Sacred Heart of Jesus. Perhaps it would be more correct to say that they are identical."*[4] *Despite the bleak horizons of the modern world,* The Messenger *could still affirm that "there is too much of real good left in the world, to permit evil completely to triumph."*[5] *An article in the following year explored the reasons for such residual optimism.*

Our readers will have remarked that our bulletin has not contained this year, as it did last year, a monthly article devoted especially to the honor and interests of the Sacred Heart of Jesus; but we trust they have not considered it on that account to have lost its character of *Messenger* of the Sacred Heart. For what is it to be a Messenger? It is to announce the tidings, discharge the commission, impart the information, serve the purposes and promote the interests of him who sends or employs the Messenger. Our little periodical, in claiming to be the Messenger of the Sacred Heart of Jesus, does not confine itself to explaining the nature and the object of the devotion to that Divine Heart, but aims to serve its interests by announcing such tidings as the Saviour wishes to be spread among men for the awakening of their zeal and the enkindling of their fervor. Whatever is dear to the Heart of Jesus, whatever He wishes men to study and ponder, whatever tends to quicken men's faith and strengthen their religious principles, whatever advances the designs which the Sacred Heart wishes to be carried out, in a word, whatever we have good reason to believe that the Heart of Jesus wishes us to announce, *that* we consider to be legitimate material for the Messenger. . . . But the month of June, by a custom now almost universal, is dedicated in a special manner to the Sacred Heart of Jesus; and our readers have therefore a right to expect in the organ and advocate of the Sacred Heart, something bearing directly on the devotion to which these days are consecrated. We invite them, then to study the LOVE OF JESUS IN HIS SACRED HEART.

God never forgets, and never changes: having made man for Himself, He never ceases to draw him to Himself. The innermost folds of our hearts are open to Him, and He knows better than we ourselves all the aspirations, all the instincts there implanted. These He sets in motion and makes use of to lead us to our end: instruments sometimes the most different, sometimes even the most opposed, become in His Almighty hand, instruments of love. Hope, fear, every feeling, when it comes from God, tends to unite us to Him by the bonds of love. But there is in the depths of our souls a sentiment whose strength no one can measure, and for which God shows a special preference: that feeling is love which challenges and demands love in return; and God who wishes our love, resolved first to exhibit His boundless love for us: "I will draw them in the bonds of love."

When we gaze upon the beauties of the universe, we are seized with profound admiration for the almighty power of Him who drew all things out of nothing. The multitude and the variety of creatures, their wondrous structure, the order that reigns among and above them all, force us, even in spite of ourselves, to see and acknowledge the infinite wisdom of Him, "by whom all things were made." But this work of power and wisdom, if looked at more closely, appears none the less a work of love. For why did God, who from all eternity was infinitely happy in Himself, display the marvellous beauties of visible nature, if not for the sake of man? And what need had He of man, He who had no need of anything outside of the Godhead? Yes, I understand it:—He wished our love; and to win it, He began by loving us. Every created thing speaks to us of our Benefactor, and reminds us of our destiny: "The heavens, the earth, the sea, and all things speak to us of Thee, O God, and bid us love Thee."—(St. Aug.)

Alas! this beautiful language of love spoken by all nature was not understood by man. He centred his affections on himself and lost sight of his Creator; and the creatures, which in the designs of Providence should have been a ladder by which to mount up to heaven, became, by attracting the affections of his heart, so many bonds by which he was held a wretched captive upon earth. Any love but God's would have been wearied and disgusted with ingratitude so monstrous: but God found in the treasures of His eternal love an unspeakable means of winning our hearts. It is no longer creatures that He will give us, but His own beloved Son: Him He will clothe with our human nature and deliver up to death. "God so loved the world that he gave His only begotten Son." And when the Word made Flesh shall have been raised upon the Cross, and shall have breathed His last sigh, then at last He shall gain our love. "When I shall have been lifted up, I will draw all things unto myself."

Would any one ever have thought that such an excess of divine love could have been met on the part of men, with coldness and ingratitude? Would any one ever have thought that our loving Saviour, far from punishing men's gratitude by casting them off, would have wished to discover another means to win their hearts? And what more can He do after giving Himself up to the disgraceful death of the Cross? He can open His sacred bosom, He can show us His Heart, the symbol, the centre, the source of love. All this He has done, and He cries out to us: "O men, ever urged by the necessity of loving, ever greedy of love, turn not your eyes from My wounded side, cease not to look at love, turn not your eyes from My wounded side, cease not to look at My loving Heart. It burns with love for you, and It alone can satisfy your craving for love. Come all ye and see, not only if there be any sorrow like unto My sorrow, but if there be any love like unto My love." . . .

The benefits which our divine Saviour has lavishly conferred upon us, we must always regard as unmistakable proofs of His love: as He Himself said, when there was question of His divinity, "if you do not believe Me, believe My works." Measured by the favors heaped upon us, that love manifests itself to us as a boundless, unfathomable ocean. Lost in the darkness of ignorance and sin, we were rescued and brought back to the light of eternal truth; dead to the supernatural order of grace by sin, we were recalled to life by His divine power; children of wrath and slaves of Satan, we were made by Him the children of God; and ransomed from our bondage, we regained our rights to our heavenly inheritance. Jesus never ceases to bestow upon His creatures whom He bought with His blood, all the perfection to which He destined them. He it is, who in the midst of the darkness that sometimes compasses our minds, flashes before our eyes the bright light of faith; who comes to strengthen our will on the point of yielding to the assaults of corrupt nature; who in the deadly struggle with our passions hastens to rouse our flagging courage, fighting with us, in us and for us. If we wished to contemplate all the benefits showered upon us by our loving Redeemer, we would have to call up before us all the years of our lives; and we should find every moment marked by some new favor. But is this the only, or the most striking proof of the love of Jesus? Can we not discover the source of all His works of love? And what is that source but His Divine Heart? Prevented [sic] and pursued with benefits unnumbered, shall we not ask Him, in our rapture of admiration and gratitude, "what is man that Thou art mindful of him, or the son of man that Thou doest visit him?" why, O my Saviour and my God, why didst Thou from all eternity fix Thine eyes on me with love? Why hast Thou in time worked out Thy merciful designs upon me? Was it to satisfy Thy burning thirst for Thy Father's glory? Was it to purchase my soul doomed to everlasting fire? Was it not rather because Thou, O my God, didst love, and dost still love me, Thy creature and Thy enemy?

. . . Why . . . did our Saviour wish to suffer so much, and to provide for our souls such copious streams of grace springing up from the foot of the Cross? Why? Look for the answer where alone you can find it, in His Sacred Heart. *"He loved us and delivered Himself for us."* He loved us! And for that love He became poor and despised. He suffered and was crucified: *He delivered Himself for us.* There is the secret, there is the mystery. It is simply a mystery of love. Henceforth we can fathom its depths and penetrate the dark shadows which the light of faith had not dispelled. The thoughts and desires, the actions and sufferings, the life and death of the God-Man are thoroughly explained by His love. We can confidently examine the different scenes of our Redeemer's life, and ask with St. Bernard; "who hath done this?" And the answer given by that great Saint and Doctor of the Church immediately suggests itself, "Love hath done it." What could confine the immensity of the God-head within the narrow prison of the Virgin's womb? *"Love hath done it."* Who could draw down the Majesty of heaven to be born in a stable and laid in a manger? *"Love hath done it."* What could make the Redeemer of the world bury thirty years of His life in the silence and obscurity of his poor retreat at Nazareth? *"Love hath done it."* And if He issued from that retreat to teach His doctrine and promulgate His law, it was love that drew Him from His solitude. If on his throne of suffering and shame He found words of pardon for those even who had fastened Him to the Cross, it was *love* that suggested them. If, in fine, in His life in the Church, in the mysterious silence of the tabernacle, in the triumph of His heavenly splendor He has never ceased to show Himself the Saviour of men despite their ingratitude for His passion and death, *"Love hath done it."* We have no reason to give for all that Jesus has done for us, except that *"He loved us and delivered Himself for us."* . . .

Now there never has been, there never will be in the world, a friend who so loved his friend, as Jesus Christ loved and still loves men. The wonderful means which His love suggested of remaining for ever with us, "surpasseth understanding." When the hour of parting was come, when men were driving Him from the world, "on the night when He was betrayed," Jesus wished to conceal Himself beneath the lowly species of bread and wine; and in the obscurity of His mysterious covering, always ready to be our nourishment, and to transform us into Himself, He remains with us, and will remain to the end of ages. . . .

Nevertheless, strange as it may appear, we have failed as yet to com-prehend the treasures of our Saviour's love. We can never behold without profound and grateful admiration the marvellous change of heart wrought in them that are lifted up from the depths of sin to the heights of sanctity; the purity and innocence of them that walk spotless through all the strifes and struggles of corrupt nature, amid the ever-recurring assaults of the world, and despite the weakness of sex and age; the long and laborious life of them that turned their back upon the world and spent their days in watching, fastings and penance; the unbending fortitude of the martyrs of every age and condition, who braved and conquered the rage of tyrants; the burning zeal of the Apostles, who in the face of countless dangers and at the price of innumerable sacrifices, spread the kingdom of God throughout the world. All these wonders wrought in souls by the grace of Jesus Christ are fit subjects for the admiration of men and angels; but they do not reveal the immensity of our Saviour's love. Who could keep an account of the good seed which throughout our life the heavenly Husbandman has cast into our hearts, but which our resistance has rendered unproductive? Who can tell how often the divine Bridegroom has knocked at the door of our hearts before it was opened to Him? Do we know all the pious thoughts, all the holy desires, all the fervent prayers, all the sacrifices of souls mastered by the love of Jesus? Even the exterior works and labors that attract most attention, tell us but little of the lively faith which inspired them, of the pure and fervent charity which animated them. Nay, is it not true, that in proportion as one is lost to self and transformed into the image of God, he becomes more generous but at the same time more studious to conceal his gifts and graces and sacrifices? . . .

. . . The brea[d]th of His love! It embraces all generations, includes all men, reaches all ages and is bounded by no limits of space; not one single soul escapes its influence. The height of His love! If you wish to measure it by the gifts it has bestowed, see what it has given us. Is it a human or an angelic nature, heaven, earth, grace, glory? Nay it has given us more: it has given us the Creator of men and angels, God. Let us acknowledge the weakness of our intellect; we can never comprehend the Infinite. The depth of His love! He came down from the heights of heaven to the abyss of our nothingness: measure, if you can, the sublimity of the one, and sound the depth of the other, and you will understand how profound, how unfathomable is His love.

In presence of a love so excessive, so divine, we ought to humble ourselves and stand confused; but let us at the same time reflect that if Jesus loves us, He also asks our love; and that if He has shown us an "exceeding great love," it is in order that our love for Him may know no other measure, than that it should have no measure. We have fallen upon days in which we witness impiety that hates, heresy that rends, faith that grows cold and forgetful. Jesus shows us His Heart overwhelmed with anguish, and asks of us reparation. His anguish is extreme: our reparation should be the most thorough. . . .

GRACES OBTAINED[6] (1869)

"Particular Intentions" and "Graces Obtained" were two regular features of The Messenger *that chronicled the cycle of spiritual activity through collective prayer for individual needs. Most of the requests involved spiritual needs; most of the "miracles" attested to were moral ones.*

We continue our record of the consoling answers received to prayer . . .

(1) A religious writing from Philadelphia, says: "With regard to the conversion of Mr. _____, it ought to be recorded. For more than fifteen years, he had been the torment and ruin of his family. Prayers, masses, almsdeeds, were offered, but our dear Lord willed that the conversion should be drawn from His loving Heart. For more than a year he has kept to his daily labors, performed his religious duties, received the Holy Sacraments monthly and at every great festival, and praise be to the Sacred Heart! he continues doing so. We have another case to record, a real miracle, but we will wait to give it."

(2) Another religious writes: "Rev'd Father, you may say my petitions are many, but I have often experienced the powerful aid of the Apostleship of Prayer, and the goodness of the amiable Heart of Jesus."

(3) The prayer in the August number, for a young lady, that her mother might consent to her becoming a religious, has been answered.

(4) "Please accept the enclosed little token of gratitude ($5) for favors obtained. . . . I earnestly recommend myself and all under my charge for the necessary graces to serve faithfully our dear Lord, and secure our eternal salvation."

(5) "Again, we beg the zealous members of the apostleship of Prayer to join with us in fervent thanksgiving for the conversion of a young man, Protestant, who is now a fervent Catholic. Some time ago, his sister, a religious, recommended him to the Prayers of the Association in one of the numbers of the Messenger, and during the month of our sweet Mother

Mary, he entered the church, made his first communion, and was confirmed.''

(6) A lady writes us: ''I have to return thanks, grateful indeed, through you to the Sacred Heart of Jesus for granting my prayers. One petition was for a reconciliation between a brother and two sisters which has taken place after five years of misunderstanding.'' The other request was on account of a domestic annoyance which disappeared almost by miracle.

A religious writing from a Northwestern city, says: ''To-day I received three applications for instruction, from two Episcopalians and one Swedenborgian. Since my published report of last year, I have, through the mercy of the Sacred Heart, received 45 into the Church. Please return thanks for it.''

A college student, writing from the South, says: ''I take pleasure, and feel it a duty in the name of my mother, to return thanks to the associates of the Apostleship of Prayer for the almost wonderful restoration of my father to health. He was recommended last February. His recovery we attribute wholly to the prayers of the association. I must make acknowledgement for many favors I myself have asked through their prayers, one of which was the return of my eldest brother to the practice of his religious duties, and also the partial conversion of my father. . . . Great fruit has been worked already from the reading of the Messenger, but of course room is left for more.''

An Ursuline writes to us: ''Please have prayers offered for us in thanksgiving for the special goodness of the Sacred Heart towards us during the past year, and beg our Lord to continue His favors towards us in future.''
. . .

A PONTIFICAL ZOUAVE[7]

As Pope Pius IX struggled to defend his temporal power against the encroaching forces of Risorgimento in central Italy, a new warrior-saint emerged in popular Catholic piety. Fictional and non-fictional accounts of papal Zouaves or ''St. Peter's Crusaders,'' risking their lives for the vicar of Christ, frequented the pages of the Messenger *in the late sixties.*

A touching ceremony took place on Saturday, the 19th of November, in the church of the English College, at Rome. It was for the obsequies of Julius Watts Russell, the scion of an illustrious English family, who but seventeen years and ten months of age, fell, fighting in the cause of the Church, at Mentana, on the 3d November. He and his elder brother Wilfrid, had enlisted together among the Pontifical Zouaves, as private soldiers, five months before; they had fought with honor side by side at Nerola, but when Julius went to Monte Rotondo, his brother, ill with fever, was obliged to remain in Rome. They clasped hands, breathed together a Pater and Ave and a Salve Regina, as Julius carrying his musket and knapsack, took his place in the ranks, at two in the morning. This was all their leave-taking for their first and last separation, and less than twenty-four hours after, the brave Julius had won the bright glory he had panted for, of giving his life-blood *pro Sede Petri.* The day before he had, according to his custom, renewed his strength in holy communion. In the battle he bore himself like a hero, speaking little, as his comrades remarked, but often praying. His cap was carried away by a ball as the fight began; several times after he had narrow escapes, till finally, near Mentana, a ball entered his brain through the left eye, and he fell. The shot was fired by a Garibaldian, at a little distance from him.

Madam Stone, who went with three Sisters of Charity to the battle field, had his body laid apart. The pious boy had with him a little manuscript prayer book, which was found. His devout, frank and generous spirit, is well expressed in the Italian words last written in it, under the heading *massima per Giulio.*[8]

> Anima mia, anima mia,
> Ama Deo e tira via.[9]

There is also a touching prayer in French, addressed to the B. Virgin for the conversion of all who even in their sins, have kept a spark of devotion to her: who knows but the conversion of some wounded Garibaldians, is due to prayers like this? The whole book is a garland of devotional jewels, in which the fervent piety of this boy Zouave appears. His innocence of manners, and his brave manly spirit, endeared him to all. An incident that occurred a short time before his death, shows his beautiful character. Some little dispute between the two brothers, grew slightly warm: Julius ended it by exclaiming, "come Wilfrid, let us kneel down and make an act of contrition, and shake hands." They did so, and they ceased their brief *amantium irae.* What wonder they should prove soldiers, who conquer themselves!

The body was embalmed in the house of a French gentleman, a friend of Julius, who had accompanied it to Rome. . . . It was laid out for a day, and visited by many thronging to see, as they said the *little Angel.* It was indeed touching to see the handsome boy in his best uniform, a chaplet of white roses on his brow, the crucifix and palm in his hands, and the scapular of the B. Virgin on his neck: a sweet and almost supernatural smile on his lips, and his countenance, made as it were, more beautiful by the wound in the eye, and the bruises of the forehead.

For the consolation of his father, a parent worthy of such a son, is reserved the blood-stained uniform he wore on the battle field. . . . Among the many Zouaves, his comrades, who during the mass and last offices, stood with lighted candles in their hands, reciting their beads for their brother in arms, and the high personages also present, the general feeling was of tender consolation and holy envy, and even Wilfrid, whose heart was pierced by the loss of such a brother, said, when all was over, that the funeral solemnity seemed like a *festival.*

The wonder and consolation of all was renewed when, before the body was enclosed in the zinc coffin, the face was uncovered for the last time. *In somno pacis,* was the idea brought to every mind by the smile, sweeter than ever, and the natural composure of the body. Towards evening it was conveyed to St. Lorenzo, and Wilfrid laid upon his brother's grave two wreaths of flowers from the Pope's garden, bidding peace to the soul of his dear Julius. Already we hope he has that peace and a palm in Heaven.

The following is the inscription prepared for his tomb:

Heic ad Martyrum cryptas,
dormit in pace,
Julius Watts Russell, Michaelis F.
anglus Praeclaro genere,
qui
pro Petri Sede strenue dimicans
in acie ad Mentanam occubuit.
III Non. Novemb. an M D C C C L X V I I
an. n. X V I I. mens. X.
Adolescens Christi miles
Vive in Deo.[10]

THE HEART OF JESUS AND THE VICAR OF CHRIST[11] (1869)

In the siege mentality that dominated conservative thought in the 1860s, ultramontane piety flowered. The following essay encapsulated the logic that made the pope the nerve center of the Mystical Body and the principal focus of the Sacred Heart.

. . . The Church traces its origin from the pierced Heart of Jesus asleep in the sleep of death on the cross, in the same manner as Eve was formed from one of Adam's ribs when God had cast upon him a deep sleep. The Church owes her existence to the Charity of the Man-God and with her existence she owes to the same charity every thing she possesses, doctrine, sacraments, graces and life. But the Charity of the Man-God has its seat nowhere else but in His Sacred Heart. The Heart of Jesus, therefore, is to the Church what the human heart is to the body of a living man, i.e. the original and constant fountain of life. But although the heart imparts life to all the body and to every part of it, it does not communicate it equally to each portion, but each is supplied by it in the manner and with that amount of nourishment due to the office it ought to discharge. The manner and quality of nourishment which the heart propels to the organ of vision, for example, differs from the manner and quality of nourishment transmitted to the organ of hearing. The brain and the nerves are supplied by the heart with a nourishment different from that with which the muscles or the bones are supplied, and the nobler the office of the organ the more exquisite and the more copious is the action of the heart upon it. To speak of the brain alone, the heart supplies it incessantly through two principal arteries with an amount of vivifying fluid incomparably greater than that diffused through the other different parts of the body, and the work effected by this fluid in that noble organ is no less wonderful than the quantity so liberally bestowed upon it.

Thus does the heart of the Man-God vivify the various members of His mystical body. "There are diversities of graces," says St. Paul, (1 Cor. xii) "to one is given the word of wisdom and to another the word of knowledge . . . to another faith: to another the grace of healing: to another the working of miracles: to another prophecy: to another the discerning of spirits: to another divers kind of tongues: to another interpretation of speeches." There are also graces adapted to the different states or periods of life as those which belong to the Sacraments; there are also graces attached to the different vocations and to the different offices of the Christian life. Following the analogy between the heart in the human body taken in relation with the various organs of the same body and the Heart of Jesus in its relation with the various members of the Church, let us illustrate further. Peter is, as it were, the brain of this mystical body and for him consequently the Heart of Jesus apportions the requisite abundance of its vivifying spirit, not for Peter's sake alone, but to benefit through him the whole body of the Church as the blood transmitted by the heart to the brain benefits through it the whole body of man. Thou are Peter, said our Saviour to Simon, Son of John, that is a rock, and upon this rock I will build my church, and so firmly shall it be built that not only no human power but not even the power of hell shall ever prevail over it. Who was Simon? Was he not a poor fisherman, obscure, timid and unlearned? Who were Peter's successors for a period of three centuries? Were they not every one objects of the most obstinate persecution and so many victims destined to death? And in after ages down to our own day, what else does the history of the Popes present to us but a series of the most virulent attacks from the mighty of the world, and revolts on the part of the spirit of error presenting itself under every variety of form?

Yet the prediction of the Man-God in favor of Peter and of his successors is verified so far and shall be so unto the end. Let the skeptic and unbeliever give the explanation he likes best of this most undeniable fact. None whatever can be found satisfactory save the realization of the solemn promise accorded to his Vicar by the Man-God. The effusion of the Heart of this Man-God in behalf of Peter and of his flock strengthens him against all attacks of human or satanic malice and power. Let Peter be thrown into a dungeon or sent into exile, let him be robbed, calumniated and slain in the person of his successors, yet he shall always emerge victorious from the onslaught. He shall always be the rock inseparably united to the divine foundation of the church and through him shall this Church always be the pillar and the ground of truth. . . .

GENERAL INTENTION: THE COUNCIL
AND ILL-DISPOSED CATHOLICS[12] (1869)

In the fall of 1869 the Catholic world awaited the opening in Rome of the ecumenical council called by Pio Nono. Conservative forces within the church looked confidently to the council to confirm the supreme moral and spiritual authority of the pope in the face of the impending collapse of his political authority. In the pages of The Messenger *the tone was increasingly apocalyptic, even affecting the monthly general intentions.*

We prayed last month for non-Catholics in good faith, of whom there are so many, especially in Protestant countries. But there is another class of men whose state is far more deplorable, and whose return may, we hope, be brought about by the council. We allude to those, who, nominally Catholics, are really in rebellion against the authority of the Church, and to whom, there is much reason to fear, even the Council may prove the occasion of formal apostasy and irrevocable condemnation.

The light cannot shine upon men with unusual brilliancy, without enlightening those who seek it and blinding those who fly from it. Jesus Christ himself tells us, that when he came into the world, not to judge it, but to save it, he became, as it were in spite of himself, the cause of the self-condemnation of those who loved darkness rather than the light, because their works were evil. (John iii, 17-19). This judgment is repeated as often as the divine Saviour makes a new effort to lead souls to salvation. The well disposed respond to his appeal, and enter the way of life; but they who do evil hate the light, and instead of coming to it, fly from it, that their works may not be reproved. (John 111, 20) Thus in all ages Jesus Christ fulfils the prophecy of the holy old man Simeon, revealing the hidden thoughts of hearts: being a sign of contradiction, a cause of resurrection or of ruin (Luke ii, 34), according as men accept or refuse the light and the life which he brings them.

We believe that the approaching Council will produce this twofold result, and that whilst bringing back many who were walking in darkness, to the way of light, a certain number of unworthy children of light will take occasion from it to reject their divine inheritance. It has been so with all preceding Councils: all have had some errors to condemn; and consequently all have reduced the adherents of these errors to the necessity of choosing between obedience and apostasy. . . .

Are there to-day, among men calling themselves Catholics, proud minds disposed to revolt against the authority of the Church, if she should think it necessary to condemn their doctrines? Would that we could doubt it; but in reading certain productions of our time, it is difficult not to recognize the language of rebellion. Rationalism, a more dangerous contagion than heresy, pervades the entire society of the present day; rationalism is that radical heresy which prompts human reason to make itself supreme judge even in questions of the supernatural order. Instead of humbly accepting the decisions of divine truth, speaking by the mouth of the Church, this proud spirit claims the right to bring them before its tribunal, and subject them to its laws. Although it cannot explain the mysteries of the smallest grain of sand, it refuses to admit the mysteries of the infinite. It arrogates to itself the right to examine everything, the holy Scriptures, the teaching of tradition, the decrees of Pontiffs and Councils; it holds nothing sacred; and when the Church, strong in the supreme power with which Jesus Christ has invested her, raises her voice against this criminal presumption, rationalism condemns the Church as guilty of violating the rights of reason.

This is the contagion which is making the greatest havoc among souls at the present time, and with which even many Catholics are more or less infected. Let it then be well understood: these unfortunate men are Catholics only in name; in reality, they are not even Christians, since that which constitutes a Christian is faith in Jesus Christ, and there can be no true faith when one refuses to submit his reason to the authority of God; and the Church is the organ of that authority. Jesus Christ has said to the pastors of His Church: "He that hears you, hears me and he that despises you, despises me." (Luke x, 16) A man must, therefore, necessarily refuse to acknowledge Jesus Christ as the Saviour, when he refuses to submit his reason to the authority which holds the place of Jesus Christ here below. Consequently, those who, although still bearing the name of Catholics, encourage in their hearts thoughts of rebellion against the Church, are out of the way of salvation.

But this puts us under the greater obligation to pray for them, that before they take the last step into the abyss, they may open their eyes to the frightful danger that threatens them. It is never without intense grief that the Church, the tender mother of souls, sees herself constrained to cut off from her those to whom she gave life. Nothing but the imperative duty of witnessing to the truth could compel her to this sorrowful sacrifice: but before striking with anathema those who have made themselves the declared enemies of truth, she warns, she solicits, she entreats them. She turns especially to God, and conjures him to enlighten these blind minds, and to soften their obstinate hearts.

Let us enter into her sentiments and join our prayers to hers. Let us reanimate our fervor, in order to obtain that the coming Council, from which we hope such good results to society in general, may not, if possible, prove an occasion of ruin to even one soul; and let us say daily, during this month:

Divine Heart of Jesus, I offer to Thee, through the Immaculate Heart of Mary, all my prayers, actions and sufferings of this day, for the same intentions for which Thou dost constantly offer Thyself a victim on our altars.

I offer them in particular for the Council and for all Catholics, unworthy of the name, whose hearts are not disposed to acknowledge and submit to Thy supreme authority. O most loving Saviour, deign to enlighten these blind souls, and make them understand that they can find salvation only in the most filial obedience to Thy holy Church. Amen.

GENERAL INTENTION: THE COUNCIL, AND
CATHOLICS WHO ARE WAVERING IN THE FAITH[13] (1869)

Our fears, heretofore expressed, are beginning to be but too fully realized. The approach of the Council is producing, upon some minds, effects similar to those produced by the approach of day upon birds, before their eyes are strong enough to bear the light. Thoughts, hitherto hidden in the bottom of hearts, begin to be revealed. Satan, who has received power to sift the wheat of the Lord, is using it to its fullest extent; his attacks upon the disciples of the divine Master are fearful; and should one of them suffer himself to be overcome by pride, or any other bad passion, the tempter drags him, Judas like, into open rebellion.

This should by no means surprise, much less shake the faith, of the disciples of the Heart of Jesus. Rather it should stimulate them to zeal and compassionate charity; to compassion for those who have fallen; to zeal, that persevering constancy may be obtained for those who are in danger of falling. We have already prayed frequently for the first, and let us not cease to pray for them, for the divine grace can restore those living stars to their place in the firmament of his Church; if the delirium of pride has cast them down, a great effort of humility may raise them up again and save them, and we must endeavor to obtain for them the grace to make this effort.

But besides these, there are many others whose urgent necessities we should earnestly recommend to God; those, namely, who have been more or less shaken in their faith by the scandals which surround us. Weak already in faith, and exposed at every step to the fascination of error, they have everything to fear from a perverseness which is daily increasing in extent and violence.

It would seem, indeed, that the moving spirit of the infernal regions had sent forth his final commands. Whilst the Church thinks only of securing to men the patrimony of truth bequeathed them by Jesus Christ, and of which Satan is struggling to despoil them, she is represented as seeking solely to enslave the mind, and stifle its noblest aspirations. The masses of the people are a prey to a disease which is consuming their very vitals and leaves them no repose; like the sick man, tossing restlessly on his bed of pain, they are given up to unceasing revolutions; institutions of every kind are tottering; the efforts of the wisest and ablest men of the time are unable to establish anything permanent; a fearful restlessness pervades and tortures society. The Church also is suffering from this sad state of things, and she alone endeavors to remedy; she proposes to re-establish the tottering social edifice on a divine, indestructible basis; she aspires only to restore strength and soundness to the nations of Europe who owe to her, not only their past progress, but their very existence also. Their only reply, however, to her maternal solicitude is a concert of blasphemies and outrages; and even men, calling themselves Christians, are not ashamed to unite with the most ungodly and irreligious wretches in accusing the Vicar of Christ, and all who profess sincere devotion to his cause, of impeding progress, and of declaring a blind war upon modern society, which will ultimately compel it to break with the Church.

To us who know the Church, and know that her desires are the desires of Christ himself, these accusations appear only absurd calumnies, but it is different with those who do not know the Church as we do, and who read them daily in works published in every form calculated to deceive the unsuspecting and excite their curiosity. In these publications, every act of the Church is misrepresented; the faults of her defenders are exaggerated and depicted in the darkest colors. It can not be surprising then that the unfortunate man who, as it were, makes this poison his daily food, should gradually relax in his faith and love of the church, and finally lose them altogether.

We must use our influence to dissuade Catholics from this fatal tendency. Let us remind them that the Church forbids, under pain of mortal sin, the reading of bad newspapers, as well as of irreligious books; and that, where the canons of the Church are in full force, it is excommunication to read such publications without good reason or without special authority. But if we cannot always induce them to abstain from the forbidden fruit, let us pray that their faith may resist its destructive influence. Let us ask light for them to detect the falsity of the accusations made against the church, and strength that, notwithstanding the assaults of temptation, they may remain faithful to her. . . .

THE SACRED HEART THE SALVATION OF NATIONS[14] (1873)

The social dimension of the Sacred Heart devotion was not restricted to the level of prayer. With a captive pope as the prime model, apostles of the devotion were exhorted to witness to the world Jesus' example, "the great lesson of submission of heart, which was to be the key of salvation" not only for the individual but society as well. Only through such humility could order and unity prevail against the anarchic elements of liberty and autonomy that modernity had unleashed.

. . . Devotion to the Heart of our Divine Lord may be said to be the highest and most complete form of homage to His Sacred Humanity, inasmuch as it involves not only the worship of His material Heart of flesh, but moreover, in a special manner, the worship of that divine love incarnate in His Heart, which was the spring of every word and action of His life. Hence it is to the *Heart* of our Blessed Lord that are to be traced all those marvellous lessons of humility, submission, charity, and all other virtues of which His whole mortal career affords us so brilliant an illustration. In studying that Heart, the great mystery of the Incarnation becomes clearer to us, and the means chosen by the Eternal for the redemption of the world, and manifested in our Lord Jesus Christ, break on us in a new light, indicating at the same time the only means by which society in the present day, the nations, the whole world, will find salvation from the evils that threaten the destruction of authority, of legitimate government, of subordination, both civil and religious—in a word, of all *order,* social and divine.

What, then, are the tendencies characterizing the Devotion to the Heart of the Incarnate God? Before, and above all, *submission.* *"Descendit de coelis . . . et homo factus est."* Such was the first lesson imparted to men by Him Who came to save them. He would teach them that the very foundation of all salvation should consist in and rest upon these two acknowledgements; the supreme sovereignty—the unlimited dominion of God, the absolute nothingness, and consequent utter dependence of the creature upon that infinite Being Who alone *is*. From thence would flow obedience to His laws, submission to those representing His authority, and lastly a spirit of subordination to all legitimately instituted power, inasmuch and in as far as it was in harmony with the order of God.

When the *Pharisees* sought on one occasion to ensnare our Blessed Lord in His speech, in order to prove an accusation against Him of stirring up the people to sedition, they asked Him if it were lawful to pay tribute to *Caesar,* in the hope that He would answer in the negative. But He in Whom dwelled the plenitude of Divine Wisdom, told them to render to *Caesar* the things that were *Caesar's,* and to God the things that were God's. And on another occasion, speaking to His disciples and to the whole assembled multitude, He commanded them to *"observe and do"* whatever the *Scribes* and *Pharisees* should say to them, although they were not to imitate their *works,* and He gave them, as the incentive of their obedience, the simple statement that *"they have sitten on the chair of Moses,"* and thus were the representatives of a legal authority.

If the sublime doctrine of the Heart of Jesus were more fully comprehended, and made to bear upon actual difficulties involving the gravest interests, how different an aspect would the world present at this hour. Whilst, on one hand, we should not witness those servile concessions, made to men in power which ultimately lead to the decadence of all that is great and noble in nations; we should, on the other hand, as a natural consequence of the right appreciation of our Lord's command regarding *Caesar's* due, everywhere see proper submission cheerfully and peacefully rendered in all cases where the exercise of authority does not trench on the rights or honor of Him from Whom all legitimate authority, all created power, emanates.

It is this *true* ideal of order, this happy combination of fidelity to God and His Church, with a spirit of submission (flowing from that fidelity) to rightly constituted visible authority, that is in the present day engaged in a deadly struggle with the spirit of the world, which inebriated with its delusive dreams of false liberty, would spurn all subordination, human and divine, to deliver up its victims, whole nations as well as individuals, to the pitiless tyrant—Revolution.

In consequence of that spirit of self-aggrandizement, which is the marked characteristic of the last few centuries, and which is ever on the increase, have men become happier, has society become less corrupt, have nations progressed in anything save material civilization, which moreover, is of such a character as to resemble *Sybarite* voluptuousness rather than that true civilization which elevates the soul, whilst it refines and cultivates the tastes?

Events will furnish the reply. A glance through the world will testify to the result of the revolt of the human will against God, against His Church, and the religious and civil powers, which are His delegates. The evil has penetrated everywhere. From the revolt against God and His Church has followed, as a natural consequence, a depreciation in the minds of men, of all visible authority. They chafe beneath its pressure, and are restless in their anxiety to cast off its yoke. Hence the fire of revolutionary spirit which is devastating the world—in some nations blazing out openly, laying waste all with its ruthless flames—in others smouldering as a volcano, ready to burst forth at any moment. To the same spirit may be traced the wreck of parental and other divinely instituted authority, and the contempt of social relationships in their rightly established order. Never perhaps, was the mass of human misery so great as at the present day. Ties which heretofore were held sacred are now disregarded; children revolt against parents and subjects against superiors, whilst the sinister aim of the people, who would endeavor to overthrow ancient institutions, together with the aristocracy of nations, is but, under the subtle and seductive name of liberty, to drag down utterly all that savors of superiority or of authority, and to wrest all power to themselves.

To the success of their project the church presents a formidable obstacle, inasmuch as she is the divinely appointed upholder of authority, and uncompromisingly teaches the great lessons of subordination which her Divine Head came down from Heaven to impart, and which He has left her the mission of teaching and preserving until the end of time. Hence, the Church of Jesus Christ is the first object of the hatred of all those whose doctrine is absolute independence, and whose motto is *"Non Serviam."* They proclaim themselves the benefactors of humanity; but how can that system render men happier, freer, or greater which is the very antithesis of the doctrine of Jesus Christ?

Submission, therefore, is the first lesson which the Heart of Jesus reveals to the world as a means of its salvation. The second all-important lesson in that school of divine wisdom is *unity*—that immense and pressing necessity of the age—that power which the enemies of God have appreciated more quickly than His friends, and which they have lost no time in turning to their own diabolical purposes. Truly, *"the children of this world are wiser in their generation than the children of light."*

Our Blessed Lord, one day when he was confuting the Pharisees, said these memorable words—*"Every kingdom divided against itself shall be made desolate,"* (Matt, xii) and the truth contained in His declaration has been but too abundantly manifested throughout succeeding ages. As by disunion the kingdom totters, the house falls, the family becomes desolate—in a word, as disunion is the signal of approaching ruin, so *unity* is the source, the bulwark, and the element of strength and of ultimate success, provided always that God *is in the midst*. The unity of the church is one of her glorious and distinctive marks. Heresies have arisen, and the heresiarchs who have originated them have fallen off as dead branches, powerless in their disunion; but the Church herself remains firm and pure and beautiful as when, eighteen hundred years ago, her Divine Founder first breathed upon her His Holy Spirit, with the promise of His abiding Presence until the consummation of ages. This unity was, again, the object of the prayers of the Heart of Jesus just before the solemn hour of His mortal life. It is the prayer of His Heart in *Heaven* now, the prayer which is ever mounting to the throne of God from the same Heart, incessantly immolating Itself in the midst of us upon our altars. And what has been the result of that divine and ceaseless Prayer? The Oneness of the church which changes not; the union amongst themselves of all those who have practically learnt to know His Heart, to desire the advancement of Its interests, and to clothe themselves with Its Spirit, and their appreciation of all that *tends* to unity, the first essential to which is the rejection of that pride of heart from whence every evil proceeds for society, for nations, for the whole world; for it must be logically evident that that which is injurious for individual men, and destructive to their interests, temporal as well as spiritual, must be so equally for mankind collectively, and *vice versa*. Hence it is that *individual* sanctification or degeneration exercises either so beneficial or so fatal an influence over entire nations. What can be more terribly manifest than the truth of this assertion at the present day?

Unity, then, in higher and nobler principles, in fidelity to the laws of God and His Church—union of Christian hearts in the one great cause, and directing all their energies and their various gifts to the attainment of a common good, is the second means which our Lord Jesus Christ indicates for the salvation of the human race; that union which He demanded for His brethren of His *Heavenly* Father, and which He declared should be the likeness of that existing between the Father and Himself.

But, it may be said, all this affects but those who profess themselves believers in the living voice of the church and in the special application which the Church makes of the teaching afforded by the Life of the Son of God, and perhaps but a limited number even amongst *them*. Our Lord Jesus Christ established His Church for the salvation of *all mankind*. *"Going, therefore, teach ye all nations,"* was His command to His Apostles; therefore the voice of the church is destined to reach every race and to penetrate every region. She disclaims all nationality, she is the mistress and teacher of truth for the whole world, and, consequently, the acceptance or the rejection of that teaching is felt by each nation, as it is by each separate soul, not only relatively to their religious tendencies, but, moreover, in their social relationships.

The *animus* which prompts the outcry of "Down with the Church! Away with priests!" is synonymous with that which causes that other cry to resound throughout the land, and which is the herald of revolution, a country's deadliest enemy, "Away with the crown, Down with the *noblesse!*" And the men who resist the authority of the one are of the same school, are instigated by the same spirit, as those who originate revolt and subsequent mutiny in armies, who set up the institution of mob-rule in opposition to legitimately constituted civil power, and who dictate the unreasonable, exorbitant, and menacing demands made by workman upon employer. . . .

. . . the Church, so persecuted, so outraged, even by those who should be ready to shed their blood in her defense, is and will be for ever, the divinely constituted guardian of Truth, the only real exponent of the great lessons imparted by the Heart of God, when walking amongst men He became the living manifestation of the Eternal Presence.

The Church alone has comprehended those lessons, and has illustrated them in her countless Saints, and it is at once the duty and the prerogative of faithful *Catholics* to shed forth their lustre still at the present day, and so to *prove* the beneficial influence which the Church exerts over nations. There is not a single *Catholic* who has not responsibility under this relationship, and not one who may not, nay does not, contribute his part, either to extend the influence of the Church or to draw down upon her teaching the contempt of her enemies. Let them, then, exhibit to the world that the same *mind is in them "which was also in Christ Jesus,"* Who *"humbled Himself—becoming obedient,"* in other words, taught the great lesson of submission of heart, which was to be the key of salvation for the human race. Let them manifest that the spirit of that divine Heart is upon them, and influences them in all their relations, social as well as religious. They who have become more fully penetrated with that spirit, and who strive despite their human passions, to reproduce the Life of the Son of God in themselves (and this is a work which can only be either appreciated or attained by the docile children of that Church, in whose midst the Heart of Jesus actually lives and still breathes forth His spirit)—they it is, we say, who will prove the most loyal subjects, the most conscientious members of society in every grade and condition. . . .

. . . Let us pray in union with the Heart incessantly immolating Itself in the midst of us upon our altars for the salvation of the entire world, and avail ourselves of every means presented to us of drawing closer the bonds which it is our Blessed Lord's desire should unite all Christian hearts. Like the coral reefs, which appear divided indeed above the blue waters of the ocean, but whose roots are, as we are told, so entwined together in the fathomless depths below as to form, as it were, but one vast impenetrable forest, so should it be with the faithful children of the church—the friends of the Heart of Jesus. Separated indeed by race, by country, by condition; wide apart as their lots may be cast, all may and should be united as one great family in the Heart of Him Who demanded for them that union in Himself which He knew would prove their strength in the evil day, and form the element of their power and influence, upon the world.

Let us then, we repeat it, pray, never losing sight of the remembrance that, whilst we pray, it belongs to us by our works to show forth the teaching of the Heart of Jesus, that thus upon us devolves the responsibility of extending the Kingdom of God on earth, and so of causing all peoples to praise Him and all nations to rejoice in His salvation.

NOTES

1. *The Messenger of the Sacred Heart of Jesus* (April, 1866), iii–x.

2. Henri Ramière, S.J. (1821–1884), French theologian and founder of *Le Messager du Sacré-Coeur de Jésus*.

3. *Messenger* (June, 1868), 231–238.

4. "To Our Readers," *Messenger* (January, 1867), 3.

5. "The Hopes of the Church," *Messenger* (January, 1868), 8.

6. *Messenger* (September, 1869), 413–414.

7. *Messenger* (January, 1868), 41–43. This article was reprinted from the Roman journal, *Il Divin Salvatore*.

8. "Maxims for Julius."

9. "Love God, my soul, and onward!"

10. "Here by the crypts of the martyrs, sleeps in peace, Julius Watts Russell, Son of Michael, An Englishman of noble birth, who, while nobly fighting for the See of Peter, fell in the battle of Mentana, On the 3rd of November in the year 1867. Aged 17 years and 10 months. Young Soldier of Christ, Live in God."

11. *Messenger* (August, 1869), 323–325.

12. *Messenger* (October, 1869), 455–457. Adapted from *Le Messager du Sacré-Coeur de Jésus* (September, 1869), 201–204.

13. *Messenger* (December, 1869), 548–549. Reprinted from *Le Messager du Sacré-Coeur de Jésus* (November, 1869), 338–340.

14. *Messenger* (January, 1873), 1–11.

XI

EDWARD HOLKER WELCH:
THE PURITAN AS JESUIT

Welch, of a Boston merchant family that traced its roots to the 17th century, was a graduate of the Harvard class of 1840. In Europe for graduate studies at Heidelberg and then Berlin, he met the Anglican priest Frederick William Faber. Faber, a prominent member of the Oxford movement who was himself slouching toward Rome, proved a crucial influence in the conversion of Welch, whom Faber had found "as wild a piece of protestantism as either the Commonwealth of Massachusetts or the university of Heidelberg c[oul]d well manufacture."[1] Welch was received into the Church (in Boston by Bishop Fitzpatrick) in 1845, some months before Faber made his more celebrated entry. After earning LL.B. and M.A. degrees at Harvard, Welch returned to Europe to prepare for the priesthood, first with the Sulpicians in France and then with the Jesuits in Italy. As he approached ordination he decided to apply for the Society of Jesus. The writings of a French Jesuit, Xavier de Ravignan (1795–1858), had first stirred in him the idea. Another important influence was a Harvard classmate and convert, Joseph Coolidge Shaw, who had gone to Europe with Welch, but under Faber's guidance had made the acquaintance of English Jesuits in Rome, and eventually entered the Society in Frederick, as a Roman Catholic priest. Shortly before Welch followed Shaw to Frederick in February 1851, the latter wrote his friend: "Ah Holker, when you have experienced the sweets of religion and the real easiness and lightness of the burden and yoke of Christ when fairly taken up as it is in His Society, you will say what the Queen of Saba said of the wisdom and greatness of Solomon, that the half had not been told her. . . . "[2] Shaw died of tuberculosis later that year. Welch seemed determined by his own life to prove the truth of Shaw's words.

Serenely austere in manner (he "seemed never to have altogether

298

shaken off . . . his Puritan stock," a contemporary remembered),[3] *he be-lieved strongly that the exterior was the reflection of the soul. Exactitude in keeping the rules of the Society was a major sign, to Welch, that the soul was sound. Yet there was a liberality about him that prevented such strict observance from becoming prissy or censorious. "Two things you still want," Faber wrote him in response to the news of his conversion, "growth in grace & perseverance in grace."[4] Long before his death, many persons in Boston and beyond felt that Welch had more than met Faber's challenge.*

SERMONS[5]

Twenty-one of Welch's Jesuit years were spent at the Church of the Im-maculate Conception in Boston. As a prominent convert of a prestigious family, his sermons naturally attracted many persons, including non-Cath-olics. But if curiosity drew them, his own power in the pulpit kept them returning. For many Episcopalians and Unitarians it led to conversion. Welch himself became known in Boston as the "receiver-general" for the large number of converts he brought into the Church.[6]

Afflictions (1863)

Welch gave this "exordium," as he labeled it, on the feast of the Holy In-nocents in 1863 at the Immaculate Conception Church in Boston. Welch's words would have had special meaning for his audience in the depths of that winter, the third of the war with no end in sight for the mutual slaughter. But in the apologia of suffering which he makes, war is but the intensifi-cation of the human condition with its "history of disappointments, cares & afflictions." For the Christian such sorrows are occasions for redemp-tion. In God's dispensation, even the horrors of civil war are the season for his special visitation.

> God can give us no stronger proof of his love than in sending them. We can give Him no stronger proof of our love than by making a holy use of them.

Gospel. Matth. 2. 13-18—Text v. 18 "A voice in Rama was heard lamen-tation and great mourning: Raechel bewailing her children and would not be comforted because they are not."

It was thus that the mothers of Bethlehem wept over their infant chil-dren torn from their arms, and cruelly put to death by the soldiers of Herod. And had they not cause for lamentation? Scarcely have these Innocent victims begun to live; and they are deprived of life. Pressed so tenderly but a moment since to the maternal breast, shielded so carefully from every danger, now they are rudely seized by the tyrant's mercenaries, and dashed to the ground, or pierced with swords. Who would have remained unmoved at hearing their cries, or at witnessing the agony of their broken-hearted mothers?

And yet, B.C., those sufferings come from God, nor could He have given these blessed Infants a greater mark of His love than in permitting their cruel enemy to put them to death. He abhorred indeed the crime of the Jewish Prince, but in His tenderness for the babes of Bethlehem He willed the effect of that crime. Yes! never would the Church have treasured the memory of these Holy Innocents, if the sword of Herod had not been stained with their blood. Had their lives been spared, few of them perhaps would have remained faithful in God's service, many of them, it is possible,[7] would have become His enemies. The never-fading flowers of Paradise, the roses of martyrdom and the lilies of virginity encircle now their brows only because their blood was shed in hatred of the name of J.C. In heaven they follow the lamb withersoever he goeth, they drink of the waters of life, and God Himself is their execeeding great reward, only because they suffered, though unconsciously, for Christ. Hail first-born of Christian martyrs! Hail blessed Innocents, meet companions for the Infant Saviour! thrice happy were you in your sufferings. A momentary pain has purchased for you never-ending felicity. The crown, which others attain only by long years of toil, you have won in the very dawn of life by the agony of an instant. Those sufferings which seemed so cruel God sent you, that you might be united to Him more speedily in Heaven, and might know Him more perfectly throughout Eternity.

B.C., it is the same with the sufferings & afflictions we are called upon to endure. In our heavenly Father's house there is a place prepared for each of us, and that we may obtain it Providence sends us those trials & sorrows which weigh upon us so heavily. "Our present tribulation," says St. Paul, "which is momentary & light worketh for us above measure exceedingly an eternal weight of glory." Like the Holy Innocents we are happy in being called upon by Providence to suffer: but more happy are we even than those blessed Infants, because in submitting as we should to these afflictions we give to God an unequivocal proof of Our love to Him and of our conformity[8] to His holy will.—God can give us no stronger proof[9] of His love than by sending us afflictions, we on our part can give God no stronger[10] proof of our devotion than by making a holy use of[11] afflictions.[12] Such is the subject of the discourse to which I invite your attention.

I. God, can give us no greater proof of His love than by sending us afflictions—I am aware that this proposition may seem false or exaggerated but I trust to be able to convince you of its truth. What, you will ask, does God show us His love taking from us those whom are dear to us,[13] in reducing us to poverty, in depriving us of health, in permitting the wicked to persecute us, in making our very existence sad and irksome to us? Yes, B.C., and we shall find that all the great servants of God have been tried by many calamities and the great Ap[ostle] tells us 2 Tim 3.12 that ''all who will live piously in CJ shall suffer persecution;'' and again he says Heb 12.6 ''Whom the Lord loveth he chastiseth: and he scourgeth every one whom he receiveth.'' The hard-heartedness & cruelty of men of which we complain so much he indeed only permits but the effect which that cruelty produces[,] the sorrow which weighs us to the earth He wills for our greater good. Every calamity then that can possibly afflict us though it seem to come from our enemies comes from Him and is a proof of His love for us, for by these afflictions he would (1.) draw us from created things (2.) he would lead us to a closer union with Himself, he would (3.) by lighter pains in this world spare us from penalties far more grievous in the world to come.

In the 1st place then God by these afflictions would draw us from the love of created things. Alas, my C B, who is there of us that has not to lament that the world and its vanities have still so much power over him. What we see and handle[14] seems near & real to us, but spiritual[15] goods are invisible and distant. In sin we see created things, instead of raising our minds to the Creator[;] we are inclined to rest in them and to love them for their own sakes. God has left vestiges of Himself in all the works of His hand, therefore all these works have something good & beautiful and we make them the object of our love, forgetting the infinite beauty of the Exemplar & prototype. ''The Creatures of God'' says the H[oly] S[cripture] (Wisdom 14,11 [) '']are turned to an abomination, and a temptation to the souls of men, and a snare to the feet of the unwise.'' As the gift of an absent friend reminds us of him so ought everything that we behold in nature, everything that happens to us or surrounds us imprint more deeply in our hearts the thought of God & fill us with new love & gratitude towards Him. But alas! as the poor heathen bows before his idol[16] & fancies it the Being which can reward or punish him, so *practically* at least we seek our happiness in things finite and created. The poor slave of sensuality seeks felicity in brutal pleasures, the covetous man[17] in wealth, the ambitious man in worldly honors. God who loves us because we are His creatures and who sees things in their true light in relation that is to eternity and not time would heal this disorder and separate us from that object which has taken His place in our hearts. He sends us afflictions. One who was dearer to us than life itself is snatched from us. ''A voice in Rama was heard lamentation and great mourning: Rachel bewailing her children, and would not be comforted because they are not.'' We are suddenly deprived of the fruits of long years of industry & toil. That young man just entering the world with every[18] advantage of rank & fortune, while he is raising the cup of pleasure to his life is suddenly prostrated by some insidious disease, deprived of health & strength, and obliged for the rest of his days to watch with all an invalid's care over the poor remains of life—others are suddenly tossed from some heighth of power to which they had climbed with so much toil: others again are reduced to such poverty that they can scarcely satisfy the demands of those who cry to them for bread, while the good name & honor of others is tarnished by the breath of calumny. Are these afflictions? Yes! B C. but afflictions sent us by God in His love. He would separate us from those created things, which have become a temptation to our souls and a snare to our feet. The idol which occupied His temple has now been removed. In luxury & pleasure, in affluence & honors[,] in health & strength, in the company of those we[19] loved[,] we[20] heard not His voice speaking to us,[21] we placed[22] a barrier between Him & our[23] hearts, and now He has swept away these obstacles. Like a kind physician who gives us bitter medicines to overcome some latent disease or like a skilful surgeon who hesitates not to use the knife that he may remove the diseased from the sound flesh, so God with more than a father's love has removed from us what was working our ruin.

2. But God would not only separate us from created things, He wishes[24] that men should love Him with their whole heart & soul & mind. And thus again the afflictions He sends us are a proof of His love; he sends them to us in order to bring about a close union with Himself. When we see that no earthly balm can soothe our pain, we turn to God for assistance. Amidst the ruins of everything that the world can give,[25] we learn to value what can never change. There are some who use as it were a holy violence to enter heaven, generous & noble souls who never forget the great end for which they were created, and who seek always God's honor & glory. But others again only enter heaven because, so to speak, they are forced to enter it. Never would they have left the broad road of destruction if Providence had not flanked it with a thousand thorns. Never would they have thought of God, if His judgements had not pressed heavily upon them. Never would they have sought that enduring peace & happiness which results from a life of virtue,[26] if the pleasure they sought in the world had not been changed into gall & bitterness. It was thus with the ancient Israelites, as the royal prophet tells us, (Ps 77.34,35) "When he slew them, then they sought him: and they returned and came to him early in the morning. And they remembered that God was their helper and the most High their Redeemer." It was thus with Manasses king of Judah, whose long course of impiety and whose final repentence the S. Scriptures record. Raised while still a child to the throne of his ancestors, he did evil before the Lord, imitated all the abom-

inations of the heathen princes, and even set up a graven and a molten statue in the temple at Jerusalem. But his sins have not exhausted the patience & mercy of the Most High. The captains of the army of the king of Assyria take him prisoner[27] and carry him bound with fetters[28] to Babylon. Who that saw this sudden change of fortune would not have deemed it a great affliction? Yesterday a king, and to-day in chains. But it is the[29] tender love of God who would convert[30] this obdurate sinner that sends this calamity. "And after that he was in distress" the inspired text adds 2 Paral[ipomena][31] 33.12 "he prayed to the Lord his God: and did penance exceedingly before the God of his fathers." Oh my C B is not a true change of heart purchased most cheaply at the price of every human affliction: With[32] what gratitude does that penitent prance on heaven and look back on God's kindness & love in stripping him for a time[33] of his earthly kingdom that he might make him possessor of an inheritance incorruptible, undefiled and that fadeth not away.

3. Finally in the afflictions which God sends[34] us are a proof of His love[35] since He is willing to receive[36] them although light & temporary as a satisfaction for our sins and desires thereby[37] to spare us at least in part punishment far more grievous beyond the grave. Who is there that is not often[38] unfaithful in the discharge of his duty? "In many things we all offend" says S James (3.2); our best actions are accompanied by many imperfections. For these innumerable faults the justice of God requires satisfaction; but like the kindness of fathers he imposes only the lightest punishment. He wishes that after death we should speedily be united to Him. He wishes to save us from that dreadful prison-house from whence no one can be released until he has paid the last farthing. Is it not then an act of His mercy and love[39] to punish thus mildly in this world the sins & faults of his servants?

My C.B. I look around me and methinks I see[40] upon the countenances of many who hear me[41] the trace of some secret care. I behold[42] a mother who is filled with anxiety as she thinks of her sons exposed to the privations, the sufferings and the dangers of war. I see a father[43] who has been deprived already of the comfort & support of his old age. I see other parents[44] still more to be pitied whose children have forgotten their duty to God and to them, only[45] mock at the[46] pious exhortations they hear, and[47] have commenced a course of disorder[48] & profligacy which must end in the destruction of body and soul. There is a widow who is struggling to support her children, but her protracted labors hardly give them bread and she feels that her own health is failing and that she must soon leave them to the mercy of strangers. Here is a husband who has just followed to the grave one who was dearer to him than all the world besides, here is another[49] who has been accustomed to every comfort, but who in his old age is reduced to penury,

here is one[50] who young as he is feels that the disease which must soon
terminate his days[51] is preying upon his vitals. The life of almost every man
is the history of disappointment, cares & afflictions. But Oh, my C Hearer,
remember that this cross which seems so heavy has been laid on your shoulders by your father in heaven. It is not the malice of men which persecutes
you, it is not accident or chance which have brought upon you these sufferings (for accident & chance are[52] mere names) but it is one who loves
you.[53] He who could give you the riches of this world if it were for your
advantage; he could spare the life of those you love; he could heal at once
that secret grief—but he wishes to separate you from those created things
that have heretofore taken his place in your heart; he wishes to draw you
nearer to Him and make you advance with giant strides in His service; He
wishes to give you an opportunity of expiating the[54] sins of which you have
been guilty;[55] it remains for us now to show that in making a holy use of
our afflictions we give to God the clearest mark of our devotion towards
Him.

II. It is impossible for man to give any stronger proof of his love for another
than by enduring sufferings for his sake. "Greater love than this no man
hath, says our divine Lord (John 15.13) than that a man lay down his life
for his friends."[56] By suffering for another we show him that we love him
not for the advantages that result to ourselves from his friendship, but for
his own merits. It proves that our[57] affection for him is disinterested. Now
in making a holy use of the afflictions which div. Providence sends us, in
submitting to them with patience, with cheerfulness and with joy, in suffering for God in one word, we show Him that we love Him for Himself.
As the author of our being, the[58] preserver of our lives and the bountiful
dispenser of every good we enjoy, God merits our constant gratitude and
love. But He is infinite in every perfection; He is truth and beauty & goodness; and therefore in Himself, and independently of all his favors to us, he
merits all the love of our hearts. If by an impossible supposition we could
expect nothing from His liberality, we should love him for himself. Now
in bearing with patience our sufferings we show him something of this disinterested love. It is no longer[59] his favors that win our hearts for his hand
now weighs heavily upon us, but it is the perfection of his nature that draws
us[60] to Him. How many love God for the prosperity they enjoy, the favors
they receive, the peace and tranquility they possess. But when He[61] seems
to hide his face from them, when the sky is overcast, and storms lower in
the distance, they are troubled[,] their confidence in God is shaken, their
love to Him grows cold, and they are tempted to exclaim as the psalmist
tells us "Then have I in vain justified my heart & washed my hands among
the innocent" (Ps. 72[73].13). Hence when Almighty God pointed out to

the fallen angel the virtue and integrity of his servant Job, 1:9,10,11. "Satan answering, said: Doth Job fear God *in vain?* Hast thou not made a fence for him and his house, and all his substance round about, blessed the works of his hands, and his possession hath increased in the earth? But stretch forth thy hand a little, and touch all that he hath, and see if he blesseth thee not to thy face—'' The fidelity of this great saint was only manifested in his afflictions. Deprived of his children and all his possessions, covered from head to foot with grievous ulcers, & sitting on the ground he cried out (v. 10) "if we have received good things at the hand of God why should we not receive evil? Let us B.C. strive in like manner to make a holy use of our afflictions in suffering for God[.] Let us give Him a proof of our disinterested love.

2. Again in suffering for Him[62] we show Him a generous courageous affection.[63] He who truly loves anyone desires the good[,] the advantage of the Being he loves—rejoices for this end to undertake great & difficult enterprises. Now as God in acting must always have in view an end worthy of Himself, those afflictions which weigh upon us[64] so heavily but which He wills must in some manner promote[65] his honor & glory. Should we not then[66] rejoice in these afflictions[?] As the eye of the soldier dying on the field of battle gleams with joy as he hears the shouts of victory bursting from the lips of his comrades[67] and as he forgets in the thought of his country's triumph[68] that his own life-blood is ebbing and ceases to feel his pain, so should the generous Christian rejoice in his afflictions because the glory of God is thereby promoted & His holy will accomplished.—Again in suffering in this manner[69] we then[70] make the most perfect[71] sacrifice we can to His divine majesty. We praise & honor him who gives of his substance to feed the poor, who devotes his time to the care of the sick, to the instruction of the ignorant. But to sacrifice the will is far harder than to give up a portion of our time or wealth. The affliction too which we at present labor under always seems to us the one for which we are the least prepared[72] and the most insupportable. In receiving it then with patience and cheerfulness we show the[73] generosity of our affection.

Finally in suffering for God we show a love most like that of our divine Saviour towards his heavenly Father. He came into this world to suffer & die in obedience to that Father's command. From the first moment of his ineffable conception the whole series of his sufferings was present to his eyes. A gracious Providence hides from our view the calamity that to-morrow may bring with it and hence the joy of to-day is unmingled with pain. But from the first moment of his mortal life the bitter chalice of his passion was presented to the life of the Infant Saviour & even then he began to drink it. "It is impossible," as S. Paul tells us, "that with the blood of oxen & goats sins should be taken away" (Heb 10.4)[.] Christ therefore took upon

himself our nature that he might suffer all that his heavenly father ordained:
"coming into the world he saith (v 5) Sacrifice and oblation thou wouldest
not, but a body thou hast fitted to me: holocausts for sin did not please thee:
Then said I, Behold I come: in the head of the book it is written of me that
I should do thy will O God."[74] And did the Redeemer ever falter, did he
ever take back the oblation he had made? Once when he had foretold his
sufferings to his Apostles & one of them[75] had said to him (Matth 15 22)
"Lord be it far from thee: this shall not be unto thee" our Lord immediately
rebuked him." "Go after me Satan" he said "thou art a scandal unto me:
because thou savorest not the things that are of God but the things that are
of men" as if he would have said, from a mistaken attachment to me and
in viewing any sufferings with mere human feelings thou placest thyself in
opposition to my will and art really my adversary. Again on the night in
which he was betrayed when the same apostle drew a sword and strove to
defend his master, the div Redeemer said to him "The chalice which my
Father hath given me shall I not drink it?" S. John 18.11 Would you have
me refuse any portion of these sufferings which my Father hath sent me and
which are sweet to me as coming from him. Accordingly my C. B. in receiving with resignation the afflictions which befall us we walk in the footsteps of our dear Lord, we show our Father in heaven a love like in some
degree to his.[76]

Precious then, B.C. are the sufferings which Providence sends us.
Sometimes when we have reflected on all that God has done for us, and on
our ingratitude to Him, have we not seemed to hear an interior voice inviting
us to suffer something for His sake, to imitate in some degree at least His
saints, all of whom were ingenious in devising mortifications? But the afflictions which His Providence sends us will become, if we make a holy use
of them far more meritorious and more pleasing to Him than any self-im-
posed penance. In our misfortunes then we will never again complain; it is
God who sends them, God who would render us worthy of that[77] crown of
surpassing beauty which He has prepared for each one of us in heaven,
God[78] who knows us, and who will never lay a burthen upon us that it is
beyond our strength to bear—Far less should we envy the prosperity & happiness of the children of the world. They seek what the world proposes to
them wealth & pleasure and fame & power. But alas! their prosperity is but
short-lived, & their happiness is only apparent.[79] Too soon their life will
be over, and their momentary felicity will give place to never ending regret.
"I have seen the wicked highly exalted and lifted up as the cedars of Libanus!["] the Psalmist says, ["] and I passed by, and lo he was not["]: and
["]I sought him and his place was not found["] (Ps. 36: 35,36)[80]

We shall never be called upon to shed our blood for Christ like the
Blessed Infants whose feast we celebrate to-day, but every one of us, at

some period of his life will have to endure trials of some kind[81]—the death of those very near to us, illness, the loss of worldly goods, the ingratitude or misconduct of those we love and for whom we have labored. Whatever be the misfortunes sent us by Providence, let us bear them with perfect resignation to the divine will, remembering what the apostle tells us in his second Ep[istle]. to the Cor[inthians] (4.17) ''That which is at present momentary and light of our tribulation, worketh for us above measure exceedingly an eternal weight of glory[.]''

16th Sunday after Pentecost: Homily upon the Gospel (1871)

Welch's preaching, unlike the Jesuit tradition in America, was consistently based on the scriptural texts of the liturgy of the day rather than on catechetical themes. It was also very concrete. He recalled all too painfully his boyhood Sundays in Episcopalian churches, where he was subjected to interminable sermons that were relentlessly abstract. Sleep was his usual refuge from this torture. Welch's own sermons were long, but his pointed illustrations and challenging topics kept his congregations' attention, even though his style was unemotional. In this homily, given in Boston in 1871, he explored the relationship of the letter of the law and its spirit in the life of a Christian.

Gosp.   St. Luke XIV 1-11. ''and it came to pass when Jesus went into the house of one of the chief of the Pharisees on the sabbath day to eat bread that they watched him. text.

1. The incident in our Lord's life which we have just read in St. Luke's gospel, and which is related only by him, seems to have taken place in Galilee, probably in the 3d year of the Savior's public ministry, and when he was about leaving that province for Jerusalem. Jesus is invited to take bread[,] that is[,] to dine with a distinguished Pharisee, and he accepts the invitation. The company appears to have been numerous, and was composed of Pharisees and doctors of the law[,] that is[,] of the most influential persons of the neighborhood. The feast was on the 7th or sabbath-day, the day of rest: for though the Jews from the time of the captivity observed this day with great exactness, they did not deem an entertainment of this kind incompatible with its observance. On the contrary as the sabbath was a day of joy they considered it a peculiarly fitting time for extending hospitality to their friends. The meals were indeed cold for the Pharisaic law forbad the lighting of a fire on the day of rest, but nothing prevented their being abundant and of the choicest kinds.

2. With regard to the motives which induced the Pharisee to invite our Lord[82] on this occasion we are left in ignorance. Had he[83] a real veneration

for him, and did he believe him to be indeed the Messiah or at least a prophet sent from God? Or was he yet undecided with regard to our Lord's character, and was he only seeking an opportunity[84] to become better acquainted with him, and to be able to form a judgement with regard to him? Or like the other Pharisees was he already his bitter enemy, and under the pretense of doing him[85] honor had he only invited the Savior[86] in order to find something in his words or actions which might serve as an accusation against him[?] In the absence of all[87] proof to the contrary we may hope and believe that he shared not the prejudices of his sect, that he had a real esteem for the Savior, and that he had invited [him] to his house to evince his respect towards him: and certain may we be that if this was indeed the case, he who was invited rewarded his host a thousand fold for his kindness and hospitality: for the single dinner given to the Redeemer that blessed Pharisee is even now eating bread at the master's table in the kingdom[88] of heaven and is to enjoy the sweet company of Jesus throughout Eternity.

3. But whatever may have been the sentiments of the host the sacred historian leaves us no doubt with regard to those which animated the greater number of his guests. He tells us, as we have seen that "they watched" the Savior, that is to say[,] they were filled with malice towards him, they closely observed him that they might find something to condemn in his discourse or in his actions.[89] Alas for them that they did not watch the Redeemer with a different spirit, observe him that they might imitate him, listen to him that they might catch each word of his heavenly doctrine and impress it on their minds, and that in thus beholding[90] his virtues they might have learned to love him, and have chosen him for their guide and model.[91] It was for their sake to win them if possible to himself that the Savior accepts the invitation today. He read their most secret thoughts, and he knew the malice with which they were filled towards him, but he came to seek and to save the lost sheep of the house of Israel, and he will not neglect the opportunity to do this which presents itself now. He foresaw the miracle he was to perform before their eyes and the proof he would thus be able to give them of his divine mission, he foresaw too that on this occasion without exposing them or appearing[92] to blame their conduct he could present[93] to their view their own secret malady and thus lead them (if only they would be led) to come to him for relief. Such were the reasons that induced him, who went about doing good, and whose meat and drink it was to perform his Father's will to accept this invitation and to come into the very midst of his enemies.

4. The company has assembled, and while they were waiting to be called to dinner a man afflicted with the dropsy enters the room and approaches the Savior.[94] Had he followed the Savior even to this festival hoping that he who had healed so many others would restore him to health, or

had the Pharisees our Lord's enemies called him there in the expectation that what actually did happen[95] would take place, that our Lord would at once deliver him from his malady and that thus they would be able to accuse the Savior of breaking the Sabbath? ''And Jesus answering spoke to the Lawyers & Pharisees saying'' To what does he answer? This form of words is nearly a Hebrew idiom equivalent to our English phrase [''']he began to speak['']. And yet with Venerable Bede we may say he answered their thoughts; he showed them that he saw clearly what was passing in their secret souls, for the Son of God ''needed not'' as St. John tells us in his gospel (2.25) that any should give testimony of man, for he knew what was in man, and in thus answering their secret interrogations, in thus reading their thoughts he performs a greater miracle than that which they are soon to behold with the eyes of the body. Will they still remain obdurate, still remain the slaves of prejudice and refuse to acknowledge the Savior? Yes, B.C., because there is no grace which we cannot resist. He who is constantly inviting us to serve and love Him will not *force* us to be His friends. ''He has left[96] man in the hand of his own counsel[,''] the Scriptures tell us[. ''] Before him is life and death, good & evil: that which he shall chose [sic] shall be given him'' (Eccle 15. 14,18)[.]

    5. And Jesus answering spoke to the lawyers & Pharisees, saying: ''Is it lawful[97] to heal on the Sabbath-day[?] Who of the simple-minded and ignorant people, *had they been asked this question would have found it difficult to answer*. If the Sabbath of the old law was a symbol of the Creator's rest after he had made the world is not this Infinite Being ever active, ever showering his favors upon all? Who preserves at each instant our lives, and thus constantly renews as it were that act by which he called us into being? Who upholds the mighty frame of the universe? who in concurring with his creatures enables them to produce those effects which we attribute to them, for instance that it may fill my lungs with the food I take that it may strengthen my body, with the water I drink that it may quench my thirst. The rest of God is not inactivity. ''My Father worketh until now['']; our Lord said on another occasion to the Jews when they persecuted him for healing on the Sabbath: [''']My Father worketh until now, and I work['''] (S John V.17)[98]

    6. But the question which the unlearned in their simplicity could so easily have answered these doctors of the law find it impossible to reply to. What response could they have made? Had they answered that it was lawful to heal on the sabbath-day they would have approved beforehand an action which they were determined to condemn: they would have deprived themselves of an opportunity they eagerly sought after[,] of bringing an accusation against our Lord. On the other hand it seemed too absurd to answer that it was unlawful, and they might easily foresee the difficulties in which

they would be involved by such a reply. Accordingly as the gospel tells us they held their peace. Where the truth was clear as day to all who were willing to see it, these doctors of the law remain in utter darkness. Does not the same thing happen in our day? How many are led astray by a false science, and find difficulties where none exist save for those who wish to find them? There is no theory however baseless even that which denies any essential difference between man and the brute beast which finds not favor in the eyes of these sages, but blinded by prejudices they refuse to admit the teachings of revealed religion, the infallible authority of Christ's Church. Ah my C.B. if we would see the truth we must ask light from on high, we must beg[99] Him who created our minds to remove from them prejudice and error, we must humble ourselves in His presence whose vision extends infinitely beyond the narrow limits of our reason, thus only can we hope to see those truths which the proud[100] who trust in themselves can never find: "I give praise to Thee, O Father Lord of heaven & earth," said the divine Redeemer[, "]because thou hast hidden these things from the wise & prudent, & hast revealed them to little ones" Mat. 11.25.

7. The Pharisees can not or will not answer our Lord['s] question, but he taking the man who had the dropsy[,] the Evangelist continues[,] healed him and sent him away. Why does Jesus take[101] the sick man, that is[,] touch him with his hands[?] a word would have been sufficient to restore him to health. He would show us, St. Cyril of Alexandria[102] answers, that even his sacred flesh on account of its union with the divine nature had a vivifying power[.] Thus on a previous occasion,[103] when a great number of sick persons came to hear him and to recover their health, "all the multitude" as our Evangelist tells us sought to touch him, for virtue went out from him, and healed all (S Luke 6.19)[.] He healed not only as God, but as the Son of man, his human nature was the instrument which the divine nature made use of.

8. And observe, B.C. that[104] before the sick man had asked for health before he had uttered a single word[,] the Savior heals him. How many favors we receive from God for which we never ask. With what unbounded liberality he supplies our wants before we are aware that they exist. Is[105] not this the model of that charity which we should exercise towards those who stand in need of our assistance. Will you wait till your aid is asked for? But there are many, and they are often the most deserving, who will never ask for it. They have perhaps seen better days and to[106] make known their poverty and want known would be to them more bitter than death; natural diffidence and modesty shuts their mouths; and renders it impossible for them[107] to expose themselves to those cruel repulses which the poor[108] so often meet with. Ye who love the divine Savior and who would imitate his conduct, look around you. Do not wait till the poor come to solicit your

bounty[;] go in search of them. Treat them with such kindness and respect, that they will no longer conceal from you their necessities[109] and then help them in so far as you [can] but with a tenderness that will not wound them.

9. Our Savior heals the dropsical man though he foresees that the Lawyers and Pharisees who are present will disapprove his action, for we are never to abstain from works of charity,[110] however much our conduct may be blamed, never to omit any duty for fear of such judgements and unjust accusations. Little matters it what men think of us, we should labor for God and then their disapproval will not trouble us. But at the same time if we can defend our conduct, if we can show those who blame us that we have done what we ought to have done then the interests of virtue and religion and the obligation[111] we are under of edifying our neighbors require that we should do so. We find accordingly that our Lord had no sooner performed this miracle and healed the sick man than[112] he hastened to justify[113] himself, to show that his conduct was free from blame, and his defence is so simple and at the same time so convincing that only[114] the most obdurate prejudice could refuse to admit it. Which of you, he asks, shall have an ass or an ox fall into a pit: and will not immediately draw him out on the Sabbath-day? If from self-interest lest you should lose an animal of value, or if from that sympathy which we feel even for a brute beast[115] in distress you deem[116] yourself justified in laboring to extricate it from a perilous position even on the day of rest though this can be done only with great difficulty and fatigue[.] Can you with any justice accuse one of breaking the Sabbath if by a single word or a touch of the hand I free on this[117] day a rational being[,] a child of God from a cruel and dangerous malady?["]

10. But unanswerable as was this argument the Jews make no reply. They could not answer him to these things[,] St Luke says. They preserve the truth but they refuse to acknowledge it. We marvel at this[118] obstinate attachment to error. But we[119] have here only an example of the fatal consequences which may ensue if once we allow a single passion to gain the mastery over us. The Pharisees hated our Lord. It is superfluous to say that he gave them no cause for their aversion. He came down from heaven for their salvation as for that of the rest of me. But he found it necessary to expose their hypocrisy[,] their blindness, their superstitious devotion to the letter of the Law while they lost sight of its spirit. And then again his blameless life, his heavenly doctrine, his wonderful miracles drew to him[120] the hearts of the people; gained for[121] him that esteem and veneration which these Pharisees so much coveted, and which to a certain extent they had enjoyed before his coming. The more clearly they saw that their aversion had no grounds, that far from hating him as a successful rival they should have venerated and loved him as a master the more their unjust aversion for him increased so that his virtues to their distorted vision seemed vices, and

truth in his mouth appeared error. In their case[122] it was envy,[123] jealousy[,] hatred which led them to deny the truth. How often since their time[124] have we seen the same sad effect follow from pride or vanity. Have we not sometimes[125] beheld[126] those who had labored long and strenuously for the interests of religion, perhaps some system they had taught was condemned by the Church;—[127]rather than humbly retract[128] their opinions[129] and acknowledge themselves[130] in error, renounce their[131] obedience to her, leave her authority and close to themselves[132] forever the heavenly portals which she alone can open?[133]

11. We see again from the conduct of the Pharisees on this occasion that however holy a practice may be in itself it degenerates to a mere superstition the moment we make all our religion consist[134] in observing it. The Pharisees were not wrong in venerating their Sabbath. The decalogue itself strictly forbad all unnecessary work[,] all secular business on that day. As we have seen the very lighting of a fire for the preparation of food was prohibited[135] by the Mosaic Law. The prophet Jeremiah speaking in the name of God forbids the Jews to carry about burdens on that day and Ezechial numbers the violation of the sabbath[136] among the great public crimes of his countrymen. We know too from our own day of rest the Lord's day which in the Christian Church has taken the place of the ancient Jewish Sabbath how advantageous[137] for the minds and body[138] is the repose of one day in the seven. The laborer, the artisan[,] the man of business worn out with the fatigues and cares of the week recovers his strength on the day of rest and returns with fresh vigor to his work when its hours are ended. But for those who lived under the old law and in the midst of idolatrous nations, who possessed[,][139] to use the language of the apostle[,] only the shadow of the good things to come (Heb X. 1) that is to say who enjoyed[140] not those abundant graces which are granted to us under the Christian dispensation[,] how necessary was the Sabbath to raise their thoughts above this world and its passing interests. In celebrating this day[141] they were constantly reminded that there was one only God the creator of all things, who having called[142] the universe into being rested from his labors on the seventh day and therefore commended his people to sanctify it. This day[143] reminded them again that they belonged not to themselves but to God, that their time was not their own to be worked or misspent; six days were to be given to labor, but the seventh to be consecrated to Him; nor could they read the commandment which obliged them to set apart the seventh day without calling to mind that[144] the God of their fathers was the God and father of all men even of the poor slave who toiled for them[;] nay that His kindly Providence extended even to the brute beast for the Sabbath which brought them repose was to be a rest for the bondsman and the bondswoman and the ox and the ass and every beast of labor.

12. But above all this great commandment of the Sabbath day taught the people of the old law that their life was not one of unceasing toil without end or aim,[145] that it was not confined to this world of sorrow & travail, that[146] even as the Most High[147] after finishing his labors had rested from them, after perfecting his work had[148] rejoiced in it and pronounced it good, so for them if they labored faithfully[149] there was to be a reward[150] from all their toils, a rest not confined to the fleeting hours of a single day but never-ending life—the Creator's eternal Sabbath.

13. I say, therefore, my C.B., that if we consider the vast importance in the Jewish Law of the Sabbath-day we shall not be admonished to see our Savior so often upbraiding the Pharisees for their fatal explanation of the precept which commanded its observance. In clinging to the letter of the commandment they lost sight of its spirit. In inventing a multitude of prohibitions which had no place in the original institution of Moses they laid an insupportable burthen on their countrymen, and brought the Sabbath itself into contempt. Above all in reducing all religion to certain exterior observances and first among them to that peculiar manner of observing the sabbath-day which they themselves had introduced they lost sight of the weightier things of the law[:] judgment and mercy & faith, they forgot that if the heart is filled with envy & jealousy and hatred[,] if we are proud[,] avaricious, unjust, if we are uncharitable[,] without compassion[,] without mercy[,] it is impossible to please God however exactly we may perform every external duty.

14. Have we not perhaps, my C.B. fallen into that error which our Lord condemns in the Pharisees, that is to say, do we not make[151] all religion consist[152] in the performance of certain mere exterior duties[?] We think we have done enough for God & our souls because we are present at the holy sacrifice of the mass on Sundays & holy days, because we[153] fail not to recite our prayers,[154] regularly approach the sacraments,[155] are members perhaps of some confraternity,[156] are just in our dealings, and[157] avoid all lewdness, intemperance and profanity.[158] But where is our[159] patience[160] in bearing with the faults of those around us or in enduring the petty annoyances of every day life? Where is our compassion for the poor and suffering?[161] Are not the defects of our neighbors a favorite subject of conversation for us?[162] We are[163] harsh perhaps and exacting towards those in our employment? Or if ourselves[164] in the service of others, we are often wanting in respect to[165] them and regardless of their interests and careless if we think we can escape observation in executing their commands? Have we any desire of advancing in perfection? In one word,[166] is that love of our fellow-man burning in our hearts and that zeal for God's glory, which should distinguish the true disciples of Jesus[?]

15. B.C. He who in to-day's gospel was the guest of the Pharisee at

dinner is seated now at His royal banquet in His heavenly kingdom, but[167] he is the same infinitely kind, beneficent Savior. His labors are ended, and it is the day of His eternal rest, but still He is ever working, ever in action, ever desirous of communicating to us some share in His own infinite beatitude. Like the man afflicted with the dropsy[,] let us place ourselves in His presence. He will surely take pity on us,[168] for He sees far better than we can our numberless sins and shortcomings, the maladies of our souls, the passions that hold us in servitude.

Stretch forth Thy beneficent hand, dear Lord, and heal this fatal pride of mine, this love of the world, this excessive attachment to created beings, this view, whatever it be, that has so often deprived me of Thy friendship and love. If men cold and hard-hearted as they are, refuse not their aid to those who are closely allied[169] to them, do I not belong to Thee, am I not Thy creature, the work of Thy hands? Deign then to lift me up from the misery into which I have fallen; strengthen me that I may walk in Thy footsteps, and follow in all things the inspirations of Thy divine Spirit; and when the labors and toils of this world are over, may it be my bless[ing] to enjoy with Thee the eternal rest of Heaven. It is the blessing I ask for myself and you in the name etc.

Boston College. Septr. 15th 1871

COMMUNITY EXHORTATIONS

From 1894 until his death in 1904, Welch was spiritual father at Georgetown. Included among his responsibilities for the guidance of the spiritual life of the community were general monthly exhortations, catechetical instructions for the brothers, and three day semi-annual retreats for those without final vows.

The following proposal for meditation was from one of his retreats or tridua for the Georgetown scholastics, probably after 1900 when Welch was approaching 80. He was still meticulously preparing his texts, now by typewriter.

Fifth Meditation of Triduum on the vocation of the Apostles[169a]

We have seen that according to St. Mark, (2.13.) Christ chose his apostles for two purposes: first, "That they should be with him": and on this subject we meditated this afternoon. Secondly, that he might send them to preach. This latter purpose we will consider this evening. During his mortal life they were to teach only their own countrymen; "Go ye not," he said to them, "into the way of the Gentiles, and into the cities of the Samaritans enter ye not: but go ye rather to the lost sheep of the house of Israel." Now however, as he is about to leave them, and ascend into Heaven, he gives them the commission of preaching to all nations. Their novitiate, so to speak, is finished, and he says to [them] (Mark.16.16) "Go ye into the whole world, and preach the gospel to every creature." These words will form the first prelude.

Second prelude. We will imagine that we see our Lord after his resurrection giving to the eleven the commission to preach his gospel throughout the world.

Third prelude. We will earnestly ask for light that we may understand what this commission is, which is addressed to us too as religious, and strength that we may faithfully fulfil it.

First Point.
(How the apostles fulfilled this command.)

(1) On the very day of Pentecost, when a vast number of Jews assembled from various countries at Jerusalem, heard of the wonders that were taking place at the house where the disciples were assembled—a sound from Heaven as of a mighty wind, parted tongues of fire descending upon every one of them and the gift of tongues accorded them by the Holy Ghost,—Peter addressed the multitude, and reminded them that the miraculous events they witnessed, had been foretold by the prophet Joel, and went on to declare to them that Jesus whom they had put to death, had risen from the grave, and ascended into Heaven. Such was the power with which he spoke that those who heard him were filled with compunction, demanded baptism, and three thousand were added to the Church. A little later, when in company with St. John, at the beautiful gate of the temple, he restored to the perfect use of his limbs, a cripple from his mother's womb, who was wont to beg at that place, and a great multitude of Jews amazed at what had been done, crowded around the Apostles, they declared to them that it was not by their own virtue or power, but in the name of Jesus of Nazareth that they had made the man whole, and five thousand more were converted. Soon we read that the number of the disciples increased exceedingly in Jerusalem, and that a great multitude of the priests obeyed the faith. (Acts 6.7)[170] Samaria receives the gospel, and the apostles travel everywhere, even beyond the limits of the Roman Empire, so that twenty four years after the ascension, St Paul could say of the preachers of Christ's doctrines; "Their sound hath gone forth into all the earth, and their words unto the ends of the world". (Rom 10.18) Our Lord's prophecy is fulfilled, contained in the parable of the grain of mustard-seed; it is indeed the least of all seeds: but when it is grown up, is greater than all herbs, and becometh a tree, so that the birds of the air come and dwell in the branches thereof.

The little band of disciples which the Saviour at his ascension left in Judea and Galilee, have founded churches every where.

(2) The apostles preached to all men without exception, to Jew and Gentile, to bond and free. Slaves at that time formed a large portion of the population, but the Apostles did not esteem them the less because they were slaves. Witness St. Paul's affection for Onesimus, a slave, whom he calls his son, whom he had begotten in his bonds, that is, while in prison at Rome, and again he speaks of him as a most dear brother. Is there not here a lesson for us? Are we not inclined to labor rather among the refined and educated than the ignorant and uncultivated? and yet these latter need our aid far more than the former. Do we not discriminate between the rich and the poor? and while we have always time for the former,[171] are we not very brief in our ministrations to[172] the latter? The rich however will always find friends: but the poor stand in need of our kindness and sympathy. When we are naturally drawn to any person, have we not reason to fear that we shall gain little merit in laboring for him: but when a person is rude, unrefined, naturally displeasing to us, we may be sure that what we do for him is done for God's sake. When the Baptist sent messengers to Christ with the question; ''Art thou he that art to come, or look we for another,'' Jesus said to them; Go, and relate to John what you have heard and seen. The blind see, the lame walk, the lepers are cleansed, the deaf hear, the dead rise again, the poor have the gospel preached to them.'' Our Lord here urges as a proof of his divine mission, not his intercourse with the great, the rich, the refined, but with lepers who were shunned by all, with the poor and the afflicted.

(3) What was the effect of the apostles' preaching? Idolatry was banished from the Empire: the false gods with their impure rites were destroyed: the sanctity of the marriage-tie—essential for man's happiness in this world and the next—was acknowledged, the horrors of slavery were mitigated, and the institution itself gradually abolished. We have already spoken of Onesimus, a slave of Philemon, a rich and honored Christian[173] at Colossae. He had robbed his master, and then escaped. Providence led him to Rome, where St. Paul converted and baptized him, and would willingly have kept him, but thought it his duty to send him back to his master, but he begs Philemon to receive him not as a slave, but as a most dear brother. The apostles in a word, taught men that with God there is no respect of persons, that He wishes all men to be saved, and that they were to labor, to use our Lord's words, not for the bread that perisheth, but for that which endureth unto life everlasting.

(4) See now the sufferings endured by them, in carrying out their Master's command to preach throughout the world. Scarcely had the day of Pentecost passed, before they were thrown into prison and scourged. James,

the brother of John was put to death, and Peter would have shared his fate, had he not been delivered from prison by an angel. St. Paul tells us what he had to endure from Jews and Gentiles, from false brethren, from hunger, cold and nakedness. In a word what our Lord had foretold, was fulfilled to the letter; "They will deliver you up in council, and they will scourge you in their synagogues. . . . The brother also shall deliver the brother to death, and the father the son: and the children shall rise up against their parents, and shall put them to death, and you shall be hated by all men for my name's sake."

(5) Yet he who tenderly loved them, who watched over them at every moment, and who had himself for their sake and for ours, drained the chalice of sufferings even to the dregs, did not leave them without consolation: always was that promise of his accomplished; "Peace I leave with you, my peace I give unto you." The Scripture, that tells us that the apostles were scourged by order of the Sanhedrin, assures us likewise that they went forth from the presence of the Council rejoicing that they were accounted worthy to suffer reproach for the name of Jesus. St. Paul in his second epistle to the Corinthians says: "I greatly abound with joy in all my tribulations." So has it been in every age— we may appeal to our own experience. If ever by God's grace we have made some little sacrifice, or endured with cheerfulness, as coming from God some little injury, have we not been at once rewarded? Have we not experienced a joy and peace we certainly should not have felt, had we refused to make the sacrifice.

Second Point.
(The command to preach the gospel has been made
to us likewise: how we can fulfil it.)

(1) Does this command to preach the gospel apply to us, religious of the Society? Yes; for the end of our vocation is the sanctification of ourselves, and the sanctification of others. We have not received the Instructions of the Novitiate, and the many spiritual advantages we have since then enjoyed for ourselves alone. We are to be, each in his sphere, the salt of the earth, and the light of the world. As the man of wealth, in the designs of Providence, is the almoner of the poor, so are we to impart to others the spiritual goods that have been granted to us in such abundance. In our Lord's parable of the talents, he who received one talent, but did not put it to profit, is most severely punished. He had not wasted his master's money, but simply failed to put it out to interest; but his master's sentence regarding him is; "The unprofitable servant cast ye out into the exterior darkness: there shall be weeping and gnashing of teeth." We can understand why the command has been given us to do all the good we can to those around us,

if we consider the value of a soul created to the image and likeness of God, and destined to live forever.

(2) How then can we gain souls to God? First, by example. Would it be possible to follow our rule exactly without exerting a most happy influence on all around us? on our brother-religious, who would be encouraged by our example: on all with whom we come in contact? here in the College with our students, our hired men and others with whom we may have to deal. If they notice our kindness and charity, our spirit of recollection, our patience in enduring little hardships, our cheerfulness and peace of mind, will they not ask themselves what it is that produces these effects? Why do we never hear from the lips of these men an angry word, an uncharitable remark? Why do they never complain, whatever happens, never murmur at any order given them? It is not in human nature to act in this manner, and they will be forced to acknowledge that it is our holy faith, the religion we profess that produces these results. Can we not ourselves perhaps remember the time when the life and conversation of some servant of God, with whom Providence brought us in contact, excited us to a desire to imitate him, to practice the virtues we noticed in him, and finally led us to give up the world, and to knock at the door of the Novitiate? We can all, though not called to teach or preach, exercise a similar influence on those around us, and thus gain souls to God. We may never know the good we have done, but God will see it, and reward us for it. We are told that the mere sight of the venerable Pontiff, St. Pius the fifth, as he walked in procession in the streets of Rome converted Protestants who saw him.

We have another remarkable instance of the force of example in St. Alban, the Protomartyr of Britain. He was still a Pagan, when the Emperor's edicts against Christians began to be put into execution in that country. He received however into his house, and treated very kindly a priest who was endeavoring to escape from his persecutors. Alban noticed the conduct of the stranger, his faith and piety, and especially his almost continual prayer. Soon he began to listen to his instructions, and in a short time became a Christian. In the meanwhile information was given to the governor that a Christian priest was concealed in Alban's house, and soldiers were sent to arrest him. That his guest might more easily escape, Alban exchanged clothes with him. He was taken before the governor, and on his refusing to offer sacrifices to the gods of the Empire, and declaring that there was only one true and living God who created all things, he was scourged, and after bearing this torment with unshaken constancy, was finally beheaded.

(3) In the second place we can gain souls to God by prayer. St. James tells us that the continual prayer of the just man availeth much. We are reminded every month of our duty to pray, and those who are priests to offer

up mass, for the intention of Father General, for our benefactors, for the heretics of the north of Europe, and all outside the Church, for the Indies and unbelievers in general, and other intentions. Our constitutions then suppose the great efficacy of prayer. The late distinguished Father Faber after his ordination was presented with a house for a small congregation he had founded—afterwards merged in the Oratory—situated in an entirely Protestant part of the country, and he was anxious to bring back to the church those who lived around him: but he and his associates began by prayer: for one month they made the conversion of their neighbors the subject of their petitions, and then only began to preach from house to house, but with such success that after some time, it was necessary to erect a church for the accommodation of their converts. Hear too what St. John of the Cross, the friend and director of St. Theresa, says: "Let those who are consumed by a restless activity, who fancy they can move the world by their sermons, and their other exterior works reflect a moment: they will easily understand that they will be far more useful to the Church, far more pleasing to our Lord, without saying anything of the good example they would give to those around them, were they to consecrate half their time to prayer. Then by one single action they would do far more good, and with much less labor than they now do by these innumerable actions to which they give all their time. Prayer would gain for them this grace, and would obtain for them that spiritual strength which they have need of to produce fruit. Without prayer all that they do is an empty sound, it is merely the blow of the hammer striking on the anvil, and reechoed in all directions. They do now little more than nothing, sometimes absolutely nothing, and sometimes even harm. May God preserve us from a soul like this, if it is puffed up with pride. The truth is it will do nothing, for it is absolutely certain that no good work can be accomplished without aid from on High''. (Cantique Spirituel) Here we might remember that the office of the apostle, the duty of sanctifying souls, of enlarging the kingdom of Jesus Christ is not confided to the priest alone. He to be sure is especially charged with this duty; and if he is what he should be the fruit of his labors will be abundant. St. Francis of Sales says: "Experience has taught me that the people are easily led to be devout when their clergy excite them to virtue both by the word of God and by good example, and that they quickly stray from the path, when their priests are ignorant, wanting in zeal for the salvation of souls, or of evil behavior.'' The priest therefore is the first to preach the gospel: but can we do nothing in the classroom, or in conversation with our students, when we are with them in the hours of recreation? St Francis Regis, while still a scholastic and a teacher, was recognized by his pupils as a Saint. Some years after his death, one of our fathers met an ecclesiastic, who asked him if the process for the beatification of Father Regis had been begun, adding that he was once his pupil,

and that he used to commit to writing at that time many things that he saw
him do, and heard him say, feeling assured even then that he would one day
be canonized. He wished, when his process was introduced to bring forward
what he had observed. Can those who are engaged merely in domestic duties become apostles? Have we not the example of St. Alpho[n]sus,[174] and
of many others? Indeed there is no position in life, in which sanctity fails
to exercise an influence. Many years there lived only three or four miles
from this college a gentleman who owned a farm[175] cultivated by his slaves,
for slavery at the time I speak of, existed in the district. Among these there
was one who was singularly exact in discharging the duties assigned him,
modest and recollected, and always the same. At times his master talked
with him: the poor man could not perhaps read, but he knew his catechism,
and when the gentleman who was then an Episcopalian asked him questions
on religious subjects, he was able to give him a satisfactory answer. Finally
the gentleman who was very intelligent, sent for books, made himself acquainted with the teachings of the church, and became a zealous Catholic,
as did all his family. His grandchildren are now living, and remain loyal to
the faith. Is there anyone who cannot be an Apostle?

Third Point.
(Means to be employed to convert souls.)

(1) Let us remember that great talents, great learning, great eloquence
do not suffice. The conversion of a soul is the work of the Holy Ghost.
"Paul may plant", the Scripture tells us, "and Apollo water, but God giv-
eth the increase." How was it that the Apostles themselves met with such
great success? St. Mark tells us, when he says; "And they going forth
preached everywhere, the Lord working withal:" that is, as the original
might be more literally translated—the Lord working with them. In truth,
unless the Lord work with us, we can do nothing. Hence the Psalmist says;
"Unless the Lord build the house, they labor in vain that build it. Except
the Lord keep the city, he watcheth in vain that keepeth it". The reason is
that it is only the Creator who can effectually move and bend the will of the
creature. Look at St. Vincent of Paul, one of those Saints who in modern
times has done most for the extension of the church. What is said of him
"He had no pretensions to oratory, but he prayed much before speaking,
and meditated deeply on the Sacred Scriptures. His heart was on fire with
the love of God and man, and all this produced a simple, warm, persuasive
sermon, that enlightened the intellect, and moved the will." "His admirable simplicity", says Bossuet, "was the characteristic of his preaching
and with it his gentleness, his love of God and of souls, together with the
purity of the sources from which he drew, which were the Sacred Scriptures, the example and preaching of Jesus Christ, and a deep knowledge of

the instincts and passions of the human heart''. The[176] reflections which present themselves to our mind in our meditations, and which incite us to correct our faults, and to strive to follow as closely as we may the example of our Lord, we have only to repeat to those who listen to us, and with God's grace they will have the same effect upon them as upon ourselves. It is the daily meditation, the drawing near to our Lord, the walking in his presence which will enable us to sanctify ourselves and sanctify others. Of what value is the applause of men, of the name of being a great orator? but what an ineffable consolation to think that we have been instrumental in turning a sinner from the error of his ways!

(2) If we would be apostolic men, we must in the second place be willing to work in season and out of season, as St Paul warns his disciple Timothy to do. In his gospel St John tells us that Nicodemus came to our Lord by night, for fear of the Jews. He was a ruler in Israel, and did not wish to be known as a disciple of the prophet of Nazareth. How did the Saviour receive him? Did he tell him that as he taught the entire day, he had need of repose at night? No, he instructs him at great length, so that after the crucifixion, treading under foot all human respect, he declared himself openly his disciple. St Philip declares that some of his most consoling conversions happened at times which were inopportune. Let nothing interfere with the work of saving a soul: and if[177] we have community-duties that cannot be put off, let us appoint a time when we can see the person who applies for instruction, otherwise he may be discouraged and never come again. The present moment is ours; delay in a matter of this kind is always dangerous. A young French officer, whose life was far from being a model one, and who was careless as to the practice of his religion, had bound himself by a promise to say the rosary every day. To whom or under what circumstances the promise was made, we are not told. One thing however is certain, that it was faithfully kept for a considerable number of years. But for every one that pledges to any rule, the occasion must come, when the rule grows irksome, and so it was with the officer in question. One day during the Crimean war, he returned at nightfall to his tent, so utterly worn out with fatigue that he threw himself at once on his bed, and instantly dropped into a sound sleep. Before midnight he awoke, or rather his Guardian Angel awoke him, and he remembered that he had not said his rosary. As may be imagined, he felt not a little disinclined to get up and recite it. For a while he lay still debating what he should do. At last he said to himself; ''I never broke my word to any man, and I will not do so to our Blessed Lady.'' He sprang up, and as one after another he told his beads, feelings of contrition for his past sins began to steal into his heart. By the time the rosary was finished he was conscious of an intense desire to go to confession. Kneeling down, he made a solemn promise to do so, saying aloud; ''I

will go to confession tomorrow morning" And why not now? asked a familiar voice out of the darkness. It was that of the army chaplain, Father Damas S.J.[177a] who through the Providence of God happened to be passing at that moment, and overheard the officer's words. Impressed by the coincidence he readily consented, and made his confession. Early on the following day he heard Fr. Damas' mass, and received Holy Communion. A few hours later the troops were called out to attack the Russians. Almost the first shot fired by the enemy struck the young officer and killed him. The Rosary had done its work. How different would have been the result, had Fr. Damas said to himself; "I am quite worn out: it is past midnight, I will let the young man wait till morning."[178]

(3) In endeavoring to extend our Lord's kingdom we must be willing to undergo very great difficulties. To how many was our Lord himself exposed. After the labors of the day, he had no home to which he could retire for rest. Again, when we endeavor to convert anyone, we have some hope at least that we may succeed; but our Lord read the hearts of men, and he knew that those obdurate Pharisees would refuse their assent to his teachings, and in so doing add to their guilt. Not only did they refuse to believe in him, but they endeavored constantly, as the gospel informs us, to entangle him in his discourse, and thus bring about his ruin: as when for instance under pretense that they esteemed his judgment very highly, they asked him whether it were lawful to give tribute to Caesar. Whatever answer he made, they hoped to involve him in the greatest difficulties. If he answered that it was lawful, he would lose his influence with the people, who relying on a passage in the book of Deuteronomy, generally regarded it as unlawful to pay tribute to a foreign prince. If on the contrary, he declared it to be unlawful, they could accuse him to the Roman authorities. Yet with unceasing kindness and patience he seeks constantly to win these hard-hearted men. Now we know that the disciple is not above his master; and if our Lord endured so much, we must be willing to endure the little trials that we may meet with: for instance the being sent to labor when our health is impaired, or in an uncongenial climate, or in a position for which we deem ourselves unfitted, or with Superiors who may seem unsympathetic. In such cases we may well say to ourselves as St. Paul said to the Hebrews; "Be not weary, fainting in your minds: for you have not yet resisted unto blood". How trifling our severest labors in comparison with those of the martyrs and of many Saints.

(4) Finally, if we would gain souls to God, we must use sweetness and gentleness. A harsh or unkind word will sometimes repel a sinner who would otherwise have made his peace with God. In such a case what an ac[count] we would have to render for our conduct! Let me suppose that someone after long struggles has overcome himself, and wishes

now to begin a new life. He presents himself at the tribunal of penance. Perhaps in his excitement and nervousness, he can scarcely utter a word. If we are patient and encourage him, he will soon recover himself, and confess with the utmost sorrow the disorders of his past life; how pleasing to God is such a confession! A brand has been snatched from the burning, a soul from the snares of Satan, a child has been restored to his heavenly Father.

Colloquy.

Divine master, how grateful should we be that thou hast called us, as thou didst call thy blessed apostles to labor in thy vineyard, to fight under thy banner, and to extend thy kingdom. Would that we had endeavored to do this during the past six months. Had we obeyed our rule with exactitude, fulfilled our duties with purity of intention, and carefully observed our vows of poverty, chastity, and obedience, we might hope that we had really served thee. With deep sorrow we acknowledge ourselves unprofitable servants: But now thou callest us again, as thou didst years ago, and we will follow thee. With the youthful [Samuel] we exclaim; "Speak Lord, for thy servant heareth". We know by experience that thy yoke is easy, and thy burthen light: whereas our many acts of disobedience to thy inspirations have brought us no real satisfaction even for the moment, and have deprived us of many graces: nay, they have filled our souls with bitterness. Grant us then, dear Lord, to change our conduct, and hereafter to walk in thy footsteps, that we may indeed be thy companions.

NOTES

1. GUSC, Welch Papers, Box 1, Faber to Welch, 1845.
2. Welch, "Father Joseph Coolidge Shaw: A Memorial Sketch," *Woodstock Letters* 26 (1897), 449.
3. "A Jubilarian Reviews His 'Primi Anni' Catalogue: 1896–1946," *Woodstock Letters* 76 (1947), 46.
4. "You Americans," he continued, "are very badly off for Saints; I do not know of any except St Rose of Lima; and I should be glad to hear that a certain wild & not overpious American whom I took a g[rea]t affection to in Germany was bidding fair to be St Edward of Boston" (GUSC, Welch Papers, Box 1, Faber to Welch, 1845).
5. GUSC, Welch Papers.
6. *Woodstock Letters* 36 (1907), 132–133.
7. Crossed out: "perhaps."
8. Crossed out: "submission."
9. Crossed out: "God gives us no greater proof."
10. Crossed out: "greater."

11. Crossed out: "bearing these."
12. Crossed out: "in a Christian manner."
13. Crossed out: "we love."
14. Crossed out: "hardly."
15. Crossed out: "invisible."
16. Crossed out: "a painted."
17. Crossed out: "mind."
18. Crossed out: "thing."
19. Crossed out: "I."
20. Crossed out: "I."
21. Crossed out: "me."
22. Crossed out: "I chose."
23. Crossed out: "my."
24. Crossed out: "would."
25. Crossed out: "earthly."
26. Crossed out: "God's love."
27. Crossed out: "the Jewish monarch."
28. Crossed out: "chains &."
29. Crossed out: "God's."
30. Crossed out: "that sends this calamity."
31. Paralipomena, or "things left out," the Vulgate title for the Books of Chronicles.
32. Crossed out: "how."
33. Crossed out: "moment."
34. Crossed out: "gives."
35. Crossed out: "tender."
36. Crossed out: "in receiving."
37. Crossed out: "in sparing."
38. Crossed out: "sometimes."
39. Crossed out: "on the part of our heavenly Father."
40. Crossed out: "stamped."
41. Crossed out: "of almost everyone."
42. Crossed out: "see."
43. Crossed out: "another."
44. Crossed out: "And there is another."
45. Crossed out: "they."
46. Crossed out: "her."
47. Crossed out: "they."
48. Crossed out: "dissipation."
49. Crossed out: "a father."
50. Crossed out: "a young man."
51. Crossed out: "take him from this world."
52. Crossed out: "these are but."
53. Crossed out: "and who shows his love towards you by this very affliction."

54. Crossed out: "those."

55. Crossed out: "hence it is that He afflicts you and that these afflictions are the strongest proof of His love towards you. Envy not the children of the world who seem to have everything that heart can desire. This short lived prosperity is all they desired all they can hope for. If God had not given them up to the desires of their own hearts, He would long since have reminded them by some calamity that this world is but a pilgrimage. Too soon their life will be over and their momentary felicity will give place to never ending regret. I have seen the wicked highly exalted, & lifted up as the cedars of Libanus: And I passed by, and lo, he was not: and I sought him & his place was not found (Ps. 36[37]:35,36). Shall we not then be grateful to God that he has dealt otherwise with us, that in his love He has sent us many afflictions and shall we not endeavor to show our love to Him making a Holy use of these afflictions: that we can with His grace do this I shall endeavor to show in a 3rd reflection."

56. Crossed out: "we show him."

57. Crossed out: "is disinterested."

58. Crossed out: "as our."

59. Crossed out: "not."

60. Crossed out: "our hearts."

61. Crossed out: "God."

62. Crossed out: "God."

63. Crossed out: "love."

64. Crossed out: "me."

65. Crossed out: "bring about."

66. Crossed out: "But if my love for God is generous & courageous I must desire His glory and therefore."

67. Crossed out: "companions."

68. Crossed out: "in his joy at the success of his country he forgets."

69. Crossed out: "our generous & courageous love for God in suffering is shown again in this that."

70. Crossed out: "must."

71. Crossed out: "complete."

72. Crossed out: "which is."

73. Crossed out: "our liberal."

74. Crossed out: "(Christ then came into this world to suffer, to make a complete offering of himself to his heavenly Father.)"

75. Crossed out: "S Peter."

76. Here there is a bracketed text, apparently an alternate conclusion: "Shall we then any longer complain when Providence sends us calamities[?] Have not a thousand created objects hitherto taken God's place in our hearts[?] Do we not wish to be more closely united to Him, in whose friendship alone we can find true peace and happiness[?] Are there not innumerable sins and disorders in our past lives which cry out against us and which demand satisfaction[?] Welcome then that affliction which has seemed to you heretofore so insupportable for it is for these reasons that the kindest of fathers has sent it to you. Is not this omnipotent Being worthy

of a disinterested & generous & courageous love—this you will show Him by accepting with joy the cross He lays upon your shoulders.

Finally if we would be the disciples of Jesus[,] if we would be worthy of the glorious name of Christians[,] we must not refuse to follow his example, we must strive to love God as he loved Him[,] we must accept whatever Providence sends us, the chalice which my Father has sent me shall I not drink it—

The children of the world seek what the world proposes to them [—] wealth & pleasure & fame & power. Alas how short at best is their happiness. We know that this life is only a time of probation [,] that as gold is tried in the fire so virtue is purified in many tribulations. God has shown His love to us in sending us many afflictions, it only remains that we should show our love to Him by accepting them, 'laying aside' therefore 'every weight and the sin that surroundeth us by patience let us run to the fight proposed unto us. Looking on Jesus the author and finisher of faith who having joy proposed unto him, underwent the cross, despising the shame & sitteth on the right hand of the throne of God.' Heb 12. 1,2[.]''

77. Crossed out: "loves us and has prepared for each of us."

78. Crossed out: "finally."

79. Crossed out: "If God had not given them up to the desires of their own hearts, He would long since have reminded them by many afflictions that man was not created for the miserable joys of this world."

80. Crossed out: "Should we not then be grateful to God that he has dealt in a different manner [alt. otherwise] with us, and that by sufferings & misfortunes He has convinced us that this life is only a time of probation and that our true home is beyond the grave. As gold is tried in the fire, so He would purify us by many tribulations. Our afflictions then are a proof of His love to us, and it only remains that we should testify our love to Him by bearing them as we ought to [alt. should] bear them."

A bracketed text follows: " 'Laying aside' therefore 'every weight,' it is the great apostle of the Gentiles who exhorts us, 'laying aside therefore every weight and the sin that surroundeth us, by patience let us run to the fight proposed unto us. Looking on Jesus the author and finisher of the faith who having joy proposed to him underwent the cross, despising the shame & sitteth on the right hand of the throne of God.' (Heb 12, 1.2)"

81. Crossed out: "and misfortunes."

82. Crossed out: "to dinner."

83. Crossed out: "unlike the others of his sect."

84. Crossed out: "did he wish in this way."

85. Crossed out: "the Savior."

86. Crossed out: "him to."

87. Crossed out: "any."

88. Crossed out: "heavenly."

89. Crossed out: "which would serve as a matter of accusation against him."

90. Crossed out: "observing."

91. Crossed out: "and consecrate themselves entirely to his service."

92. Crossed out: "without."
93. Crossed out: "expose."
94. Crossed out: "He was not one of the invited guests nor did he belong, as it would seem clear from the sacred text, to the family of the host."
95. Welch has inadvertently inserted a "that."
96. Crossed out: "set man."
97. Crossed out: "the Savior then asks the lawyers & Pharisees."
98. Crossed out and in brackets: and then again was it not evident that strictly as the law forbad all work on the day of rest it made an exception [alt. exempted] in favor of certain kinds of work, those connected with the public services of religion? The Jew had but to turn his eyes towards the Temple and he saw there on every sabbath two lambs without blemish sacrificed to the Lord Most High, and that same day too the twelve loaves of proposition were baked and placed before the Lord. To this the Savior referred when on another occasion he said to the Jews: "Have ye not read in the law that on the sabbath-days the priests in the temple break the sabbath and are without blame? (Mat 12.5)
99. Crossed out: "ask."
100. Crossed out: "those."
101. Crossed out: "touch."
102. Crossed out: "as several of the fathers."
103. Crossed out: "as our Evangelist tells us."
104. Crossed out: "he heals the sick man."
105. Crossed out: "it."
106. Crossed out: "they cannot."
107. Crossed out: "to beg from door to door and."
108. Crossed out: "poverty and want."
109. Crossed out: "want."
110. Crossed out: "never to omit any."
111. Crossed out: "even."
112. Crossed out: "that."
113. Crossed out: "that it."
114. Crossed out: "nothing."
115. Crossed out: "when we see it."
116. Crossed out: "feel."
117. Crossed out: "that."
118. Crossed out: "their."
119. Crossed out: "alas! B.C. this a."
120. Crossed out: "gained for."
121. Crossed out: "drew to."
122. Crossed out: "of the Pharisees."
123. Crossed out: "aversion to our Lord."
124. Crossed out: "we have seen in the history of the Christian Church."
125. Crossed out: "too frequently."
126. Crossed out: "We have seen opinions promulgated systems taught by."
127. Crossed out: "But the infallible Church the pillar and ground of the truth

finds [alt. found] it necessary to condemn this [alt. any] system they had taught, to repudiate these opinions they had promulgated, and he whom we thought her dutiful child.''

    128. Crossed out: ''what he had taught.''

    129. Crossed out: ''teachings.''

    130. Crossed out: ''himself.''

    131. Crossed out: ''his.''

    132. Crossed out: ''himself.''

    133. Crossed out: ''holds the keys [that] shuts & opens.''

    134. Crossed out: ''merely.''

    135. Crossed out: ''prohibition.''

    136. Crossed out: ''these sabbaths.''

    137. Crossed out: ''even in a national point of view.''

    138. Crossed out: ''body and.''

    139. Crossed out: ''enjoyed.''

    140. Crossed out: ''possessed.''

    141. Crossed out: ''with devotion.''

    142. Crossed out: ''formed.''

    143. Crossed out: ''They were.''

    144. Crossed out: ''was the.''

    145. Crossed out: ''but was a preparation for a happier state of.''

    146. Crossed out: ''but.''

    147. Crossed out: ''Creator.''

    148. Crossed out: ''to speak.''

    149. Crossed out: ''there would be a rest where they would receive the reward of all their toils so for them.''

    150. Crossed out: ''a rest after their labors.''

    151. In parentheses: ''reduce.''

    152. In parentheses: ''to.''

    153. Crossed out: ''never.''

    154. Crossed out: ''we.''

    155. Crossed out: ''we.''

    156. Crossed out: ''we.''

    157. Crossed out: ''we.''

    158. Crossed out: ''This we say to ourselves with great satisfaction, and we imagine that we have done enough.''

    159. Crossed out: ''how little.''

    160. Crossed out: ''we have.''

    161. Crossed out: ''Do we not often speak of.''

    162. Crossed out: ''are.''

    163. Crossed out: ''not.''

    164. Crossed out: ''we are.''

    165. Crossed out: ''towards.''

    166. Crossed out: ''where.''

    167. Crossed out: ''still.''

168. Crossed out: "we have no need of words."
169. Crossed out: "united."
169a. GUSC, Welch Papers.
170. Crossed out: "Soon."
171. Crossed out: "we."
172. Crossed out: "with."
173. Crossed out: "citizen."
174. Alonso Rodriguez, S.J. (1533–1617), a temporal coadjutor, who for 46 years was porter at the college at Palma, Majorca.
175. Crossed out: "which was."
176. Crossed out: "these."
177. Crossed out: "when."
177a. Amédée de Damas (1821–1903).
178. Crossed out: "midnight."

SELECTED BIBLIOGRAPHY

Bangert, William V., S.J. *A History of the Society of Jesus.* St. Louis: The Institute of Jesuit Sources, 1972.

Bossey, John. *The English Catholic Community, 1570–1850.* New York: Oxford University Press, 1976.

Chinnici, Joseph P., O.F.M. *The English Catholic Enlightenment: John Lingard and the Cisalpine Movement, 1780–1850.* Shepherdstown, W. Va.: Patmos Press, 1980.

Curran, Robert Emmett, S.J. "From Saints to Secessionists: Thomas Hughes and *The History of the Society of Jesus in North America." Studies in Catholic History In Honor of John Tracy Ellis.* Edited by Nelson H. Minnich, Robert B. Eno, S.S. & Robert F. Trisco. Wilmington: Michael Glazer, 1985, 239–259.

—. " 'Splendid Poverty': Jesuit Slaveholding in Maryland, 1805–1838." *Catholics in the Old South: Essays on Church and Culture.* Edited by Randall M. Miller and Jon L. Wakelyn. Macon: Mercer University Press, 1983, 125–146.

—. " 'The Finger of God Is Here': The Advent of the Miraculous in the Nineteenth-Century American Catholic Community." *The Catholic Historical Review* 73 (January, 1987), 41–61.

Daley, John M., S.J. *Georgetown University: Origins and Early Years.* Washington: Georgetown University Press, 1957.

de Guibert, Joseph, S.J. *The Jesuits. Their Spiritual Doctrine and Practice: A Historical Study.* Translated by William J. Young, S.J. St. Louis: The Institute of Jesuit Sources, 1964.

Dolan, Jay P. *The American Catholic Experience: A History from Colonial Times to the Present.* New York: Doubleday & Co., Inc., 1985.

Durkin, Joseph T., S.J. *Georgetown University: The Middle Years (1840–1900).* Washington: Georgetown University Press, 1963.

Edwards, Francis, S.J. *The Jesuits in England: From 1580 to the Present Day*. Tunbridge Wells, Kent: Burns & Oates, 1985.

Ellis, John Tracy. *Catholics in Colonial America*. Baltimore: Helicon Press, 1965.

Fenwick, Benedict Joseph, S.J. *Memoirs to Serve for the Future Ecclesiastical History of the Diocess [sic] of Boston*. Edited by Joseph M. McCarthy. Yonkers, N.Y.: United States Catholic Historical Society, 1978.

Guilday, Peter. *The Life and Times of John Carroll: Archbishop of Baltimore (1735–1815)*. 2 vols. New York: The Encyclopedia Press, 1922.

Hennesey, James, S.J. *American Catholics: A History of the Roman Catholic Community in the United States*. New York: Oxford University Press, 1981.

—. "Several Youth Sent from Here: Native-Born Priests and Religious of English America, 1634–1776," *Studies in Catholic History*, 1–26.

Hughes, Thomas S.J. *The History of the Society of Jesus in North America: Colonial and Federal. Text*. 2 vols. London: Longmans, Green, and Co., 1907, 1917.

—. *The History of the Society of Jesus in North America: Colonial and Federal. Documents*. One volume in two parts. London: Longmans, Green, and Co., 1908, 1910.

The John Carroll Papers. 3 vols. Edited by Thomas O'Brien Hanley, S.J. Notre Dame: University of Notre Dame Press, 1976.

Melville, Annabelle M. *John Carroll of Baltimore: Founder of the American Catholic Hierarchy*. New York: Charles Scribner's Sons, 1955.

Modern Spiritual Exercises: A Contemporary Reading of the Spiritual Exercises of St. Ignatius. Translated by Davil L. Fleming, S.J. Garden City, N.Y.: Image Books, 1983.

INDEX TO INTRODUCTION

INDEX TO TEXT

Other Volumes in This Series